*The Emergence of the
Modern European World*

For my children

The Emergence of the Modern European World

From the Seventeenth to the Twentieth Century

EDWARD WHITING FOX

with the editorial assistance of Susan Harris Shefter

BLACKWELL
Cambridge MA & Oxford UK

First published in the USA 1991
First published in the UK 1992
Reprinted 1993

Blackwell Publishers
238 Main Street
Cambridge, Massachusetts 02142, USA
108 Cowley Road
Oxford, OX4 1JF, UK

Library of Congress Cataloging in Publication Data
Fox, Edward Whiting.
      The emergence of the modern European world : from the seventeenth to the twentieth century / Edward Whiting Fox, with the assistance of Susan Shefter.

        p.   cm.
      Includes bibliographical references and index.
      ISBN 1-55786-050-5 – ISBN 1-55786-126-9
      (pbk.):
        1. Europe – History – 1492–   I. Shefter, Susan Harris.   II. Title.
      D102.F69   1991
      940.2–dc20   91-8309
                                                                            CIP

British Library Cataloguing in Publication Data
A CIP catalogue record for this book is available from the British Library.

Typeset in 11 on 13pt Sabon
by Graphicraft Typesetters Ltd., Hong Kong
Printed in the USA

This book is printed on acid-free paper.

Contents

Maps

Acknowledgments

For the last dozen years, since this book's inception in a different project, Susan Shefter has worked tirelessly to help to bring it to completion, especially by keeping track of the successive versions of the manuscript. Without her devoted editorial assistance and personal commitment it would not have been published. I also deeply appreciate Glenn O. Nichol's thoughtful and professional contribution of a chronology and a guide to further reading.

I would like to thank Richard Rosecrance for conversations largely focused on the manuscript during a series of weekly luncheons, Martin Schefter for reading the entire manuscript and making a number of excellent suggestions, Leonard Hochberg for discussions about the need for such a book, for encouraging me to write it, and for introducing it to his wide acquaintance in the field.

My thanks also to my daughter Elizabeth Fox Genovese for her insights on Freud; to my son Edward W. Fox Jr.; my sons-in-law Eugene D. Genovese and William Scott Green, for dealing with copy ambiguities, and to my wife Elizabeth S. Fox for the final job of copyediting when I was incapacitated.

Finally, I would like to express my gratitude for the gracious and decisive part played by my editor John Davey in bringing this work to its present conclusion.

Introduction

This volume presents a narrative history of the world in which we live today – the modern world – from its emergence in seventeenth-century Europe to the present. Most surveys of this subject focus upon the rise of the nation state, chronicling the pursuit of military power and the consolidation of territory under central governments. In this book, however, these developments are seen as only one strand of the story; equally important in shaping the modern world was an expanding pursuit of commercial wealth, which knit port cities together into a growing community with an organic existence of its own.

The commercial community was as much an oceanic phenomenon as the administrative state was continental. Of course waterborne trading systems had flourished in the Mediterranean since ancient times, and later in the Baltic, producing unprecedented riches in periods of peace. But it was the opening of the Atlantic (and eventually the world ocean) to a vastly expanded trade in bulk goods that established the base for the generation of unimagined wealth, and ultimately for the transformation of the European economy into its current global form.

The history of the commercial community is comparatively difficult to follow, partly because it lacked the clearly defined territorial base and formal governmental structure of the nation state. Instead it consisted of a widespread and complex network of waterborne communication systems connecting islands and the fringes of continental masses. Although governments took part in this trade in various ways, it was essentially and increasingly a private undertaking, which enriched the participating port cities rather than the administrative capitals of territorial states. Oriented toward the sea, the port cities characteristically had little integral relation to the land-based governments of their hinterland except where they served as vulnerable objects of forceful exploitation or willing sources of capital investment.

The two overlapping systems of economic and political development within the European world gave rise to conflicting attitudes toward social organization. The land-based states were generally organized in orderly and rigid bureaucratic hierarchies, which found eloquent defenders in the eighteenth-century French *philosophes*, with their ideal of the perfect government perfectly implemented. By contrast, the members of the commercial community, lacking any firm territorial foundation, were compelled to operate by common consent, and to order their relations by mutual agreement, often arrived at through parliamentary procedures or diplomatic exchanges. These divergent patterns of thought and practice were reflected in the institutions that grew up in the two different types of society and have continued to figure importantly in conflicts between them ever since. In our own times the tensions of the Cold War can be understood at least in part as an extension of the land–water dichotomy that first emerged in seventeenth-century Europe: to the east, the vast land-based territorial state of the Soviet Union is heir to the administrative-military tradition, while across the Atlantic to the west, the United States reveals its origins and membership in the oceanic trading community.

1

The Dawn of the Modern World

It is a commonplace among historians of Europe to describe the seventeenth century as the beginning of "modern" times, in that it saw the end of medieval society and the beginning of the historical era in which we still live. Significantly, it was in the seventeenth century that Europeans first used the word "modern" to characterize their own society, and what they seemed to mean was close to what we mean by the term today.

Many aspects of the European world would reveal modernizing tendencies in the seventeenth century. Perhaps the most striking break with the past occurred in the realm of scientific investigation, with the introduction of a completely new emphasis on direct observation, reinforced by the use of instruments — particularly microscopes and telescopes. Equally important was the application of mathematics to theoretical analysis, as in calculating the path of the planets around the sun. In spite of the extraordinary progress we have made in the sciences since that time, we are still working today with the same basic scientific approach. Moreover it was this way of thinking that made possible the accelerating progress of technological innovation that was to transform the material basis of life in the western world.

Another seventeenth-century phenomenon that seemed modern then and still does today is the emergence of what we now generally term the "state." Beginning in the late Middle Ages, a growing number of kings had struggled against the vigorous opposition of their nobles to transform their feudal monarchies into administrative governments, and in the seventeenth century the monarchs clearly began to exercise the upper hand. In France and Spain, and on a smaller scale in the German and Italian principalities, absolute monarchies began to take firm territorial shape, organized by administrative agents, with the chief objective of increasing the royal income. To this end the king taxed the urban classes and the peasants, though he usually had to exempt both the nobles and the clergy as the price of their support. Following the French model, the monarchs of Russia, Prussia, and Austria also developed bureaucratic states during this century, seizing control of eastern Europe from defeated Sweden, decadent Poland, and the declining Ottoman Empire.

It was also during the seventeenth century that the attitude toward religion began to change, so that differences of doctrine nearly ceased to be a cause for war. This was not the result of any lessening of faith — there was in fact an important religious revival in this century — and few societies yet enjoyed internal religious toleration, but there did come to be a general acceptance of a variety of established churches among the different political units of the European world. This was hardly a situation we would now call modern, but it still represented a significant change in that direction.

Finally, the seventeenth century saw the opening of Atlantic commerce, a development which would prove to have momentous significance for the future course of western society. Since medieval times, the Atlantic had served as a water route for trade within Europe, but no true transatlantic commerce took shape until the English, French, and Dutch colonies were established in North America in the mid-1600s. The oceanic commercial economy that now grew up was similar to the one that had united the ancient Greek cities, but on a vastly larger scale, and it proceeded to generate the unprecedented wealth that would become the unique characteristic of the modern European world.

Along with its riches, this new economy produced its own inherent attitudes toward authority and political organization. Like the commercial community of the ancient Aegean, this much greater one of the Atlantic nurtured a spirit of negotiation and compromise among its members, and ultimately within the participating societies as well. Although the Atlantic never produced an equivalent of the Delian League of the ancient Aegean, or the Hanseatic League of the medieval Baltic, its major maritime powers

(England, Holland and Sweden) did instinctively unite to resist the attempts of France's Louis XIV to control the lower Rhine and its adjacent coastline. Further, the port cities of this community regularly resisted efforts by the territorial rulers of their own hinterlands to subject them to administrative control.

London was the largest and richest of all the Atlantic ports, and served as the effective capital of the new commercial community – enjoying such a privileged position in large measure because its island setting virtually guaranteed it immunity from military attack and control by the land-based powers of the Continent. Not coincidentally, it was England and Holland, the chief beneficiaries of the Atlantic trade, that saw the development of both the largest and the most prosperous urban, or "bourgeois," classes in European society, and the first constitutional governments to be established anywhere in the world.

The political history of Europe in the seventeenth century revealed a clearly discernible pattern that reflected these developments. In France, two remarkable ministers laid the foundations of an administrative monarchy that would dominate not only France but all of Europe in the second half of the century. In England, by contrast, two kings who were bent on creating a similar administrative monarchy produced instead an open revolt, which ended with the execution of the second monarch. Each of these stories reached its climax at the end of the century, in England with the Glorious Revolution and the establishment of limited monarchy as a model for the Atlantic community, and in France with the imposition of an absolute monarchy which would be imitated throughout most of the rest of inland Europe.

THE RISE OF THE ADMINISTRATIVE MONARCHY IN FRANCE

The history of the European Continent in the first half of the seventeenth century was dominated by a series of bloody conflicts that have come to be known collectively as the Thirty Years War. In general terms, this was a civil and religious war fought by the Holy Roman Emperor and his Catholic supporters against Protestant princes for control of the empire. But the significance of the conflict lay less in the many specific issues over which the participants fought than in the sheer scale of the war, which was unprecedented at this time. This was the first war that involved all the major powers on the Continent, and the first that was fought to establish a balance of power among them. It was also unprecedented in the devastation it wreaked on the civilian population of the Continent; the loss of life has been compared to that caused by famine and plague in the fourteenth century. By the time a settlement was reached (the Peace of Westphalia, in 1648), a new standard of military strength had been set for any European ruler who wished to maintain his position against the others, and the subjects of these rulers had a keen new interest in the ability of their royal armies to protect them. In France this combination of motives led the monarchy to develop the superior military strength that would ultimately make it the dominant power on the Continent for the next two centuries.

At the beginning of the seventeenth century the French monarchy seemed to be disintegrating in civil and religious war. It was finally salvaged, however, by the young Bourbon Henry of Navarre, who changed his faith for the third time (from Protestant to Catholic to Protestant to Catholic) with the quip, "Paris is well worth a mass." Then in 1598, to protect his former co-religionists and pacify his new realm, Henry IV issued the famous Edict of Nantes, which granted Protestants the right to conduct services in any places in which they were then established and to maintain a considerable number of fortified towns for a period of eight years. While these concessions probably represented the minimum the Protestants would have accepted, they also constituted a serious infringement on the royal prerogatives, and would later cause difficulties. In the mean time, however, the peace they provided allowed Henry to reorganize the royal administration.

Henry was assassinated by a Catholic fanatic in 1610, leaving the newly pacified realm to his nine-year-old heir, Louis XIII, with the queen mother Marie de Médicis as regent. For fourteen years Marie managed to maintain her position by buying the contemptuous support of the great nobles with concessions and pensions; eventually this policy was repudiated by the young king, leading to a series of crises at court. In the course of these struggles Marie brought into the court a promising young provincial bishop named Armand de Richelieu, whom she persuaded Louis to appoint to his council in 1624. This was all Richelieu needed: with consummate skill he won over the young king, and proceeded to lay the foundations of a policy that would make the monarchy the dominant institution in France, and France the dominant power in Europe.

These achievements established Richelieu as one of the greatest statesmen of all time. He created basic law and order in the provinces by establishing the authority of the royal agents, particularly in the area of tax collection. Then, with the treasury replenished, he was able to develop a masterful foreign policy in which he both outmaneuvered and outfought France's rivals.

Louis XIV

When he died in 1642, Richelieu left not only the administrative base of an absolute monarchy but also a carefully trained protégé, the Italian Cardinal Mazarin, to carry on his work. Shortly after Richelieu's death Louis XIII also died, and the French throne went once again to a minor, this time the five-year-old Louis XIV, under the regency of the queen mother Anne of Austria. The real authority was exercised by Mazarin, however, until his death in 1661. If Mazarin lacked Richelieu's force of character, and ruled by manipulating the queen, his devotion to the institution of the monarchy was no less, and his efforts on behalf of the royal exchequer were even more successful than those of his master. Thus the day after Mazarin's death, when the young Louis XIV surprised the royal council by assuming full control of the government, the new king had an unequaled administrative apparatus at his command, which was ready to be turned into the absolute state that would dominate and dazzle Europe throughout his reign.

Mazarin had in his turn prepared a successor to carry on his work, Jean-Baptiste Colbert, a professional bureaucrat who had held a number of government posts and managed the cardinal's vast personal fortune as well. When the young king's superintendent of finances tried to assume personal power, he was promptly replaced by Mazarin's protégé, whose activities were wide-ranging and tremendously important in furthering the royal policies. Meticulous rather than brilliant, Colbert began by rigorously reforming the antiquated and inefficient tax collection system. By imposing simple standards of honesty he greatly increased the total intake, although he made no progress in eliminating the nobles' exemptions from direct taxation. Colbert also concerned himself with industry and trade in an effort to increase the country's wealth. Curiously, he failed to recognize that agriculture was still by far the most important tax base, and that the luxury industries he cultivated had a very limited potential to produce income – at least unless they could be offered on the oceanic market. To that end he tried to build up a merchant marine, and to protect it, a navy. Altogether his efforts to manage the economy were only moderately successful, but his tax reforms made Louis XIV by far the richest monarch on the Continent.

The uses to which this new fiscal wealth was put were all connected with the emerging administrative state. These included the country's system of roads and canals, the navy, the royal court at Versailles, and most importantly of all the army, which another great minister, Louvois, was in the process of transforming into an efficient fighting force. Louvois not only quadrupled the size of the army (from under 100,000 troops to over 400,000), but he also replaced the mercenary regiments "owned" by their colonels with troops that were raised, paid, supplied, trained, and commanded by royal officers, thus creating the first modern army and setting a new standard for all would-be European rulers.

Like many of Louis's official servants, Louvois came from a distinguished professional family; his father and later his son also served as ministers of war. Such officials were hardly of humble origin, as is sometimes suggested; they were rich and educated, as well as able, and those who were not nobles by birth usually acquired titles from the king. They did owe their positions entirely to the king, however, who made it one of his principal policies to exclude all great landed nobles and princes from positions of power. At the same time he kept the nobles under his close scrutiny by requiring their presence at his lavish court, for which he built the vast palace complex of Versailles, some ten miles southwest of Paris. There, every aspect of the king's daily existence was made the focus of a near-oriental degree of ritual, requiring the attendance of his courtiers.

Behind the brilliant façade of the court, however, the dominating institution of the monarchy was the army. Making war, it was said, was the "métier du roi" (the business of the king), and it was to be the lifelong obsession of Louis XIV. (At the end of his life he is supposed to have said, "I loved war too much.") This pursuit of glory began almost immediately with his assumption of power following the death of Mazarin. The cardinal's last triumph had been to negotiate a treaty with Spain, which brought a nagging war to a conclusion by settling the Franco-Spanish boundary on the crest of the Pyrenees, essentially as it is today, and transferring to France some Spanish territory in the Netherlands that bordered France. Finally the Spanish king signed a marriage contract between his daughter Maria Theresa and Louis XIV, though with the stipulation that, in return for a large dowry, the French king would give up his wife's rights of inheritance in Spain and the Spanish possessions. Clearly Louis had as little intention of honoring this renunciation as there was likelihood that the dowry would be paid; thus the treaty, though it ended Franco-Spanish warfare for a time, also served to launch the French king on his policy of expansion. As his actions would demonstrate, he hoped both to place a Bourbon on the throne of Spain and to acquire Spanish Habsburg lands along the left bank of the Rhine.

As soon as his father-in-law died, in 1665, Louis claimed the Spanish possessions in the Netherlands for his wife, arguing that her renunciation of her inheritance had been invalidated by the fact that her dowry had not been paid. This was the first move in a campaign to realize his territorial ambitions, which led to a series of wars. In the first, he was frustrated by an alliance of the maritime powers: England, Holland, and Sweden. After a brief interval he launched a second war, this one against the Dutch, whom he blamed for his earlier defeat. Having bribed his cousin Charles II to take England out of the alliance, Louis was able to invade Holland, but his success provoked a popular uprising in that country which brought the ultra-patriotic William of Orange to power. That stubborn prince opened the dikes and flooded the country to force a French retreat. In a series of treaties, Holland then received back all French-occupied territory, while Spain ceded the County of Burgundy to France. Within five years, however, the French armies again began occupying with impunity cities along the Netherlands frontier, as well as in Alsace along the Rhine.

At this peak of his power, in 1685, Louis made the worst mistake of his long reign: without provocation or apparent reason, he suddenly revoked the Edict of Nantes. It was with this edict that the Bourbons had ended the French religious wars and established their dynasty, by guaranteeing limited toleration of the Protestants. Whatever threat to the monarchy the Protestant minority may have once posed had long since been eliminated by Richelieu when he ended their right to fortify specific towns and cities. Now, faced with forced conversion to Catholicism, some 200,000 of the wealthiest and best-educated citizens of France fled to Holland, Scotland, or North America. Also when the Great Elector of Brandenburg responded to Louis's action by inviting the refugees to settle there, many accepted, providing that emerging state with some of its ablest public servants, and injecting a sprinkling of French names into the Prussian aristocracy.

While religion was no longer an issue that could kindle open warfare, Louis's belligerent step provoked a hostile reaction throughout Protestant Europe, gaining widespread sympathy for William of Orange in his efforts to resist the renewed French threats. As a result, he was able in 1688 to form the anti-French League of Augsburg, with the Austrian Habsburgs, the kings of Spain and Sweden, and several German princes. At this point he was called to England to assume the throne vacated by James II in the "Glorious Revolution," thus adding that country to the alliance. The French responded with a preemptive invasion of the Spanish Netherlands and then crossed the Rhine into Holland, but in spite of their military superiority they were not able to win a decisive victory on land, while at sea the English and Dutch gained the definite upper hand with their victory at La Hague in 1696. As a result a peace treaty was signed the following year by which the French recognized William of Orange as king of England and conceded to Holland all captured territory, together with the right to garrison border fortresses on the French–Netherlands frontier as a guarantee against invasion. In effect this treaty marked out the two poles which now existed in the rivalry for control of the European world.

Frustrated by the growing strength of the Atlantic powers, Louis turned his attention to his other main objective, the Spanish throne. The childless Habsburg king of Spain died in 1700, after publishing a will that left the crown to Louis's grandson, Philip of Anjou. Louis immediately accepted for the young prince and dispatched him to Spain to occupy the empty throne. Fearing that this was Louis's first step toward annexing Spain, his opponents now united in yet another effort to contain his ambitions: this Grand Alliance included England, Holland, Sweden, the Austrian Habsburgs, Savoy, the Holy Roman Empire, and many German states. The ensuing war raged across the Continent from the Netherlands to northern Italy, with skirmishes as well in North America and India. With by far the largest and most efficient army, the French appeared quite capable of meeting this formidable challenge; but if the Grand Alliance had no comparable army, it did have two generals of extraordinary skill: England's John Churchill, later Duke of Marlborough, and Prince Eugene of Savoy. Under their command the allied forces managed to outmaneuver the French armies, finally pushing Louis's monarchy to the edge of bankruptcy and military collapse.

Two events suddenly brought the war to a close. The fall of a ministry in England led to the recall of Marlborough, and the death of the Habsburg emperor in Vienna suddenly made Charles – the Habsburg then struggling to keep the throne of Spain – also heir to the family's Austrian possessions, thus threatening to revive the empire of Charles V. Since hardly anyone was prepared to accept this concentration of lands and power in the hands of a single ruler, and since the Alliance had lost its greatest general, both sides felt a compelling disposition to negotiate. The result was the Peace of Utrecht (1713), after Westphalia the second general European treaty, which among other complicated details: (1) recognized the Bourbon Philip V as King of Spain and her American colonies, (2) compensated the Austrian Habsburgs for the loss of Spain by giving them the Spanish possessions in the Netherlands and northern Italy, (3) recognized Brandenburg and her territories as the Kingdom of Prussia, and (4) promoted the Prince of Savoy to King, giving him Sicily, which he soon had to exchange for Sardinia. The English got Nova Scotia, Newfoundland, and the Hudson Bay territories from France, and also Gibraltar from Spain.

For Louis XIV the gains from his fifty years of military and diplomatic campaigning were actually meager. He had finally established his grandson on the throne of Spain, but with the condition that Spain and France should never be united. In addition he had pushed forward his eastern and northern frontiers as much as fifty miles, thus gaining considerable rich territory, but only at the cost of long, exhausting wars that brought France perilously close to collapse at the end of his reign.

THE REJECTION OF ABSOLUTE MONARCHY IN ENGLAND

The early Stuarts

During the century (1598–1715) in which the Bourbons were creating their absolute monarchy in France and establishing that country as the dominant military power on the Continent, the Stuarts (1603–1714) were struggling unsuccessfully to achieve something comparable in England. While there were a number of parallels in the two stories, the dissimilarities were much more important. The founders of the two dynasties both came from collateral lines of royal descent and frontier principalities (Scotland and Navarre), but their kingdoms were completely different. Where France was only emerging from the chaos of the religious wars, England had just completed, under Elizabeth, one of the country's greatest reigns. The French king, Henry IV, was a genius at political manipulation, who knew instinctively how to turn his country's misfortunes to his own advantage, while England's James I was so inept that he aroused opposition from his prospering subjects, largely over abstract issues of his royal prerogatives. Believing that he ruled by divine right, he had particular difficulty in coming to terms with a Parliament that was equally convinced that its approval was necessary for all new legislation, especially if it involved the appropriation of taxes. Still, despite stormy confrontations (in one of which the king attempted to dissolve Parliament and imprison its leaders), the first Stuart reign did not lead to any open break, and Charles I succeeded his father in 1625 without challenge. From that time on, however, relations between the king and Parliament would deteriorate rapidly, to end in civil war.

The period from Charles's accession to the opening of the Civil War corresponded almost exactly with Richelieu's ministry in

France (1625–42), and there is evidence that Charles had the Continental model of an administrative monarchy in mind as he sought to establish his own. He realized that such a project would require him to have a standing army at his command, and that to create such an army he would have to have the right to impose taxes on his own authority. Clearly Parliament saw the issue with the king in much the same terms, and considered the proposed royal army and taxation to be directly threatening to their own interests.

Perhaps the best explanation of the differences between the French and English stories is that the subjects of Louis XIII had recently come through a time of devastating civil war, and thus were willing to sacrifice abstract rights in exchange for physical security, whereas Charles's subject had no such motive for giving up any of their powers to the king. In addition, the chief servants of the French crown were men of extraordinary ability and devotion, which could hardly be said of the Stuarts' favorites. Finally, France provided the large, rich agricultural base required by a military monarchy, whereas England's growing wealth derived from commerce rather than land, and thus did not offer the same kind of support for a standing army.

Charles I began his reign by marrying the sister of Louis XIII, thus bringing the French concept of monarchy into the center of the English court. But the English Parliament also established its opposition to the king's plans from the start, by granting him the traditional rights to customs duties for only a single year. Being in urgent need of funds, Charles called new elections, which seemed only to increase the opposition. With his need for cash mounting, the king made still another attempt in 1628, with his third Parliament. This body opened proceedings by passing a "Petition of Right," which in effect outlawed martial law in time of peace. When Charles accepted this condition, Parliament voted him subsidies, but when he then collected customs duties without authorization, his favorite and chief advisor, the vain and incompetent Duke of Buckingham, was assassinated. The turbulence spread to the Commons in the next session of Parliament, provoking Charles to try to govern without Parliament for the next eleven years. Raising money by a variety of dubious expedients, he aroused the most opposition with an attempt to exploit his right to collect taxes from port cities to protect them against the threat of invasion; although there was no visible hint of danger, Charles collected the tax every year, and even extended it to include inland cities. While this issue was generating political opposition in England, the king suddenly undertook to require religious uniformity with the Church of England from the Scots, who were then in the process of establishing their own Presbyterian church. When he moved to enforce this policy, the Scots took up arms and defeated him in two minor engagements known as the Bishops' Wars. Unable to continue the struggle, Charles was forced to agree to pay a substantial indemnity to the Scottish army, and thus had to go back to Parliament for cash.

The result was what came to be known as the Long Parliament: convened in 1640, it would not finally be dissolved until 1653. From its start, Charles and the Commons were in open conflict, and the issues were always the same, with the king insisting on, and Parliament denying, his right to raise taxes on his own authority. In addition Parliament opposed any development of a royal army, and defended the independence of the courts. Finally, a series of mounting confrontations between the king and Commons led to Parliament mobilizing an armed force of 20,000 men and 4,000 cavalry, while the king called for his supporters to rally at Nottingham. It was the start of the Civil War.

Although the majority of the population remained neutral, factions formed around the king and Parliament. A great deal of historical effort has been expended in trying to establish just what motivated the two sides; but perhaps the most important clue lies in their geography. That is, although both factions found supporters in all areas of the country, in general the king's followers came from the agrarian north and west, while those of Parliament came from the more developed south and east, especially London and certain Atlantic ports. There is a logic in this division, and the key factor was London.

London had become an important port in the later Middle Ages, with the development of the Atlantic link between the Mediterranean and the Baltic; but it was only with the opening of the transatlantic trade in the seventeenth century that London began to rival and then surpass Paris as the largest European city. This spectacular growth was due in part to London's wresting from Amsterdam the position of chief entrepôt between the Baltic and the Atlantic, but even more important in its development was the city's relation to southern England. Located near the head of the Thames estuary – the highest point of the river reached by the ocean tide – London was accessible not only from the sea but also from the entire river valley, which now became the richest farming area in western Europe. When the city began to require vastly more food, the landowners along the river and its tributaries turned to intensive commercial farming – which was made possible by the fertility of the valley and the availability of cheap water transport along the river and its tributaries. The resulting mass production of crops reduced their cost, making profits for the enterprising farmers while providing the city with cheap food, the essential source of energy for all of its expanding activities. London not only became a shipping center but also produced many of the goods – such as textiles, hardware, and many luxury items – that it exported. Thus the city unified southeastern England in what now became the most prosperous local economic system in Europe, just as it was also becoming the center and metropolis of the new Atlantic trade.

What this new commercial society did not require or want was an absolutist bureaucratic state on the Continental model. Secure on their island from foreign invasion, the traders and manufacturers had no interest in supporting a standing army which could be used to impose the king's unlimited fiscal exactions on them. Moreover, because the local squires served as Justices of the Peace, maintaining order and administering justice, England had no need of royal officials; as a result, the English king had neither troops nor bureaucrats to enforce his will. On the other hand, England's remaining feudal nobles, living far from London on their large self-sufficient estates, felt no threat from the king and tended to rally to his cause against the commercial upstarts – including those nobles who had invested in commerce or commercial agriculture – whom they envied and feared.

With their feudal heritage, the king's supporters had the military advantage at first over their Parliamentary opponents; when they failed to use it, however, they gave time to a country squire named Oliver Cromwell to organize a highly effective army in the Parliamentary cause. Drawing on an unusually well-educated and politically committed class of small landowners, including many religious dissenters (whether Puritans, Presbyterians or other minor sects), Cromwell used their ability and dedication, and his own military genius, to weld together a disciplined and mobile force which excelled in the intermittent war of raids and sieges that followed.

The conflict reached a turning-point when Cromwell, assisted by the Scots, gained control of the north with a major victory over a badly outnumbered royalist army at Marston Moor. The following year Charles suffered another major defeat, which ended his resistance. Taking refuge with a Scottish force, he received terms from Parliament which he rejected, hoping to take advantage of divisions among his foes. However, his Scottish protectors were unwilling to fight for him, and turned him over to Parliament, whereupon he was seized and imprisoned by its army. He then escaped and returned to Scotland, and this time the Scots took up arms in his defense, since he was after all a Stuart, and a Scot by descent. But they were finally defeated by Cromwell, who was determined to rid England of this "man of blood," as he bitterly called the king. Following this action, a regiment of Puritan soldiers proceeded to march into the House of Commons and expel or arrest some hundred members who were thought to be too sympathetic to the king. The residue of sixty or seventy members – called the Rump Parliament – was now entirely under the control of the army, and obligingly voted to bring Charles to trial. He was sentenced and beheaded early in 1649.

Following his execution, the Rump abolished the monarchy and proclaimed the Commonwealth – a synonym for republic. If it drew its only legitimacy from Parliament, the new government was actually ruled by the army, under Cromwell. There is no little irony in the defeat and replacement of the king by just such an absolute ruler and standing army as the Parliamentary resistance had been intended to forestall. But because Cromwell was a conscientious statesman as well as a superb general, his regime was moderate, except in his murderous suppression of a Catholic revolt in Ireland that had been incited by the royalists. In this Cromwell showed no mercy, massacring the garrisons of two towns which had refused his summons to surrender. Thousands of Catholic lords lost their lands to Puritan soldiers in this defeat, and the unpopularity of these new settlers, after the atrocities committed by the Puritan army, embittered Irish relations with England for centuries.

Impatient with bickering and corruption in the Commonwealth, Cromwell introduced a new constitution, assuming the title of Lord Protector. In theory his regime was based on a unicameral Parliament, to which the members were appointed, but as soon as they quarreled with him he dissolved it, demonstrating to all where the power really lay.

The Restoration

Cromwell continued to rule until his death, when he was succeeded by his lazy, inexperienced son. But the country did not want continued army rule, and the regime was dissolved. Although it had been guilty of almost none of the excesses normally associated with military government, the Commonwealth had been authoritarian and unresponsive to public wishes, and this inherent rigidity was aggravated by its uncompromisingly Puritan complexion. If Charles's attempt to enforce conformity within the Anglican church had been a disaster, the army's Puritanism was in some respects even less tolerable – as in its "blue laws," which antagonized many by prohibiting such popular pastimes as gambling, cockfighting, and the theater. Even the army recognized this, and by reconvening the survivors of the original Long Parliament, cleared the way for new elections in preparation for the restoration (1660) of the late king's son, as Charles II.

Although as eager as his father had been to emulate the kings of Europe and enhance the power of the throne, this prince had learned one thing from his decade in exile: he "did not want to go on his travels again." This meant that unlike his cousin Louis XIV, who was about to assume absolute power in France, Charles II had to rule with the support of Parliament. Knowing better than to try to further his aims by defiance and arbitrary acts, he set out to develop his influence within Parliament. In this effort he initiated political practices – notably the formation of a court faction within Parliament – that would develop into the party system that has characterized British government ever since. The Tories, as they came to be called, upheld the monarchy and the Anglican

Church, while their opponents, the Whigs, defended Parliamentary rights and toleration for Protestant dissenters. During this period these "parties" were nothing more than loose coalitions of lords and gentry, the Tories counting more country squires and nobles among their number, and the Whigs more of the prosperous merchants from London and other ports. Since the Tories were Charles's natural supporters, he persecuted and even executed a few of the leading Whigs when they were convicted of conspiring against the Crown to seize control of Parliament.

The enthusiastic public welcome that greeted the new monarch represented in part a revulsion against the extremes of Puritan rule. Indeed the main preoccupation of the Restoration Parliament which had brought him back was to curb the rights, both political and religious, of all dissenters from the established Church of England, whether Protestant or Catholic, both of whom were barred by statute from holding public office or attending universities. On the other hand Charles granted a general pardon to almost everyone who had fought against his father, and advocated religious toleration for all in an effort to help the Catholics, whom he favored. Gradually this division between king and Parliament would develop into an irreconcilable rift that would finally bring down Charles's successor, James II, and ensure the preeminence of Parliament and its laws in the government of England.

In seeking every means of freeing himself from Parliament's control, Charles took advantage of the opportunity presented in 1670 when Louis XIV proposed a secret treaty of cooperation. About to launch a war against Holland, Louis hoped to neutralize England by offering Charles a huge subsidy that would enable him to dismiss Parliament if it moved to aid the Dutch. Since he had no interest in the war, this proposal suited Charles to perfection; but Parliament, although it did not learn of the secret terms of the Treaty of Dover until much later, suspected the worst – correctly, as was eventually disclosed, since Charles had promised Louis to reveal his secret Catholicism and try to reconvert England as soon as it was feasible. As a result, most members of Parliament began to view all Catholics as partisans of the French and supporters of the Stuarts' absolutist ambitions.

With the help of able ministers and carefully orchestrated bribes in Parliament, Charles was able to defuse the opposition and even bring England into the war against Holland for two years. The remainder of his reign, however, was largely occupied by a continuing contest with Parliament over religious toleration and the possibility of a Catholic successor to the throne. Because Charles fathered no legitimate offspring, his legal heir was his brother James, the Duke of York, who made no secret of his own Catholicism and even took a Catholic princess as his second wife. Although legislation was proposed in Parliament to exclude Catholics from the succession, it was never passed, largely because James's heirs, in turn, were his daughters by his first wife, both of whom had been raised as Anglicans.

When Charles died, therefore, James II succeeded without any Parliamentary opposition. Almost immediately, however, one of Charles's illegitimate sons launched an abortive invasion from Holland to seize the throne. When the attempt collapsed, James took the occasion to purge suspected rebels, try to reinforce his authority, and establish religious toleration for his fellow Catholics, while also raising many of them to high places in the army, navy and government. By continuing this disastrous line of action James succeeded in uniting both Parliamentary parties against him in a common defense of the Church of England. Finally, as matters approached a climax, a son was born to the new queen.

The revolution of 1688

With the probability now that James would be succeeded by a Catholic heir, seven eminent Whigs and Tories sent an invitation to William of Orange, Stadholder of Holland and husband of James's elder daughter Mary, to assume the throne and save England from Catholic rule. William, who was just then in urgent need of English help against the French, sailed for England with a few thousand men. The desperate James tried to make belated concessions, but finding no response, he ignominiously fled to France, although in fact he had at his command a strong army and even stronger navy which could have repelled William without difficulty. This "Glorious Revolution" of 1688 – so-called because it took place entirely without bloodshed – was to establish permanent constitutional government in England.

To make certain that the relations between Parliament and the

Crown could never again be in question, Parliament spelled them out in the Bill of Rights of 1689. Among other provisions it specified that no law could be made or rescinded without Parliament's approval, and no money raised for a standing army without its consent. This document also provided for jury trial, due process, reasonable bail, and life tenure for judges, as well as the right of citizens to bear arms. In its miscellaneous character this Bill summed up the conclusions about government which had been reached by the large majority of Englishmen in half a century of struggle and debate.

William had no trouble persuading his new subjects to join the war against the hated French, thus restoring England to the leading role in world affairs that its civil strife had prevented it from assuming ever since the death of Elizabeth. In particular the English were threatened by Louis XIV's attempts to seize the Spanish Netherlands, the best staging area for an invasion of their island. To conduct the war William oversaw the organization of the Bank of England, inspired by the Bank of Amsterdam, which was supported by Parliamentary credit and served systematically to draw the funds of the wealthy merchants into the royal coffers. Once this institution was in place William had far more cash at his disposal than Louis could raise in taxes or by piecemeal loans; and it was in part because of this better funding that superiority at sea was decisively gained by the English. Despite many victories on the Continent, Louis was forced to conclude peace without attaining any of his goals.

When William died a few years after Mary, he was succeeded by Mary's sister Anne, who immediately joined another alliance against Louis XIV in the War of the Spanish Succession, from which England emerged as the chief challenger to French hegemony. With the strongest fleet and largest treasury of the age, the little island kingdom, which Louis had been able to manipulate with bribes a quarter of a century before, now forced him to the brink of personal defeat and national collapse.

THE EUROPEAN WORLD

During the second half of the seventeenth century, more than three-quarters of Europe's hundred million inhabitants lived on and worked the land. Of the rest, at least half lived in the small market towns (with populations of 1,000 to 3,000) that dotted the hinterland, serving the peasant villages and resident landlords. Interspersed at much greater distances were provincial or regional capitals, usually with populations of 5,000 to 20,000. Most of these cities had once been the seats of feudal courts, but they were now likely to serve as administrative and judicial centers for the new monarchies; accordingly, they were linked to their royal capitals by the new roads that the rulers were building during this period. Much the largest of the inland capitals was Paris, with a population of some 500,000 while some (like Potsdam, with a population of 3,000) were no larger than rural market towns. Whatever their size, however, most such inland cities had to be located in a fertile valley of a navigable river, because of the prohibitive cost of transporting food any distance over land.

Finally, there were dozens of commercial cities, located at the best ports on navigable water. The oldest, dotting the Rhine–Elbe corridor and the shores of northern Italy, had by now lost their old luxury trade and persisted mostly as regional market towns and trade centers. At this time, however, a whole new category of tidewater ports was springing up around the Baltic coast and particularly along the shores of the North Atlantic. Even those that were old medieval sites, like London or Amsterdam, were essentially new cities in the seventeenth century, and often resembled their counterparts in the New World (such as Philadelphia or Boston) far more than their inland sisters. Some of these ports were even planned (for example St Petersburg), and almost all of them were rich by any contemporary standards. With the notable exception of London, however, few had a population of more than 50,000.

The vast majority of the population who worked the soil lived lives of unmitigated toil and deprivation. Characteristically they farmed village lands collectively for their own subsistence, and the estates of the landlords for rent. With the general spread of rural peace in the second half of the century, the peasants in western Europe probably had a slightly easier time than they had had earlier, but in France these gains were soon offset by the monarchy's ever greater demands for taxes. In eastern Europe, for a variety of reasons, the lords were able to increase their authority over the peasants at this time, returning them to a serfdom that bordered on slavery (they could in fact be bought and sold), especially on the huge estates that lay along the Vistula and other large rivers.

In the New World, the transatlantic economy had given rise to commercial farming of the tropical crops that were most in demand in the European market. Huge plantations were established by European colonists in tropical areas of the Americas – above all, on the islands of the Caribbean – and African slaves were imported to work them. Although the Spanish and Portuguese had long since introduced African slavery in their colonies, this was the period that saw the beginning of the massive shipment of Africans to the New World, as the basis of the profitable mass production that was being achieved through the plantation system. The whole purpose of the commercial plantations was, of course, to produce the maximum surplus to sell in the urban markets of the commercial system, and since the New World lacked a peasant population that could be put to work on these plantations (the native Americans had also proved useless for this purpose), the importation of the hardy African workers appeared to be a rational means to this ruthless end. (It is worth noting in this context that the commercial community of the ancient Aegean had also resorted to slave labor to achieve mass production on its plantations.)

In all of the various types of European cities more than half the population lived at a level comparable to, or worse than, that of the rural peasants. By far the largest part of the population in any city consisted of the astonishing number of day laborers, beggars and criminals who crowded its alleys and basements. Of the laborers the largest number were porters, who did the work of transporting water, fuel, and building materials on their backs. (Human workers were far cheaper to sustain than animals, and there were few city streets wide or smooth enough to make a cart useful.) In addition the cities housed a small middle class of tradesmen and craftsmen who provided the goods and services required by their fellow residents; the large majority of these people also enjoyed only a very modest standard of living. The fledgling Atlantic commerce improved the lives of very few at this time, and the overwhelming fact of life for most Europeans, in the seventeenth century as before, was that the available means of raising and distributing food simply did not produce enough surplus to support more than a tiny leisured elite. Most of these favored few were nobles, whose wealth derived from land but who lived in the cities if they could afford to, with the richest ones congregating in the royal capitals. Even for the most privileged members of the society, of course, life offered little comfort and much hardship, as we think of these conditions today.

In the cities, the elite was increasingly coming to include two new categories beside the resident wealthy nobles. In the inland cities and capitals there would usually be a few rich commoners, generally on their way to buying a title and noble status, who owed their success to service of the crown, or to the commercial farming of land near the city. A striking contrast to this group was provided by the "merchant princes" of the port cities, who made huge profits (and sometimes suffered corresponding losses) from the large-scale production and commerce involved in ocean trade. On the whole they tended to live in their own cultural world, developing a separate style of comfort and elegance (which was often less lavish than that of the great nobles), and generally ignoring the hinterland society. The principal exception to this pattern of life was their readiness to lend unlimited sums to the rising monarchies. This curious symbiotic relationship is an indication that the new commercial elite at first had few ways to reinvest its unprecedented profits, and of those by far the most important and available was the royal treasury.

Outside the Atlantic economy there were few ways to increase one's wealth except through inheritance and marriage, or occasionally royal favor. The standard preoccupation of large property owners, whether noble or untitled, was simply to preserve the family patrimony, not increase it. In the inland cities, therefore, the historical cliché of the ever-rising bourgeoisie should be regarded critically. There the striking phenomenon was not so much economic as demographic dynamism: the population was growing faster than the economy in these areas, thus leaving increasing numbers of young townsmen struggling to find a place for themselves. One of the few developing sectors in their society was the monarchy, and such new employment as existed tended to be in law and public service rather than in business.

As it had been since the dawn of civilization, the development of an advanced culture was still largely a product of city life, due to the greater economic resources and larger community that size provided. This tendency was strikingly manifested in the physical appearance of the cities themselves during this period, with the proliferation of a dramatic style of architecture called the baroque. Although it was first used for churches, it became above all the style of the royal courts and capitals, setting an elaborate stage for the drama of power and privilege that was being played out by the new monarchies. One of the greatest examples of this use of the baroque style was Louis XIV's palace at Versailles, which became the symbol of royal residence to be imitated in all sizes from one end of Europe to the other.

In England, however, the baroque style was generally rejected in favor of a revival of classical simplicity. One of the few exceptions to this rule was St Paul's Cathedral, designed by Sir Christopher Wren, one of the great masterpieces of baroque architecture. Wren is also admired, however, for his many beautiful London churches in the classical style; and it is their simple lines and pointed steeples that crossed the Atlantic to reappear in the wooden churches of New England.

A similar divergence between England and the Continent could be seen in other arts, and perhaps most importantly, in the entire range of intellectual activity, from social and political criticism through philosophy to science. The Civil War provoked a whole new literature of political thought in England, which culminated in the essays of John Locke, celebrating the Glorious Revolution and spelling out the new concept that authority is legitimate only when based in the consent of the governed. Needless to say this idea contrasted strongly with the contemporary justifications of absolute monarchy produced by royal spokesmen at Versailles, notably Jacques Bossuet, bishop of Meaux, or even France's later defenders of "enlightened despotism." While Bossuet's defense of Louis XIV's monarchy was a highly systematic description of a logical hierarchy of power, Locke's theory of the ideal government starts from an examination of the needs and rights of the individuals who made up the body politic. Not only did these two attitudes serve the radically different interests of the two governments, but they also seemed essentially to reflect two divergent ways of regarding the world, which in turn can be attributed to the societies in which they were produced. The centrally administered territorial state on the Continent was a hierarchical system in operation, whereas no such authority could be established over the Atlantic community, with the result that its governance was left to the mutual agreement of its members.

Even in the field of science it seems possible to discern a similar difference of approach between Continental and English thinkers. The most important Europeans tended to emphasize mathematics within a context of philosophical speculation, whereas the English scientists focused on the empirical method. In France, for example, René Descartes undertook to deduce a proof of the existence of God from the proposition, "I think, therefore I am." Blaise Pascal, also a Frenchman, and Gottfried Leibniz, a German, continued this speculative tradition, which in spite of their mathematical achievements (Leibniz invented calculus simultaneously with Newton) ultimately led away from the method that would prove most fruitful in the sciences. The greatest scientist of the age was the English Isaac Newton, who used direct observation as the basis of his explorations, and for the next century at least it would be the English with their empiricism who would dominate science. After Newton one of the most important contributors was William Harvey, who demonstrated the circulation of the blood; and after him came too many to mention except collectively, by noting the founding of the Royal Society in 1662. This institution, established under generous royal patronage, may have been inspired in part by the French Academy, which Richelieu had created in 1636 to bring forty of the wisest and most literate Frenchmen together to serve the king. But as naturally as the focus of the French Academy was on literature, and its purpose enhancement of the monarchy, the function of its English counterpart was the pursuit of scientific knowledge for its own sake. And while the influence of each institution would be important in the development of its own country, the activities of the Royal Society had a great impact on all science, and therefore on the subsequent history of the entire world.

2

The Eighteenth Century

Although Louis XIV had failed to conquer the left bank of the Rhine, he did make France by far the greatest military power on the Continent – a power which it had required a coalition of half of Europe to contain. As a result, the administrative monarchy he established in France was taken as a model for survival by the rest of Europe's rulers, and one of the principal themes of the eighteenth century was the emergence and development of a series of similar states capable of playing an independent part on Europe's stage. Although these began as military organizations, they also served as vehicles of political and administrative reform, some of them to the extent that they became known as "enlightened despotisms."

During this same period a nearly inverse development was taking place on the Atlantic. Where at the beginning of the century there were half a dozen naval powers of roughly comparable strength, by the end of the Seven Years War (1763) there remained no single serious rival to Britain's fleet. Unlike the French state on land, however, British naval hegemony did not invite imitation, primarily because it posed no threat to the other commercial countries. This was due in part to the temper of Britain's ruling elite, but also to the nature of the element in which these countries operated. It simply was not feasible to impose an efficient rule and administration on an oceanic base. The one time the British ignored this fact of life – in their effort to control their American colonies – they paid dearly for their error.

Britain's great wealth and power derived not from military rule but rather from her capacity to organize and facilitate the growing Atlantic commerce. This commercial system depended on the growing exchange of goods between the port cities on both sides of the Atlantic. One of the problems of understanding this phenomenon is the deeply ingrained habit of considering these trading operations as primarily British or French or Dutch, when in fact they were primarily Atlantic. This does not mean that there were no rivalries, or even skirmishes, between the merchants and seamen of different countries, but rather that any continued commercial success depended on the voluntary cooperation of the participating members for their mutual benefit. Inevitably the two radically dissimilar systems of social organization – the Continental military monarchies and the Atlantic commercial community – produced quite disparate institutions, which were explained and justified by very different systems of ideas.

Culturally the eighteenth century saw the consolidation of the modernizing tendencies of the previous century, and their evolution into a civilization recognizably similar to our own. This can be illustrated by some of the formal titles that the eighteenth century has acquired. As the "age of reason" it was the period in which the idea gained currency that men, not the gods or fate, were responsible for human destiny, and that their rights and obligations must be evaluated in the light of reason rather than of divine revelation. The eighteenth century has also been called the "age of democratic revolution" because of the revolt of the American colonies against Britain, and the overthrow (or actually the transformation) of the French monarchy. From these two crucial developments emerged the first significant attempts to involve the general population in the management of public affairs – even though otherwise these "revolutions" were not as similar as their common name implies.

The same period also encompassed the "industrial revolution," which would initiate economic changes even more radical than those taking place in politics, although the two spheres would powerfully interact. And finally on the Continent the eighteenth was the century of limited war and formal diplomacy, as monarchs struggled to establish themselves on the French model, while overseas it witnessed the origin of the modern commercial empires. Although the Atlantic nations did not penetrate the other continents to any great extent during the eighteenth century, with the major exception of North America, they did begin the process of establishing control of the world's oceans and some of their coasts. It was this system of oceanic communications that sooner or later would introduce to the rest of the world the rationalism, democratic values, and economic development that would transform eighteenth-century Europe into the society we know today.

THE NEW MONARCHIES

When he died in 1715, Louis XIV left France exhausted, with his goal of pushing her borders to the Rhine only half-fulfilled. Even so, she was still the dominant power on the Continent – larger, richer, better organized and administered, and militarily far more powerful than any other European state. Both at home and abroad Louis XIV had established his own personal style as the model for royal conduct and magnificence. Although his reign was followed by a debilitating regency and two incompetent successors, no one would seriously challenge Bourbon authority in France for three-quarters of a century; and no other European monarch would attempt to play a major role on the Continent without following Louis's example by reorganizing his realm into a centralized administrative-military state. Even those hundreds of minor principalities (especially in western and southern Germany) that were too small to pretend to great-power status would strain their resources to pattern their courts after Versailles – all too often with comic-opera effect. Thus in style as well as substance, Louis XIV's personal domination of France and Europe during his long reign (1661–1715) would be continued by his successors and imitators through most of the eighteenth century.

The chief purpose of the new-style monarchs was to impose an effective rule over an extended territory that had previously been subject to local feudal lords. Because they were new, relatively efficient, and in principle dedicated to "enlightened" administration, these monarchies were admired by contemporary intellectuals and social critics, who saw in them instruments for reform and progress, even though their authority was based in force.

The only existing restraints to the arbitrary exercise of royal power were local institutions of medieval origin, such as provincial

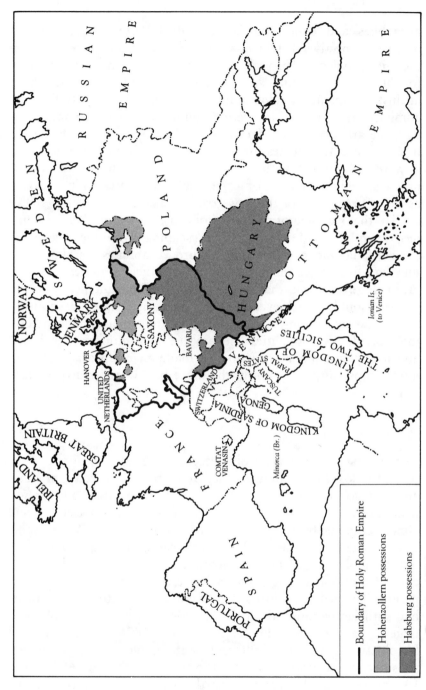

MAP 1 *Europe, 1721*

Boundary of Holy Roman Empire

Hohenzollern possessions

Habsburg possessions

assemblies and courts (in France called "estates" and "parle-ments," respectively), which were in fact bastions of feudal aris-tocratic privilege. Through these institutions the old nobility fought a stubborn and surprisingly successful rearguard action against the spread of royal authority, so that in actuality the new administrative monarchies were all built upon major compromises with the aristocrats they pretended to have reduced to obedience. In every case, the greatest magnates – those too powerful to crush – were bought off with high offices or recognition of special privileges, while the mass of lesser nobles were pressed into service as the officer corps of the new royal armies.

To the vast majority of Europeans, however, "enlightened despotism" offered new hope of escaping from the thicket of ancient anarchic customs and absurd disabilities within which they had lived since medieval times. The efficient, impersonal and rational government that was considered "enlightened" in this context could be achieved only by authority; thus "despotism" was necessary to bring about reform. But reform also depended on the individual personalities and abilities of a number of remark-able new young monarchs who now made their appearance, begin-ning – most surprisingly – in the more backward area of eastern Europe.

Peter the Great

At this time Russia was hardly accepted as European by the West. Its Orthodox faith barely entitled it to be considered Christian, and its vigorous rejection of everything foreign since its liberation from Tartar subjugation at the end of the fifteenth century had almost completely isolated it from western Europe. At the same time, however, the tsars had been engaged in a struggle with their unruly nobles (called boyars) that was quite similar to the feudal conflict that was taking place in western Europe during the same period. Toward the end of the seventeenth century, Tsar Alexis had sufficiently consolidated his authority to be able to subdue a huge peasant uprising, and at his death in 1676 the succession of his oldest son was not challenged by the nobles. His two younger sons became co-tsars at the death of their brother in 1682, and a few years later the younger of the two, Peter, overthrew the regency of their sister and assumed full personal authority, in 1689.

Although only seventeen years old at the time, Peter was already seven feet tall, a giant in every respect, with a truly superior mind and superhuman energy as well as a volcanic temper. From the outset his purpose was clear: to reverse the traditional Russian distrust of everything foreign and new, and to learn as much as possible about Europe, putting this knowledge to use in modernizing his backward country. To bring Russia into European affairs he would have to establish ports on the Baltic Sea in the north and the Black Sea in the south; and to do this would require a modern army and navy. Finally, to be free to carry out any policy, he would need to crush the still independent boyars. (As a symbol of his authority the young tsar forced these luxuriantly bearded nobles to conform to the current clean-shaven European style, and actually barbered some of them himself.)

To establish his position in the Baltic, Peter began building the entirely new port city of St Petersburg at the head of the Gulf of Finland. Intended to serve as his capital and "window on the west," this was the largest planned city yet undertaken in Europe, and to design it Peter brought in some of the best Italian and French architects of the time. Once he had moved the government there from Moscow – the center of boyar resistance – Peter felt free to prepare for war against Sweden, then the dominant power in the Baltic region. To provide his backward country with some of the modern techniques it lacked, he personally undertook a study mission in Europe, traveling incognito, and actually working for a time as an apprentice in a Dutch shipyard. What he brought back to Russia was not only modern naval and military techniques, which he imparted to his officers in person, but also the modern concept of the administrative monarchy, which he implemented by replacing customary institutions with a new bureaucracy directly under his control. His object was not merely to control the nobles, but also to make them responsible for collecting taxes, and for providing him with military or civil service. One important consequence of this approach was to increase the nobles' authority over their peasants, thus reversing the current trend toward the relaxation of feudal serfdom. Faced with this threat, some of the peasants fled to the country's uninhabited eastern frontier, where they lived as free herdsmen and woodsmen known as Cossacks. Gradually these pioneers opened up Siberia, and even in Peter's reign provoked a border conflict with China which had to be settled by diplomatic negotiation and a treaty.

In 1700 the anticipated war with Sweden began at Narva, where Sweden's young Charles XII, a spectacular battlefield commander, completely overwhelmed the inexperienced Peter. But in spite of his tactical abilities Charles had little strategic sense, and he wasted the next years on a pointless campaign in Poland after which he attempted a foolhardy raid on Moscow with the aid of some rebellious Cossacks. Peter, who had managed to regroup his forces, was able to isolate his opponent deep in Russia and crush him at Poltava in 1709, using Russia's vast distances in a tactic that would be repeated in future famous Russian victories. Charles was lucky to escape with his life, while Peter acquired Estonia, Livonia, and other Baltic territories from Sweden, thus establishing Russia as a Baltic power with a solid opening to the west.

When Peter died in 1725, Russia suffered a troubled succession and period of confusion, but the foundations he had laid for a modern administrative state would survive to serve his successors and provide another much-imitated model for other rulers of the period. He had succeeded in subjecting largely independent landed aristocrats to the authority of a royal bureaucracy, which in turn financed and operated a modern professional army. The implementation of this program meant the construction and mainte-nance of effective communications (roads) throughout the huge empire, but it had little effect on the basic economy, which con-tinued to rest on the nobles' self-sufficient estates, or clusters of estates around market towns, with some internal commerce mov-ing along the large rivers. Although St Petersburg became a flourishing Baltic port, it had little economic connection with the rest of Russia. Even its appearance was "oceanic," in that it resembled Bordeaux or Philadelphia far more than it did Moscow or any other Russian city. Finally it should be noted that the changes brought about by Peter the Great were almost as signif-icant for the rest of Europe as they were for Russia, since after his reign Russia became involved in virtually every general European war, frequently as the decisive factor because of her nearly limit-less reserves of manpower. Even so, it was some time before the significance of Peter's achievement was fully recognized in the west. A crude, uncouth genius, Peter had transformed Russia from a backward state – on a par in western minds with Turkey, India and China (all of which it bordered) – into the largest and one of the most powerful of European monarchies. There was nothing in Russian history, geography, class structure or economy that predestined her for this triumph, or doomed her rivals Poland, Sweden and Turkey to collapse. Instead, in this period of absolutism, it seems to have been the personality of the despot that determined the course of history.

Poland

While Peter was turning Russia into a competitive European power, Russia's southwestern neighbor, Poland, was disintegrating into anarchy. Culturally the Poles were oriented toward the west far more than the Russians were; for example, they used the Roman rather than Cyrillic alphabet, and they belonged to the Catholic rather than the Orthodox branch of the Christian Church. Their territory was centered on the valley of the Vistula and the ancient cities of Warsaw and Cracow, but it extended as far north as the Niemen River and southeast nearly to the Black Sea. Like Russia before Peter, Poland was dominated by aristocratic landlords; but since these nobles were no more devoted to their independence than the boyars had been, it is difficult to explain why no central administrative authority was established, allowing the monarchy to retain its elective character. One factor was certainly the lack of an accepted and resourceful ruling house that produced monarchs of the quality of Peter in Russia, the Hohenzollerns in Prussia or the Habsburgs in Austria. Whatever the cause of Poland's political incoherence, the consequence was her partitioning and assimilation by her three chief neighbors, who thereby brought the anarchic nobles into authoritarian regimes after all.

The rise of Prussia

In 1701 the reigning Hohenzollern assumed the title of king in his Prussian lands, as Frederick I. His successor Frederick William used this oddly shaped territorial base to build an army which was the largest in Europe in relation to the population (some 80,000 troops out of some 8 million inhabitants). While he was too cautious to risk any of his magnificent troops in battle, Frederick William drilled them to a state of perfection which would make them a formidable fighting force in the talented hands of his son who succeeded him in 1740 as Frederick II. Having been raised according to his father's rigid concept of military discipline, the young prince had no love for army life and seemed a most unlikely candidate for martial glory. No sooner was he on the throne, however, than Frederick II launched his army in a lightning attack on the Austrian province of Silesia which revealed him to be a field commander of the greatest skill.

The occasion for this raid was the recent succession of a princess to the Habsburg inheritance in Vienna. Because the late Emperor Charles VI had lacked a male heir, he had left his Austrian throne, though not his imperial title, to his daughter Maria Theresa. If this unusual arrangement provided ample excuse, by the standards of the time, for military intervention by ambitious neighbors, the results at least suggest that Charles's apparent doubts about the military capacities of his gifted daughter were justified. The war which Frederick started for possession of the rich province of Silesia actually began a struggle for the leadership of Germany which would not be resolved for more than a century. Inevitably the fighting involved other powers: the king of Bavaria laid claim to Maria Theresa's inheritance, whereupon the French, still instinctively hostile to Habsburg power, gave him their support. This then brought the British in on the Habsburg side, but in reality only to fight the French, which they did in India, North America (King George's War), and at sea. The results of all this widespread activity were few: Frederick's seizure of Silesia was recognized, but Maria Theresa's succession was confirmed, at least for a time.

One important effect of the war, however, was to establish Frederick as a military genius. With the development of firearms, particularly the musket, battles and wars could be won by the skillful deployment of troops as well as by their sheer numbers or reckless courage. The commander's objective became the concentration of his firepower on a limited portion of the enemy's troops, with the hope of breaking their line and thus dividing their forces. This tactic required a high degree of professional discipline in the soldiers, particularly in their ability to execute marching maneuvers under fire, which in turn made them too valuable to risk in any but a favorable situation. As a result, wars became relatively orderly contests between professional (often mercenary) armies, which attempted to outmarch one another in an effort to seize a superior position, or alternatively to avoid fighting at a disadvantage by retreat or even surrender. In this game Frederick had an instinctive ability to size up a situation and take full advantage of any opportunities it offered to corner and defeat his enemy; thus he became the decisive factor in his country's impressive military success.

Austria and the Seven Years War

Although Maria Theresa's inheritance was much larger than Frederick's Prussia, and should therefore have given her military superiority, the new queen was no match for her opponent on the battlefield. She had neither a general of Frederick's skill nor a unified modern army; rather she had to raise separate units of troops from each of the Habsburg possessions with the backing of the local nobles. Although this antiquated system had been good enough to drive the Turks out of Hungary, it was not good enough to keep Frederick out of Silesia. Finally the queen and her advisors responded to the challenge by creating a single fiscal system for all her territories, as the necessary base for the development of a unified army. This reform was strictly limited to military affairs, however, and left the great nobles firmly in control of local government (and in Hungary even exempt from taxes). The army it created won few victories, but it did serve to keep the Habsburgs a major factor in European affairs for the next hundred years.

The peace of 1748 that recognized Frederick's conquest of Silesia was accepted by the other European monarchs because even with this addition Prussia was still the smallest of the major European powers and did not appear to pose any threat to the others. Maria Theresa, however, was for from reconciled to the loss, not merely to her prestige but also to her income, since the great estates along the Oder River could export surplus grain to the Baltic trade and earn important cash returns. Forced to bide her time, the queen did her best to build up her forces until in 1756 her opportunity seemed to have come. The French, her traditional enemies, now offered her support in an attack on Frederick that was motivated by England's decision to form an alliance with Prussia as a Continental balance to France. This "diplomatic revolution," as it was called, was primarily the product of France's growing struggle with Britain particularly overseas. The British chose Prussia this time instead of their traditional Habsburg ally in part because of Frederick's military prowess, but probably more because of their new common interests in the Baltic and the easy access this sea route provided to the British for the delivery of subsidies and supplies to Prussian ports. Thus only Maria Theresa had an immediate objective in going to war at this time, but the rise of Prussia and the growing rivalry between France and Britain made a general European conflagration almost inevitable as the new powers struggled for European hegemony.

The ensuing Seven Years War raged from 1756 to 1763, and proved the final defeat of France's challenge to Britain overseas, in India as well as North America (where the conflict was known as the French and Indian War). On the Continent, Russia joined France and her allies, putting Frederick in an apparently hopeless situation since his troops were now vastly outnumbered as well as surrounded on three sides. With the help of English money to supply new troops, however, Frederick staged a brilliant campaign, repeatedly escaping defeat, until a sudden change of regime in Russia brought a new young tsar to the throne who regarded Frederick as his personal hero. Shifting Russia's alliance to the other side, Peter III saved Prussia from disaster and put an end to the hopes of its opponents, thus bringing the war to a conclusion. In Europe peace was restored essentially on the basis of the *status quo ante*; overseas, however, the British won an overwhelming victory, as the French were driven out of both India and North America, retaining only a few islands off Newfoundland and in the Caribbean.

THE ATLANTIC COMMUNITY

From the beginning of the eighteenth century to the end of the Seven Years War (1763), a number of critical changes had taken place in the European world. On the Continent, France was no longer the single power but had been joined by four or five others, including the reorganized Habsburg possessions, Prussia, Russia, and even Spain. On the Atlantic, however, the opposite process had taken place. Where there had been three leading maritime powers at the end of the seventeenth century (Holland, Portugal, and England), and four others to be reckoned with (Spain, France, Denmark, and Sweden), by the end of the Seven Years War Britain had assumed an unassailable superiority at sea.

The building of new land powers had been a simple matter of following the French example: establishing a central administration, working out compromises with the nobles, and creating and perfecting a large standing army. The process of Britain's rise to naval superiority, however, was more complex. The first element was the vast general expansion of Atlantic trade which occurred around the turn of the century, and the second was Britain's emergence as the dominant factor in that new system.

Economic growth is a difficult phenomenon to describe in historical narrative, since its progress is seldom marked by events as precise and decisive as battles and reigns. In this case, however, a marked acceleration occurred in Atlantic commerce toward the end of the seventeenth century, which was destined to transform European society.

Since the later Middle Ages, Mediterranean merchants had been sending ships up the Atlantic coast of Europe to the North Sea and the Baltic, but it was not until the Portuguese reached the Far East at the end of the fifteenth century that transoceanic commerce had been attempted. The first cargoes that were brought back to Portugal, mainly pepper, made colossal fortunes for the merchants; but the quantities involved were so much larger than those that had been arriving in the Near East by caravan that the price collapsed, and pepper became a glut on the market. When the English and Dutch entered the trade, emphasis had shifted to coffee and then tea, with some fabrics thrown in.

The major product used to buy these eastern luxuries was silver, which was then in good supply in Europe, primarily because of the Spanish mining operations in the New World. Curiously, however, neither the importation of treasure into Spain nor its export to the Far East did much to strengthen the economies of Europe. The Spanish used their wealth to buy basic necessities (such as food and textiles) from northern Europe, rather than to develop their own productive capacity, and the East India trading companies of England, Holland, and France simply passed on this gold and silver to the east to pay for the luxuries they imported, so that it offered no stimulus to European production.

The slave trade

Gradually, however, a "New Spain" made up of soldiers and officials began to emerge on the islands and shores of the Caribbean. To maintain themselves in any comfort these expatriates had to establish large estates – on the traditional feudal model – and to depend on exports from Europe for many amenities. To pay for these, they needed products to exchange, and fundamental to this production was the establishment of a reliable labor force in the colonies. From the beginning, the Spanish, and the Portuguese in Brazil, had found the native Indians unsatisfactory as laborers, and had turned to importing slaves from Africa, to work first the mines and then the estates.

Slave trading on a small scale already existed on the West African coast before the Portuguese became the first Europeans to arrive there by sea. The original buyers were North African merchants who traversed the Sahara by caravan, and the slaves were simply one of the valuable commodities the traders could obtain in West Africa, along with gold and ivory. Generally the suppliers of all these commodities were local rulers or their agents, and the slaves were enemy captives who had been taken in wars or raids. The European traders were welcomed into this market, particularly because they could pay in firearms, a product of the greatest interest to rulers everywhere. The Portuguese made the first European purchases of African slaves in the middle of the fifteenth century, taking them back to Portugal as curiosities. But it was with the beginning of European settlement of the New World, and above all the development of the labor-intensive sugar-producing plantations in the Caribbean, that the Europeans began the wholesale transportation of African slaves across the Atlantic.

This slave trade grew steadily for three and a half centuries, eventually transporting some ten million Africans to the western hemisphere, and involved merchants from almost all of the Atlantic ports of Europe. Through the sixteenth century the Portuguese dominated the trade almost exclusively, providing the slaves for their plantations in Brazil. In the seventeenth century, first the Dutch and then the English and French took over the trade and expanded it, supplying not only the Portuguese and Spanish colonies but increasingly their own, as their governments acquired islands in the West Indies and began turning them into huge sugar-producing factories.

It was the French who first introduced sugar cane into the West Indies, in 1640, finding that the soil and climate of the islands were ideal for the crop. They also found that despite the vast amount of labor required to produce it, sugar yielded even vaster profits when sold in the insatiable European market. By the beginning of the eighteenth century a flourishing plantation economy had sprung up in the West Indies, producing mostly sugar-but also tobacco and a few other specialized crops, and the profitable "triangle trade" was well established that linked the islands with their labor supply from Africa and their markets in Europe. This commerce was further facilitated during the seventeenth century by major improvements in ship design which made it easier both to hold a course against adverse winds and to carry bulky cargoes over long distances.

As the English colonies began to grow up along the North American coast, their merchants also entered this trade, particularly by importing sugar from the Caribbean to be turned into rum, which they then exported to both Europe and Africa. In the southern colonies, meanwhile, the tropical climate and ready supply of slaves and markets led to the establishment of a plantation system based on the Caribbean model, that was to expand and dominate the culture of the South until brought to an end by the American Civil War. As far north as Virginia those who owned land in this region were typically "gentlemen" with huge holdings, which they assumed would be cleared, planted, and farmed by a servant class, as such estates would be in Europe – and by now, imported Africans were established as the peasants of this part of the New World. As in the West Indies, the African slaves in the American South soon greatly outnumbered their European masters, who were therefore never entirely free from the fear of slave revolts, and often enforced their rule with brutality to prevent any attempts at resistance. The slave system was less harsh on the mainland than on the islands, however, if only because the climate was found unsuitable for growing sugar cane, which of all the plantation crops involved the most grueling labor to cultivate and process; in addition the American landowners generally lived on their plantations, whereas those in the West Indies usually enjoyed their profits in Europe while leaving the operation of their plantations, and the power of life and death over their slaves, in the hands of unregulated overseers.

Effects of transatlantic trade

During the eighteenth century the growth of the port cities on both sides of the Atlantic led to a mutual trade in staples, especially food and fuel, that eventually became even more profitable than the trade in slaves and plantation products. This commerce included such commodities as salt from the marshes along France's southern shores, fish from the North Sea and grain from the Baltic; but the greatest single item in bulk and value was coal for London's endlessly growing needs. Carrying all these goods along the European coasts as well as overseas demanded huge fleets of merchant ships, and since much of Europe had been mostly deforested even before the shipbuilding boom began, the builders had to find their supplies along the wooded coasts of the Baltic or northeastern North America. Access to such naval stores, including pitch as well as wood, was therefore of great strategic significance in both peace and war.

Because wood was in such short supply, the growing cities turned to other materials for domestic fuel where they could; thus Amsterdam ran on peat and London on coal. Simply because of London's huge demand for coal, England had much the biggest shipbuilding industry in the European world, and by far the largest merchant marine. And because there was little difference between most fighting and cargo ships, this meant that Britain automatically had the largest reserve fleet, as well as the most important naval construction facilities – which she now began to use to build and maintain the greatest navy in existence.

During the period between the Peace of Utrecht and the Seven Years War (1713–56) there was comparative peace on the Atlantic. Holland had slipped into a position stably subordinate to England, while in France the regent for the child successor to Louis XIV was intent on amassing the largest fortune possible during his brief period of power, and that purpose seemed best served by peace and trade. French ports prospered, largely from the slave and sugar trades, and made fortunes for the merchants, but without creating any substantial base for future naval power remotely comparable to that of Britain. This was unimportant so long as peace persisted, and even after the end of the regency, the young Louis XV's government continued the policy of friendship and cooperation with the British. With Prussia's invasion of Silesia in 1740, however, the French could not resist the instinctive urge to support an enemy of their traditional Habsburg rivals. Thus France joined Prussia just as the British, worried by the aggressive behavior of this neighbor to their own king's Hanoverian possessions, went to Austria's defense. As a result Britain and France were again at war, and the arena in which they clashed was now inevitably the Atlantic and North America. While this conflict, called King George's War, remained minor in itself, it launched a renewal of the Anglo-French struggle which would continue intermittently for half a century and more.

By the middle of the eighteenth century, the British had a string of flourishing settlements along the Atlantic shore of North America, and the French were well established in the St Lawrence valley. Even though the various British colonies were founded by different groups for different reasons, they all prospered with the growing Atlantic economy; and as their populations increased, they began to move inland with their farms and villages to occupy land used by the Indians. The conflict inherent in this situation was seriously aggravated by the French, whose colonizing efforts took a very different line.

From the early days of exploration, the French had followed the rivers, going up the St Lawrence and down the Mississippi, and had befriended the Indians, both to convert them and to trade with them for furs. Always a luxury in Europe, furs were in great demand, and British and French trappers and traders had long competed to supply this market. Since the French did not settle and occupy the land – except in Quebec – they did not threaten the Indians, and were therefore able to make common cause with

NORTH AMERICA

Mackinac I.

St Louis

Mississippi

Fort Niagara Montreal Quebec

PROVINCE OF

Fort Pitt

WEST FLORIDA

New Orleans

PA.   N.Y.   Saratoga   QUEBEC

MD.   St. Lawrence

VA.   N.J.   CONN.   N.H.   MASS.

Salem   Annapolis   Cape Breton I.

Philadelphia   Boston   NOVA SCOTIA

GA.   S.C.   N.C.   DEL.   New York   Cape Cod

Yorktown   R.I.   Halifax   Louisbourg

Gulf of Mexico   Chesapeake Bay

Wilmington

Charleston

EAST FLORIDA

Saint Augustine

NORTH ATLA

Bermuda

CUBA

San Salvador

Jamaica

HAITI

Caribbean Sea

Puerto Rico

Curaçao

Antigua

Lesser Antilles

Barbados

Trinidad

SOUTH AMERICA

| 0 | | 600 miles |
| 0 | | 800 km |

MAP 2   *The North Atlantic on the eve of the American Revolution*

them against their mutual enemy, the British. With French firearms and encouragement, the Indians regularly attacked inland British settlers, provoking reprisals and a growing determination on the part of Britain to eliminate the French in North America. Since the British government had already sent troops to defend their colonies in 1756, when the Seven Years War erupted in Europe, it was hardly surprising that the smoldering conflict in North America now flared up into what the English would call the "French and Indian War." Although hostilities in Europe had been precipitated by the struggle over Silesia between Maria Theresa and Frederick of Prussia, the British and French did most of their fighting against each other, at sea or in the colonies. Outfought in both of these arenas by the British, the French finally lost their outposts in India and were completely crushed in North America by the time peace was made in 1763, finally concluding the last general war in Europe for nearly three decades.

THE AMERICAN REVOLUTION

In the eighteenth century, for the first time since the Reformation split the world of medieval Christendom, there was again a universal language of ideas in Europe. The tone was set by intellectuals whose objective was to rethink man's relation to society, just as the great seventeenth-century scientists had reconsidered man's place in the physical universe, without reference to divine revelation. One important question that was now addressed was how the authority wielded by society (the state) over the individual could be justified in the absence of religious doctrine.

This question received its most famous and influential consideration in the work of the English John Locke, who argued that only that authority exercised by the governed themselves, or their chosen representatives, could be considered legitimate. In France, the *philosophes* (philosophers), as the social critics of the day called themselves, focused on the necessity of reforming society to abolish the evils they deplored. In their view most of these evils derived from the irrationalities and superstitions of the past; in particular they denounced the jumble of inherited rights and privileges enjoyed by the nobles, who were entitled to own land and collect rent from the peasants who worked it, yet did not serve any very useful social function in return. In trying to define a better society the *philosophes* turned their imagination to a fictitious "state of nature," in which man had lived in newborn innocence, without the encumbrances of custom or property. Many thought they saw such an ideal society in construction in the New World, where their fellow Europeans were settling a virgin land, unimpeded by any preexisting rights of ownership. (That the native Americans might have had some such rights was not a possibility that occurred to many Europeans at this time, whether philosophers or settlers.)

Many of the British colonists also thought of themselves as involved in a social experiment, and attempted to shape their new society so as to avoid Europe's worst problems. By contemporary standards their average level of education was high, and in many cases their political awareness was sharpened by the fact that they or their forebears had come to the New World in search of religious freedom. Since the new land was free of ancient feudal claims, the colonists found their liberties threatened only by what seemed to them an arbitrary claim of sovereign authority by the king and his government in Britain.

Matters came to the point of open confrontation very slowly, with few of the colonists desiring or even considering independence. As in the English Civil War a century before, the critical issue in the growing conflict was the right of the king to maintain a standing army and to impose taxes for this purpose. Up to the middle of the eighteenth century the British colonists had been involved in extensions of all four of the wars between Britain and France that had taken place in Europe, and thus had needed British troops to reinforce their own militias against their tough French and Indian opponents. In 1763, however, the British finally put an end to the French threat in North America with their victory over French forces in Quebec; thereafter the British colonists no longer felt the need of a British military presence, and were therefore in no mood to accept the imposition by the king of special new taxes to help defray its costs. These taxes were actually a ministerial decision taken with the support of Parliament, but they were issued in the name of King George III, and came through with the force of a royal decree establishing "taxation without representation." The apparently easiest solution to this problem – offering the colonies Parliamentary representation – was actually impractical due to the slow and irregular nature of transatlantic travel. It seemed clear that the government in Britain had no choice but to withdraw the hated taxes or risk rebellion by the colonists. The best minds in Parliament (mostly but not exclusively Whigs) knew that the issue should not be forced, but during the crucial period they were out of power. Meanwhile a dazzling array of talents in the colonies began one of the most extraordinary political debates in modern history. With all of "enlightened" Europe as an eager audience, the colonial leaders began to develop the logic that would take them inexorably to their Declaration of Independence in 1776, through a shaky confederation and long war to final victory over the British in 1781, and finally to the United States Constitution in 1787.

In the military contest the British seemed to be in the best position at first, with complete control of the sea, and thus the ability to transport and supply regiments capable of overpowering any local forces along the coast. By contrast, the colonial troops were forced to live off the land and move awkwardly through the interior; as a result they had great difficulty concentrating sufficient strength at any one point to successfully confront the British, who if they did could also quickly slip away by sea.

For all the superiority of their position, however, the British lacked the numbers to occupy and take charge of the hinterland. These basic power relations were dramatized at the outset of the war, when the British troops sent to destroy the colonial military stores at Concord were barely able to accomplish their mission and retreated quickly to the coast (1775), while two months later in Boston they easily dislodged the colonial forces from Bunker Hill despite vigorous resistance. Then when General Washington was able to concentrate his Continental army on the heights overlooking Boston, the British simply evacuated the post, only to occupy New York a few months later.

In 1777 a major British campaign to split the colonies by capturing the Hudson valley ended in disaster, encouraging the Continental Congress to draft articles of confederation creating the "United States of America." A British victory seemed unlikely so long as colonial morale could be maintained, so these signs of rebel resolution and success encouraged the French to seek revenge against their old rivals by offering aid to the colonies. In addition to moral support, the French could provide powerful naval assistance; while their fleet was no match for the British, they could stop the convoys moving the British troops up and down the coast whenever Britain's Atlantic fleet was at sea. And this is exactly what happened to bring the war to an end at Yorktown (1781): the main British army was bottled up by a flotilla of French battleships and forced to surrender to Washington before the British fleet could be sent to its rescue. As a result, the treaty of peace recognizing the new American republic was signed in Paris in 1783.

If the French experienced a sense of victory over the British through this action, it did nothing to alter the basic balance of power either in Europe or on the seas. The British fleet continued to enjoy overwhelming superiority, while even this minor campaign further eroded the precarious situation of the French treasury. On a different level, however, American independence had a decisive impact on the European Continent. American representatives – particularly Benjamin Franklin – had enjoyed great personal popularity in Paris, thus widely publicizing the colonists' cause. And the young Marquis de Lafayette, who had served as a volunteer under Washington, returned to Versailles as a hero, thus reflecting a glow of even royal approval on the idea of the revolution. It was as if the intellectual and immaterial spirit of the age of reason had been given form and substance in the inspiring actions of the British colonists and their French allies. The reasonable inhabitants of a free new world had defied tyranny and shown the way to a more enlightened existence to all who would follow.

3

The French Revolution

In one of the more famous attributions of modern history, Louis XV (1715–74) was supposed to have said, "After me the deluge." the message of this prophecy seemed to be that all was not well in France, and that some catastrophic reaction was impending. Perhaps the king intended to refer only to the moral outrage provoked by his debaucheries and general excesses, but there were indeed real troubles in France, that were both widespread and deeply rooted.

In the middle of the eighteenth century there had been a serious crop failure in France which produced a rash of local protests and disorders. Partial famines were common and unavoidable throughout Europe because subsistence agriculture can never produce more than marginal surpluses, and these could not be transported far; when poor weather reduced the yield, the peasants ate less but generally survived, while the urban poor, depending entirely on the dwindling surpluses, were in a much more precarious situation. What made the mid-century crisis worse than usual in France was a population explosion that had outdistanced the capacity of the land to absorb it; this meant that more and more people were forced into the cities and towns, where they were faced with outright starvation by any crop failure that reduced the supply of grain. The resulting food riots plagued France for the rest of the century, and contributed crucially to the ultimate débâcle.

Another menacing problem began to preoccupy the king's ministers following the Seven Years War (1756–63), when the tax income fell into chronic deficit and the royal budget could be balanced only by ever larger loans. Actually from its beginning in the fifteenth century, the monarchical state in France had been financed largely by loans from bankers, whose source of capital was either silver mines or the commerce in the Mediterranean or Atlantic. On the whole this fiscal arrangement had proved mutually beneficial: the merchant bankers had few other opportunities for investment, and the king used the money to expand his administration, thus contributing to the economic development of the realm as well as the growth of his tax income. Indeed, for a while the king's revenues increased more rapidly than the interest charges on the rising debt; but eventually the process of expansion was carried so far that the royal administration began to cost more than it produced. This transition coincided with the extraordinarily heavy expenses of the Seven Years War (particularly the cost of trying to match the British at sea), leaving the government with no way to meet the carrying charges on its debt except by further borrowing – a procedure which normally leads to bankruptcy.

Thus when the young Louis XVI came to the throne in 1774, clouds of the threatening storm lowered on the horizon. In an effort to head off the looming fiscal crisis, he appointed a series of able and conscientious ministers with instructions to reverse the pattern of deficit financing. Not surprisingly the ministers proposed a number of necessary fiscal reforms, including the abolition of both the nobles' exemption from most direct taxes, and the practice of "tax farming" – that is, obtaining cash from a bank in exchange for the right to collect as much tax income as possible under existing laws in a given district. But since the overextended treasury would have collapsed without the large sums advanced by the bankers, these expensive intermediaries could not be replaced, any more than the feeble king could withstand the violent opposition of the court nobles to any loss of their fiscal prerogatives. As a result the king regularly abandoned the reform-minded ministers, only to appoint new ones who would make the same recommendations and be dismissed in their turn. Critics of the regime blamed the king for not imposing the reforms by edict, and while he obviously lacked the character to attempt this, it is also true that the only agency that could have enforced such a radical program was the army, whose officers were all nobles and thus vigorously opposed to it.

Although most of the land was owned by nobles, their estates were characteristically divided between domains – usually a small half – which they owned outright, and land which was rented and farmed collectively by the peasant villagers. Since the rent for the peasant lands had long been fixed, it had been eroded with the inflation that had plagued Europe since the sixteenth century. At about this time, therefore, the nobles were beginning to resort to legal tricks to increase the peasants' dues, just as the monarchy was also raising the royal taxes. Not only the king's ministers but even spokesmen for the nobles recognized that the peasants could not survive these mounting pressures indefinitely, but neither side felt able to reduce its own demands. The nobles tended to think the king should repudiate his debt to the bankers, which is how the medieval kings had usually dealt with the problem, but the king's ministers realized that this course would be suicidal since it would cut off the flow of future loans on which the monarchy was now dependent for survival; they generally recommended the abrogation of the nobles' privileges instead.

THE IMPASSE

Lacking the personal force to impose a workable solution, the king made an effort to persuade the nobles to sacrifice their privileges voluntarily, convening an assembly of their representatives at Versailles in 1787. Predictably, the nobles were not persuaded, and they advised the king to summon the full Estates General to resolve the crisis. This body was a national assembly of medieval origin which had not met since 1614. Traditionally it had consisted of representatives of classes called estates, the first estate being the clergy, the second the nobility, and the third everyone else. Since the nobles dominated the clergy through the bishops, who were all nobles, they felt sure of defeating any proposal in the Estates General that touched their privileges, by a vote of two estates to one. This was in fact the way it had worked in the sixteenth century, when the third estate, then consisting largely of representatives of the towns, was regularly left to bail the king out of trouble with "voluntary" money grants.

The Estates General

Once the king agreed to convene the Estates General, it became clear that no one knew how to go about it. A countrywide project was therefore proclaimed, to collect any information that the oldest inhabitants could remember hearing from their elders about the process used for the last previous meeting in 1614. With this help, officials finally worked out a plan for each estate to elect 300 deputies, which spokesmen for the third estate insisted on modifying to give them double that number; since the nobles counted on each of the three estates meeting and voting separately, they did not seriously oppose this increase.

The voting was organized in at least three stages: parishes, towns, and finally regional assemblies, which chose the deputies to the Estates General. At each stage the voters not only elected representatives to the next group but also drew up lists of grievances about the government. Since almost all adult males were eligible to vote, this complex procedure meant that virtually the entire male population of France became involved in a national political debate throughout the spring of 1789. Certainly nothing like this had ever happened before and it is doubtful if it has since. With astonishing regularity, the principal complaints listed in the grievances concerned the irrational nature of the regime and above all the lack of a simple, comprehensive code of laws. Almost no one complained of the monarchy as an institution or even of its absolute authority.

The Estates were directed to meet at the beginning of May, 1789, at Versailles – Louis XVI's enormous palace ten miles outside of Paris – because the king wanted to be there for the hunting season. When the three delegations finally assembled, something irreversible occurred. While the bishops and great nobles already knew one another, the lower clergy and the deputies to the third estate suddenly found themselves together with hundreds of like-minded colleagues, from all over France, who all agreed about the political and moral as well as financial bankruptcy of the regime, and the means and objectives of its reform. This discovery transformed the archaic medieval institution of the third estate into the body that would call itself the National Assembly.

From the beginning, events took on the aura of high drama. The nobles appeared in magnificent court attire, a riot of color and rich fabrics, while by royal order the deputies of the third estate wore sober black and remained standing throughout the ceremonies. Ignoring this humiliation, the third estate promptly demanded that the three orders meet in a single body. Because their earlier demand for 600 delegates had been granted, and also because – as they had discovered – they could count on the support of many of the lower clergy, this arrangement would give them a probable majority on any issue considered by the assembly. Predictably, the nobles objected and the king wavered; then, most unpredictably, the third estate voted to constitute itself a "National Assembly," and invited the other two estates to join them. The king then closed their meeting hall "for repairs," and the displaced but determined deputies met in a nearby indoor tennis court, vowing never to disband until they had given the country a constitution.

At this point a shrewd, opportunistic bishop named Talleyrand made a key move. Sensing which way the tide was flowing, and seeing an opportunity to establish himself at its fore, he persuaded the dissident lower clergy to join the new National Assembly, thereby tipping the balance of power decisively in its favor. The rest of the upper orders now had little choice but to follow, as the king finally requested them to do. With these modest steps the revolution had begun.

THE CONSTITUTIONAL MONARCHY

The fall of the Bastille

These events were followed with great interest by the rest of the country, and indeed by the rest of the European world, but nowhere with the same intense passion as in Paris. In spite of the removal of the royal court to Versailles, the city had remained the effective capital of the realm; it was the center of administrative offices, financial institutions, and courts, as well as of the intellectual life of the country – from the Academy through the university and special schools, to the salons of the *philosophes* and the clubs and cafés of the journalists and political adventurers. Needless to say, all shades of opinion could be found in this huge population, but in general there was an explosive potential popular support for radical reform. The people who made up the active Paris "mob" of demonstrators and street fighters seem to have actually been predominantly small shopkeepers rather than day laborers or indigents; this meant that they had some education and so were all the more open to radical ideas. Their dual motivation was a hatred of privilege, as represented by titles and wealth, and a passion for equality; yet they were also ardent defenders of private property. In addition to simple enthusiasm there seems to have been no lack of ambitious self-interest to maintain the momentum of events. For example, the Duc d'Orléans, the enormously rich cousin of the king, apparently saw himself as a possible replacement for Louis on a "constitutional" throne, and is thought to have supported agitators and demagogues to feed the revolutionary fervor of the Paris populace. In any case the Paris "mob" would play a key role in all the events that followed, beginning with their historic attack on the Bastille.

The occcasion for this uprising was a rumor that began to circulate almost immediately after the National Assembly was created, that the king intended to disband it by force, and that troops were moving into the vicinity of Versailles for this purpose. In fact such an action would have required more resolve than Louis was capable of mustering; further, he was unlikely to think it in his interest to call in the army, since that would put him at the mercy of the nobles who were its commanders. In Paris, however, the rumor was enough to enable some purposeful leaders to organize a well-directed mob attack on the garrison fortress of Paris known as the Bastille. In revolutionary mythology the Bastille has become a symbol of royal tyranny, but its true significance was military. If it had actually been invested with the troops who were believed to be en route to Versailles, it would have dominated the city, but since it was entirely undefended, it was quickly seized and destroyed, on July 14, 1789. Once deprived of a fortified base in the city, however, no professional army could contend with an enraged, and by now well-armed, urban mob; thus the loss of the Bastille made military intervention in Paris impossible and left both the royal court and the National Assembly at the mercy of the city.

Recognizing their true situation, some of the royal family and greatest nobles fled the country. Their first purpose was to escape personal danger, but they also hoped to enlist armed support, especially from the Habsburg in-laws of the king, to save the regime. These émigrés were followed by many others as the revolution gained momentum. In the mean time, peasants in scattered areas of the provinces were beginning to engage in acts of violence against their local lords, pouring out of the villages with pitchforks and torches to storm and burn the châteaux, and occasionally murder their inhabitants as well. Undoubtedly one factor behind these widespread outbreaks was the unfulfilled expectation of change that had been raised by the long electoral exercise of the preceding spring. As news of lynchings and arson reached Versailles it caused panic among the nobles and in an all-night session of the Assembly (August 4) they took the lead in rescinding virtually all of their special rights and privileges. Although some of this legislation was later rescinded again, or modified to provide for indeminification of the nobles, few peasant obligations to the lords actually survived after that night. All rents ceased, and the village lands were divided among the residents. The peasant phase of the revolution had taken place.

The new order

In Paris the revolution was taking on a new momentum. When the royal officials proved unable to cope with the mounting violence in the streets, they were replaced by a provisional city government made up of the electors chosen in the first round of the earlier national election, reinforced by a newly improvised National Guard. While these new authorities were struggling to maintain some semblance of order, anonymous masters of the mob were planning to complete their seizure of the revolution. On October 5 a disorderly crowd of women (or perhaps men disguised as women, to forestall retaliation) marched the ten miles to Versailles to demand that the king provide more bread for Paris. (This was the occasion when the queen, Marie Antoinette, told that the people had no bread, was supposed to have responded, "Then let them eat cake.") The real purpose of the march emerged, however, when the leaders of the group refused to return to Paris without the royal family. Although by this time a contingent of the National Guard had arrived to protect the king, Louis refused to risk bloodshed, and docilely accompanied the marchers back to the capital, where he became a virtual prisoner in his palace of the Tuileries. At this development the members of the National Assembly realized that they would lose all authority if they remained in Versailles without the king and except for 200 deputies who resigned they decided to follow Louis to Paris. With the government now entirely within the city walls, the revolution was to be increasingly at the mercy of the mob.

Undeterred by this move, the Assembly proceeded with its self-appointed task of recreating the government as a constitutional monarchy. After formulating a "Declaration of the Rights of Man," it gradually elaborated a constitution that was a strange mix of English parliamentary elements, benevolent despotism, and the immediate needs of the revolutionary regime. With equally great self-assurance it also undertook the reorganization of the administrative system, abolishing the old provinces and replacing them with 83 smaller "departments" centered on the principal towns. However the destruction of the old administrative units proved much easier to accomplish than the actual implementation of the new ones. Local government was largely left to local improvisation, which in practice tended to mean the disintegration of all administration, without any systematic or effective replacement.

Finally, since few taxes had been collected during all this confusion, the Assembly moved to meet the government's now disastrous fiscal deficit by the bold step of seizing the huge landed properties of the Church and offering them for sale. To justify this confiscation it was argued that the lands had originally been given to the Church only in trust, which it had abused. From this it followed that the government now assumed responsibility for paying the salaries of the clergy, thus turning the priests into civil servants. To transform the Church lands into negotiable wealth, the government issued paper currency against the proceeds of future sale, an action which led directly to runaway inflation.

At a national anniversary celebration of the fall of the Bastille (July 14, 1790), the king went through a public ceremony, if with obvious private reservations, of accepting the draft constitution and the many reforms passed during the previous year. Actually, however, the new regime was far from complete. In particular, efforts to balance the powers of government could not be reconciled with the realities of the situation. No second legislative body could be established without reviving the hated second estate (the nobility), and to give the king effective power would risk his using it to oppose reform.

As the Assembly struggled with these problems as well as the day-to-day affairs of the country, the deputies inevitably began to organize in groups and parties around common interests. These took the form of political "clubs," of which the most important were the Jacobins, so-called because they met in a former Jacobin monastery, and the Girondins, originally a faction of the Jacobins whose leaders came largely from the department of the Gironde in southwestern France. Although both groups were radical, they gradually separated to become the polarizing elements in the Assembly, with the Jacobins favoring a strong central government and the Girondins advocating greater local self-rule and dispersal of authority. This division reflected the place of origin of the deputies. The Jacobins were characteristically the young professionals from the small towns of the interior who had played such an important part in the election of the third estate. They stayed in close contact with their towns through a national network of local Jacobin clubs, and cultivated the more radical views of the *philosophes*, favoring the concept of enlightened despotism. The Girondins, by contrast, came largely from the port cities and frequently had close connections with the Atlantic trade; as a result they were distrustful of a strong central administrative authority, which would tend to prey upon, rather than contribute to, the prosperity of their regions.

While these politicians were striving to develop a national policy, the king wavered between going along with the powerful tide of reform and hoping to stem it, with the aid of disaffected elements in France and elsewhere. The new civil constitution of the clergy seemed to offer him an opportunity to gain allies, since nearly half of the country's clerics refused to take the oath of loyalty to the government that was now required of them as civil servants. Finally, however, Louis decided to seek aid abroad, and attempted to flee the country with his family (June 20, 1791). Traveling in two royal coaches, the ill-disguised party was recognized and captured a short distance from the frontier, to be brought back to Paris and a more secure confinement in the Tuileries. At first the Assembly "suspended" the king for this action, but it then quickly reinstated him, since at this point virtually no one yet envisioned a government without a king. Louis's attempted flight, however, gave a powerful impetus to the growing sentiment for a republican form of government.

The National Assembly, sensing the need for a change, finally put into operation the draft of the new constitution. Elections were called for a legislative assembly, which took office in September 1791.

THE REVOLUTIONARY REPUBLIC

The fall of the monarchy

While the first acts of the revolution were being played out in Versailles and Paris, the rest of Europe watched with mixed emotions. To some it seemed the dawn of the new world proclaimed by the *philosophes* and anticipated by the American Revolution. To the more privileged and conservative, however, the news from France — particularly that brought out by the émigrés — was fraught with terrible menace. Even so, Europe's royal rulers were slow to react. Having long been dominated by France, they at first enjoyed a sense of relief as the overbearing French monarchy was engulfed by domestic problems, and wondered if the new situation might be turned to their own territorial advantage. Sooner or later, however, they began to worry about the precedent that was being set.

Many of the émigrés settled in the Rhineland to be near France, while others headed for the Habsburg court at Vienna, where they expected sympathy and support from the family of their queen. In Vienna they were received at first with embarrassment by a government that had no desire to become involved in the troubles of France. However, Louis's unsuccessful flight alarmed the king of Prussia and the Habsburg emperor; in late

August 1791 they met to discuss the situation, issuing a communiqué which, although very mild, was read in Paris as a threat to the revolution. Thus some already-glowing embers of belligerence were fanned in France, and during the course of the ensuing fall and winter of 1791 relations deteriorated further between the revolutionary government and the Habsburg–Hohenzollern alliance. Why the two camps should suddenly feel the urge to go to war has never been fully explained, but in the spring, war finally broke out.

In France it was the new Legislative Assembly that declared war and deployed its armies along the northeastern frontier. But because the upper ranks of the French army had been reserved for the greatest nobles, many of the most important commanders had emigrated, and the government suspected the loyalty of those who remained (with reason, in at least one case). The confusion and distrust that resulted led to serious early reverses in the field.

Suddenly France seemed vulnerable to invasion and the revolution threatened by intervention. When the Prussian commander of the allied forces issued a manifesto threatening reprisals for any mistreatment of the king, there was a violent reaction in Paris. A mob stormed the Tuileries, slaughtered the royal Swiss guard and forced the king to flee to the Assembly for asylum. Under pressure from the mob, that body then stripped Louis of all authority and confined him to prison (August 10, 1792).

The Terror

The city was seething with rumors of widespread treason among opponents of the revolution. The mob was now completely out of control, and acknowledging its own powerlessness the Legislative Assembly voted for the election of a Convention to draw up still another constitution – officially turning the government over to the "revolutionary forces" of Paris, which were dominated by the Jacobins and the mob. With the leaderless French armies in retreat and foreign occupation an imminent threat, mass hysteria swept the capital and half a dozen other cities, leading to the massacre of political prisoners awaiting trial for suspected anti-revolutionary sentiments or acts (September 1792). Just when the revolutionary cause seemed lost, however, the French troops pulled themselves together and stopped the allied advance, in a small but decisive action at Valmy.

The following day the newly elected Convention met. In its first session it abolished the monarchy and proclaimed the Republic, complete with its own "revolutionary" calendar; then it turned to the business of disposing of the king. Rightly suspected of correspondence with the enemy (the Habsburgs), Louis was tried, found guilty, and executed in January of 1793. The trial and execution greatly sharpened the differences between the Jacobins and Girondins in the Convention: while there was little dispute about the king's guilt, the Girondins opposed the death penalty which was demanded by the Jacobins. It carried by a single vote. The execution also helped provoke a royalist revolt in western France, and most importantly it brought Britain, Holland and Spain into the alliance against revolutionary France.

With 749 members, the new Convention was too unwieldy a body to deal with these enemies of the revolution at home and abroad. Accordingly, it delegated its executive power to two committees, Public Safety and General Security, both of which soon came entirely under the control of the Jacobins. The committees were now confronted with a new rash of difficulties, from wild inflation and mounting food shortages to widespread outbreaks of counter-revolutionary insurrection, particularly in such port cities as Lyons, Bordeaux, and Nantes. To meet these threats the Jacobins instituted a group dictatorship under the fanatical Maximilien Robespierre, who imposed a Reign of Terror (1793–4). Believing the population to be riddled with traitors to the revolution, the Jacobins created tribunals to try suspects with little ceremony, proclaiming a mandatory death sentence for anyone not immediately cleared of all suspicion. Ironically these summary executions were usually carried out with the machine invented by Dr Guillotin as humane alternative to hanging.

The Terror operated on different levels. Originally a response to a "spy scare," it was used by the Jacobins to eliminate their political enemies, including those in the Convention; the deputies enjoyed no immunity, and some thirty Girondin leaders were sent directly to their death by a single vote. After thus consolidating their power in the Convention, the Jacobins used the Terror to eliminate enemies of the new order wherever they could be found throughout France. Taking advantage of a rhetorical decree known as the *levée en masse*, which commanded all citizens to aid the war effort to their utmost, the Convention sent officials in pairs through the provinces to encourage local Jacobin clubs and revolutionary committees to denounce citizens whom they suspected of lack of enthusiasm for the revolutionary cause. In the convenient confusion of party and country that has become so familiar in succeeding centuries, those labeled opponents of the revolution were tried and often executed as enemies of the nation.

One important internal threat to the Jacobins came from the organized armed resistance of a movement based in the port cities, which sought to turn the republic into a federal system in which the "provinces" – actually the cities – would exercise substantial autonomy. The cities of Nantes, Bordeaux, Lyons, and Marseilles all had to be reconquered from these federalists, who were finally crushed with mass reprisals. The citizens of Toulon actually turned their city over to the British fleet in an effort to save it from the revolutionary forces: it was soon retaken, however, thanks in part to the skill of a young artillery officer named Napoleon Bonaparte, who was promoted to general because of this success, which he would use as the first modest step in a fabulous career.

At the same time, the revolutionary troops were confronted with a peasant revolt in the lower Loire, which had been provoked by government efforts at conscription in the region. Led by an unlikely coalition of royalist nobles and radical clergy – who had provided essential poor relief in this impoverished area before the confiscation of Church lands – these rebellious peasants held out until 1800, apparently offering a base for British intervention which was never seriously exploited.

All of this internal turmoil, combined with foreign invasion in the north and east, may serve to explain, if not excuse, the crimes of the Terror. But there is no apparent explanation for the fact that the Terror continually increased in violence, even after these threats to the revolution had subsided – finally reaching a wild climax in Robespierre's manic attempt to create a synthetic "revolutionary religion," which had the effect of transforming the Terror into a virtual inquisition. This pathological behavior was finally brought to an end when Robespierre, in an ecstasy of virtue, announced to the Convention his intention of sending to the tribunals all deputies guilty of graft or other civic immoralities. Inevitably this threat united in firm opposition all the deputies who feared they might be on Robespierre's list, whereupon they brought about his rapid downfall and execution, with the enthusiastic approval of the general public, who clearly had had enough of terror.

The Directory

The following period of reaction (known as Thermidor, from the new name for the month in which Robespierre fell) brought the liquidation of the remaining Jacobin fanatics, the closing of the political clubs, the return to the Convention of the surviving Girondins, and even the reemergence of some monarchists. More important, it saw the beginning of what would become a major military offensive, and the implementation of yet another constitution, in a regime known as the Directory.

When the Convention finally returned, after the Terror, to its original task of producing a new constitution, its new leaders were painfully aware of the dangers of a single omnipotent assembly. The new constitution carefully balanced two separate chambers of the legislature and an executive body composed of five members, called Directors, each of whom presided in turn. To make quite sure they were establishing a regime they could control, however, they added the proviso that two-thirds of the new deputies must be chosen from members of the Convention. This measure provoked a popular demonstration (supposedly royalist in inspiration) which the architects of the regime put down with a force commanded by General Bonaparte. By using some field guns (a "whiff of grapeshot," in Carlyle's phrase), Bonaparte dispersed the crowd and cleared the path for the transition. Such use of force involved some risk of provoking a mass reaction, but Bonaparte took this chance in order to ingratiate himself with the current ruling clique. At about the same time he also married Joséphine de Beauharnais, the former mistress of one of the Directors, thus further establishing his membership in that group.

The main task of the new Directory turned out to be a very different one from that of the Convention, because of the sudden success that the French military forces were now enjoying. Where the Convention had struggled to reorganize the nation's defenses and supply the hard-pressed capital with food, the new government found itself called upon chiefly to supply three remarkable armies which were now launched on unprecedented campaigns of warfare and conquest. Because this business was highly lucrative, the Directory earned an unrivaled reputation for governmental corruption – in a dramatic pendulum swing away from Robespierre's Republic of Virtue.

On the eve of the revolution the French army was clearly the best in Europe, having been thoroughly reformed and reequipped by Louis XVI. It had passed through a shaky period in the early months of the war (1792) when a number of its highest officers defected, but it emerged stronger than before with the promotion of able and ambitious junior officers to replace the nobles. By the fall of 1794 it had taken the offensive, occupied Flanders and invaded Holland, where it set up a puppet regime called the Batavian Republic. In this first foray beyond their borders the French forces found themselves welcomed by local populations as agents of the Enlightenment and liberators from the *ancien régime*, and they were even offered large money subsidies in gratitude.

This unexpected success inaugurated the next phase of the revolution, in which for the next several years French armies would march back and forth across cental Europe and northern Italy, proclaiming their mission to free all subject peoples and exacting tribute in cash or treasure wherever it was not promptly offered. Suddenly "revolutionary warfare" was proving a very profitable activity. With this new source of income, in fact, the Directory was freed from the necessity of raising any revenues, and as a result lost all interest in and contact with the provinces. Instead of trying to collect taxes, it spent the foreign subsidies on contracts for army supplies, siphoning off large bribes in the process for the personal enrichment of its members.

In the spring of 1796, two French armies invaded Germany (one in the north, the other in the south), while a third, under General Bonaparte, followed the Mediterranean coast into northern Italy, which was both a Habsburg preserve and a route to Austria. Quickly overrunning Piedmont and Lombardy, in what turned out to be more a triumphal march than a campaign, the French were again received as saviors, and offered huge indemnities by the "liberated" cities. The following year Bonaparte returned to Italy; pausing briefly after crossing the Alps to set up "republics" in Genoa and Milan, he proceeded to occupy Venice. From there he offered the Austrians the treaty (of Campo Formio) by which France received the Austrian Netherlands and the left bank of the upper Rhine, thus achieving Louis XIV's goal of a Rhine frontier, while giving Austria Venice in compensation. The success of this Italian campaign, as much political as military, established Bonaparte as the most important among a group of brilliant young generals of revolutionary France, thereby further whetting his inordinate ambition.

Bonaparte found himself with no more objectives in Italy, but determined not to let his fame cool he planned and launched a fantastic expedition against Egypt. Since the British had effective control of the Mediterranean, it is not clear what he expected to achieve by this project, nor why the Directors approved it. As it turned out, it did serve to keep his name before the public, and even enhanced his reputation because of the exotic glamour of his destination, even though as a military undertaking it was a dismal failure. With improbable luck Bonaparte managed to get his troops to Egypt, but soon after they arrived his fleet was bottled up and then largely destroyed by the British navy. Bonaparte dealt with this situation by abandoning his troops, now helplessly trapped in Egypt, and slipping back to France just in time to make a bid for power in Paris.

In 1798, while Bonaparte was in Egypt, a new alliance had formed and declared war on France; this second coalition included Britain, Russia, Portugal, and the Ottoman Turks. At first the Russians and Austrians pressed the French hard in Switzerland and Italy, but when they seemed to be on the point of invading France itself, the tide turned. The British, who had done badly in Holland, later made a separate peace with France (at Amiens in 1802); the Russians withdrew from the alliance, and the war collapsed.

At the same time, however, the French government was also collapsing. The Directory had by now not only thoroughly discredited itself by its corruption, but it had also lost control of its one essential constituency, the army, which had become wholly independent through its remunerative career of conquest. Unlike earlier revolutionary governments, moreover, the Directory had no roots in the provinces; its two assemblies were made up largely of political adventurers who had survived the Convention, and the new delegates, chosen in a series of partial elections, had been screened by the assemblies to weed out opponents of the regime. This procedure assured the Directors control of the government, but it also deprived them of all popular support. In addition it meant that the Directory felt no interest in or responsibility for the provinces, and in a country formerly run by a central administration this neglect led to the collapse of the remaining local services. Roads went unrepaired and unpatrolled, with the result that banditry flourished, leaving the cities and towns isolated and demoralized.

Brumaire

The Directory had neither the will nor the resources to deal with such general disintegration. When it was challenged in 1799 by a Jacobin revival in the assemblies, one of the Directors, Emmanuel Sieyès, used this threat to put in motion his plan to overthrow the Directory. Using the prestige of the army, through the personal participation of a popular general, he intended to replace the Directory with an authoritarian regime capable of wielding the necessary power. To carry out the coup Sieyès picked Bonaparte, knowing him to be a protégé of the political clique behind the Directory and thinking he would therefore be a safe figurehead for the new regime. Little did he realize that the young general had rushed back from Egypt precisely because he anticipated just such an opportunity, which he fully intended to turn entirely to his own advantage.

The ensuing coup of Brumaire (named for its month) would almost certainly have failed had there been any serious opposition. As an excuse for demanding power Bonaparte was supposed to denounce a Jacobin plot to the two legislative assemblies; with his troops outside their meeting place, he appeared before the deputies only to find that they recognized his true purpose and turned on him. Dragged fainting from the hall, he was saved by his brother Lucien, who was president of the assembly, and who rallied the troops to march in and dissolve it by force, proclaiming the Consulate. Once this was accomplished, however, Bonaparte forcefully seized the reins of power. Quickly revising the constitution Sieyès had prepared, he made himself the "First" of the three Consuls who were to replace the five Directors, and the only one with power. To aid him there were to be a number of small consultative, and largely appointed, assemblies, while administrative officers, called prefects, were appointed to each department to restore local services and establish a rigorous system for collecting taxes. Bonaparte's goal was nothing less than a thorough reorganization of the government which would assimilate the revolutionary reforms in a new administrative system.

In 1802 Bonaparte issued still another constitution, naming himself "Life Consul," with the right to appoint his successor and absolute authority over all branches of government. It was at this point that he adopted the royal style of using only his first name, Napoleon. Despite these actions, however, it would be wrong to view Bonaparte's regime as simply a naked dictatorship which had subverted the short-lived Republic. In one sense Napoleon fulfilled the revolution, by implementing the reforms demanded by the lists of grievances drawn up for the meeting of the Estates General in 1789. That the new regime was viewed in this light at the time is evident from the overwhelming support the new constitution received in a plebiscite, and from the readiness of everyone except the most doctrinaire Jacobins to serve in the new administration. The Life Consulate – which would become the empire in two years with few changes except of title – was in fact the true implementation of the doctrine of enlightened despotism. It was authoritarian, but it used its powers to carry out the rationalization of government and to defend these reforms from internal reaction and foreign intervention.

Probably the most important reform accomplished by Napoleon's regime was to open up careers in its victorious armies to young men of ambition and talent. Under the old regime there had been little opportunity for careers of any sort except through inheritance or marriage. Even the lesser nobility, who had little choice but to serve their king as junior officers, could not rise about the rank of major, so that Bonaparte would never have commanded an army if there had been no revolution. The expanding armies of the revolution, however, could increasingly absorb those young men crowded off the land by the growing population, and at the same time offer them the possibility of promotion on the basis of ability rather than birth. It was primarily a result of the talents, energies, and ambitions thus liberated, including those of Napoleon himself, that all of Europe soon found itself at the mercy of the revolutionary armies – at least until the rest of the Continent was provoked into making comparable changes in order to liberate itself from French domination.

4

The Industrial Revolution

During the period between the end of the American Revolution (1783) and the consolidation of the French revolutionary regime under Bonaparte (1799), an altogether different and even more momentous "industrial" revolution was taking place in England. The impact of this development is still felt at every turn by all the heirs of the European tradition, and at least indirectly by most of the other inhabitants of the world as well. It is responsible for the material changes that have transformed our civilization in the last two centuries, all but totally separating us from our long historical past and bringing us to our most extraordinary achievements as well as to the brink of cataclysmic dangers. Not only has it produced vast material riches for some of the world's population, but it has also increased exponentially our powers of destruction, both through weapons and through the environmental degradation that may ultimately prove an even greater threat to our survival.

According to a well-established tradition the industrial revolution was the inevitable culmination of the long and gradually accelerating development of technology that had its origins deep in the human past. Nothing could be further from the truth, as the actual originators of the process would have been the first to tell us. It is true that from the beginning of the Middle Ages, Europeans demonstrated an ingenuity in using and improving traditional tools and techniques which had no counterpart in the ancient world. To explain this difference it has been suggested that the ancients had little interest in devices that would merely save the labor of slaves; but this argument is hardly convincing for periods when slaves were in short supply. Another possible explanation is that the scarcity of wood in the Mediterranean world inhibited earlier experimentation with the simple machines that came into use in forested Europe, such as wind and water mills, used especially for grinding grain, and the wheels and looms used for spinning and weaving. What is often overlooked, however, is the fact that, for all the fascinating refinements Europeans had made in the traditional crafts, the human body always remained the chief source of energy for the production of goods. Looms, for example, were powered only by the weavers themselves, and therefore could not be larger than the human reach nor heavier than human strength could work. Although water power could be used in limited ways, it could not drive the looms because they were too small and fragile, and the obvious solution of making heavier looms with more metal parts was impractial because of the short supply of iron. Thus in spite of continued technical improvements, most machinery had reached the limits of its practical size and complexity by the beginning of the eighteenth century – until some new source of energy could be harnessed to produce, as well as to drive, metal machines. The new source of energy that would serve this function, and thereby inaugurate the industrial revolution, was the coal-powered steam engine. The people who made this critical breakthrough, however, were not attempting to rescue technology from its dead end, but simply improvising a method to raise water out of flooded coal mines.

The story begins with the opening of the Atlantic trade in the early seventeenth century, and the dramatic growth of London as its central port, fed by the new commercial agriculture of the Thames valley. The very success of this operation, however, created another problem of comparable size. From early in his prehistoric past, man has required fire no less than food to survive: many vegetable foods, including grains, must be cooked in order to be digestible by man, while meat is also made safer and easier to eat (as well as better-tasting) by cooking. Just as important, the great land masses of the northern hemisphere had severe winters and would not have been habitable without the heat of domestic fire. The obvious fuel was wood, but this was frequently hard to get, particularly in urban areas. Many regions that produced abundant crops either lacked trees altogether or had been deforested over the centuries, and since firewood was even more difficult to transport than food, its supply could pose serious problems.

By the time London began its transformation into the capital of the burgeoning Atlantic community, southern England had been effectively denuded of its forests, and was quite incapable of providing the necessary firewood to the city it was so successfully supplying with grain. Thus some other source of fuel was needed, and in the seventeenth century this problem was solved by exploitation of the coal at Newcastle, which could be carried up the Thames River to London. The resulting trade not only removed a potential limit to London's growth but rapidly became the second largest business in England after the grain trade. The accelerating demand for coal pushed mining operations ever deeper until the mines were flooded, thereby creating a sudden commercial crisis of grave proportions. Since a huge investment was at stake, equally large financial resources were brought to bear on the problem. Its ultimate resolution required a half-century of purposeful trial and error, which ended not merely by saving the mines but also by harnessing their coal to two completely new purposes: the production of good-quality iron in unprecedented quantities and the transformation of heat into power by a rotary steam engine. These two developments passed the critical transition into the realm of practicality at almost the same time (1782 and 1783), and together launched the industrial revolution, by making possible the transformation of the old stalled technologies into metal machines that could be driven by the new steam engines.

The men whose ingenuity brought about this revolution had a very clear idea of what they had accomplished and where their inventions could next be applied. For all their remarkable vision, however, they barely glimpsed the future – the nineteenth and twentieth centuries – and seem not to have been aware that they had introduced the first new major source of energy since the beginning of agriculture. To understand the specific nature of this crucial transition it is necessary to turn back to seventeenth-century London.

THE COAL TRADE

London's phenomenal growth in response to the stimulus of the new Atlantic economy was made possible by the expansion of the agricultural capacity of the Thames valley and the adjacent coastal areas. Specialization in crops and the development of new techniques led to the production of far more wheat and other foods than had ever previously been achieved, while the natural canals provided by the rivers of southeast England facilitated transport of these goods to the city. To meet the need for a corresponding increase in fuel supplies, London turned to coal, as its rival port of Amsterdam would turn to peat.

The transition to the new fuel had begun in the sixteenth century, but had proceeded slowly until a great fire destroyed much of London in 1666; as the city was reconstructed, both new and restored buildings were equipped with coal-burning furnaces. While Britain was fortunate in its many large coal deposits, transporting adequate quantities to London still posed a major problem. Moving such a heavy material overland was far too cumbersome and costly (the expense of mining the coal was doubled in only a few miles), which meant that it had to be transported almost entirely by water. Moreover, because of the quantities involved, it was all but essential to carry it in large ocean-going ships rather than on river barges. Given these requirements, the new trade was quickly centered in Newcastle, where large veins of coal came to the surface in hills above the Tyne estuary, making it easy to load ocean-going vessels that could then be sailed down the North Sea coast and up the Thames.

By the eighteenth century the coal trade had become the largest and most lucrative segment of the new ocean commerce. Some idea of its size is suggested by the fact that it was the primary support of England's shipbuilding industry, which was much the largest in the European world. It was also the basis of Britain's growing naval superiority, since it maintained shipyards in constant operation that could be turned to building warships at any time and provided a reserve fleet of ships and seamen that could be readily converted to combat use. During this same period the French could not afford to keep even a single shipyard in continuous operation for combined commercial and naval use, while England had seven.

The steam engine

To supply this huge fleet of coal ships, the mines at Newcastle were worked at an unrelenting pace. The shafts were pushed deeper and deeper into the earth until at the beginning of the eighteenth century they reached the water table and began to flood. In the past this problem had usually been solved by crude pumps, driven by oxen or horses harnessed to walk in a circle and turn a winch. At Newcastle, however, the scale of operations was such that a radical new solution was required. To meet this emergency some managers of the mines attempted to construct large atmospheric pumps that used coal as a source of power. This type of pump involved lowering into the water a hose to which an air-tight chamber was attached; the chamber was partly filled with water, then heated until it was full of steam, and finally cooled so that the steam condensed, creating a vacuum that drew water up the hose from the mine. Although it was an improvement over the conventional method, it was still far short of satisfactory, and the mine operators continued their search for some better way of accomplishing their task.

The next technique they tried was the piston pump. Moving a piston up and down in a tight-fitting cylinder would also create a vacuum that would lift up the water. The necessary stroke of genius was to see that a piston in a cylinder could be pushed and pulled by expanding and condensing steam, thus creating an engine that could drive the pump. To translate this concept into a practical machine, however, taxed the talents and resources of all concerned. The result was the cumbersome Newcomen engine. Because of its inefficiency it was useful only where the coal to drive it was plentiful and cheap, but it did serve to keep mines in operation.

The final step in the development of a practical steam engine was initiated inadvertently by a professor at the University of Glasgow, who used a model of the Newcomen engine to illustrate his lectures on heat. When the machine failed to function properly, he called in the university instrument-maker, James Watt, who saw at once that the trouble was not in the mechanism but in its design. Although it took him several years, by 1783 he had produced an efficient, flexible engine with rotary motion, which could not only be used to drive a practical piston pump but could also be applied to a whole new range of tasks extending far beyond the mines.

Unlike most of the existing machines – such as looms – which were largely made of wood, all of the steam pumps that had been tried, including Watt's engine, were made of metal. This was absolutely essential because of the heat involved, the pressures produced, and the need for close-fitting parts. To begin to realize the potential of the steam engine to drive other machines, it would also be necessary to build them of metal. But before this was possible, two other developments were required: the first was the large-scale production of good-quality iron, and the second a practical machine tool technology capable of producing metal machines.

Although iron had been known and worked from the second millennium BC, it had always been produced in small quantities and used for special purposes, such as the cutting edges of tools or weapons. The main limit on production was the need to smelt the ore with charcoal, which produces greater heat than wood. To make the charcoal, very large quantities of wood were used in relation to the finished metal, and while iron deposits were generally plentiful in the European world, trees had long been in critically short supply. Thus it would have been impossible to produce enough charcoal-smelted iron to build large numbers of steam engines and other metal machines for them to drive.

Quite naturally, when the British began to use coal for domestic fuel, the iron-makers tried to adapt it to their purposes, but with very discouraging results. In the process of smelting, the molten iron absorbed the sulphur in the coal, making the end-product extremely brittle. However, there was now both the incentive and the opportunity to continue experimenting with ways of improving coal-smelted iron. The first of workable quality was finally produced, by extraordinary coincidence, in the year before Watt completed his steam engine. A virtually unlimited supply of good-quality iron soon became available, and new techniques for working and shaping the metal were now required. It was found that these skills had been developed on a small scale by the craftsmen who built the scientific instruments used by the members of the Royal Society and the university faculties. All that remained was to make machine tools that could be driven by the new steam engine to make ever more engines, and an endless variety of machines.

Without all these other developments, the coal-powered steam engine would have had a very restricted application. But harnessed together, coal and iron provided the energy and tools that would enable man to work his will and satisfy his wants beyond his wildest dreams.

THE NEW INDUSTRY

Putting the first steps of industrialization together required a very large investment of human energy, but once the process was completed, coal demonstrated its remarkable quality of releasing far more energy than was required to extract it from the earth. By contrast, preindustrial agriculture produces only a marginal surplus of energy beyond what is required to support its work force. The labor of small numbers of miners provided sufficient coal not only to turn out vastly more cloth than could many craftsmen, when used in steam-driven looms, but also to lift more coal out of the mine, thus yielding more energy as its own energy was expended. This self-generating capacity of the new fuel was the key to the subsequent explosion of productivity that created the modern industrial world.

Only an enterprise involving such vast investments as the London coal trade could have supported such a radical solution as the steam engine. Similarly, only a market as dense and profitable as London would have provided an incentive for applying the new techniques to the traditional crafts. After its original use to pump water and lift coal from the mines, the new technology was first applied systematically to the production of textiles. A series of improvements in hand-loom design had increased the demand for thread far beyond what could be met by conventional spinning procedures, and since thousands of spindles could easily be driven by one engine, the problem was perfectly suited to the application of steam power. It was not long before the consequent abundance of thread created pressure to harness the looms to steam as well. A rotary-powered loom was invented in 1784, but its operation was so rough that it broke wool thread in the process. For this reason, it was first used for the stronger cotton fibers, producing a low-quality cloth at a speed and in a quantity that bore no relation to any previous method. By the turn of the century cheap cotton cloth was within the financial and physical reach of everyone in Britain; as British economic historians are fond of recounting, one effect of this bounty was that underclothes, previously a luxury of the rich, were now available to the general public. A longer-range consequence of this development was that the mills were soon demanding far more raw cotton than could be obtained from India, their original source of supply, and thus provided the incentive that led to the establishment of slave-run cotton plantations in the southern United States.

At first England's textile mills were improvised structures that were scattered around the edges of towns where coal and cotton were available, and where workers could be hired. The large commercial and banking interests of London and other port cities seem to have taken little part in mobilizing this new industry; instead, local workmen with a flair for the new techniques managed to put the machines together and operate them with little outside help, usually plowing their profits back into more machinery. Though the earliest factories could be established without seriously disturbing the existing social order, the rapid concentration of more and more mills in favorable locations drew workers from beyond commuting distance. Suddenly masses of poor newcomers were entering the cities and seeking shelter wherever they could find it. Unfinished cellars of existing houses were rented and cheap new housing was thrown together by unscrupulous speculators, producing unsanitary and dangerous living conditions that were equaled only by the grim conditions within the mills themselves.

Working conditions

Descriptions of the lives of the early factory workers are so horrifying, in fact, that they raise the question of how any free people could be induced to accept such misery. There is ample evidence, however, that the rural poor poured out of their country villages to volunteer for the new jobs, with an alacrity that can only mean that they were fleeing from a still worse fate. There was some rural unemployment at this time, caused in part by the spread of commercial sheep farming to feed the growing market for wool; but by itself this displacement of farm labor did not involve large enough numbers to account for the rush to the factories. In the end it is hard to avoid the conclusion that rural existence itself simply did not hold the attractions that have often been imputed to it by urban social critics. Certainly it was monotonous and isolated, while the rewards for its backbreaking labor were meager and uncertain. The long hours demanded of the factory workers probably represented little change from what they had been used to, and the wages paid by the mills must have seemed deceptively large to people who had rarely used cash. Whatever the explanation, the factory owners had no difficulty recruiting workers, and it did not occur to them that they had any responsibility to help the workers create a viable new existence around the factory. The resourceful men who made the machines, built the factories, and operated them understood their virtually unlimited potential for making goods and therefore money; but it was only with experience that they came to learn about the costs and problems that were also involved.

Geographical factors

The factory with its steam-driven machines acted as a funnel through which huge quantities of raw materials – drawn from a variety of sources – were processed, to emerge in correspondingly large quantities of manufactured goods that were distributed in turn to widespread markets. In terms of the volume of production the human labor involved was minimal, but in comparison with the traditional dispersed cottage industries, the factories required a dense concentration of workers. All of this meant that the factories had to be located near, or with good water access to, the sources of raw materials and fuel, and a market or shipping port. Thanks to her generous coal deposits and many navigable rivers and harbors, England enjoyed a variety of locations that met these conditions, and dozens of new factory towns and cities sprang up, the two greatest of which were Manchester and Birmingham. Located inland from the port of Liverpool, where American cotton arrived, Manchester was the center of the new textile industry, and one of the first "planned" industrial cities. To the south, in the heart of the coal and iron regions, the new metal-working industries collected around Birmingham, in contrasting disorder.

As the factories and factory towns grew, cheap transportation became ever more important, and England's natural waterways were augmented first with canals and then with roads and eventually railroads. Imports of food into the new cities came increasingly from outside the country, since England's own population was being diverted to the factories, and it was cheaper to buy the necessary food with the profits from the factories than to raise it by the traditional methods at home. In short, England was being transformed into the world's first industrial country.

It is striking how fully, not to say uniquely, England provided the necessary conditions for all these developments. First there was the river system that originally allowed the growth of London, through the intensification of food production and its transportation to the city, thus creating an urgent need for fuel. Next there were the superb coal deposits readily available to meet this growing need, and abundant iron close to the coal. And finally there was England's established position in the center of the Atlantic commerce; not only did she build the most ships and carry the largest part of the trade, but she also provided its essential banking services. Nowhere else in the world was this crucial combination of assets reproduced in such remarkable proximity. Once the industrial transition is analyzed in these terms, it becomes difficult if not impossible to imagine it taking place in any other setting; and indeed it was to prove effectively impossible to reproduce anywhere else without direct and substantial aid from England.

MECHANIZED TRANSPORTATION

From the early Middle Ages Europeans had traveled incessantly. By far the most common form of locomotion was walking, but those few who could afford it rode horses or mules. Carts followed rudimentary wagon tracks to carry crops from the fields to the center of the village, town or city; but cross-country carting was virtually impossible, since roads as we know them hardly existed. For the most part, travelers of whatever sort followed paths across the fields and along the river banks, the traders and merchants leading horses or mules that carried their trade goods in saddle bags and the itinerant peddlers carrying their wares on their backs. Besides what little could be carted in from the surrounding fields, supplies for the towns and cities were brought by barges on the local rivers. Virtually all European cities were located by necessity on waterways that could be used to transport those cumbersome staples of existence: food (grain), fuel (firewood), and building materials (stone). The larger the city, the more it depended on its river: Paris was fed by grain barged down the Marne from the rich fields of Champagne, and London by the Thames from its even richer river valley.

The prohibitive cost in energy of moving food and fuel any distance over land had rigidly restricted the territorial size, and therefore the productivity, of Europe's economic units. In the Continental hinterland these seldom had a radius of over fifty miles, and sometimes as little as ten. Although much larger, the sea-trading communities of the ancient Aegean, the medieval Mediterranean, the Baltic, and the early modern Atlantic were limited to the coastlines of their sea and river systems. Thus although the first phase of the industrial revolution provided the Atlantic economy with an apparently unlimited potential for the production of material goods, its territorial limitations were still the same. The second phase of this revolution, therefore, involved the extension of this economy far beyond the port cities through the mechanization of transport.

Roads

Western Europe had practically no highways of any kind until the seventeenth century, but by the middle of the eighteenth century all large and most small cities were connected by some kind of road that carried mail and coach services. Even though the bulk of this traffic consisted of passengers, increasing quantities of goods – mostly luxuries – were also being moved, with much difficulty. The royal engineers who laid out and built the new roads were curiously slow to solve the main problems of their task. Not until the 1780s did two English engineers develop practical methods for establishing the essential elements of good highway construction –

stable foundations, effective drainage, and solid surfacing – and these were applied only gradually to the existing systems. This meant that under most circumstances heavy carts cut into the soft surfaces and mired in frequent mud holes along the way. Where such difficulties constrained the growing industry, new methods began to be developed to cope with them. Private companies were chartered to build and maintain toll roads, called turnpikes, that could be used for transport as well as travel. Although large numbers of these were constructed, most were for short distances where the traffic was particularly heavy. Proving to be a temporary expedient at best, they were soon replaced by improved public roads.

Railways

A more limited, but ultimately more significant, solution was developed in a number of mining areas to get the coal or ore over the few miles to the waterside. First it was found that parallel planks laid across a road made a cheap and sturdy surface that would bear the weight of heavily laden carts. As the quantity of coal or ore increased, these wooden tracks were strengthened with an iron strip, leading eventually to the introduction of the iron rail, recognizable as the forerunner of today's model. Thus the rails, like the steam engine, were developed by and for the coal trade.

While the carts on these earliest "railways" were pulled by horses, the coal field operators and their mechanics recognized from the start that the traction could be supplied by steam. Early in the nineteenth century, an altogether impractical but prophetic steam-propelled cart was made to run briefly in a London suburb; but to serve any useful purpose, a smaller, lighter, and more powerful engine would be necessary. While improved steam engines were being developed for this task, the problems of rails and wheels were also being resolved, so that when the first practical locomotive was built in 1829, there was also a well-designed rail line under construction between Liverpool and Manchester; in fact the locomotive (Stephenson's *Rocket*) was built to compete for a prize offered by the Manchester–Liverpool rail company for an engine that would meet certain specifications of size, power, fuel consumption, and speed.

If railroads were a product of the industrial revolution, they were also an essential element in its development and expansion. While the railroad building boom that was to transform the European world belongs to a later date, some of its characteristics are foreshadowed in this early phase. From the beginning the most profitable use of the rails was to connect fixed resources (coal) to docksides for further distribution, or docks (Liverpool) with fixed factory sites (Manchester). The mechanization of these first key segments of the transportation system, however, stimulated the development of more extensive rail lines that would transport passengers along the routes they used most heavily, and finally the increase in rail traffic of both kinds would necessitate improving the roads from the terminals into the adjacent country.

Shipping

In the same way, the increasing volume of goods arriving by rail at the river and ocean ports required greater shipping capacity. While it would be some time before steam propulsion would be competitive for ocean navigation, it promised to facilitate river traffic from the outset. Few rivers in western Europe or North America were as adaptable to barge use as those of southeastern England: some had too fast a current (the Rhine) or banks that were too steep for tow paths (the Hudson), yet these would become readily navigable by steam-propelled craft. Because boats could carry larger, more cumbersome engines and greater quantities of fuel than locomotives, practical demonstrations of steam propulsion on water preceded those on land by nearly twenty years.

The frequency with which the first rail lines connected an inland point of production with a port emphasizes the close relation between the new industry and the oceanic economy. It is not clear that profits of the Atlantic commerce were invested in the first factories, which were oriented toward small-scale textile and hardware production for their immediate localities, but the expansion of the factory system rapidly came to involve large-scale importation of raw materials, and equally wide dispersion of finished products. For operations on this scale, nothing less than the entire Atlantic commercial community would provide an adequate market. As English mills poured their goods overseas in ever greater volume, they also drew back comparable quantities of cotton, grain and other staples, thus vastly increasing the productivity of the oceanic economy. For the next century Britain would be the center and chief beneficiary of this system.

With the industrialization of transport – that is, the application of steam to land and water propulsion – the oceanic economy expanded increasingly into the European hinterland, but at an uneven rate and to a varied degree, leaving many large pockets of subsistence farming. Beyond Europe, borne on the rising tide of inexpensive textiles and hardware generated by English mills, it reached the vast markets of the Far East and traveled up the rivers of Africa and the Americas. This process of growth and penetration would continue for a century or more, until it appeared that industrial Europe had enmeshed the whole world in its far-flung network of wealth and power.

INDUSTRIAL CIVILIZATION

By a strange coincidence, the industrial revolution occurred in Britain at almost the exact same time as the political revolution in France. This very simultaneity, however, seemed to reinforce the exclusive character of each development. Although French ideas of equality did penetrate the English working population, they evoked no mass reaction, while prerevolutionary French borrowings of English industrial innovations – early versions of coal smelting and the steam engine – were largely lost in the succeeding political turmoil. This tendency to mutual isolation would be massively reinforced by the Napoleonic Wars. Thus the first impact of the new industry on society was experienced exclusively in Britain, and a British stamp was placed on industrial civilization.

The new industrial society in Britain differed fundamentally from its preindustrial predecessor, first in its rapid urbanization, then in its increasing wealth (as measured by per capita production of consumer goods), and finally in the growing role of money in social as well as commercial and political relations.

Urbanization in itself was hardly new, for "civilization" had begun with the first concentration of the population in cities. But the new coal-fueled industry produced a new kind of city, and would also transform most of those surviving from the past. The concentration of mills in favorable locations created sprawling urban agglomerations, overflowing with the new mill hands and their families. At first the workers crowded into all manner of existing spaces; then local agents built new housing, often in the form of rows of crude cottages. Given the hours of work required by the factories (twelve seems to have been a daily minimum), and the fact that women and children worked along with the men (though for lower pay), there was no time or energy left to make these minimal structures livable with even the most basic amenities of existence. Food was purchased at nearby shops and consumed with little preparation; as a result, the average diet was wholly inadequate – largely bread supplemented with beer, or increasingly gin, which was produced by factory methods and sold for almost nothing.

Although life in the country villages was hard and should not be sentimentalized, it did presumably provide a social structure, coherence and tradition that was totally lacking in the new concentrations of immigrants to the city. Even the Church, which managed to serve most rural parishes to some degree, failed to function at all in many of the new cities. That this situation was totally unacceptable and called for radical modification was early recognized by some articulate workers, occasional mill-owners, and an increasing number of other responsible citizens, including politicians. From the outset workers formed mutual benefit associations of various kinds, while the new evangelical Protestant sect of Methodists took a special interest in the city poor. Before long the government began to inquire into mill town conditions and to prescribe some legal measures for their amelioration.

The fact that these social problems were concentrated in urban centers made them visible to those who had the power to change them, in a way that comparable hardships in traditional village life had not been. As a result, the living conditions of factory workers tended to improve, at first very gradually and then more rapidly. Considering their abysmal level at the outset, this slight rise hardly justifies the many abuses of the system, but it does tend to discredit the widely held view that industrialization itself created mass poverty. The basic problems were the original low level of wages, which were set partly in terms of existing rural rates and partly by the limited resources of the mill owners, and the uncertainty of employment. In the first generation the employers were often simply enterprising craftsmen, who worked and lived with their employees and reinvested their profits in their plants; as a result they had neither the financial reserves nor the sense of obligation to keep their mills operating or their workers paid when they had no immediate orders to fill. Production would start and stop fitfully, so that temporary but repeated unemployment was a constant threat. Gradually, however, the larger and more successful firms brought greater stability to factory employment.

The workers themselves also began to improve their situation. Very slowly they groped toward a labor movement with the authority to negotiate with mill owners. In addition they sought opportunities to educate themselves and their children. The fact that women and children were hired for inhumanly long hours at miserable pay has given the whole system a particularly ugly reputation, but again the likelihood is that life in the rural villages was even worse, for women and children as well as for men. For women in particular, factory employment may have represented an improvement over their previous condition in that it served to liberate them from the absolute and narrow restrictions of rural domestic life, offering at least a possibility, which they did not have before, of change for the better.

The mill hands were not the only new residents of the growing cities. In addition to the factory owners and their immediate assistants, there was also a whole new category of professionals – bankers, lawyers, journalists, and doctors, among others – who served and were supported by the new industrial wealth. Having little to do with the old landed aristocracy (although many came of gentry stock), this new elite was wholly urban in orientation, well-educated, conscientious, and self-assured. Under the label of the "upper middle class" in Britain and the "bourgeoisie" on the Continent, they would become the target of endless polemics by radicals and conservatives alike, who both denounced them for their alleged devotion to money as the ultimate value.

As the English moved into the industrial age they were lured by visions of untold riches and haunted by guilt for the misery they saw around them in the burgeoning factory towns. While it would be the middle of the century before the new industrial sector would dominate the economy, even by 1800 it was a powerful adjunct to commerce. With the assistance of the energy now released by coal, workers could produce many times the quantity of goods turned out by craftsmen in the same length of time. The effect was to release human energies from the traditional tasks, now performed by machines, to undertake other activities, including the creation of new wealth on an absolutely unprecedented scale. The ultimate effect was to remake Great Britain and the rest of the European world, which was expanding overseas at an ever-accelerating pace.

5

The Napoleonic Empire

Napoleon was once asked what his impact had been on the French Revolution. He answered, "I finished it," using the French verb "achever" which can equally well mean either "completed" or "destroyed." In fact he did both. He brought to a speedy end the revolution of mobs and coups, insurrection and terror, food shortages, inflation, and neglect of public services and security. But he implemented the revolution against governmental incoherence and incompetence, as well as privilege, quite faithfully, according to the popular demands recorded in the lists of grievances drawn up in 1789.

On seizing power Napoleon moved first to make peace with France's adversaries in Europe and then to reorder life in France, notably by reducing the jungle of customary law to a series of succinct and remarkably effective codes. At the same time he reestablished efficient central administration by appointing prefects as his representatives in each of the new "departments," and provided a fiscal base for his government by creating an equitable new system of taxation. Finally he instituted the first system of universal military service. Together these reforms provided a framework for the nation which had been implicit, but had eluded realization, in the earlier phases of the revolution.

Napoleon governed this new state single-handedly, giving himself the official title first of life consul and shortly thereafter of emperor, looking to ancient Rome for this nomenclature as for much of the style of his regime. In place of a legislature he created a complicated series of consultative, deliberative and administrative bodies whose members he appointed from elected panels.

Much has been made of the dictatorial nature of this rule, and indeed there were no effective constitutional checks on Napoleon's personal power. In practice, however, he tended to abide by his own rules, at least sufficiently to win him the overwhelming support of the French people. The major difference between Napoleon's government and modern dictatorships was that he had no "party." His model was rather the "enlightened despot" idealized by the *philosophes*, and his power depended on popular approval and the loyal, efficient service of the community leaders he appointed as the administrative officers of his realm. For Napoleon and for most of his subjects as well, there was no contradiction in the inscription on the gold coins that read, "Napoleon, Emperor of the French Republic."

For fifteen years Napoleon dominated France and much of the rest of Europe, as much by his genius as by the force of French arms. Not the least of his talents was a flair for discerning and exploiting ability in others; indeed it was his own extraordinary capacity that helped him recognize the potential of others and use it without fear of creating rivals. Thus he overawed his own marshals as completely as he did an entire generation of Europe's best professional soldiers, by his sheer ability to win battles. Similarly, in an age of brilliant diplomats he easily outmaneuvered all the others, leaving his mark on Europe for a century or more. At home it was much the same story; not only did he govern France with complete assurance but he also reordered the government along lines that still hold today. In drafting legal codes he exhibited the same superiority over the country's greatest legal minds that he did over the other generals in the military field. No one in western history had so dominated his age since Alexander the Great. One measure of this superiority is that virtually without exception historians have failed to organize the history of Europe in the first fifteen years of the nineteenth century around any other theme than the rise and fall of Napoleon Bonaparte.

THE CONSULATE

With General Bonaparte's show of force on the 19th of Brumaire (November 10, 1799), the Directory had disintegrated and disappeared, leaving Sieyès and his co-conspirators a clear field in which to establish still another regime. Sieyès produced the constitution he had prepared for the occasion, which granted Bonaparte a figurehead role in the new government, and Bonaparte promptly rewrote it, giving himself the title and authority of first consul and reducing Sieyès's other two consuls, as well as four assemblies, to purely consultative roles. This was hardly according to Sieyès's plan, but since he had no political base, and Bonaparte had the troops of the Paris military district under his command, there was no contest.

Although Bonaparte enjoyed virtually unlimited power in the new regime, he retained the underlying principle introduced by Sieyès. This replaced the direct democratic election of deputies by an arrangement in which the four "representative" bodies of the national government were appointed by Bonaparte from lists of "notables" provided by a very indirect process of election. This form of selection had the effect of creating a partnership between Bonaparte and a national elite, and implemented to a surprising degree Sieyès's formula of "confidence from below, authority from above" – an expression of the essential concept of enlightened despotism.

Administration

With the new government securely in his grasp, Bonaparte moved to restore and reorganize the national administration. His first step was to appoint "prefects" to assume control, under his direct orders, of the public services in each of the departments that had been created by the revolutionary government. Under each of these new officers he created a hierarchy of sub-prefects and mayors, replacing the locally elected officials who presided over such local government as had sprung up during the revolution. At the same time Bonaparte established an efficient and equitable system of assessing and collecting taxes, and a program of national conscription for military service.

To implement these and other reforms – including the creation of the new law codes – Bonaparte realized that he needed a period of peace. Accordingly, he made overtures to the members of the Second Coalition, but these powers spurned the offer, since their armies were now largely on the offensive in central Europe. At this rebuff Bonaparte took immediate action: leading an army across the Alps he relieved the beleaguered French forces in northern Italy and finally defeated the Austrians, forcing the Habsburg emperor to make peace. By the terms of the Treaty of Lunéville in 1799, Austria ceded the left bank of the Rhine to France (thus formally accomplishing Louis XIV's dream), with the understanding that the German princes who lost territory as a result would be compensated on the right bank. This rearrangement of German political units began Bonaparte's program of consolidating the existing countless tiny principalities and free cities of western Germany into some thirty new states, under rulers he chose to retain for their friendliness and subservience to France; this satellite Germany would hereafter serve as a buffer between France and the more threatening German states of Prussia and Austria. In the Lunéville settlement, moreover, Austria recognized France's satellite republics in Italy, Holland, and Switzerland. It was at this time also that Spain ceded Louisiana to France, and shortly afterwards the Pope signed a concordat with Bonaparte in which he formally accepted the jurisdiction of the French government over the clergy and church lands in France, as well as the total state control of education, which had formerly been a church monopoly. By this time the Second Coalition had disintegrated, and unwilling to continue the fight alone the British agreed to the Treaty of Amiens in 1802, thus bringing a brief peace to all of Europe.

Bonaparte took advantage of the acclaim in France that followed on this new success, proclaiming himself "life consul" and announcing a new constitution which further consolidated his personal power. The system of consultative assemblies was simplified by reconstituting the "senate" as a royal council.

During the period of peace following Amiens, Napoleon gave his attention to the legal commission charged with codifying the laws. The law that had prevailed under the old regime had been largely customary, with endless local variations. It had been the object of widespread and vigorous criticism in the lists of grievances of 1789, and the revolutionary government had a clear and urgent mandate to reduce it to a brief, clearly written form that any citizen could understand. The task proved more difficult than the idea, however, and was put off during the turbulent years of the revolution. Finally the Directors made a start, which Bonaparte now proceeded to develop. The results were brilliant – Napoleon would later call it his finest achievement – and went far toward fulfilling the original revolutionary program.

The new code not only provided the desired simple text, but also incorporated some of the most important reforms that had been implemented in the revolution. First, it confirmed the equality of all male citizens before the law, thus putting a final seal on the abolition of official privilege. As corollaries of this basic right it also recognized freedom of individual conscience and occupation, as well as the right to security of person and property. One important provision established the right of children to inherit fixed portions of their parents' property, as a way of preventing the restoration of the great landed estates of the old regime. In general the code served to protect above all the interests of small property-holders, including, for example, strict laws against charging excessive rates of interest. It was a system designed to favor property, but it was weighted heavily in favor of the small landowner and shopkeeper and not of the rich, whether landlord or entrepreneur. Unfortunately even in revolutionary France the Rights of Man were not thought to belong to women, who would be grossly discriminated against by the laws of all western nations for another century.

Renewal of the war

Since neither France nor Britain had made any important concession in the Treaty of Amiens, tensions between the two countries continued and the peace lasted less than a year. A major cause of friction was Napoleon's commitment to high tariffs, which he not only extended to his newly conquered territories (notably the formerly Austrian Netherlands) but also raised considerably. This was in the old mercantilist tradition of manipulating foreign commerce to provide revenues for the royal treasury, and inevitably such interferences in the trade of the Continent's port cities affected Britain's basic interests in the Atlantic.

In 1803 Napoleon challenged Britain's hegemony in the Caribbean by sending a sizeable army to reestablish French control over the island of Haiti. There a remarkable ex-slave named Toussaint l'Ouverture had led a successful revolt against the planter regime and established an independent black government. Napoleon's sudden interest in Haiti seemed to be related to his recent acquisition of the Louisiana territory from Spain, and it is likely that he sought to establish an island base from which to move into his new North American possession. Whatever his intentions, however, he met with disaster when his expeditionary force was completely destroyed by the combined effects of Haitian resistance and yellow fever. Recognizing his untenable position in the New World, Napoleon abandoned his plans for a transatlantic empire, and sold Louisiana to the United States.

At this juncture Napoleon discovered a conspiracy against his life; it appeared that the plotters intended to replace him with a Bourbon prince, and he suspected it was to be the young Duc d'Enghien, then residing across the German border in Baden. Napoleon had the duke kidnapped and then executed, although it turned out that the young man was obviously innocent. This injustice provoked protest throughout Europe but Napoleon ignored the reaction, using the threat against his life as an excuse to inflate his power and status still further. France was no longer a republic, he announced, but rather an empire, and he proceeded to stage a theatrical coronation of himself as emperor – a move which received massive popular endorsement in a national plebiscite. This redefinition of the nation provided Napoleon with an occasion to invite back to France all émigrés who had fled the revolution and succeeding regimes, provided they would swear allegiance to the new French Empire. It was also accompanied by a revival of old titles and honors that had been abolished by the revolution; Napoleon found these useful, just as the monarchs had, to reconcile and bind their recipients to his regime, even though they now no longer had the old meaning in terms of wealth and privilege. It was Napoleon's boast at this point that had finally unified the French people in a single nation, after decades of social fragmentation and disruption brought about by the revolution, and there is much evidence to suggest that he did.

THE CONTINENTAL SYSTEM

With the proclamation of the Empire, Napoleon's foreign policy appeared to change; from efforts to establish peace he turned to preparations for war. Actually the Peace of Amiens between Britain and France had never been more than an uneasy truce on both sides of the Channel. In France the unemployed army officers, who faced retirement on half-pay, posed a threat that Napoleon only partially met by creating the Legion of Honor, an official organization for the distribution of decorations and stipends as rewards for distinguished service. In Britain, unrest mounted as Napoleon suddenly raised French tariffs (in 1803) to a level that effectively excluded British textiles. While the trade affected by this move was hardly decisive for the British economy, the new tariff touched a sensitive nerve and was taken as an act of war in Britain.

The French tariffs were only a current expression of the age-old conflict between a land-based power and the trading cities along its shores. The ocean ports of France, and those of the Continent as a whole, were linked to Britain by shipping ties which not only fostered their prosperity but also supplied much of their staple needs. Like all other territorial rulers, Napoleon saw his ports as a source of government revenues, but just as in other such cases, his attempt to control their trade for his own purposes ultimately disrupted it and hence threatened the very survival of the cities that depended upon it.

Trafalgar

Even before war was declared, in 1803, Napoleon had begun to assemble troops at the Channel port of Boulogne, in highly visible preparation for an invasion of England. In the course of a year he concentrated some 100,000 troops along the coast, and requisitioned a thousand barges, ostensibly to carry the invasion forces across the Channel. Whether Napoleon seriously intended to try such an attack is not absolutely clear; one would think that his experience with Nelson in Egypt would have revealed the hopelessness of challenging the British at sea. In any event Napoleon proceeded with his dubious plan, commanding the admiral of the French fleet to make every effort to lure Britain's main Atlantic squadron to the Caribbean, after which the French ships were to "slip back" to cover the invasion. Finally in the summer of 1805 Nelson did pursue the French to the West Indies, but he gave them no opportunity to return to the Channel unchallenged, forcing them to sail to Spain, then their ally, for supplies and reinforcements. It was off Spain's southwest coast, at Cape Trafalgar, that Nelson finally moved in, destroying both the French and Spanish fleets in one of the most famous sea battles of history. It would be over a century before British sea power would again be challenged.

The mastery of Europe

Anticipating the disastrous outcome of his admiral's maneuvers, Napoleon had abandoned his plan to cross the Channel, and shortly before Trafalgar sent the waiting troops on a lightning campaign into central Europe. There a new Third Coalition – consisting of Austria, Russia, Sweden and Britain – was mobilizing for an attack on France. After a brilliant victory over the Austrians at Ulm, on the upper Danube, Napoleon pushed on to occupy Vienna. At that juncture the main Austrian army headed back from Italy to meet Napoleon, and the new young Tsar Alexander led two Russian armies to aid the Austrians. Trapped by the three converging forces, Napoleon completely routed them at Austerlitz, in his most famous victory. The Austrians sued for peace and the Russians withdrew in haste. Even Prussia, which had been on the point of joining the Coalition, signed a treaty with France instead.

The territorial terms of Austria's settlement with France were complex and temporary, but their general thrust was to confirm French possession of the left bank of the Rhine and French hegemony over Italy, where France now received Venice from the Habsburgs. It was at this point that Napoleon deposed the Bourbons in Naples (who had become English puppets) and replaced them with his brother Joseph. Next he placed his brother Louis on the throne of Holland and created the Confederation of the Rhine in western Germany, composed of the newly consolidated principalities that he had been putting together since the beginning of his career. Clearly a French protectorate, this Confederation included most of Germany except for Prussia, Brunswick and Austria. The Holy Roman Empire now no longer existed even in name, and Francis I formally relinquished its crown, though he did retain an imperial title, as Emperor of Austria.

At this point the inept young king of Prussia and his superannuated generals declared war on the French, apparently under the illusion that they still wielded the military power of Frederick the Great. In the battles of Jena and Auerstadt the French annihilated the Prussian armies, and Napoleon occupied Berlin a few weeks after the opening of hostilities (1806). It was from the Prussian capital that he published the Berlin Decrees, closing all European ports to British trade, and christening this policy the Continental System.

Thus far Napoleon's main military objectives had been to consolidate his hold on the left bank of the Rhine and establish his influence in northern Italy and western Germany. Now it was chiefly the British who remained to be dealt with, for as long as Britain was secure she would encourage and subsidize Napoleon's enemies on the Continent. The irreparable loss of his fleet at Trafalgar had put an end to Napoleon's hopes of attacking England across the Channel by military means; he could only launch an economic war against his greatest rival, and this he attempted to do from his new base in Prussia.

Although Prussia had operated on the European stage as a conventional military, land-based monarchy, it did possess a section of Baltic coast with several important ports including cities at the mouths of the Oder and Vistula rivers, both of which served as outlets for large Prussian grain exports. Napoleon was thus able to use his land power to close some valuable ports to British trade, in what was clearly only the first move in his design of closing the entire Continent to Britain with the hope of bringing her to terms. Britain was Napoleon's sole target in this policy, and he failed to realize the destructive impact it would also have on Europe's coastal areas. Indeed, his interference in the Baltic trade – taken together with his call to the Poles to revolt – quickly persuaded Tsar Alexander that French policy was in serious conflict with Russia's interests. As a consequence he came back into the war against Napoleon (1807), only to suffer another crushing defeat at Friedland.

Peace between Napoleon and Alexander was arranged at a dramatic meeting on a raft in the Niemen River near Tilsit, on the border between Russia and Prussia. Essentially the two rulers divided Europe between themselves: Napoleon offered the defeated tsar recognition of a Russian sphere of influence in eastern Europe (including a free hand with the Turks), but in exchange obtained his promise not to interfere in France's domination and reorganization of western and central Europe. In particular, Alexander agreed to the harsh terms Napoleon imposed on Prussia, including the reduction of its territory by half (all land west of the Elbe was ceded to Napoleon), the imposition of a huge indemnity, the limitation of its army and the closing of its ports to British trade. This Treaty of Tilsit is generally considered to represent the high point of Napoleon's career; with Russia's formal concessions he had essentially achieved his ambition of becoming the acknowledged military master of Europe. It remained to be seen if he could also use this power to bring Britain to capitulation by closing the Continent to her goods.

Unlike twentieth-century economic warfare, Napoleon's Continental System was intended not to deprive the enemy country of critical supplies but rather to bankrupt it, by cutting off its markets for export. The blockade of the Continent did bring Britain to the brink of monetary collapse for a brief period, but before long the lack of critical imports began to cause unbearable shortages in the Continent's ports. The prompt and nearly universal reaction was massive smuggling – which in French-occupied territories took on a patriotic aura.

The first serious break in the system came almost immediately in Spain. In an effort to close Portugal's ports to the British, Napoleon had offered to help Spain conquer her small neighbor in 1807. The ensuing campaign succeeded briefly, driving Portugal's ruling dynasty into exile in Brazil. A year later, however, the British sent a small expeditionary force to help their Portuguese ally against the Spanish invaders. In response, Napoleon brought 100,000 French troops into Spain, and with the excuse of suppressing smuggling, forced the king and his heir to abdicate, placing his own brother Joseph on the throne. This produced a massive popular reaction against the French in Spain, which was only aggravated by their brutal efforts to suppress it. Widespread guerrilla warfare gradually turned Spain into a major military front for Napoleon, and finally forced the French to occupy the entire country (1809), at a considerable cost in men and money.

In the mean time, the coastal populations of Prussia, Holland and even France had developed smuggling into an industry on such a scale that the French had no possibility of stamping it out, particularly since their own officials were generally the eager recipients of enormous bribes. Napoleon's response was to sell licenses for illegal imports, so that at least be got a cut of the profits.

With little coastline to threaten the Continental System, the Habsburgs had been gathering and reorganizing their forces without too much interference from the French. By 1809 the Archduke Charles thought he read in the Spanish revolt the beginning of a general European uprising against the French, and mistakenly decided that it was time to renew the war. In one summer campaign Napoleon completely routed him, occupying Vienna once again and dictating the Treaty of Schönbrunn. In this arrangement the Habsburgs were forced to cede territory to France and various of its client states, and to sign an alliance with Napoleon which was to be sealed by his marriage to the Habsburg emperor's daughter Marie-Louise. To reinforce his "royal" status Napoleon had long felt the need of both a male heir and formal recognition from Europe's hereditary royalty, two objectives he hoped to achieve by this union. He therefore divorced his childless wife Joséphine, and eventually he did produce a son by Marie-Louise, although this intended heir would not in fact inherit anything.

Napoleon now controlled almost all of continental Europe, from the Atlantic to Russia in the north and the Ottoman empire in the south. Only Sweden was independent, and Portugal was just beginning to be liberated by the British. Further, all the territory within the natural boundaries of the Pyrenees, the Alps, and the Rhine River had been consolidated within France itself, in what could be described as the logical end-product of the Bourbon concept of the administrative monarchy. This expanded France was the heart of the Continental System, which besides serving as a blockade against Britain was also viewed by its architect as an extension of France's own economy.

The French nation itself was effectively administered from Paris for the purpose of producing taxes and military conscripts, in return for which the inhabitants were provided with efficient public services; and it is important to note that the regime was generally popular until Napoleon's fall. Surrounding France were its satellite states, ruled by the emperor's relatives or favorites. Napoleon's brother Louis was king of Holland, his brother-in-law

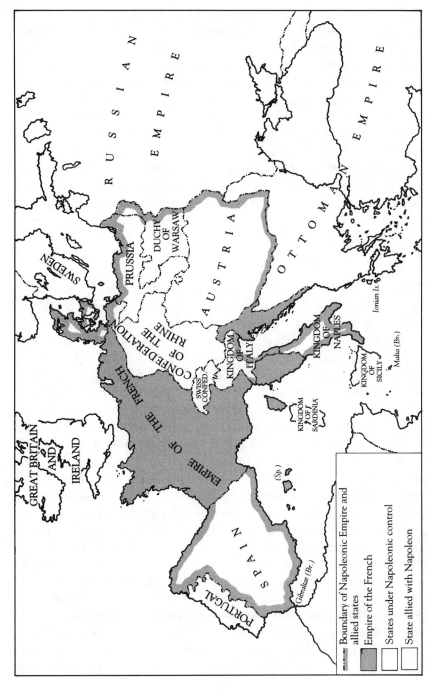

MAP 3   *Europe, 1812: the Napoleonic Empire*

Murat king of Naples, and his brother Joseph king of Spain, while Napoleon himself was king of northern Italy. In Germany Napoleon controlled his newly created puppet principalities of the Confederation of the Rhine, and in eastern Europe he had divested Prussia of her Polish provinces and formed them into the puppet state of the Grand Duchy of Warsaw. From all these satellite states Napoleon expected indemnities and armies, and above all compliance with the Continental blockade, in return for the "enlightened," rational regimes he imposed. And finally from the category of forced allies – notably Prussia and Austria, but also Denmark and Norway – Napoleon expected military support; he did not, however, interfere with their internal affairs except in occupied Prussia.

Strains on the system

Originally the more socially advanced parts of Europe (particularly the Rhine and Po valleys) had responded favorably to French reforms and administration, but by 1810 that welcome had worn thin. In the more backward areas, where the peasants or serfs actually had the most to gain from French rule, the popular reaction had always been hostile, as in Spain. But Napoleon's most costly mistake was probably his attempt to impose the Continental blockade on his subjects and subject territories. Just as he obviously understood the administrative integration of a vast continental area, he seems to have had little understanding of an oceanic trading system and its hold on the Continent's coastal population. In Holland his brother Louis abdicated his throne rather than attempt to force the blockade on his Dutch subjects, at the cost of both their prosperity and their essential supplies. Napoleon's immediate response was to incorporate Holland and the North Sea coast into France, just as he had already taken over central Italy and the Dalmatian coast, and would add Catalonia (Barcelona) two years later. But these desperate measures failed to put an end to the British trade that was so vital to the ports of these areas. Further, Tsar Alexander was hardly likely to abide by the terms of the Tilsit treaty and punish his own Baltic ports by closing them to Britain; indeed within a year of Tilsit he was in secret contact with both the British and the Habsburgs, exploring the possibilities of

joining forces to curb the insatiable demands of the Emperor of
the French Republic.

THE WARS OF LIBERATION

Napoleon's downfall was even more rapid than his rise. It is
traditional to say that he had reached the apex of his power in
the years 1810 to 1812, and certainly his authority and influence
reached their greatest territorial limits at this point, when the
frustration and failure of the Continental System had not yet
emerged as a troubling factor. His absolute control of the French
administrative regime always enjoyed the overwhelming support
of the French population, and for the most part it was also
docilely accepted in the areas that Napoleon had assimilated to
France – both in the Rhineland and along the Dalmatian, Italian,
Dutch, German, and Spanish coasts. Beyond the frontiers of
France proper lay the satellite states of the Confederation of the
Rhine and the kingdoms of Italy, Naples and Spain; ruled by
puppets or relatives of Napoleon, these states tended on the whole
to benefit from French influence, and with the important exception
of Spain they showed no inclination to challenge the emperor's
will. All that appeared to be beyond his reach was Russia to the
east and Britain to the west, the one separated by distance and the
other by the sea. The decaying Ottoman Empire offered neither
threat nor opportunity to Napoleon, while the still independent
Swedes appeared to put themselves voluntarily under Napoleon's
sway in 1810 when they invited one of his generals to become the
heir to their childless king.

On this vast theatre Napoleon exercised two principal forms of
power, one administrative and the other military. Both had their
limits. Effective as the French system of government was, it produced strains and antagonisms when it was extended beyond areas
in which the French language was spoken; the Dutch in particular
were completely alienated by the experience of being ruled in
French. Beyond the borders of French administration, Napoleon
operated as the invincible military commander; his repeatedly
demonstrated ability to defeat any regular armies put in the field
against him established his hegemony in one degree or another
right up to the borders of the Ottoman and Russian empires. This

power also had its limits, however: his armies could not march beyond the water's edge, nor travel too far from their source of supplies and reinforcements, nor conquer foes who would not fight conventional battles. The only weapon Napoleon could devise against the menace of the British was the blockade, but he was unable to implement it effectively and even if he had done so it would probably have done little damage to Britain. Worse, his attempt to enforce the blockade trapped him in futile efforts to stamp out the smuggling which was not only profitable but also entirely necessary for his coastal subjects. Inability to pursue this policy successfully seemed to drive Napoleon to attempt to apply his military power – his greatest strength – in ways that were fatally inappropriate to its nature. First he tried to use his armies to fight people rather than other armies, then he led his troops beyond a logistical point of no return.

The Spanish rising

The turning-point in Napoleon's fortunes may well have been his decision in 1808 to close the port of Lisbon to the British. To this end he proposed to the king of Spain a joint campaign to be followed by the division of Portugal between the victors. The offer was accepted, the plan was carried out, and the French seemed to have closed the last principal gap in the blockade. Napoleon anticipated that the British would come to the aid of their Portuguese allies, and he sent an army of 100,000 men to Spain, ostensibly to guard the coasts against the British but in reality to replace the king with a French satellite government that would run the country more efficiently in line with French interests. At this the Spanish populace rose in revolt, beginning a guerrilla war that would continue until the French were finally driven out. At the same time, the British landed an expeditionary force in Portugal that would also harass the French from the rear. Neither of these forces could be brought face to face with the French to be destroyed in a classic Napoleonic battle. Instead they gnawed away at their superior foe, keeping the French continually on the defensive.

Interestingly, Napoleon never tried to win over the Spanish people, who were among the most impoverished and oppressed peasants in Europe, by invoking French revolutionary reforms, even though in France the peasants were the most important base of his power. Outside France Napoleon did not bother to appear as other than conqueror, a disdainful approach that probably cost him dearly by stirring fierce nationalist resistance. In any event the struggle in Spain demonstrated to an incredulous Europe that the French were not as invulnerable as they had appeared, at least if opposed by a desperate population. The Spanish paid an appalling price in atrocities suffered, but the damage they inflicted on the French was irreparable.

Nationalism in northern Europe

Although the archduke Charles was disastrously premature in reading the Spanish situation as a sign of general French collapse, the hopes raised by Spain's resistance did bear useful fruit in Prussia and the smaller German states. As a result of its defeat in 1806, Prussia had virtually ceased to exist as a conventional power; a remarkable group of reformers now took command of Prussia, however, deciding that drastic measures were clearly the only alternative to national disintegration. Inspired by a new wave of German nationalism, and learning from Napoleon's own success, they set to work to create a new Prussian state and army. Serfs were freed (although not given land), careers were opened to talent, universal military training was instituted, and army discipline was modified to accommodate a new class of educated urban volunteers. The French were not unaware of these developments, nor blind to their implications, but a national German awakening was not something that could be cornered on a battlefield and crushed. They did make some efforts to check the tide of nationalist feeling in Prussia, but succeeded only in fueling it all the more.

In 1810, when his brother Louis abdicated the throne of Holland, Napoleon annexed the country, together with the German North Sea coast, thus bringing them into open conflict with their French overlords, while their trade with the British was not effectively suppressed. At about the same time, the Swedes asked Napoleon to help them find an heir to the throne of the childless king; he selected the independent-minded Marshal Bernadotte, who surprisingly proceeded to serve the interests of his new state at the expense of the old. Immediately upon taking charge of Sweden's foreign policy he arranged a settlement with Alexander, recognizing Russia's recent conquest of Finland (formerly under Swedish rule) in return for the promised compensation of acquiring Norway from Denmark. More important, he joined Russia in making peace with Britain, and thus reopened the Baltic to English trade.

The invasion of Russia

Confronted with this gradual erosion of his authority and prestige, Napoleon sorely needed some demonstration of strength. He therefore decided to find an enemy to defeat in battle, and the only European ruler who was in any position to offer resistance was Alexander. The two emperors had a list of differences, but the particulars were doubtless secondary to Napoleon's desperate need to flex his military muscle once again. It is not clear at what moment Napoleon decided to attack Russia, but he began demanding contingents of troops from his allies and satellites, and moving up his own forces, until he had half a million men under arms in eastern Europe. Then in June of 1812 he crossed the Niemen River into Russia, with what must have been the largest single army to take the field in Europe's history. Clearly he expected that Alexander would try to block his path and thereby offer him the chance to win a resounding victory. Nothing of the sort occurred. The Russian army retreated before him, allowing the French to destroy Smolensk without resistance, and making a stand only at Borodino, less than a hundred miles before Moscow. Napoleon claimed a victory, but both sides suffered severe losses and the Russians withdrew in order.

Continuing their advance, the French found Moscow deserted. Then in a few days fires began to break out and rage unchecked in the city, leaving it uninhabitable for the approaching winter. Frustrated, and now forced to retreat, Napoleon proposed a truce to Alexander, who of course rejected it. Finally, after wasting a month in unaccustomed perplexity, Napoleon began his retreat in mid-October, far too late to escape the advancing winter. In the long march back across Russia the French forces suffered a devastating defeat, even though no armies were raised against them.

They found all villages and towns in their path deserted and destroyed so that they were unable to find supplies, they were harassed by bands of guerrillas, and finally they were overtaken by a particularly savage winter. Their suffering and losses were unspeakable, with not more than a quarter of Napoleon's half million men surviving to cross the Russian border. Napoleon himself rushed ahead to Paris, to attempt to deal with the inevitable reaction to his débâcle.

Defeat

As the shattered remnants of the French army struggled across Germany, the anti-Napoleonic forces began to prepare for action. The Prussians, still nominal allies of France, signed a treaty with Russia and sent a small force to join the Russian army that was now moving west behind the French. During the spring and early summer of 1813 there was indecisive fighting in northern Germany. Austria reentered the war, signing an alliance with Prussia and Russia, and fought a major battle at Leipzig in which Napoleon's forces were defeated and driven out of Germany (October 1813), leaving his satellite Confederation in shambles. At the same time in the south, the British under Wellington had driven the French from Spain and pursued them into France.

The Allies were now in a position to dictate terms to Napoleon. Having no interest in prolonging the war by invading France itself, they offered Napoleon peace within the borders of the Rhine, the Alps and the Pyrenees. Unable to relinquish his entire imperial design in such short order, Napoleon simply let the offer lapse, and the campaign continued. For the first time the allies had a superior supply of reserves, thanks in part to Prussia's new spirit and army, and could afford losses that Napoleon could not. Thus they pushed the French back from defeat to defeat, and in April of 1814, after a brief but fierce skirmish outside the gates on March 30, they entered and occupied an undefended Paris. After vainly offering to retire in favor of his infant son, Napoleon finally abdicated. Not only was there no popular call for him to retain the throne, but it was Napoleon's own marshals who insisted on his surrender, and his ministers in Paris who were busy arranging the return of the Bourbons and the orderly transfer of power to Louis

XVIII, brother of Louis XVI. The French state, which was largely the work of Napoleon, continued to function smoothly and effectively without him, in the hands of the able men he had trained to run it.

Even Napoleon's unequaled military genius was disarmed once his generals refused to obey him; but to be sure he did not find fresh resources, the allies shipped him off to Elba, a tiny island off the Italian coast, with the promise of a subsidy of two million francs and the right to retain his imperial title. It was a comic-opera solution that very nearly turned into grand tragedy. Napoleon endured only a few months of exile with his refugee court. Then, hearing of dissension among the allies, he made a desperate attempt to take advantage of this possible opportunity. Escaping from the island without difficulty, he sailed for France and made directly for Paris, gathering veterans as he moved. The Bourbons and their entourage packed and fled, and the capital received Napoleon once again.

The principal allies reacted to this development with expedition, putting large forces into the field under the command of Britain's Duke of Wellington, who gave his adversary little time to rebuild his military base of power. Napoleon tried to prevent the massing of a huge allied invasion force by meeting the troops where they were assembling in Belgium. After a few days of minor engagements he met Wellington at Waterloo; it was a long, hard-fought battle, but the arrival of a Prussian contingent late in the day turned it into a crushing defeat for the French. Once again Napoleon abdicated, and once again he was confined to an island, but this time it was St Helena, in the South Atlantic, and he was securely guarded as a prisoner under house arrest. This brief return to power, called "the Hundred Days," provided less an epilogue than an anticlimax to his career, and to the fifteen years of Napoleonic rule in France that had both fulfilled and brought to an end the ideal of enlightened despotism in the form of an administrative and military monarchy.

6

The Concert of Europe

The allied powers that finally brought Napoleon to defeat had one common overriding objective: to bring peace to Europe as a whole. Napoleon's downfall at Waterloo took place a quarter of a century after the Estates General had convened at Versailles and ignited the revolution in France, which in turn had led to war in Europe. Only the elderly could now remember growing up in a stable world. The Continent had suffered great material destruction, human misery and general confusion during these years of warfare, and it is only with this fact in mind that the story of the postwar years can be understood.

The representatives of the powers who undertook to reconstruct their world saw peace as threatened equally by war and by revolution. Traditionally Europe's rulers had waged war to conquer territory, which in itself was their principal source of wealth and power. In the eighteenth century, therefore, the emergent monarchs had learned that their individual security depended on preventing any one ambitious ruler from amassing enough territory to dominate the others – in short, that the relative strength of each should be kept in balance. With revolution these rulers had had less experience, and therefore had not yet developed a technique for its avoidance. No ruler of the age, however, had failed to note the fury of the Paris mob, or the explosive force of the armies of revolutionary France, and most concluded that harshly repressive measures would only provoke subjects to similar excesses. At the same time their conservative instincts warned them that too lax or liberal a regime might invite and start the avalanche, as royal concessions had done in France. What they wanted was not to push the clock back, as has been charged, but simply to stabilize and reinforce the status quo.

At the Congress of Vienna the representatives of the powers managed to put together a mutually acceptable settlement by June of 1815, even agreeing to reconvene as required to adjust their diplomatic structure to changing social and political circumstances. Ironically, however, it was this last prudent provision that ultimately served to destroy the system it was intended to preserve. Inadvertently the allies restored to power a few highly reactionary regimes, and when these provoked revolutionary protests and revolts, the conservative members of the alliance could not resist the temptation to use its machinery to suppress the uprisings. While this intervention achieved its immediate purpose of restoring order, at least temporarily, it also alienated the British and led to their withdrawal not only from the alliance but also from the affairs of the Continent in general.

The reaction of the British was the product not of any sympathy for radical regimes but rather of a deep aversion to interfering in the internal affairs of other countries. To some degree this attitude derived from their experience with the American colonies, but in general it reflected their interests as the center of a commercially based oceanic community. (England's rule of Ireland was, however, a flagrant exception to this general orientation and policy.) In practice, Britain's opposition to intervention made it impractical for the other powers to attempt it in areas that could be reached only by sea, notably Greece and Spanish America. But on the Continent, in Spain and Italy, the allies could impose their will. The result was success for nationalist uprisings in Greece and the Spanish American colonies, but defeat for revolutionary movements in Italy and Spain in the 1820s.

After a brief period of quiet, a number of small revolts swept across the heart of Europe in 1830. The first, in Paris, forced the abdication of the king, the second in Brussels secured Belgium's independence from Holland. Other attacks on authority occurred in some smaller German and Italian states, but had only limited success at best. And finally the Poles drove the Russian garrison from their country, only to have the tsar's troops return to reestablish full control. Without any question these sucessive outbursts were directly or indirectly influenced by events in France, giving rise to the belief that some general assault on constituted authority had been launched in Europe. Yet each outbreak differed significantly from the others in the details of its means and aims. The most that can be urged as a common cause is a general sense of restlessness coupled with a determination to adjust old institutions to new aspirations.

The mood or style of this period, at the time and since, has been called Romanticism. The chief characteristic of this phenomenon was a reaction against the extreme rationalism of the eighteenth century, and one of its important sources was the work of Jean-Jacques Rousseau, who probed the role of what we would call the subconscious in human conduct. In the Romantic perspective a new emphasis was placed on subjective perceptions, and on the importance of the individual in general, particularly as "hero" or "artist." Romantic influence can be seen in much of the artistic and intellectual achievement of the time. One of the important early Romantics was the English poet William Wordsworth, another was the German poet Schiller, and in France the movement's leader was Victor Hugo. In all three countries most young artists and writers went through a Romantic phase, and the movement can also be viewed in part as an expression of the restlessness of a young generation that had been encouraged in its aspirations by the ferment and change brought about by the revolution and Napoleon, yet found its hopes frustrated by a society that was still essentially static and closed.

IN QUEST OF PEACE

The Quadruple Alliance

As the armies of Austria, Russia, Prussia and Britain were converging on Paris in the spring of 1814, the diplomatic representatives of these powers met at Chaumont in eastern France, where they signed a twenty-year treaty of alliance that committed them to work together to restore and maintain the peace of Europe. A few weeks later, the forces of this Quadruple Alliance occupied the French captial, where their delegates, joined by those of the secondary powers of Spain, Portugal and Sweden, formulated the terms of Napoleon's surrender and abdication, and drafted what would be known as the First Treaty of Paris. Their principal task was the disposition of the emperor and his family, and the establishment of a new regime in France.

Napoleon was offered the little island of Elba (off the north-west coast of Italy) as a place of exile, together with a sufficient subsidy to maintain a modest court. To replace him the allies decided, on the advice of Talleyrand, to restore the Bourbon dynasty in the person of Louis XVIII, younger brother of the late Louis XIV. Talleyrand's role in this arrangement is not without interest; originally a bishop and prominent figure in the court of Louis XVI. this adept statesman had already managed to time his changes of allegiance so as to come out on top after the Revolution and again after Napoleon's seizure of power, serving the emperor both as foreign minister and as presiding officer of the Senate. Sensing a change in the wind after Tilsit, Talleyrand had begun negotiating with Napoleon's enemies while still in office, and as a known traitor to Napoleon he now had the liveliest possible reason for seeing that the emperor was not allowed to retain the throne of France. Under the circumstances this objective did not prove difficult to achieve.

The Bourbon claimant was the only readily available figure to assume the throne, and if he generated little enthusiasm he provoked even less opposition. Having disposed of Napoleon, the peacemakers had little further interest in dismantling the "imperial" government he had set up, and it continued to function with no significant interruption and amazingly little modification. The legal and administrative institutions underwent changes mainly of personnel, while the central executive organs in Paris – the Imperial Senate and Legislature – were replaced in the new Bourbon constitution by Chambers of Peers and Deputies which would differ from their Napoleonic counterparts chiefly in name.

The final treaty was completed in a few weeks. Although it left intact the governmental reforms that had been established by the revolution and Napoleon, it did deprive France of all her major conquests, reestablishing her boundaries as those of 1792. But even this arrangement involved little change, because most of the territories in question were now already in allied hands. Significantly, the victors took great care to avoid any act or gesture that would be humiliating to the defeated French. No French territory was seized, no indemnity was exacted.

In all these decisions it is easy to see the primary objective of Europe's leaders in 1814. They were determined to deprive France of the military superiority that had allowed her to dominate the Continent – by the elimination of Napoleon and the return of the conquered territories – but they were at least as eager to avoid provoking a new outburst of patriotic zeal for expansion among the French. The mildness of their terms was clearly the product of neither unselfish benevolence nor any lack of resolve on the part of the victors, but rather of their overwhelming desire for peace and their shared philosophy of how it was to be achieved.

For twenty years France's overwhelming military might had kept Europe in constant turmoil. But behind its conventional military superiority lay the new revolutionary energies which year after year had provided the French armies with an endless supply of able soldiers and superior officers. In order to contain French military power, therefore, the allies had not only to deprive France of her swollen territorial base but also to avoid provoking a new nationalist outburst – either by refusing to recognize the revolutionary reforms or by subjecting the country to humiliation. And finally, the allies recognized the danger of weakening France's military position too much, lest it destroy the general balance of power in Europe that they were eager to maintain.

The Congress of Vienna

When the allies turned from France to the rest of Europe, they found their principles more difficult to apply. Realizing that they would need much more time to resolve these problems, they accepted the invitation of the Habsburg emperor to meet at Vienna in the fall. The city itself proved to be an awkward choice; more like a large provincial town than a major capital, Vienna was strained to its limits by the company that assembled there in September. Each of the principal powers sent a small but distinguished delegation to support its chief negotiator. These official guests, however, were swamped by a host of displaced petty princelings who descended on the conference in the hope either of winning some indemnity for their lost territories or of merely enjoying the imperial hospitality. Presiding over this heterogeneous assembly was the Habsburg emperor, who held open house – with daily banquets, balls, and entertainments – for all visitors of rank, whether they were formally invited or not.

Amidst this social hubbub the chief representatives of the powers met informally but regularly at the residence of Prince Metternich, the Austrian foreign minister. The only head of state to attend was Tsar Alexander, while for Britain there was the foreign secreaty Lord Castlereagh and for Prussia the foreign minister Prince Hardenberg. And finally from France the irrepressible Talleyrand arrived uninvited, to be ignored at first and then gradually included in the chief working group.

In the drama that ensued, the leading parts were played by star performers. Both Alexander and Metternich were young (about 40), handsome, gifted (especially in languages) and colorful. Alexander was distinguished by a strikingly split personality, which left his associates in constant doubt whether they were dealing with a model "enlightened despot" or a mystical reactionary. Metternich displayed a vanity matched only by his interest in pursuing the ladies; these activities just missed involving him in a duel with Alexander. The British Lord Castlereagh, though no less aristocratic than his colleagues, was as pious and principled as they were cynical and worldly, while the Prussian Prince Hardenberg was so deaf that he could take no useful part in the discussions. Ironically, the dominant figure came to be Talleyrand, who won his leading place at the bargaining table by the sheer virtuosity of his performance.

The task that confronted these emissaries was the restoration of a stable and peaceful Europe. The French case had been comparatively easy to settle, first because the country had traditional boundaries which contained a contiguous, integrated territory of sufficient size to command international respect, and second because the French people had no widely felt unfinished business, in terms of either territorial ambitions or revolutionary reforms. The same could not be said for the rest of Europe. In all of Europe that lay between the Baltic and Mediterranean, the Atlantic and the borders of the Ottoman and Russian empires, Napoleon had rearranged the map, changing institutions and rulers with a reckless, if sometimes inspired, abandon that had no precedent in European history. By a process of amalgamation he had reduced some three hundred tiny territorial units in western and southern Germany to about thirty medium-sized states. While occupying Italy he had extended French administration to part of the peninsula and Bonapartist rule to the rest. And in the process of these various adjustments he had placed himself, a brother, or a favorite on more than half a dozen European thrones, both old and new.

At first glance it might well appear that all these various regimes, as creatures of Napoleon, were proper subjects for some degree of suspicion. Quite sensibly, however, the powers decided to recognize the status quo wherever no overriding considerations prevailed. This moderation was obviously intended to avoid provoking popular resistance to what would be perceived as reactionary policies. At the same time the powers refused to countenance any further unification of the German states, or even the granting of constitutions, which they saw as likely to invite further revolutionary demands.

The only significant cases in which this moderate approach was not followed involved either events beyond the powers' control, or their efforts to maintain or revive the Continent's balance of power by the manipulation of territory. In the first category there was the return of the pope to Rome, and with him the restoration of reactionary regime in the Papal States. Just to the south, in Naples, the Congress had recognized Napoleon's brother-in-law Murat as king, in exchange for his defection from Napoleon; but when Murat then reversed himself during Napoleon's brief return to power, he was driven out, and the resulting power vacuum was quickly filled by the old repressive Bourbons. Meanwhile their equally unrepentant cousins were restored to power in Spain by popular demand. All three of these repressive regimes would cause problems for the alliance. However it was the question of territorial equilibrium that would most threaten the stability sought by the Congress.

With Napoleon's departure and the return of France to her 1792 boundaries, the dominant military power on the Continent became Russia. By western standards her sources of manpower were unlimited, a fact that lent both force and menace to Alexander's insistence on establishing an outpost for his armies in a revived kingdom of Poland. This threat to the heart of Europe was hardly eased by Alexander's protests that he would not assimilate Poland into the Russian Empire, but rather rule it personally as a constitutional monarch. Nor did it help that his proposed new kingdom would be constituted in part from territory that had been acquired by Austria and Prussia in their earlier partitions of that unhappy country. When the allies proposed that Prussia be compensated for her territorial losses by the restoration of her Polish provinces, Alexander demanded that the necessary land be found in the west. His will prevailed, and the Congress ended by giving Prussia much of the Rhineland, with fateful consequences.

Confronted with the tsar's refusal to compromise on these crucial issues, Britain and Austria, with the encouragement and support of Talleyrand, finally drew up a secret agreement to take joint military action against the Russians. At just this point, Napoleon returned to France and launched the campaign that led to Waterloo. Amazingly, this cataclysm neither interrupted the negotiations nor weakened the anti-Russian block, but it did have a sobering effect, and rather than go to war with Russia they finally settled for a negotiated resolution that limited the tsar to rule of a smaller Poland than he had wanted.

Having reestablished the original borders of France, the allies needed to reinforce them against possible further French adventures. In the north, the old Habsburg Netherlands were attached to the kingdom of Holland; to the east – where France ambition was most feared – Prussia was given a solid block of Rhineland territory; and in the south, France's invasion route to Italy was barred by the cession of the French county of Nice to the kingdom of Piedmont. In addition, the Habsburgs were compensated for the loss of the Netherlands by the acquisition of Lombardy and Venetia and the crowns of several lesser principalities. Finally, with the major exception of Prussia, the German states were left much as Napoleon had rearranged them, and following his example, organized into a loose confederation.

A few days before Waterloo, the delegates signed the "Final Act" of the Congress, which included a far-sighted provision for further meetings from time to time, as events revealed a need to review and revise their work. They then proceeded to France to sign the Second Treaty of Paris and oversee the second Restoration. Although this settlement called for some border rectifications

MAP 4   *Central Europe and Italy, 1815: after the Congress of Vienna*

and a stiff indemnity, it was still a surprisingly moderate settlement considering the circumstances; and the first of the subsequent congresses, that of Aix-la-Chapelle in 1818, was called only to dismantle the occupation and welcome France back into the concert of Europe.

THE CONGRESS SYSTEM

When the delegations of the great powers left Vienna in 1815, they had reason to hope that they had established a durable and flexible peace. And in fact it would be 40 years before two major European powers would confront one another on a battlefield again, and a century before there would be a general war. In spite of this unprecedented period of peace, however, political turbulence led almost immediately to revolutionary outbreaks in one country after another. As a result, the attention of the powers began to shift from the problem of maintaining a balance of power in Europe to the new threats to internal law and order. Britain now found herself alone in choosing a policy of non-intervention, and under the leadership of Alexander and Metternich the alliance increasingly come to function as an engine of repression. Ironically, this repression of internal uprisings would be carried out chiefly through two agencies that had been created to reinforce international peace, the "congress system" and the "Holy Alliance."

At the end of the Vienna meetings the powers had agreed to meet at periodic intervals to make whatever adjustments might be necessary to reduce tensions – a plan that was dubbed the "congress system." In addition, Tsar Alexander, in a characteristic fit of mysticism, had drafted a treaty by which Europe's rulers would promise to govern their relations with one another according to Christian principles. While this proposal, which the tsar called the "Holy Alliance," was generally greeted with irreverent consternation, few princes felt they could afford to openly reject such a pious project. Only the pope, the sultan of the Ottoman Empire, and the king of Great Britain excused themselves from signing the document, the first two on the grounds that – in rather different ways – it would be inappropriate for them to promise to conduct themselves as Christians, and the king with the explanation that his signature would be unconstitutional unless countersigned by a minister. In any event, both the congress system and the Holy Alliance seemed innocent enough when they were established, but as the Quadruple Alliance held its five successive annual congresses, its function as a "holy" alliance came to be defined increasingly as that of snuffing out all revolutionary conflagrations in Europe.

The first post-Vienna Congress met in Aix-la-Chapelle in 1818, mainly to recognize France's fulfillment of her obligations to the allies and therefore to withdraw the occupation forces. At this meeting, however, the tsar suddenly proposed a new treaty by which all European rulers woud guarantee not only each other's boundaries and territories but their regimes as well. Britain's foreign minister, Castlereagh, was horrified, and made it quite clear that his government would never participate in any such undertaking. Thus although Britain would participate in the congresses that followed, this first gathering opened a decisive gulf between her and the Continental powers which would only widen as time passed.

Reform movements

The tsar's concern may have been provoked by the activities of liberal students in Germany – the nearest such unrest came to Russia. A recent student "festival" had been held, ostensibly to celebrate the 300th anniversary of Luther's break with Rome, but actually to reinforce the hopes of reform that had been aroused by the French example. The whole affair was peaceful and law-abiding, but it demonstrated that German students counted on the continuing liberalization of government institutions and the eventual unification of their country. Actually much of their motivation – like that of the young French revolutionaries a quarter of a century before – was the desire to create a larger field of opportunity in which to exercise their talents. For the most part university students came from business and professional families; thus they were not poor (even if chronically short of spending money), but they felt stifled in the close confines of Germany's petty states.

In Italy the rising generation was being alienated in a more extreme way. In one or two duchies in the north, as well as in the

Papal States and the kingdom of Naples, aggressively reactionary regimes attempted to eradicate all French influence. The results, again, were to block the aspirations of the young for a national system of legal and efficient government in which they could find some future for themselves. Not having universities as a base, the Italian radicals created secret societies, called Carbonari (charcoal-burners), because they met clandestinely in woodlands.

Revolution in Spain

The first open break with the established order actually occurred in Spain, where the Bourbons had been defended and restored by ferocious popular resistance to the French invasion under Napoleon. In the course of the war King Ferdinand VII had granted a constitution (1812), which was actually more administrative than liberal, but following the French defeat he cancelled this reform, with considerable assurance that he had the support of the public. However, he had failed to take into account the younger army officers, who had been impressed by the efficiency of the French army and system of government; again it was the younger generation of professionals (in this case military) who were most seriously disaffected. The situation was then gravely aggravated by a series of revolts in Spain's American colonies that deprived her of desperately needed revenue. Encouraged by Russia and Austria, Ferdinand mobilized troops and organized an expedition to reassert control of his overseas possessions.

Assembling at Cadiz, the troops saw the lamentable condition of their ships and realized they had no chance of surviving the crossing. They mutinied, and instead of restoring order, their officers seized the opportunity to organize a march on Madrid to force reforms – including the restoration of the constitution of 1812 – on the derelict regime. This was one of the earliest "revolutions of the colonels," that would recur repeatedly, and for much the same reasons, on the fringes of the European world from then until the present. The king, who became a prisoner of the army, restored the constitution, which had been based on the first revolutionary constitution in France (1791), with power divided between a single legislative chamber and the king. Perhaps more significantly, the constitution also divided the country into administrative departments on the French model, thereby laying the base for an efficient central government. Before any substantial reforms could be implemented in Spain, however, the conservative European powers persuaded France to intervene and crush the rebels. When they restored the king to his absolute authority the French actually urged him to retain the constitution, but he opted for savage repression instead.

The Spanish Empire

For the conservative members of the alliance, the restoration of the old regime in Spain was only a first step to the reconquest of that country's rebellious colonies in the New World. Since the sixteenth century the Spanish monarchy had depended heavily on the gold and silver it imported from its American colonies to cover its basic expenses. Although the production of the mines had long been dwindling, it was still important when the Napoleonic Wars cut the Continent off from the Atlantic. The effect of this blockade was not only to deprive Spain of its treasure but also to leave the colonies to their own devices.

From the beginning, service in the Spanish royal colonial administration had been limited to officials born in Spain. Even colonists of pure Spanish descent, who constituted a property-owning elite, were systematically excluded from government service. Thus alienated, these "creoles," as they were called, seized on their wartime isolation to take matters into their own hands. With the examples of the American and French revolutions before them, they inevitably dreamed of independence, which they proceeded to achieve under the inspired leadership of a remarkable statesman named Simon Bolivar.

The rapid establishment of a series of independent republics in South America was taken as a scandalous affront by the members of the alliance. Thus with the Spanish monarchy restored at home, their next objective was to assist it to reassert control over the wayward colonies. The fact that neither Spain nor her backers possessed the requisite shipping for such an undertaking did not deter them in the least. Their efforts to organize the project, at the last congress (at Verona in 1822), led the British foreign minister Canning to send word to the American President Monroe urging him to issue a general warning against European intervention in the New World. The result was the Monroe Doctrine, and ultimately the continuation of Latin American liberation without European interference.

Southern Europe

While this Spanish drama was unfolding, revolutionary uprisings also occured in Italy and Greece. Encouraged by the original success of the rebellion in Spain, Italian dissidents overthrew the reactionary regime in Naples in 1820, while a year later rebellions also broke out in the north, most notably in Piedmont. Order was restored by Austrian intervention, but a revolutionary movement had been born in Italy that would eventually unify the whole peninsula under a wholly new regime.

Meanwhile, in the east, Greek patriots began their War of Independence from the Turks in 1821. Although European public opinion warmly favored the Christian victims of Ottoman oppression, the prospect of Greek liberation raised some deeply disquieting specters for the powers. For quite some time they had feared the imminent disintegration of the Ottoman Empire because of Russia's obvious intention of filling the gap by seizing Constantinople and the Straits (linking the Mediterranean to the Black Sea) – from which vantage point she could dominate traffic on the Mediterranean as the Turks had never attempted to do. Indeed this prospect frightened Castlereagh as much as it did Metternich, with the result that they joined forces to persuade Alexander not to intervene on the side of the Greeks. The struggle then became particularly confused by the emergence in Greece of both rebellious Turkish governors and dissident Greek patriots, and it dragged on (with occasional intervention by the British, French, and Russian navies) until 1829, when Greece was finally granted full independence by the Ottoman ruler.

At about this time Russia finally attacked Turkey, but made little headway, and withdrew in 1833 after persuading Turkey to close the Straits to warships of all nations. By this time the Russian threat to western Europe was clearly receding. Alexander had died in 1825 and the occasion had been market by Russia's version of a colonels' revolt, when idealistic young officers demanded a constitution to establish a more enlightened and efficient government. Although they were quickly rounded up and disciplined, their actions revealed a current of unrest in the very country that had led the reactionary movement in post-Napoleonic Europe.

THE REVOLUTIONS OF 1830

The fall of the Bourbons

During the decade of the 1820s, the political restlessness that had marked Europe's postwar transition was effectively damped down by the repressive policies of the alliance. Only in Latin America and in Greece did struggles for liberation continue and succeed. In the summer of 1830, however, a popular uprising in Paris forced the abdication of the Bourbon king Charles X, a development that was followed by a series of revolts in the Netherlands, Switzerland, Italy and Poland. The event in France apparently triggered the other outbursts, but there was otherwise little similarity among them in their causes and outcomes.

With the restoration of Louis XVIII, post-Napoleonic France possessed one of the most stable regimes in Europe. When Louis died in 1824, however, he was succeeded by his eccentric brother Charles X, whose ideal of kingship was drawn from a mythical view of the Middle Ages. At this point in history his assertion of a right to absolute and arbitrary rule represented less an ultra-reactionary stance than an unbalanced mind, which soon involved him in a serious struggle with the Chamber of Deputies. Although his quarrel happened to be with the "lower" house, its members were hardly advocates of revolution; in fact they were elected by the 90,000 largest taxpayers of France, which meant the largest landowners – at least half of whom were former nobles. In opposing Charles these landed aristocrats clearly were not challenging the established order, but rather trying to prevent an irresponsible romantic from provoking a dangerous popular reaction. The king responded to their position with clumsy moves, threatening an absolutist coup. This prospect so alarmed the principal bankers' consortium that they now entered the conflict and attempted to take control of the situation. They mounted a poster and press campaign in Paris calling for public demonstrations against the king's maneuvers; the shopowners responded by closing their doors, thus putting thousands of workers on the streets in beautiful summer weather and thereby creating an instant, if not altogether purposeful, mob. Rather than using force to clear the streets, as a true reactionary would probably have done without hesitation, Charles surprised everyone by suddenly fleeing.

Caught unprepared by this move, the authors of the melodrama almost lost control of it. At this point, Lafayette – of American revolutionary fame – arrived in Paris from his nearby country home to take over what he assumed would be a new Republic. In no mood to replace one romantic with another, the bankers now rushed forward their own candidate, the financier Duc d'Orléans, who as a member of the royal family could mount the vacant throne as King Louis-Philippe. This arrangement was made with little difficulty, and the only change that was made in the form of government was a revision of the constitution to increase the electorate from 2 to 5 percent of the largest taxpayers among the adult male population (an increase in the number of voters from 90,000 to 225,000). Because the principal taxes were levied on land, this selection still favored the landed aristocrats, but the increase now brought in urban property owners as well; for this reason the new regime was referred to as the "bourgeois monarchy." Although the shift also brought more small-town professionals into the electorate, where they were free to seek political careers, it did not dilute the effective control of the king and his banking partners. Thus although the coup would be known as the revolution of 1830, it was really only a "revolution of the bankers," which replaced an irresponsible eccentric on the throne of France with one of the wealthiest and most purposeful financiers in Europe.

Belgian independence

This French adventure was followed a few weeks later by an even more theatrical coup in Brussels, the time and place of which had been widely advertised in advance. When the Congress of Vienna had decided to divest France of the former Spanish Netherlands, which Napoleon had annexed, it could think of nothing better to do with them than add them to Holland, despite important differences of language and religion between the two regions: Holland was Dutch-speaking and predominantly Protestant, whereas the old Habsburg Netherlands, also known as Belgium, was French-speaking and Catholic. To make matters worse, Holland's king insisted on making Dutch the sole official language for his newly expanded nation, thereby disrupting the Belgian school system and effectively barring French-speaking Netherlanders from public service. These grievances were sufficiently frustrating to incite the population of Brussels to a massive demonstration. Like the one in Paris, this show of resistance had surprising success, toppling the regime and thus ending Dutch rule in Belgium.

These adjustments in France and Holland were reluctantly accepted by the Quadruple Alliance. While he would have liked to defend the status quo, Metternich knew better than to move troops into France, or even Belgium; at the same time the British would not accept the return of the Netherlands to France, as the inhabitants themselves would probably have preferred. As a result the alliance settled for recognition of the new regime in Paris, and of the independence and neutrality of Belgium, where a constitutional monarchy was to be established.

In the mean time, inspired by the easy success of the Paris and Brussels insurrections, restless students in several German states frightened their local monarchs into granting constitutions. The contagion spread next to northern Italy, where students and young army officers attempted some minor military actions, but all were too near Austria to escape prompt repression. (One young participant in a revolt at Bologna, who barely escaped with his life, was the nephew of Napoleon and would himself later become emperor of France.)

The final outbreak of the revolutionary contagion that swept across Europe occurred in Poland, where the nobles had been preparing to assert their independence from Russia. When the tsar proposed to use his Polish army to repress the revolutions in Paris and Brussels, the troops revolted and drove the Russian garrison out. Characteristically torn by dissensions among themselves, however, the Poles were no match for the Russian army, which returned not merely to restore Russian control but this time to integrate Poland into the Russian Empire as well. Most of the Polish leaders then fled to western Europe, where they became social heroes and resident consultants to would-be revolutionaries.

A comparison of the issues and actors in these four different theaters of revolution reveals surprisingly little similarity. In Paris an eccentric king was challenged by a Chamber of Deputies made up of aristocratic landowners, and was brought down by the country's wealthiest bankers – with the brief assistance of an obliging urban mob. The whole affair came off so well that it lent a certain popularity to the idea of revolution, but it actually had no base in the mass of the population. In Brussels the issues were altogether different: there the Belgians were protesting linguistic, religious and "ethnic" oppression; their movement for independence found its principal support among the educated and ambitious youth, who found their way to careers blocked by their inability to speak Dutch. In Germany and Italy the outbursts were produced by similarly frustrated young men whose careers were blocked by the narrow boundaries and antiquated regimes of their petty principalities. And finally, the revolt in Poland was conducted by landowning aristocrats against a foreign occupying power; here the greatest similarity was with the Greek War of Independence, which had been waged largely by Aegean merchants to free themselves from the corruption and inefficiency – as well as brutality – of Turkish rule.

ROMANTICISM

For at least a century the intellectual and artistic life of Europe had been dominated by the rationalism of the Enlightenment. This influence had imposed a rigorous classicism on the culture of the French Revolution itself – as illustrated, for example, by the style of the painter Jacques-Louis David. Outside France, however – notably in Germany and England – the French Revolution had been welcomed by the younger generation as a harbinger of a new spiritual as well as political freedom. Two of the earliest admirers of the revolution were the poets Wordsworth in England and Goethe in Germany, both of whom became important leaders of the new intellectual and artistic movement that would be called

Romanticism. Like other Romantics who were originally inspired by the revolution, each later turned against it, as it succumbed first to the Terror and then to Napoleon's authoritarian regime. Ironically, however, Napoleon's conquests had the overall effect of reinforcing the Romantic reaction against rationalism, especially in Germany, as nationalism in the subject territories took the form of an assertion of the indigenous culture against the rigid rationality imposed by the French administration.

Whatever their sources, the European world welcomed the new ideas and attitudes of the postwar decades that would make up the Romantic movement. Although it is referred to as a single cultural phenomenon, the movement really included a wide variety of impulses in different countries and areas of culture, including many contradictory elements. Perhaps most fundamentally, the Romantic movement was the reaction of a younger generation against its elders and their values, and as such it was manifested in almost all aspects of life, from manners and dress to literary and artistic styles, political attitudes and actions, and religious practices and beliefs.

The young Romantic tended to defy established morality and conventions, break the classical rules of composition in painting and poetry, and in general proclaim his right and duty to remake the world according to his own private vision. Often this rebellious pose served to cover a lack of talent or training, and much of the artistic outpouring of the age was simply bad; at the same time it had to be recognized that the arts and letters had succumbed to an arid formalism in the eighteenth century, and certainly the outstanding figures in the new movement were artists and thinkers of genius.

The first important figure of the Romantic movement was Jean-Jacques Rousseau, a powerful critic of the Age of Reason and its pretensions, who wrote in the middle of the eighteenth century. In the next generation and across the Rhine, the giant of German literature J. W. Goethe created what was probably the most important manifesto of Romantic values in his poetic drama *Faust*. In this work a professor sells his soul to the devil to discover those truths which mere learning had failed to reveal, and is finally redeemed from his bargain by pure love. In England the Romantic movement was expressed in a magnificent revival of lyric poetry, by a group of poets that included Wordsworth, Coleridge, Keats, Byron and Shelley. Finally in France, a generation of Romantic poets and dramatists followed the lead set by the novelist Victor Hugo.

Another art form that was powerfully affected by the Romantic revolt was painting. The work of the new generation of artists differed profoundly, in both style and subject, from that of the era dominated by David. Leaders of the rebellion against the formal neoclassical style were Eugène Delacroix (1799–1863) in France, and John Constable (1776–1837) and J. M. W. Turner (1775–1851) in England. These were painters of enormous talent, who would undoubtedly have burst the bonds of any conventional style, but who found a welcome freedom in the Romantic revolt. While they all revelled in a riot of color, the French and English artists basically took very different directions in their innovation. Delacroix stressed drama and swirling action, looking back to the paintings of Rubens, who had been out of favor with the classicists, while Turner and Constable painted landscapes and sea scenes which anticipated the work of the later Impressionists in their bold experimentation with light and color.

Similar developments occurred in most forms of art, including music, the theater, and the novel. One of the most important influences that reshaped all of these arts at this time was the dramatic increase in the size of the paying public that took place during the nineteenth century. While the publication of both books and periodicals had proliferated in the eighteenth century, and public performances of plays, concerts and operas were well established, the "public" that bought the literature and attended the performances had been limited to a fairly small elite, and much intellectual and artistic production was still dependent on the patronage of monarchs or wealthy aristocrats. Although such subsidy did not end abruptly, it was gradually replaced in the post-Napoleonic period by royalties, state support, and above all the massive participation of the educated middle class as consumers of the arts.

One consequence of this development was that artists and writers were now addressing a new audience, with different tastes and interests from those of its eighteenth-century counterparts. In contrast to many of the aristocratic patrons of the eighteenth century, this new public was indifferent, if not hostile, to the concerns and standards of the Enlightenment. Instead, their tastes in the arts reflected an attraction to passion, drama, violence, and eroticism. In the popular literature heroes now regularly confronted overwhelming odds, often in bizarre or occult settings; the emphasis on the exotic often led authors or painters to imagine scenes in the New World, the Near East, or in another time – particularly the Middle Ages, a period that had been much despised in an Age of Reason that was based importantly on admiration of classical (basically Roman) culture.

A whole cult of things medieval now grew up within the Romantic movement. People became interested in their own ethnic history and culture as it had developed in the centuries after the decline of the Roman Empire. Old folk tales and songs were collected and imitated, and European history itself was defined as a subject of interest and inquiry. Europe's own rich heritage of historic monuments began to be valued, as only classical "antiquities" had been in the previous century. Castles and churches – by then in general disrepair – were rediscovered and admired, often as much for as in spite of their sad condition; the confusion on this point actually led to the occasional new construction of "ruins" to lend the proper Romantic air to some new estate.

With this revived interest in the Middle Ages came a corresponding revival of appreciation for the medieval forms of religious expression. This was not a return to the religious conventions and convictions that had been disrupted by rationalism and the French Revolution; rather it was a discovery of the aesthetic appeal of worship in the setting of the Gothic churches, where religious feeling would be heightened by the inspiring architecture, the glow of the stained glass windows, and often the anachronism of organ music – since the only music that had actually filled the cathedrals in medieval times was the primitive plainsong.

For some, a renewed interest in religion led to a rediscovery of the political virtues of the "Christian monarchy." It was this concept, rather than any reactionary purpose, which inspired in Charles X the extreme behavior that led to the revolution of 1830. Five years before, he had personally planned an elaborate coronation ceremony for himself which he believed to be a revival of medieval customs; the resulting ridiculous affair – climaxed by the release of white doves in the top of the cathedral at the moment of his anointment – was much more approximate to a Hollywood extravaganza than actual medieval practice. It was when Charles gave indications of attempting to interject similar elements into the everyday affairs of state that his richest and most important subjects lost patience with his posturing and removed him from the throne.

Some Romantics were genuinely reactionary in politics, but many more were radical or revolutionary. The young officers and students who led the insurrection in Italy and Germany, as well as the patriots in Greece and Poland, tended to affect the manner of Romantic literary heroes. The cult of the hero was central to the movement, and ironically the ultimate hero for many romantics, including radicals and nationalists, came to be Napoleon, who in manner and style had been the ultimate embodiment of the classical and rational ideals of the eighteenth century. Although Napoleon had actually pushed cynical realism toward its ultimate expression, his extraordinary personal achievements made him a symbol for the Romantics of the triumph of the individual over the reactionary inertia of established society. By the sheer overwhelming force of his will, personality and intellect Napoleon had changed the course of history and then become its victim – his final tragic fall only reinforcing his heroic status as a Romantic figure.

7

Pax Britannica

It was at the Congress of Verona (1822) that the British Foreign Secretary, George Canning, officially brought to an end Britain's intervention in the affairs of Europe, after more than a century's vigorous effort to maintain a balance against French ambitions on the Continent. Not only did he refuse to join the delegates of the other great powers – Austria, Russia, Prussia and France – in authorizing armed intervention against the revolutionary regime in Spain, but he also seized the occasion to denounce the principle of interference in the internal affairs of independent states. Toward that end he was instrumental in urging the American President Monroe to issue his Monroe Doctrine, declaring that the intervention of a European power in the internal affairs of any state in the western hemisphere would be opposed by the United States as dangerous to her peace and safety. Clearly this was a warning to the Continental powers not to become involved in the wars of independence that were sweeping through the former Spanish colonies. Since none of the European states had the naval capability to threaten the liberated colonies, the Monroe Doctrine was perhaps more of a boast than an ultimatum, but it did serve to mark an important turning-point in European history. In 1822, for the first time since Louis XIV set out to conquer the Low Countries, France was no threat to anyone but the revolutionary regime in Spain. And indeed all of the great powers that had contended for the mastery of Europe – Austria, Russia, Prussia, and France – were now absorbed by the problem of maintaining their authority over their own subjects.

In the mean time Britain's interests and ambitions had been

expanded and transformed quite beyond anyone's – including Canning's – comprehension. From the late seventeenth century, England had been the center of the new Atlantic commercial community, thanks chiefly to the expansion of grain production in the Thames valley that had fueled the great London market. Unchallenged since the Seven Years War (1756–63), the British navy, now reinforced by the London coal trade, completely destroyed its only remaining rivals, the fleets of France and Spain, in the battle at Trafalgar in 1805. The only remaining serious threat to England was the possibility of a united and hostile Europe, which came close to realization in Napoleon's Continental System. That attempt to isolate England, by sealing her off from the North Sea and Baltic ports, appeared to succeed briefly but then backfired, provoking smuggling and eventually rebellion along Europe's shores. Further, although the interruption of her normal European trade first brought England to the brink of bankruptcy, it also forced her to develop every alternative overseas, thereby greatly expanding her commercial wealth.

In Britain the quarter-century of the French Revolution and the Napoleonic Wars had been precisely the period in which the industrial revolution began. When the Continental System was established, it meant that British merchants were faced with the necessity not merely of replacing the northern European ports for their staple trade, but also of finding outlets for the flood of cheap goods (primarily textiles) that were beginning to pour from their new factories. When the Continent was closed to them, therefore, the English turned to Europe's overseas colonial possessions, which were by this time freed from their mercantilist controls and eager to trade. What took place then was an expansion and transformation of the old Atlantic commercial system into a new one which would reach all but the polar areas. In every important sense Britain was the center of the new system, and she exploited her position to the full. This did not necessarily mean fastening military, administrative and commercial controls on every valuable territory available, in the manner of the eighteenth-century mercantilist powers. Rather, the British now developed a wide range of relationships with their overseas trading partners, extending from direct rule imposed by force to a totally free exchange of goods. At this point because of Britain's unassailable naval as well as economic power, she was faced with no competitors in this phase of expansion, and one result of her naval presence around the world was to enforce a peace on the high seas that was called the "Pax Britannica." In this way British domination of the new oceanic trading community was undoubtedly beneficial to the subordinate members, and generally their prosperity was enhanced by their commercial relations with Britain. At the same time, Britain's ever-increasing edge over the preindustrial societies with which she traded gave her a growing power over them, and to the extent that her interests conflicted with theirs, her actions and decisions could also have unfortunate, if perhaps ultimately unavoidable, destructive effects on them.

POSTWAR DEPRESSION AND REFORM

The Napoleonic Wars had exacted a high price from the British government. The extraordinary costs of the war included not merely the maintenance of the army and navy but also huge subsidies paid to Napoleon's enemies, and were almost more than the treasury could bear. At the same time, Napoleon's Continental System interfered with England's European trade, for a while dangerously reducing the royal revenues. For the British public, however, the war was a period of general prosperity – perhaps the first example of the modern phenomenon of a wartime boom. Britain's new industry was turned to producing military supplies, particularly textiles for uniforms, and new overseas markets were found to absorb the surplus production no longer going to Europe. One effect of Napoleon's naval blockade of the Continent, in fact, was to cut off France and Spain from their New World possessions, leaving the latter free to establish their independence, in some cases, and in all cases to trade with the British.

Irish troubles

One significant result of the wartime boom in England was that for the first time many workers earned enough to be able to eat meat – previously a prerogative of the rich – thereby causing a shortage of that commodity. In response to this demand, English landowners in Ireland turned massively to cattle raising, for which their land was particularly well suited. This shift mean dispossessing their peasant tenants, who were now crowded into smallholdings and forced to subsist on potatoes. The potato was an import from the New World that was just coming into wide use throughout Europe at this time because it produced more calories per acre than any other crop previously known to Europeans. In the case of Ireland, however, dependence on the potato as the staple crop proved disastrous, for the crisis caused by the shift to cattle raising came at the same time as a blight which destroyed the potato crop for two years in a row (1846–7), causing widespread starvation.

From their earliest intervention in Irish affairs, shortly following the Norman conquest, the English had been unable either to subdue or to abandon this neighbor island. If Ireland were to be independent, England's European enemies could always threaten invasion by way of the island – as indeed they had as recently as 1797, when the French tried to land a force to support an Irish uprising. But complete subjugation of Ireland also seemed impractical, although Cromwell had given it a brutal try, particularly since the Reformation had added a religious difference to the original ethnic one between the populations of the two islands. In 1801, one more attempt to resolve these tensions was made with the "Act of Union," which created Irish seats in both houses of the British Parliament. This was similar to the settlement reached with Scotland in 1707, but with the crucial difference that the Scots were allowed to keep their Presbyterian Church, while the English stubbornly refused to recognize Catholicism as the legitimate religion in Ireland. As a result, the Act of Union only set the stage for an intensified struggle that would play a large part in, and often dominate, British politics for a century and more.

Economic difficulties

When the Napoleonic Wars were finally over, Britain emerged with the largest government debt ever recorded in her history. At the same time, however, she also had the first coal-driven, mechanized industry in history. The country's leaders were fully aware of the significance and potential of this industrial achievement, and to maintain Britain's priceless monopoly of industrial machines and techniques Parliament passed a series of bills prohibiting their export, and also prohibiting the emigration of those capable of reproducing the critical apparatus. This short-sighted policy did not prevent the spread of English ideas and methods, however, and soon gave way to a much more effective exploitation of Britain's lead through the deliberate export of her industrial revolution, which would prove almost as lucrative as the export of the finished manufactured products.

Just as the Napoleonic Wars had created an economic boom in Britain, the restoration of peace in Europe brought about what was perhaps the first modern postwar depression. The huge orders of military supplies ceased, and some 400,000 men were demobilized in Britain, producing massive unemployment. The factory workers, who had been earning unprecedented amounts, and who now no longer had farms to fall back on, were suddenly without wages or any other means of obtaining food.

The need for reform

At this juncture (1815) the large landowners and grain producers used their considerable influence in Parliament to pass the so-called "Corn Laws," which forced up the price of grain by imposing tariffs which made its importation impossible except when home-grown wheat reached famine prices. This move marked two important developments. First it was a response to the fact that Britain had begun to import food for the first time, and second, it called forcibly to the attention of the factory workers their vulnerability to Parliamentary action, and their vital need for political representation. During the Napoleonic Wars the new factories had offered sufficient jobs and wages to keep most workers content, but the Corn Laws, coming together with the postwar economic collapse, suddenly made Parliamentary reform an urgent issue for the less privileged portion of the population.

Ever since the Glorious Revolution (1688), political power in Britain had rested firmly in Parliament rather than with the king, but even the House of Commons represented only a small elite and the new manufacturing cities had virtually no voice in it. This injustice became the prime target for both the workers' protests and the efforts of liberal political leaders in the postwar period.

The movement for Parliamentary reform first took the form of public meetings and demonstrations – some large enough to cause official concern. Two at least were met by force, and followed by repressive legislation. The climax of this policy of confrontation came when troops fired on a huge crowd that had gathered in a field near Manchester. Sobered by this bloodshed, both sides retreated to more moderate behavior, and gradually a program of reform began to take shape.

Following the death of Castlereagh, on the eve of the Congress of Verona (1822), the cabinet was reorganized in a liberal direction. In quick succession the barbarous old code of civil law (with some 200 capital offenses) was modified and rewritten, a series of tariff reforms facilitated the importation of cheap grain, and finally the laws which outlawed union activity were repealed and replaced by an ambiguous arrangement that established a rigorously limited right to strike.

At this juncture a Catholic was elected to Parliament by an Irish constituency. According to existing law, no Catholic (or "Dissenter" from the Church of England) could hold public office, but the cabinet (under the Duke of Wellington as prime minister), while opposed to Catholic emancipation, was even more afraid of Irish revolution. The result was an Emancipation Bill that enabled Catholics not only to serve in Parliament but also to hold any public office except for that of lieutenant governor of Ireland, lord chancellor of England and the monarchy itself. While this measure avoided an immediate confrontation with the Irish, it was only a first and very small step toward a resolution of the basic "Irish problem." At least it gave the beleaguered ministry time to deal with some other urgent matters.

By 1830, wide public support had developed for reforms to make Parliament more truly representative. Not only were the old electoral districts out of date, giving no representation to the new factory towns, but the existing electoral system resulted in a House of Commons to which some two-thirds of the members belonged only by virtue of privilege or corruption. Needless to say, forcing such a body to reform itself was not easy, but the public demand was so vigorous that between 1830 and 1832 three versions of reformed election laws were passed by the House of Commons, only to be blocked by the House of Lords – the ultimate beneficiaries of the existing system. Finally, with the country in an uproar and fanned by winds of revolution from the Continent, the liberal ministers persuaded the king to create enough new peers to swing the vote for reform in the House of Lords. This action set a pattern, to be followed in later crises, which effectively subordinated the upper to the lower house. The actual reforms, although headed in the right direction, were very modest. The worst electoral abuses were eliminated but property qualifications for voting were retained, leaving the bulk of the public still disenfranchised. The major effect of the reforms was to transfer political power from the old landowning elite to the newer commercial and industrial elite.

A number of other significant reforms were put through in this period of political ferment. The slave trade had been prohibited in 1807, but it was not until 1833 that the government followed this act with the emancipation of slaves in all of England's colonies. Even more important in England itself was the Factory Act of 1833, which made a very minor but essential beginning to the control of what was called "wage slavery." A series of parliamentary commissions had recently revealed working conditions in factories, particularly those affecting children, which had caused a national scandal. For a number of reasons children had been heavily involved in factory work from the beginning. Their small hands were able to reach into the machines for cleaning – with all the horrifying risks involved. Even more important, however, they were more tractable than adults, and above all much cheaper, particularly when hired in lots from orphanages. The very reforms of the Factory Act were a shocking indictment of the current system: children under the age of nine could not be employed, those between nine and thirteen could work only 48 hours a week (or nine hours a day), those over thirteen years old only 69 hours a week (or twelve hours a day). Nevertheless, the Act – together with the parliamentary inquiries upon which it was based – did serve to awaken the national conscience to industry's abuse of the poor, and to begin legislative efforts to improve the lot of the factory worker.

Unable to participate in the political process themselves, the workers were now able at least to form unions, as well as a National Association for the Protection of Labor (1830). In 1834,

Robert Owen, a successful industrialist who was also a utopian socialist, helped organize the Grand National Consolidated Trades Union, which rapidly reached a membership of 500,000. Its avowed purpose was to mount a general strike for an eight-hour day, but it succeeded only in sparking a series of local confrontations which frightened the government into some severely repressive actions. The Grand National Union was dissolved and the labor movement was seriously set back as a result.

In 1837 King William IV died and the throne passed to his eighteen-year-old niece, Victoria. Queen Victoria's reign, from 1837 to 1901, would prove to be one of the longest and most important in European history. From the beginning, because of her youth and irreproachably respectable upbringing, Victoria presented a welcome contrast to her elderly, dull, and dissolute predecessors. Unquestionably she had both important talents and a real vocation for her position but her success was due above all to the good fortune of coming to the throne at the beginning of what may well have been her country's greatest period.

EMPIRE IN INDIA

The East India Company

In 1600 a group of English merchant-adventurers had received a charter from Queen Elizabeth to form the East India Company, with exclusive rights to import goods from the Far East to England. Like other trading companies of the period, they bought products abroad that were rare or unobtainable at home, and hence could be sold there at a high price; in this case the company purchased chiefly spices, tea and coffee, from trading ports along the coasts of India and Indonesia. Although great fortunes were expected – and occasionally made – from such luxury trade, it seldom had a major impact on the economy of a European country. Thus the East India Company had existed for well over a century before it played a significant role in British affairs. In the mean time it had no support from the government in its rivalry with Dutch companies for Indian port facilities and local influence.

It was from this modest beginning, however, that Britain

would eventually acquire all of India as an imperial possession. To begin to understand this dramatic development it is necessary first to look more closely at India, the great "subcontinent" lying behind the few coastal trading posts that attracted the Europeans. About half the size of the United States, India is cut off from the rest of the Asian land mass by the Himalayas, the largest mountain range in the world. The peninsula nevertheless suffered at least eight major overland invasions in historical times, most of the invaders coming from the same central Asian groups that had mounted the great Mongol invasions against China and Europe.

The greater part of India's population has always lived in the rich agricultural area just south of the mountain boundary, which is fed by three great rivers. To the south of these river valleys lies a vast semi-arid plateau, and a population that could not compete with that of the north in prosperity or culture. For the invaders, therefore, the prize was always the rich agricultural north, and the result was that the economic base that might have supported a unified Indian state was under repeated attack, while the poorer south had no focus for its own unification.

At the time the English East Indian Company was formed, most of the peninsula was under the rule of conquerors known as the Mughals, probably meaning Mongols. These conquerors had established an efficient administration over most of the country, and produced one of the world's great rulers in the Emperor Akbar (1556–1605). Akbar maintained peace and prosperity to a degree previously unknown in India, and fostered art and culture as well. Even so, the Mughals remained foreign conquerors, and Muslim rulers of primarily Hindu subjects. A century after Akbar one of his successors attempted to force the conversion of the Hindus to Islam; it was a colossal failure that turned the country back toward anarchy and prepared the way for British intervention.

Actually it was the French who set the next phase of Indian history in motion. During the middle of the eighteenth century, France and Britain were locked in a struggle for supremacy not only in Europe and North America but also in India, where agents of a French East India Company were now established and challenging those of the English East India Company. This contest generally took the form of supporting rival Indian princes, and it came to a head when the local ruler of Bengal, with French encouragement, attacked the British in their station of Calcutta. Capturing the city, he was responsible for the death of a number of British prisoners who were packed into an inadequate room that was to be known as the infamous "Black Hole of Calcutta." The situation was turned around by a British Company clerk turned temporary commander, Robert Clive, who proved himself a military genius. With the company's army alone, he drove the Bengali forces out of Calcutta and took the nearby French station, then with the support of a single battalion sent from Britain he went on to defeat the main army of the prince, thus making the British *de facto* rulers of the rich province of Bengal. Although the company had resorted to arms strictly in self-defense, it now found itself taking over the taxes and land rents of its newly conquered territory, which produced income on a vastly larger scale than had the old luxury trade.

During the next quarter-century, unrestrained by any governmental authority, the officers of the company proceeded to exploit their position in Bengal by every means available. They did not turn to commercial farming directly, but they encouraged the large landowners to raise commercial crops by using their peasant tenants as laborers. While this produced an enormous fortune for the company, it was at the cost of widespread starvation among the peasants. The news of this rapacious misrule reached England, and Parliament finally intervened by appointing a Governor-General to administer the company's territory. He brought about the intended reforms in Bengal, but it proved impossible to limit British involvement to this province alone, as Parliament had hoped to do originally. With Mughal power disintegrating in the north and native princes contending with each other, the British could hardly have remained in India without becoming involved in this general struggle. Gradually British authority – direct and indirect – spread from its Bengali base, and with it the establishment of orderly administration. This process continued uninterrupted while at home Britain was absorbed in the renewed French challenge under Napoleon, and by the time peace was restored in Europe the relationship between Britain and India had been completely altered. From 1820 to 1880 British exports to India would increase eightfold, her trade with the subcontinent taking second place only to that with the United States. The explanation for this commercial explosion was Britain's rapidly expanding capacity to produce cheap goods – especially cotton cloth – for which India provided a virtually inexhaustible market. Although the old luxury trade continued, it became incidental to this new development, which became a major factor in Britain's industrial economy.

By the 1820s the East India Company was maintaining a military establishment of over 200,000 men, about three-quarters of whom were native Indians (called Sepoys, from a Persian term) under British officers. The actual number of British troops in India seems never to have exceeded some 60,000 at any one time – hardly enough, even with the Sepoys, to conquer or occupy a land with a population even at that time of over a hundred million. To a very large extent, therefore, the task of the English forces was simply to quell strife among the local princes and eliminate bandits from the countryside. To achieve these goals the British were forced to develop communications: roads, canals, and eventually telegraph and railroads. With this went an extension of civil administration, and a uniform legal system. Perhaps the key English contribution to this gradual pacification and unification of the subcontinent was the English language, which gave India a single lingua franca for the first time in history.

The company had begun with a rigorous policy of respecting local customs and prohibiting any imposition of British influence, including proselytizing by Christian missionaries. In the nineteenth century, however, this policy began to change as Parliament extended its responsibility in India. It admitted missionaries, abolished the slave trade and slavery, and outlawed the practices of infanticide and suttee – the cremation of a widow on her husband's funeral pyre. To broaden the base for their regime the British also founded schools and universities to educate future civil servants – in English.

With a new sense of India's importance, the British felt a growing apprehension as they became aware of Russian expansion in central Asia. They could hardly hope to match the forces of the tsar if he should decide to follow the traditional invasion route into India through Afghanistan and the Khyber Pass. To avoid such an unequal confrontation, therefore, they attempted to support independent buffer states along the border, and to gain control over the few states in northern India that remained independent. In a series of frontier campaigns they suffered some serious defeats, which damaged their military prestige, especially among the Sepoys. Although they finally completed the conquest of India in 1856, they were now stretched thin and vulnerable; a year later the Indian Mutiny broke out. The bulk of the Sepoys rebelled against British rule, placing a descendant of the last Mughal on the throne in an attempt to end foreign domination. Within a year the British managed to regain command, mainly because two elite bodies of their native troops, the Sikhs and Gurkhas, remained loyal. Nevertheless the British had suffered serious losses, both military and civilian, provoking a furore in Britain, where the whole crisis was blamed on the inadequacy of the company. The inevitable result was to bring India under direct British rule. In 1858 the remnants of the company were dissolved and replaced by an official British administration, under a Viceroy who reported directly to the Cabinet in London.

Direct rule

While British interests continued to prosper under the new regime, the native population benefited from a program of reforms – political, social, and economic – that was now undertaken. New schools were founded, responsible positions in the civil service were opened to Indians, and extensive public works – roads, irrigation systems, and railroads – were built. These measures were paralleled by a thorough and highly effective reform of the native armed forces, intended to increase both their efficiency and their loyalty to the British. Ultimately the pacification of the country, and its gradual unification through the development of communications (especially railroads) and the spread of the English language, began to create a national Indian society and a widely-shared vision of a self-sufficient Indian nation.

Two serious problems, however, were created for the Indian populace by the British presence in their country. The traditional Indian handicraft industries – particularly those dealing with textiles – were destroyed by the massive importation of British manufactured goods, which also forced the Indians to produce raw materials that Britain needed (such as cotton) to export to her in exchange. Thus a whole class of craftsmen was thrown out of work in India, while peasants were also forced off their subsistence farms to make room for the new large commercial plantations. This was an early example of the dislocation caused by the introduction of industrial products into a preindustrial society, which in the coming century would be repeated all around the world. An even more severe problem was the population explosion that followed the British reforms, since by reducing chronic warfare, improving sanitation, and above all increasing the food supply through irrigation, the British removed many of the old and brutal curbs on life expectancy in India. This pattern too would be repeated over and over as Europe's ties with the unindustrialized world increased.

The British government's assumption of authority over the East India Company brought it closer to China, where the East India Company had also been operating independently for over a century; actually its contacts had been limited to Canton, which was the only port where the Chinese government allowed foreign merchants to call. For the Chinese, involvement with the British merchants had been much more harmful than beneficial, and when the British government stepped in, it was only to prevent the Chinese from defending their own interests against their scandalous exploitation by the British in India through the trade in opium. For over a century the use of opium had been spreading in China, in spite of official prohibitions against its import, and most of this opium was grown in India and brought to China by British merchants. In 1839 the Chinese seized and destroyed a considerable quantity of the contraband in Canton, and the British government took this occasion to establish its authority in China, demanding recompense for the opium, which the Chinese naturally refused. With this excuse the British mounted an expeditionary force from India that moved up the river beyond Canton to Nanking; having absolutely no modern weapons, the Chinese were helpless before this modest attack and had no choice but to capitulate. In the Treaty of Nanking (1842) that the British dictated, they were granted special access to the Chinese market, the possession of Hong Kong and several other ports, and the right of trying their own nationals in China in their own courts. These measures effectively prevented the Chinese from controlling the opium trade, which grew rapidly thereafter, making a fortune for the

British middlemen at a frightful cost to the Chinese. By thus establishing their superiority in China, moreover, the British set a precedent for other western powers who were later able to demand and receive similar subservience from China.

In 1869 the French opened the Suez Canal, thereby cutting in half the length of the sea route from England to India. This statistic was crucial in the transformation of India from a rather remote interest of the British to what in 1875 they would begin to boast of as their "empire" – presided over officially by Queen Victoria as "empress" and ruled in fact by her viceroy, who was installed at Delhi, the former capital of the Mughal dynasty. The Mediterranean, which had been a backwater in the preceding stages of European overseas expansion now became a vital British interest, as her route to the east and "lifeline of empire." A new phase of European imperialism was now launched which was to have enormous consequences not only for India but also for most of the rest of the non-western world.

WORKSHOP OF THE WORLD

While British soldiers and civil servants were creating the Indian empire, their compatriots at home were busy adjusting British society to the strains and challenges of the new industrial economy. The industrial revolution had launched a process of ever-accelerating expansion, with new factories spawning other factories in an almost biological progress. Because the initial profits were seldom consumed, they were usually reinvested in new machines, which led to greater productivity and generated more wealth. This in turn was spent to build more factories, and more factories meant more workers, more cities to house them, more food to feed them, more raw materials for them to use and more manufactured goods to be sold. This torrent of production had its impact on every aspect of British life.

The rapid growth of the urban working class led to hopes that workers could influence national affairs through political or trade union action, but a militant nationwide working-class movement did not develop in Britain. The reasons were complex. For one thing, although the living conditions of the factory workers now seem dreadful to us, at that time they were better than those of the agricultural worker, and they were also better than those of the factory workers on the Continent. This did not mean that the British workers were, or perceived themselves to be, fairly used by their employers, but it did mean that they had something to lose. There were two other influences that contributed to relative moderation in the political activity of workers in Britain. First, most of Britain's radical leaders were brought up in the Methodist tradition, which was egalitarian but also tolerant and essentially nonviolent. Their counterparts on the Continent, by contrast, drew on the uncompromising tradition of the Enlightenment, and therefore tended to be more absolutist in their ideology.

At one point Britain's growing labor force tried to organize itself in a National Union, mounting a campaign for full political suffrage that was organized around a nationwide petition called the Charter. When this movement failed to achieve its objective, workers fell back to forming local unions that worked out compromises with local employers. This pragmatic approach proved satisfactory on the whole because British industry continued to expand and prosper. As a result there was no serious unemployment, and working conditions were gradually improved. Everyone realized, however, that a major social confrontation could be averted only by uninterrupted economic growth.

Repeal of the Corn Laws

The national issue that provoked the most conflict at this time was the continued enforcement of the "Corn Laws," which protected British grain producers by prohibiting the importation of cheaper grain from abroad. As industry expanded, the increasing influx of workers from the country to the cities increased the demand for commercial food (especially wheat), thereby raising the prices; at the same time, however, great grain-producing areas were beginning to be opened overseas that could pour cheap supplies into England's cities if the Corn Laws were repealed. It was not only the workers who demanded repeal, but also, significantly, the newly rich class of the factory owners, who had to pay higher wages as prices rose, and who also sensed that by importing grain from overseas they would be creating new markets for their own products in return.

In the mid-nineteenth century Britain was still the only industrialized country in the world, so her much valued textiles and hardware could be paid for only with raw materials or hand-made luxuries. Since the latter category never became commercially significant, it was basically Britain's purchase of raw materials and food supplies that gave other countries the purchasing power to buy British goods. In other words, what we think of as Britain's industrial economy was really a much larger oceanic economy, in which Britain's industry played only one part, and its prosperity was completely dependent upon her economic partnership with the coastal periphery of the western world. The Corn Laws were finally repealed in 1846, having been dealt a death blow by a serious crop failure that occurred in England in 1845. From that point on, Britain was as dependent on imports for its basic food supply as its textile industry had become dependent on cotton from the slave states of the American South.

The expansion of industry

By this time British factories were increasingly involved in the export of the industrial revolution itself. The first stage of this development was to ship to Europe and North America the machines and steam engines that were necessary for constructing factories that would produce consumer goods. The second stage was to supply railroads which could both open the interior of the country to imports from the coasts and prepare a base for the development of heavy industry that would produce the machines themselves. The first practical railroad was built in England in 1825, and it was widely recognized then that it was only a matter of time – and not much time – before rails would be laid in Europe, North America, India and beyond. By the 1840s this unprecedented international development was under way, with England providing the equipment, locomotives, cars, and most of the rails, as well as the trained personnel to install them and a very large part of the capital to pay for them. By the middle of the century all of Europe's large cities had put out rail tentacles to a coast, a river, or the neighboring countryside, and by the 1860s a skeleton system of main lines linked the Continent's capitals. Ultimately these railroads would serve to integrate the national economies and governments in the countries where they were laid, but their first effect was to greatly extend and strengthen Britain's ties with its commercial empire.

As the industrial economy expanded in Britain and spread abroad, it was always accompanied by a sharp increase in population. Experts are extremely cautious about claiming a causal relation between the two developments, but it is probably safe to assume that at least some of the population growth was due to the real, if still inadequate, improvement of the workers' diet that took place as the industrial economy became more productive. Further, the phenomena that accompanied overcrowding ceased to operate as a population curb in Britain, and later in Europe, because of the new ease of overseas emigration. Among the British the largest emigration by far was to the United States, but there were also the large territories of Canada, Australia, and New Zealand where British emigrants could feel at home.

During the third quarter of the century the British pursued their efforts toward reform: in the Reform Bill of 1867 — which further extended the suffrage though leaving it well short of universal, in a failed attempt to grant Ireland "Home Rule," and in a piecemeal but extensive program of social legislation covering housing, health, public education and unemployment. Although they were not declared with the same fanfare as they had been in revolutionary France, some Rights of Man had also emerged from the industrial revolution which were generally agreed upon by the British as social goals, and pursued as such with vigor and intermittent success.

MEDITERRANEAN POLITICS

Turkish decline

With the development of the Atlantic economy in the seventeenth century, the eastern Mediterranean had become a commercial backwater, leaving the Turks with an inadequate economic base to support their crumbling Ottoman Empire. The Islamic provinces along the coast – from Syria in the east through Egypt, Tripoli and Tunisia – maintained a nominal allegiance to the sultan but were effectively independent. Egypt, however, maintained a semblance of coherent government, as a legacy of Napoleon's invasion, which had forced her leaders to make some reforms. Tripoli and Tunisia were sinking into anarchy and piracy, as was Algeria farther west.

Across the Mediterranean to the north, the empire's Balkan provinces, largely Slavic in ethnicity and Greek Orthodox in religion, were still exploited as occupied territories by regional Ottoman governors, whose brutal tyranny was mitigated only by their lethargic incompetence. When the Greeks revolted in their War of Independence, they put the European powers in a quandary. Since all educated Europeans had been brought up in the classic tradition, the cause of Greece was immediately popular. When the tsar proposed aid for the rebels, however, he was suspected of expansionist ambitions, which – given the weakness of the Turks – were taken as a serious threat by the other powers. The Habsburgs now suddenly realized their own interest in the Balkans and their vulnerability to Russian power, while the British, who had shown little interest in the area after Napoleon's débâcle in Egypt, recognized that if Russia should gain control of Constantinople she could dominate the eastern Mediterranean and open a route to India's vulnerable northwestern frontier. These fundamental concerns led to ever-increasing tensions and a series of international crises. The only solution acceptable to the European powers seemed to be to facilitate the inevitable disintegration of the Ottoman Empire, but without allowing the collapse of the court at Constantinople.

War in the Crimea

What this meant, in practice, was the protection of the sultan while he modernized his administration and armed forces. In a series of border clashes with the Russians, the Turks gave intermittent signs of vigor, while the western powers corrected the balance wherever the Russians gained too much advantage. This complicated process led in 1854 to the outbreak of what official histories call the first major European war since Waterloo. The Crimean

War, as it was called, was barely European, and could be called major only because it was international, not because of the participants' commitment to the conflict. The first move was made against Russia by the new emperor of France, Napoleon III, apparently to establish his prestige in Europe; the British and the Turks then joined in for their own strategic reasons. Initially it looked as though the would-be belligerents would find no place to fight, but Britain's objective – to eliminate the Russian threat to Constantinople – led logically to an attack on the Russian naval base on the Crimean peninsula in the Black Sea.

The Allied European expeditionary force was small, and except for the French contingent, badly mismanaged. As a result the campaign dragged on for two years before the Allies captured the Russian base. The whole affair would hardly be worth mentioning except for some indirect results. For one thing it was the first war to be reported by professional journalists for newspapers with large circulations. The effect in Britain, especially the accounts of mismanagement and human suffering, was widespread public outrage, leading to both sweeping reforms of the armed forces and the organization of the first civilian medical field service. This forerunner of the International Red Cross was organized by a ruthlessly determined young woman of conventional upper-class origins, named Florence Nightingale, who simply imposed her will on the British government. The war also served as the occasion for some diplomatic gesturing by Cavour, the prime minister of Piedmont, who took his little country into the war on the side of the allies to win international recognition of his king, under whose rule he confidently expected to unite the Italian peninsula.

The Crimean War was brought to a formal conclusion in 1856 at the Congress of Paris, which its host Napoleon III obviously hoped to use as an occasion for reorganizing Europe according to his own grand design. The British were no more amenable to this form of collective action than they had been to the now conservative version presented by Metternich a quarter of a century before, and peace had to be made in a more piecemeal fashion. Principally, the Black Sea was demilitarized, and Turkey's independence was guaranteed in a collateral treaty between England, France, and Austria. Thus Britain acted to forestall the emergence of Russian power into the Mediterranean even before the Suez Canal

(1869) would turn it into her "lifeline of empire." Ironically, the most important consequences of the war occurred in Russia, where the new young Tsar Alexander II (1855–81) read his country's defeat as a clear mandate to launch a major program of reform, beginning with the emancipation of the serfs, which he proclaimed in 1861.

With the suppression of the Indian Mutiny and the imposition of direct rule in India, British interest in the eastern Mediterranean grew, and was vastly increased when the opening of the Suez Canal in 1869 halved the length of the sea route between England and India. Six years later the British government bought the controlling interest in the Suez Canal Company, and the following year Queen Victoria was proclaimed Empress of India. If the Crimean War in mid-century had marked the beginning of English interest in the Mediterranean, a quarter of a century later the former backwater had become a major British highway, vital to Britain's interests as ruler of a commercial, and increasingly territorial, empire.

CRISIS IN NORTH AMERICA

Rivalry Between North and South

Although it had only recently fought for its political independence from Britain, the United States steadily increased its participation in the British economy during the nineteenth century until it was Britain's chief trading partner. One important effect of this relationship for the United States was the expansion of the plantation system, and thus slavery, in the southern states. With the development of the textile industry in England, early in the nineteenth century, the southern United States became England's principal supplier of cotton. This new demand taxed the exhausted soil of the old plantations, lying along the rivers of the coastal states, and encouraged the planters to move west into the Gulf states and the lower Mississippi. There they built new plantations along new river shores, reviving the old slave economy which had been in decline along the eastern coast. Although the slave trade was now suppressed, the slave population within the United States was growing, and it was now moved west to work the new lands. It was this new extension of the controversial institution of slavery which aroused political opposition in the northern states, where slavery had been abolished, and led ultimately to the confrontation of the Civil War.

Along the northern coast of the United States, only a few of the rivers were as navigable as those of the South, but many could be used to run mill wheels and thus supply power to small factories that were now being fitted with the new metal machines. This use of water power did not constitute full industrialization because the area produced little iron and less coal, but it did produce consumer goods that competed with those coming from Britain. In 1825, however, the Erie Canal was finished, connecting the Hudson River to the Great Lakes and the rich new farming area of the upper Mississippi. Once this cheap transportation was established, the American midwest began to pour grain into Britain's manufacturing cities. Only three years after the canal was opened, the first western rail line was in operation. With American farmlands thus supplying cotton for England's mills and food for its workers, and with the British factories turning out railroad equipment to extend their penetration of the American continent, the United States quickly became the second center of the oceanic economy.

During this early phase of the industrial revolution in the United States, her water-powered factories were not fully competitive with their British rivals, and their owners naturally favored a high tariff to protect their domestic market. Just as naturally, the South favored free trade and easy access to British goods. While the political forces of the two regions were fairly evenly balanced at the start, the expansion of the southern plantation culture threatened to give the South a decisive advantage in national politics, prompting several northern states to consider seceding from the Union.

Slavery

Divisive as the tariff issue was, however, it quickly fell behind that of slavery in importance. The anti-slavery sentiment that had swept England and France in the first quarter of the century had also reached the United States, gaining support not only in the old

Puritan strongholds such as Massachusetts but also as far south as
Virginia. With the onset of the cotton boom, however, the southern planters suddenly began to view slavery as the indispensable
foundation of their system. No longer able to obtain slaves directly
from Africa, since Britain's closing of the Atlantic slave trade in
1807, the owners of the new western plantations turned to the old
plantations for their supply.

The westward expansion of the plantation system greatly intensified the political conflicts surrounding the creation of new
states. The national abolition of slavery in the United States would
require a constitutional amendment, which had to be passed by
two-thirds of the Senate, and each state had two senators, regard-
less of its population. Initially the South seemed to have a safe
margin, because slavery had already been established in the new
Gulf Coast states before they were admitted to the Union, and
westward migration was at first slower in the North than in the
South. Then, however, the Erie Canal and the first railroads
pierced the barrier of the Alleghenies, opening the upper Mississippi valley to large-scale settlement and farming. Although this
area would soon produce grain for the British market on as great a
scale as the South produced cotton, it was done without the use of
slaves or the plantation system.

Pushing ahead of the plantations along the Gulf coast, pioneers
next made their way into Texas, which was largely uninhabited,
although nominally it was part of Mexico. In 1836 these American
settlers took advantage of the lack of effective Mexican government to declare their independence, and then in 1845 sought
admission to the Union. Thus goaded into action, the Mexican
government declared war on the United States. Although the
Americans were hardly better prepared for combat than their
opponents, they had infinitely greater resources on which to draw.
In 1847 they managed to improvise an invasion that actually took
Mexico City, leading to Mexico's surrender and its cession not
only of Texas but all the territory due west from Texas to the
Pacific (New Mexico and Upper California). Almost simultaneous-
ly the British settled their unresolved dispute with the United
States over the Oregon Territory, establishing the boundary be-
tween the United States and Canada as it is today. Thus suddenly
America had acquired a full Pacific coastline. The following year

(1849), gold was discovered in California. San Francisco became the Pacific port for a frantic gold rush, which was linked to the east coast by the great clipper ships that were built to carry this trade around the Horn.

Soon it became clear that the broad unsettled swath across the interior of the continent would be populated and organized into states just as rapidly as transportation systems could be established. In this the South had the initial advantage, thanks to its many navigable rivers. Although the application of steam propulsion to sea-going ships was still in the future, it was early adapted to paddle-driven river boats, which now became a key feature of the southern way of life. By the 1840s, however, railroads began to proliferate in the north, particularly between the central Atlantic ports (New York, Philadelphia and Baltimore) and Chicago. One effect of these lines was to open up the Pennsylvania coal fields and link them to the Lake Superior iron mines, thus creating an American iron and steel industry that would gradually rival and then surpass that in Britain. At mid-century, therefore, in spite of the luxurious standard of living enjoyed by many plantation owners, the South was falling rapidly behind the industrializing North in wealth and economic power.

It was during the second quarter of the century that the politics of the Union became polarized. The institution of slavery was coming under increasing moral censure, and although at first the cause of emancipation tended to be viewed as of interest primarily to fanatics, it rapidly became widely politicized, thanks in part to a series of heavily biased Supreme Court decisions favoring slavery. What made slavery such a divisive issue was the lack of any common ground between the South and Northeast. If people from the West and Northeast had significant political differences, they did at least share basic values; the South and the North, on the other hand, were different societies. Besides the planter aristocracy and its slaves, the bulk of the population in the South consisted of small farmers whose land was too poor and too remote from water transport to enable them to raise or market cotton. Cities were few and small, supporting little of the urban middle class that was growing so rapidly in the North. As was to be expected in a slave society, work was generally held to be demeaning in the South, whereas ambition was admired in the North. But perhaps the most crucial difference was in education. From their earliest days the northern colonies had developed what was probably the best and most widely available system of public education in the Atlantic world, with which the South had nothing to compare. Much has been made of the role of the Puritan tradition in shaping the northern view of slavery, but probably it was chiefly the Puritans' general commitment to literacy that had the most influence. Educated, literate northerners were generally more open than their southern compatriots to ideas about social reform, and above all to the idea that slavery was morally indefensible.

The Civil War

Although it is now fashionable to seek causes of the Civil War in economic issues, it was really on the moral plane that the battle was joined. The political union of the United States made it possible for the majority to impose its moral standards on the minority, and since they had the upper hand, the northern reformers simply could not resist the temptation to impose their abolitionist convictions on the South. The precipitating cause of war was the election to the presidency of Abraham Lincoln, who was unalterably opposed to further expansion of slavery. Seven southern states promptly voted to secede from the Union and form the Confederate States of America. Considering that the United States had begun its independence by "secession" from British rule, it is possible that Lincoln would not have taken this as an act of war had not Confederate troops fired on a fort (Sumter) whose commander refused to recognize their authority. Lincoln responded by calling for a declaration of war and the mobilization of 75,000 state militia troops.

In spite of its inherent superiority in manpower, industrial plants and wealth, the North was quite unprepared for the conflict. The South, on the other hand, had provided the bulk of the Union's small professional army and was able to draw on these forces to form a trained Confederate army, commanded by the country's finest general, Robert E. Lee. Under Lee's remarkable leadership the Confederate armies were able to prolong the war for four years, even though there was never any question of their winning ultimate victory.

Only gradually did the North develop a strategy, dividing the Confederacy first from north to south along the Mississippi and then from west to east, all the while keeping the southern coasts sealed by a naval blockade. The Union forces were only able to prevail over Lee in the main theater of the war when they finally completed their plan by reaching Savannah, thus cutting off the southern troops from their essential sources of supply. Because the Confederacy had little industry, it was largely dependent on England for arms and other manufactured products, purchased with the money earned from the sale of cotton. Since the navy was traditionally as northern in its orientation as the prewar army had been southern, the Confederacy could not fight a conventional war at sea but was limited to blockade-running, with fast, armed merchant ships, some of which were especially built for the purpose in British yards.

Somewhat surprisingly, both the British and the French tended to favor the South, although both countries had been active in suppressing the slave trade and freeing slaves in their own colonies. In Britain there was fear that interference with the cotton supply would cause mass unemployment and grave social disturbances. In fact no serious shortage of cotton developed in Britain, but her relations with the North were nevertheless strained by its blockade of the South.

The French in Mexico

Similar considerations may have influenced the French, who were beginning to create their own textile industry. Probably, too, they hoped that a Southern victory would avert Federal opposition to Napoleon III's adventure in Mexico, where in 1860 a revolution brought a liberal government to power. When the new government suspended payment on the country's foreign debt, Napoleon seized on the default as an excuse to send troops – ostensibly to collect the debt, but really aimed at the creation of a French "empire" in Mexico. By 1863 a large French army occupied much of the country, including Mexico City, and in 1864 an Austrian archduke was dispatched by Napoleon to be crowned emperor, as Maximilian I. As soon as the American Civil War was over, however, the United States forcefully demanded the withdrawal of the French forces. Obviously the Monroe Doctrine had been in suspension during the Civil War, but as a result of the Union victory it was now restored to full force. Unable to resist this pressure, and also worried by Prussia's aggressive moves in Europe, Napoleon III ordered his troops home in 1867, leaving Maximilian to be captured and executed by the Mexicans a few months later.

Canada and Alaska

At the same time that the French departed from Mexico, the British presence in Canada was diluted by the North America Act (1867), which gave Canada independent status as a Dominion, and Russia sold its claim to Alaska to the United States. Further, it was in the same year that the first transcontinental railroad was completed in the United States, symbolizing the unification of the east coast with the west. What these events foreshadowed was the rapid consolidation and development of the United States. Immigrants from Europe began to pour into the growing country in unprecedented numbers, with many making their way west. Huge new industries were organized to produce steel, build railroads, mine coal, drill for oil, and produce and ship lumber, wheat, and meat. With few exceptions the major market for all these goods was the United States itself, while at the same time the United States was also surpassing Europe as Britain's largest customer, thus greatly reinforcing the Atlantic trade. With her new ports on the west coast, moreover, the United States was also beginning to play a role in a new oceanic economic community that was taking shape in the Pacific.

VICTORIAN SOCIETY

The Atlantic community of the nineteenth century was far more than a British commercial empire. United by the English language, it developed a common culture based on Britain's style and morality as well as its wealth and products. This cultural influence dominated the life of Britain's "Dominions" – Canada, Australia and New Zealand – penetrated and stimulated the young United States, and placed its exclusive stamp on the native elite in India. It also had a lesser but still significant impact on the rest of the modern world.

The culture that Britain exported with her manufacturing is commonly called Victorian, after the monarch who not only reigned throughout its heyday but also exemplified it and even shaped it to a degree. Although it was wholly British, it was also largely new, thanks to the industrial revolution. Victorian culture, like any other, was supported by the wealth of the society, and nineteenth-century Britain was incomparably richer than any previous society had ever been; at the same time much of this wealth, and the leisure it permitted, was now bestowed on a new segment of society.

Traditionally, wealth and position in Britain, as in most of Europe, had derived from ownership of land, but the new wealth of the nineteenth century was produced in cities. Few of its beneficiaries owned land, or even came from the old merchant oligarchy whose wealth had come from the Atlantic trade of the previous century. Characteristically the early mill owners were simply ambitious workmen, who chanced to find their enterprise exceedingly profitable. Within a few decades their proliferating fortunes were supporting not only their heirs but also a whole new class of professional associates – including bankers, lawyers and doctors. This growing middle class had no land but plenty of money, and they used it to create their own new urban society, building large, comfortable town houses in a profusion never before approached. Similarly the coastal cities of the United States – such as Boston, New York and Philadelphia – began to build streets of fine brownstone-front houses only slightly less elegant than their London models. Since the new wealthy class did not see their children's success in terms of preferment at court or in the church, they took great interest in education. During this period the ancient universities of Oxford and Cambridge were shaken out of their eighteenth-century hibernation and completely overhauled, to provide the first modern version of what we call a "liberal education," as well as an "undergraduate life," that included athletic competition. At the same time the old "public" secondary schools (called 'private' in the United States) were expanded and reorganized to prepare the sons of the new rising elite to enter the universities in large numbers.

At the center of Victorian culture was the family, comfortably installed in its town house and supported by a large staff of domestic servants. The home was the setting for much of the social and public life of the society, including serious discussions that were well nourished by extensive reading of books, periodicals, and newspapers. In these circumstances the gulf was narrowed between public and private morality, and people began to expect politicians to meet the same standards that applied in the family. Members of Parliament were expected to be, and so increasingly came to be, both honest and informed.

Obviously not all members of Victorian society met its published standards; still it did produce an educated, industrious, enlightened, and conscientious elite that took its public and private responsibilities with utter seriousness. It also established a model of respectability in public and private behavior that was aspired to by all who could afford it. Even the royal court was run by Victoria as a proper and respectable, if somewhat extravagant, private home.

The new Victorian culture not only changed manners and morals from what they had been in the eighteenth century, but also provided the able, educated, and disciplined leaders that were needed by the new industrial society. This elite included not only the industrialists, bankers, doctors and lawyers, but also the engineers and scientists, teachers and scholars, politicians, journalists, and practitioners of all the arts – who were now producing for a large public for the first time. Not surprisingly, one of the most successful art forms of this literate society was the novel, which increasingly dealt with the social problems brought on by industrialization. Victorian architecture, on the other hand, was not particularly impressive in artistic terms (though it has its admirers). Except for the town houses, the most characteristic edifices of the era were the new railway stations that were becoming the vital centers of the expanding cities. Much of the other building was in new mills, and the proliferating iron bridges for the railroads.

John Stuart Mill

Undoubtedly the most representative and important spokesman for the new elite was John Stuart Mill. A child prodigy, he had

been educated by an ambitious and successful father to the point
of nervous breakdown, but after his recovery he became the principal economic analyst of the oceanic community, as well as the
chief theorist of British government. His greatest concern in politics was the threat of unlimited democracy, which could subject the
minority to the tyranny of the majority, and he proposed to meet
this threat with proportional representation. His elevation of this
problem to a central concern clearly demonstrates the difference
between the aims of British parliamentary politics, with its two
parties alternately in power, and the Enlightenment ideal that
prevailed on the Continent, of a single national policy, for the
good of all, that was imposed by the ruling elite.

One of Mill's most interesting views was his passionate support of equal rights for women, a cause in which his wife Harriet
Taylor Mill was a pioneering advocate and writer. In this area the
Mills were far ahead of prevailing opinion in Victorian England or
anywhere else at this time, yet they pointed to the fundamental
contradiction between the subordination of women and Victorian
liberalism which represented a significant crack in the edifice of
patriarchy, and provided women with their first opportunity to
organize a movement to secure their rights. (In particular the Mills
emphasized the inconsistency between the antislavery position and
the virtual enslavement of married women to their husbands by
laws that barred them from owning property, obtaining a divorce,
or retaining the right to their children after a divorce.) In addition,
the value placed by Victorian culture on the home and education,
together with the growing size and prosperity of the middle class,
meant that increasing numbers of young women were gaining
enough education to want the same opportunities their brothers
enjoyed – to obtain higher education, pursue careers, earn income,
and participate in the national political life. The movement to
obtain these opportunities took shape in the middle of the century
in England and America, and shortly afterwards in many other
countries, and would continue for some seventy years before it
succeeded in bringing down the major barriers to equality. Every
victory in this struggle had to be wrested by women from an
entrenched opposition, and although they had won the right to
own property by the end of the century, they would not gain the
right to vote in most countries until after the First World War.

Darwin

Without question the greatest intellectual achievement of the Victorian age was the formulation of the theory of biological evolution. Although the hypothesis of evolution had been familiar to both British and European scientists since at least the beginning of the century, it was the painstaking documentation of this theory by the English naturalist Charles Darwin, and his publication of *The Origin of Species* in 1859, that announced the theory to the literate world, instantly producing an intellectual shock wave which has not yet entirely receded. In many ways the theory was comparable as an advance in scientific understanding to the discovery of the solar system, and it had a similarly staggering impact on modern man's concept of the universe and his place in it.

For some time geologists had known that the earth revealed a fossil record of the appearance and extinction of thousands of different species of plant and animal life over a history of hundreds of thousands of years. Chronologically, moreover, species showed a general progression from the simple to the complex. This evidence flatly contradicted a literal understanding of the Biblical story of creation, but scientists had not been able to come up with an alternative theory that would explain the development of this family tree of life. As a biologist, Darwin had puzzled over this question for years. It was the work of Thomas Malthus on population that gave him the clue he needed. Reading Malthus's doctrine that an ever-expanding population was always forced to compete for a fixed food supply, Darwin suddenly saw plant and animal populations as faced with the same challenge; in that situation, he deduced, the particular species that were best adapted to their immediate environment would have the best chance of surviving to reproduce themselves, thus producing a self-generating process of natural selection. The biochemical mechanisms that governed hereditary and genetic mutation would not be discovered until later, but Darwin hypothesized that new genetic features would occur accidentally within a species, would then be passed on to future generations, and that those hereditary features that helped a species to survive and reproduce would be perpetuated, while those that did not would die out.

Once a coherent theory of evolution was published, it entered the public consciousness with explosive force, posing a challenge to the Biblical account of creation which could not be ignored as easily as the puzzling geological evidence alone. Just as unsettling, Darwin's theory was ministerpreted by some as a justification of selfishness and aggression in human society and an indication of the natural superiority of whichever persons or peoples had gained dominance over others. Darwin himself, as well as most of the educated elite from which he came, avoided these vulgar and dangerous extrapolations. To most Victorians, however, the theory of evolution tended at least to confirm their impression of their own inherent superiority.

8

The Demographic Revolution

Perhaps the most momentous development to take place in Europe during the nineteenth century was the doubling of its population. In 1800 western Europe was estimated to have slightly more than 200 million inhabitants, most of whom lived on the land as peasants or in small towns supported by the subsistence agriculture of the countryside. Inland cities seldom had more than ten to twenty thousand inhabitants, while the largest ocean and river ports would have only twice that number. London, with nearly a million and a half inhabitants, was then in a class by itself. On the Continent there were fewer than a dozen major capitals with populations that ran into the hundreds of thousands; the largest was Paris, with a population of half a million. By the end of the century, however, the population of Europe had doubled to exceed 400 million, of whom more than half now lived in cities. Thus while the peasant population had remained essentially stable (or even begun to decline), the number of city-dwellers had increased some fivefold. Europe had been transformed from a rural to an urban society.

Since populations cannot expand beyond the limits of available food, this dramatic explosion in human numbers meant that during the nineteenth century the food supply in Europe also doubled in size. This enormous expansion depended as much on improved transportation as on increased production. The traditional subsistence farming of Europe's peasants could produce only a limited marketable surplus, so that any increase in demand had to be met from commercial farms. In the era before railroads, however, it was prohibitively expensive to transport food over land; therefore such efficient farms could exist only where there was a water route to an urban market. Port cities had always imported food from waterside plantations, and both London and Paris were fed by river systems that provided both rich farmland and convenient water transport. On the other hand, the rivers of the European interior tended to be too shallow or swift for easy navigation, and as a result, most inland cities had to depend on their immediate surroundings for food until the railroads offered them wholly new possibilities for growth.

The speed with which the railroads remade Europe was breathtaking. Considering that the first successful steam locomotive began operating in England in 1830, it is astonishing to find rails being laid in France, Belgium, and a number of German states before 1840. Then in the next decade the main lines of a complete Continental system were projected and launched, as European governments became involved in the process. In Britain it had been the new industry that created the railroads and financed their development; on the Continent, however, there was and would be little industry until rail transport was available. The only agencies capable of raising the extraordinary amounts of money required for the task were the state governments, and their involvement meant that the pattern of construction would be determined more by political than by commercial considerations. Whereas in England the first successful railroad ran from Manchester to Liverpool, linking this major industrial center to the nearest deep-water harbor, on the Continent construction characteristically began in the capitals and was pushed out into the countryside.

Although the Continental governments' main purpose was to reach the national frontiers and then beyond to other capitals, the immediate effect of the new lines was to open new farmlands to the big city markets for food. Thus, to take two principal examples, by the mid-1840s Paris was drawing food from the valley of the Loire, and Berlin from that of the Oder. Furthermore the construction of the rail lines created an economic boom that drew all manner of people to the cities just as it was making it possible to feed them. The result was an explosive expansion and fundamental transformation of Europe's major cities.

It was not merely the cities that were transformed, however, but also the entire Continent. Previously Europe had been a predominantly rural society. Not only had the vast majority of its population worked the land as peasants, but its privileged aristocracy had drawn its strength and wealth from owning the land worked by the peasants. To be sure, cities existed and were important both as administrative stations for the emerging monarchies and as centers of commercial wealth; but for all this they remained subsidiary to the rural world of peasants and nobles. By the end of the nineteenth century, however, power and wealth had shifted wholly and irrevocably from the countryside to the growing cities, which would not only dominate the history of the twentieth century but would also produce a whole new urban culture, often characterized as "bourgeois."

The term "bourgeois" (or in German, "bürger") originally meant nothing more than "townsmen" in early medieval Europe when the first towns appeared. As the towns grew, the term became restricted to those who "belonged" to the town, in the sense of owning property and having some say in its affairs. Even so, this would include at one end of the social scale the smallest shopkeepers, and at the other a few rich merchants and bankers. Within the dominant land-based society of that time, however, even the wealthiest bourgeois were usually at a distinct social disadvantage in any encounters with the nobles, and to the aristocrat, "bourgeois" was a term of scorn – a connotation that sometimes still attaches to the word, long after the demise of its noble originators.

In the nineteenth century the well-to-do bourgeois class mushroomed in size and significance along with the cities. Many more of the new city dwellers, however, were unpropertied workers who performed humble services or, increasingly, manned the new factories that began to cluster around the growing cities. As in the medieval towns, it was only those who owned property who were termed "bourgeois," while whose who did not gradually came to be known and to think of themselves, as "proletarians." They were to the emerging urban industrial society what the peasants were to the old agrarian order, but with important differences.

First, the peasants were born into an age-old social and economic system, the order of their lives deeply embedded in custom.

The new proletarians, by contrast, were thrown into already crowded and unhealthy cities to live in improvised housing and find precarious employment as day laborers. Second, the peasants, because they produced food, tended to be assured at least a minimum of nourishment, while the workers were dependent on their daily wages – when they had work – to buy whatever they ate from whatever the markets had to offer. Finally, the peasants were clustered in small villages scattered across the countryside, while the proletarians were herded together in the sordid intimacy of slums and factories. The result in the cities was an inherent confrontation between the haves and have-nots, and a smoldering mutual resentment that was seldom matched in the rural world of the hinterland. This is not to say that the peasants were better off than their urban counterparts; that an increasing number of them did not think so is suggested by the mounting exodus from the country to city that took place as the century wore on. Nor is it clear that the bourgeois were worse exploiters of the poor than the landed aristocrats had been; actually the evidence suggests that they had more sense of responsibility to their society as a whole.

With their new wealth and opportunities, and facing the new problems of urbanization, the bourgeois gradually remade Europe's culture. Indeed the society we know today, in its best as well as its worst aspects, is largely a product of this transformation. Primarily through the medium of education, the bourgeois gave new forms and roles to the arts and above all to the professions, from law and medicine through engineering and politics. Perhaps most remarkable, it was the bourgeois themselves who produced the most searching and telling criticism of the society they were creating. Thus it was this group which produced not only almost all of the century's teachers, scholars, writers, artists, scientists, lawyers, and statesmen, but also virtually all of its revolutionaries.

THE REVOLUTIONARY TRADITION

The major events of the history of nineteenth-century Europe – including the demographic transformation of European society – can be viewed largely as the working out of the implications of the

French and industrial revolutions. By 1815 the French people had implemented the bulk of their agenda of 1789, and they had also introduced their goals and procedures directly or indirectly to most of the rest of Europe. Some areas had been brought under French administration others had been given French constitutions and rulers, while others were organized as satellite states; still others were merely occupied or invaded by Napoleon's France, but even these did not wholly escape French influence. In virtually all countries, partisans of liberty or justice – or even mere efficiency – would work to realize the entire program of the revolution. This would include constitutional government based on manhood suffrage, equality before a national law, and an impersonal and effective administration of the country. Thus in 1815 each segment of Europe, according to its experience, had its own docket of unfinished revolutionary business, in the guise of a program of reform.

At the same time a large number of Europeans emerged from the Napoleonic Wars with a lively sense of the value of the new British industry, and a determination to bring it to the Continent as soon as possible. The industrialization of Europe began with the restoration of peace, and followed a very different course from the one it had originally taken in Britain. In Europe, coal and iron were widely scattered and remote from most major cities and ports. An efficient transportation system would be necessary, therefore, before any massive concentration of industry could be developed like that in the English Midlands. It was the character of Europe's rivers, most of which were too shallow or swift for easy navigation, that necessitated the building of railroads; but there was no possibility that the Continent could develop the industrial capacity to build and install railroads from its own resources. In other words, Europe's first rails would have to be produced and laid by Britain. Furthermore, the vast amount of capital required to finance the job could be found only in Britain, and the only institutions in Europe with sufficient credit to borrow such sums were the state governments. All these factors meant that the new rail systems in Europe would be shaped initially by political rather than economic considerations. Lines would be laid not primarily to connect the coal fields with raw materials or markets, as they were in England, but rather to link the capital cities with the provincial cities and national frontiers, in order to strengthen the administrative control of these areas by the central government. In fact the first economic effect of these rails was actually to discourage industrialization, by facilitating the influx of British goods from the ports to the interior.

When the new industrial economy finally did begin to emerge in Europe, however, it grew within the framework of the national rail systems. The end-product of this development would be newly powerful nation states, in which the new efficient administrative apparatus was integrated with the equally new national industrial economy. Although these states would continue many of the functions and traditions of the military monarchies of the eighteenth century, they were essentially very different institutions. Not only would they become incomparably richer, thanks to their growing industries, but also their new rail communications made them far stronger, both at home and abroad. In addition these same factors would foster the growth of a whole new urban population, much of which would live in precarious dependence on the new industry; lacking even the meager security of traditional village life, these people could hope for aid and rescue only from the state.

Socialism

The idea that the state was responsible for the material welfare of its citizens seems to have originated during the French Revolution, with the government's confiscation of Church lands and its inheritance therefore of the Church's responsibility for all charitable works. Disseminated with demands for French-inspired democratic reforms, the idea rapidly developed importance in the political ideologies that took shape in the nineteenth century. The advocates of state responsibility for social well-being were called "socialists," because they concerned themselves with social as well as political inequities. Although the term did not come into common use until the 1830s, the phenomenon was already familiar; to appreciate how suddenly the socialist movement made its appearance, one need only look at the most radical leaders of the French Revolution, who were all staunch defenders of private property. When an agitator named Gracchus Babeuf demanded the abolition and equal distribution of all private property, the following he attracted among the Parisian poor was too small and disorganized to constitute any threat. The mobs that dominated Paris were led by, and largely composed of, shopkeepers and artisans, who were ready to defend their property, however modest; similarly the peasants, who comprised by far the largest and most powerful revolutionary group in the country, had seized and divided much of the farmlands early in the revolution, and had no intention of losing it to urban radicals. Ultimately Babeuf did catch the horrified attention of the Directors, when they learned that he was plotting to overthrow the government and carry out his program of expropriation, but this "conspiracy of the equals," as it was called, was quickly suppressed and its leader executed. Babeuf's ideas survived, however, and gathered converts as the cities grew and their propertyless poor increased. Without question he was a major source of the socialist thought and action that would be generated in France and spread through Europe as the nineteenth century progressed.

The other widely recognized precursor of modern socialism was also French. Born into a great aristocratic family, Henri de Saint-Simon not only managed to survive the revolution but even took advantage of it to make a fortune speculating in Church lands. Much of this wealth he lavished on extravagant dinner parties at which he expounded his theories of social change. Although he himself never attempted to build a movement or instigate political action, he attracted a number of devoted disciples, who at his death (in 1825) dedicated themselves to the implementation of his ideas.

Saint-Simon's propositions actually led to many different and often contradictory conclusions. He himself explained that the true nature of society had been revealed to him by the incredible ease with which Napoleon was replaced by the Bourbons, only to drive them out for the Hundred Days and then be replaced by them again in the Second Restoration, all of this without disturbing the functioning of the nation. In fact, he asserted, if ten thousand of the most prestigious figures in the land – the greatest nobles, landowners, army officers, and clergy – were all killed in a single night, the country would continue to function as though nothing had happened. If, however, it were to lose only three thousand of the leading men of science, art and industry, France would become a body without a soul, because "a nation is nothing but a great industrial society." In the ideal nation he envisioned, science would provide the key to human progress through industrial production. This progress in turn would require peace and international cooperation – beginning, Saint-Simon hoped, with a political as well as economic union of France and Britain, to be followed by a world federation.

Although Saint-Simon obviously admired Britain's capacity for self-government and industrial production, he had little confidence in the British concept of "enlightened self-interest" as an organizing force. His own preference for "scientific" management clearly drew on the tradition of the *philosophes* and enlightened despotism. Thus, though he had scant respect for the state as it existed, he influenced most subsequent socialists to count on government intervention to achieve their goals. Further, while he never questioned the right of private property, he was deeply suspicious of unrestrained economic individualism, particularly as it was expressed in market competition and the unlimited accumulation of money, or "capital" as it was coming to be called.

While money was hardly an invention of the eighteenth or nineteenth centuries, it did begin to play a quite different and far larger role as the industrial revolution developed and spread. Previously the principal repository and measure of wealth had been land, exploited for the most part by subsistence farming. Since this depended on a stable resident labor force, the first purpose of this wealth was to feed – however poorly – the serfs or peasants who did the work. Although some rents or wages might be paid in money and some crops sold for cash, the economic system depended almost entirely on the local production and consumption of food within the social structure of villages, manor houses, and market towns.

It would be a gross error to assume that this system of economic relations provided a fully satisfactory life for the peasants, but it is also true that those who migrated to the cities found urban existence threatening and precarious. Whether they worked in the new factories or in traditional occupations such as the building trades or baking, they were paid money wages, which stopped any time employment ceased. Since without money the city workers could buy no food, the fact or threat of unemployment locked them in a desperate competition for work which kept all wages low.

One of Saint-Simon's basic convictions was that the reform of society at which he aimed could be carried through only with religious zeal. Christianity was exhausted as a meaningful agent of social action, he was convinced, and would have to be replaced by a new "scientific religion," which he called the "new Christianity" in the title of one of his most important works. At his death, his followers took this instruction literally and tried to establish a religious cult, complete with ritual, clergy, uniforms, and a common domicile open to men and women on equal terms. This unconventional behavior immediately alarmed the authorities, and led to a sensational trial, which ended in convictions on charges of subversion and immorality. The sect was dissolved, but Saint-Simon's followers continued to pursue his goals and exert an important influence on French affairs, particularly through the writings of his young secretary, Auguste Comte. Comte devoted the rest of his life to systematizing the Master's ideas in a grand theoretical structure, which became the basis of the new academic field of sociology and defined the quasi-religious philosophy of "positivism" which was to have an enormous impact on the intellectual history not only of France but also of much of the rest of Europe during the second half of the century.

Perhaps the most remarkable thing about Saint-Simon's thought was its prophetic quality. At the time of his death the industrialization of Europe had barely begun, but he clearly anticipated many of its problems and potentialities, and understood its workings – particularly the key role of transportation in the process. Moreover his basic instinct was to develop and organize the new economic forces rather than to resist or blunt them, as many other reformers sought to do. Among this latter category the best known was an eccentric French genius named Charles Fourier, who dreamed of establishing model communities in which all members would be equal and would voluntarily take turns at doing the necessary work. The "phalanx," as he called his community, was intended to be self-sufficient – an unmistakable reaction against the emergent industry, with its ever greater division and specialization of labor, resulting in the increasing regimentation of the workers. Fourier's description of his phalanxes was so vivid and attractive — at least to intellectuals — that a number of such utopian communities were actually established, mostly in America. They survived for varying lengths of time, but had little impact upon the larger-scale social and economic conditions they protested.

Another prominent social critic in France was a journalist named Louis Blanc, whose attention had been caught by the plight of the workers in the new factories. Convinced that they were being exploited, Blanc hoped to ease their day-to-day existence, rather than to reform society as a whole. His prescription was simple: the government should buy a factory, help its workers form a cooperative organization to run it, and leave them to achieve their collective salvation. Because they would be working for themselves, they would work harder and produce more and better goods than they would for an employer, thereby making greater profits. Indeed these profits would be so plentiful that some could be donated philanthropically for the purpose of purchasing other factories to be turned over to their workers, and so on. Whether this self-generating plan aroused much interest among the workers is not clear, but Blanc's work was widely read and greatly feared by mill owners. Blanc counted on the government to buy the first mill to be turned into a "social workshop" (as he called his cooperatives) and start the process. Needless to say, the July Monarchy of Louis-Philippe had no such intention, but when the revolution of 1848 erupted in Paris, it was Louis Blanc and his plan that would be adopted by the mob.

PARIS, 1848

The fall of Louis-Philippe

Almost from the day after the revolution of 1830, the politically alert had begun looking for the next installment. On the whole this anticipation was the product of the wishful thinking of traditional Jacobins — which is to say, educated young men in quest of careers. In the Germanys these young men tended to be students, but in France they were characteristically members of the professions; in either case their aims were to open political and government careers to talent, by extending the suffrage in France, or supporting constitutional government and national unification east of the Rhine. While there was much political effervescence at this time, there was little if any serious plotting to seize or replace constituted authority. Instead, subversive threats were whispered and inflammatory tracts circulated, while everyone watched Paris for the signal that would set off the next round of revolution.

Despite this long anticipation, the outbreak which finally occurred in Paris in 1848 took everyone by surprise. The immediate cause was not, as had been expected, the assassination of King Louis-Philippe by some wild revolutionary hero, but rather a press campaign against him launched by the same bankers who had put him on the throne by a similar maneuver eighteen years before. These opponents hardly intended to trigger a full-scale revolution, but merely to break the king's personal power, which he was using to appropriate to his own account the most lucrative of the railroad bonds, from which they had hoped to make huge profits themselves. To this end they added their support to a political campaign for electoral reform, particularly an extension of the currently very limited suffrage which would open more careers to would-be politicians. Matters came to a climax when the reform leaders announced a huge rally – called a "banquet" to get around a police regulation against political meetings – for which the government refused to grant a permit. Although both sides tried to avoid a confrontation, things got out of hand and the streets suddenly filled with a vast and angry mob.

What neither the bankers nor the politicians had appreciated was the extent to which Paris had changed since 1830. With the passage of an important law in 1842, construction had begun on a national rail system. One line was pushed out from Paris to the Loire valley, greatly increasing the capital's potential food supply. At the same time speculators began competing for the state bonds floated to finance the rail construction, thus creating a financial boom and countless paper fortunes. The result of the two developments was a rush to Paris, both by investors eager to spend their easy money and by provincial workers in search of jobs. Building became the biggest business in the city, and the luxury trades flourished beyond all precedent. Then in 1846–7 disastrous weather throughout much of Europe drastically cut the supply and raised the prices of food, thus threatening the urban poor with starvation and subjecting the new economy to strains that deflated the market for railroad bonds. Fortunes were lost overnight, and the free spending that had gone with them suddenly stopped. In Paris thousands of transient laborers were thrown out of work, and it was these cold, hungry, desperate men – who cared little about electoral reform and less about railroad bonds – that the machinations of the bankers and the protests of the politicians had mobilized in the streets.

The bewildered king responded to the riots with political concessions, which had no effect on the workers, since their demand was for jobs. When they began building barricades, the king finally called out the troops, thereby provoking clashes in which both demonstrators and bystanders were killed and wounded. At this the mob turned against the king, who was lucky to escape by the rear of the Tuileries palace as the rioters stormed the front; after officially abdicating in favor of his grandson, Louis-Philippe then fled for his life. Meanwhile the mob converged on the Hôtel de Ville, where from a second-floor balcony a self-appointed provisional government announced a Republic. At this juncture an armed worker managed to scale the wall and threaten the leaders into proclaiming the "right to work" and adding several radical politicians, including Louis Blanc, to their group. The dominant figure in the provisional government was no radical, however, but rather the relatively conservative orator and poet Alphonse de Lamartine, who repeatedly calmed the mob with his hypnotic if empty eloquence.

The Second Republic

The most urgent task confronting the new ministers was to provide some sort of livelihood for the mass of hungry workers. To meet this need they instituted a huge program of public works, called the National Workshops, which guaranteed a job to any worker who applied. Although the title was clearly intended to echo Louis Blanc's "social workshops," that was the only similarity to his scheme of worker-owned factories. What was needed was immediate relief for the unemployed, and that was provided in the simplest way, with direct daily wages to all who enrolled.

Because no proof of residence was required, thousands of poor people poured into Paris from the provinces to get this dole, thus doubling the size of the mob and its threat to law and order. Remarkably, this unstable situation produced no new revolutionary impulse, and the provisional government was able to exert a moderating influence for a surprising length of time. Even Louis Blanc used his considerable prestige to prevent excesses. As a result, three enormous demonstrations, which might well have shattered all semblance of peace, were defused, and the government maintained its precarious control.

The second problem facing the new republic was the necessity of reestablishing legitimacy for the government by holding elections for a new National Assembly. Because it would have been utterly impossible to prevent the Paris mob from voting, the provisional government accepted universal manhood suffrage. To everyone's amazement, this apparently radical concession produced an overwhelming majority for Lamartine's moderate Republicans – largely because the peasants, who still constituted more than half the population, voted massively against the state-subsidized program of the National Workshops, which they were forced to support with a land tax.

The "June Days"

When the leaders of the Paris mob realized the extent of their defeat in the elections, they organized a march on the new Assembly and dispersed it. Although both order and government were quickly restored, the event triggered a nationwide reaction against the mob and their Workshops. Thus encouraged, the Assembly passed a law requiring all Workshop members from the provinces either to return home or else to enlist in the army. Recognizing this challenge for what it was – an attempt to cut their number by half and thus destroy their influence – the members of the Workshops decided to fight. With murderous intent the government now withdrew its troops from the city, thus allowing the insurrection to come to a head and consolidate its position. Then the army returned and utterly crushed the rebels in five days of the bloodiest street fighting yet seen in Europe.

The property-holders of France – a category that included the peasants – were frightened by the self-assertion of the new mass of dispossessed and unemployed, and took it as an attack not just on the current political regime but also on the entire society and its foundation in private property. In actuality the insurgents' demands were limited to the "right to work" – that is, the obligation of the state to provide employment for any worker in need – and the recognition of a ten-hour working day. But innocuous as these goals may seem to us, there is no doubt they were seen as dangerously revolutionary at the time. Thus although the Workshop forces were decimated in the fighting, they were also subjected to fearful reprisals in the aftermath, with some 40,000 of the survivors being deported to France's colonies. In addition, the government maintained martial law in Paris for the rest of the year.

The efforts of the French to construct a new political regime were dominated by the widespread panic arising from the events of these "June Days." The Assembly that was elected in the spring of 1848, to give the country a new constitution and decide the form of its government, was deeply conservative, and imbued with the primary objective of restoring and maintaining order. This they believed could best be accomplished by a strong executive. Accordingly, with no acceptable royal heir available, they opted for a president on the American model – that is, one chosen for a four-year term by direct popular election. There was no attempt to retreat from the universal male suffrage that had been established by the provisional government, in part because no one had the slightest idea what sort of president it would produce.

Louis Napoleon

What it produced in the election that followed was an overwhelming victory for a man who had come to France only three months earlier and who had no apparent qualifications for the job except his name. Louis Napoleon Bonaparte was probably the son of Napoleon Bonaparte's brother Louis – although even that is not entirely certain – and had grown up in Italy and Germany. Although he was not quite unknown in France, the attention he had previously attracted had been less than favorable. As a young man he had broken into the courtyard of the army barracks at Strasbourg and invited the garrison to revolt and restore the

Napoleonic Empire. Instead they locked him in the guardhouse, where he remained until the government expelled him to America. Four years later he reappeared, this time on a beach near Boulogne, having crossed the Channel in a chartered excursion steamer, and followed by a handful of "troops" in rented uniforms. This "invasion" was promptly rounded up by the local constabulary and Louis was confined to a fortress in the provinces. After a few years of reasonably comfortable incarceration (during which he wrote some socialist tracts), he managed to walk away in borrowed workman's clothes and went to London, where he lived well, supported by his wealthy mother's estate. Then with the fall of the July Monarchy in February 1848, he returned to France to reassert his claim to being Napoleon Bonaparte's legitimate heir, and to take advantage of the new opportunities that suddenly presented themselves. He got himself elected to the National Assembly, then by skillfully exploiting the unpopularity of his chief opponent, won election to the presidency by a landslide in December of 1848.

From the outset of his presidential term Louis Napoleon's sole objective was to transform his office into that of emperor. While he did not publicly proclaim this purpose, he pursued it relentlessly, by cultivating the army, consolidating his support among the conservatives, and seeking confrontations with the Assembly, which he correctly judged to be the only — and insubstantial — obstacle to the restoration of the Napoleonic imperial throne.

The Second Empire

On December 2, 1851, a year before his term ran out, President Bonaparte used the army and police to arrest his principal political opponents and to occupy the Assembly. He then announced his assumption of power and proclaimed a new constitution, to be subjected to an immediate plebiscite. Some resistance was offered, a few barricades went up in Paris, but the support of the army proved decisive; the coup was accomplished, and the political opposition was crushed by the huge majority Napoleon received in the plebiscite.

In the regime that issued from this coup virtually all power rested in the president, who was merely aided by a subservient advisory council of state, senate, and legislative assembly. One year later, in still another plebiscite, Napoleon sought and received popular ratification of his assumption of the title of Emperor, as Napoleon III (since the son of Napoleon I had been known as Napoleon II although he had never ruled).

This meteoric rise of a nonentity to absolute power as head of the French government continues to demand explanation by the historians. Republican politicians in France have firmly established the interpretation that Louis Napoleon's original election to the presidency was a complete accident, after which he maintained himself in power by trickery and force. But this view ignores the truly astonishing electoral statistics: in the election of 1848 Louis Napoleon received 5,500,000 votes, compared with 1,500,000 for his nearest rival, and in subsequent plebiscites he won majorities of 7,500,000 to 650,000, and later 7,839,000 to 253,000.

It is not traditional to treat this regime as the logical product of the revolution of 1848, but the principal change brought about by that uprising was the adoption of universal male suffrage, and it was the vastly expanded electorate resulting from this new ruling that brought Louis Napoleon to power and kept him there. In these circumstances, what the success of Louis Napoleon must have indicated was the continuing appeal to a large segment of the French population – mostly the conservative peasants – of Napoleon Bonaparte's legacy and his role of "emperor." And just as Napoleon I had come out of the French Revolution to return France to the traditional form of the state, with the First Empire, Napoleon III emerged from the social and economic upheavals of 1848 and drew on the same tradition to reunite the nation in his Second Empire.

GERMANY AND THE HABSBURG EMPIRE, 1848

Germany

News of the Paris revolution was greeted with wild enthusiasm throughout the Germanys and the Habsburg Empire. In the small Rhineland states, crowds of intellectuals – students, lawyers, doctors and others – clamored for liberal reforms and constitutions, which panicky rulers hastened to grant. In the major capitals, the bulk of the population – including the hordes of recent immigrants from the countryside that were pouring into every important city on the Continent – staged massive demonstrations, creating dangerous mobs which, in spite of general efforts to avoid confrontation, would sooner or later come into conflict with government troops.

Two opening events set the tone and direction of what was to follow in central and eastern Europe. In a euphoric mood, some fifty Rhineland liberals met in Heidelberg and issued a call for the election of a national assembly, by universal manhood suffrage, to draft a constitution for a united Germany. At the same time in Budapest, the liberal Magyar opposition in the Hungarian legislature, which had been negotiating with the Habsburgs for a measure of political reform, suddenly brought the proceedings to a standstill with a demand for full Magyar autonomy.

In each case the "revolutionaries" demanded liberal reforms, a constitution, and recognition of nationalist aspirations. The reforms they listed were usually fairly moderate concessions of civil rights, especially the freedom to write and speak politically. It was assumed that the new constitutions would embody such liberal provisions, as well as establish some element of representative government, but few of the constitutions granted at this time failed to recognize the incumbent monarch or attempted to establish genuinely democratic regimes. What was expected of a constitution was the provision of a set of publicly recognized procedures for governing the political unit for which it was drafted. Finally all these reforms were usually demanded in the name of the "nation," which meant the dominant segment of the population, with the inescapable democratic implication that a "nation" had an inalienable right to rule itself and ultimately to define itself. In practical terms national self-definition tended to follow linguistic lines, so that in the German Confederation the predominance of the German language had a powerful unifying effect, while in the multilingual Habsburg Empire, administrative unification through the language of the rulers (German) had inevitably meant alienating the other large linguistic groups that now were demanding the right to rule themselves in their own tongue.

The Habsburg Empire

In March of 1848, the Habsburg cities from Prague to Milan all erupted in demonstrations. In Vienna, seat of the imperial Habsburg court, the university students seized the initiative, demanding standard civil rights and the dismissal of the chief author of imperial repression, Chancellor Metternich. In the vian hope of avoiding further trouble, Emperor Ferdinand I sent his old chancellor packing (to exile in England), and then promised to call a constitutional assembly. At the same time, in line with this policy of concession, the Habsburg minister in Budapest accepted a body of legislation, called the March Laws, which would grant Hungary autonomy under a liberal constitution.

When news of the revolt in Vienna reached Milan, a mob seized the city, and after five days of fighting forced the Habsburg garrison out of the fortifications. At this point Venice also revolted and declared a republic, further intensifying the revolutionary fever that was sweeping the Italian peninsula. Although he was no leader of Italian nationalism, King Charles Albert of Piedmont felt compelled to declare war on the Habsburgs in support of the Milanese rebels, simply to prevent an outburst among his own subjects. His forces were joined by volunteers from the rest of the peninsula, but the Piedmontese army was still no match for the Austrian forces in Italy, which finally crushed it at Custozza, forcing the Italians to abandon their independence movement.

In the mean time, the situation in Vienna had seriously deteriorated for the Habsburgs. The government issued a constitution, but also dissolved the students' revolutionary committee and the national guard, a paramilitary organization of substantial citizens that had been formed after the French model. This led to a new wave of violence that forced the imperial family to flee Vienna, leaving the city in the hands of a revolutionary "committee of public safety."

Taking advantage of this situation, Czech nationalists in Bohemia called a Pan-Slav Congress to meet at Prague. It began by denouncing Austrian rule and ended by igniting an armed insurrection, which the imperial military governor promptly suppressed by bombarding the city and imposing martial law. This action, closely following the defeat of the Piedmontese army by the Habsburgs, seemed to mark a turning of the tide in the Habsburgs' favor, which they solidified by bombarding their own capital into submission, thus providing a public demonstration of the total bankruptcy of imperial policy. The generals now took matters into their own hands (December, 1848), and forced the abdication of the imbecilic Emperor Ferdinand in favor of his nephew Franz Joseph, who would reign until 1916.

The new emperor's first challenge came from Hungary, where the Habsburg forces were driven out and a republic was declared. In desperation the young ruler accepted an offer of aid from the tsar, whose army promptly crushed the rebels in Budapest, allowing the Habsburgs to restore their authority and exact severe reprisals (August 1849). In the mean time, a charismatic young revolutionary named Mazzini had established a republic in Rome, and stirred up enough national enthusiasm to induce the Piedmontese to attack the Austrian occupation forces once again. This time the would-be liberators suffered such a crushing defeat that King Charles Albert abdicated in favor of his son, who became Victor Emmanuel II. In Rome the republic was attacked and taken over not by the Austrians but by the French under Napoleon III, who defended this opportunistic act as protecting the interests of the pope in the name of all Catholics.

Moves toward German unity

While the Habsburgs were thus contending with their unruly subjects, the German states were also in ferment. Almost simultaneously with the initial outburst in Vienna, a huge, if relatively peaceful, mob took over Berlin. With the police hopelessly outnumbered, King Frederick William saw little choice but to call out the army. In the unintended but inevitable clash that followed, several hundred demonstrators were killed, and it was apparently genuine revulsion at the bloodshed which moved the king suddenly to grant all the concessions the demonstrators had asked for, including the convocation of the Prussian Assembly.

While this body was convening in Berlin, the National Assembly called for by the Heidelberg intellectuals finally met at Frankfurt to draft a constitution for a united Germany. The deputies to this assembly were predominantly members of the liberal professions, particularly professors and lawyers, many of whom had been politically active as students in the German universities during the period of protest against Habsburg hegemony and repression. As soon as it was convened, in May of 1848, the Assembly plunged directly into its main task of drafting a constitution, an exercise in which the collective erudition of the members raised the intellectual quality but lowered the practical productivity of the debates. From the beginning, however, the deputies found themselves involved in immediate political decisions as well as theoretical and legal problems. They began by dissolving the moribund Diet of the German Confederation, which they proposed to replace by a provisional government presided over by the Archduke John, an uncle of the Habsburg emperor, who would have the grand title of Imperial Regent but neither a bureaucracy nor an army at his command.

The first problem to test this arrangement was a contest that developed between the Confederation and Denmark for the two southern duchies of Schleswig and Holstein. These political units were dynastic possessions of the Danish crown, but now they refused to recognize the accession of a new Danish king, Frederick VIII, on the grounds that his claim to the throne was through the female line. Because Holstein was a member of the Confederation, and Schleswig had a large German population, the Frankfurt Assembly responded to the situation by inviting Prussia to send forces to counter those of Denmark. England and Russia immediately warned Prussia against intervention, and an armistice was signed (September 1848) by which all troops were to be evacuated and the duchies administered jointly by Denmark and the Confederation. This shaky arrangement inevitably led to further trouble, but in the mean time both the Frankfurt and the Prussian assemblies went back to work, and in due time produced the instruments of government for which they had been convened.

In December of 1848 the Prussian Constituent Assembly was dessolved and the government promulgated a new constitution based on its work. Although it provided for a two-chamber legislature (lords and deputies), executive power remained with the monarchy, and while the principle of manhood suffrage was recognized, it was also diluted by a three-class system of voting which gave the largest taxpayers a grossly disproportionate representation in the lower house.

By March of 1849 the Frankfurt Assembly also produced its constitution for a federal state. This was to be governed by two elected parliamentary houses and presided over by a constitutional "emperor of the Germans." The assembly invited the King of Prussia to assume this imperial post, but his opposition to the plan sealed its doom; among his objections to it was that as a ruler by "divine right" he would be stooping to accept the office of emperor offered by a popularly elected body. Although it was not then put into effect, the form of government arrived at by the Frankfurt Assembly would serve as a model for later attempts at German unification. It established the principle that only German territories could be included in the federation, and that the individual states should be represented in the upper house while the lower one should be elected directly by manhood suffrage. Austria was excluded from the planned union because of her ties with her non-German provinces, thus leaving Prussia by far the dominant force in the federation.

Without any doubt there was strong sentiment throughout the German-speaking world for some form of political unification. In an effort to turn this to Prussia's advantage, Frederick William offered his own draft constitution as an alternative to the Frankfurt model. The king's plan was for a "Prussian Union" which would yoke the other German states to his country; this "inner confederation" would then serve as the nucleus of a central European bloc that would be completed by the Habsburg empire. To this end Frederick William invited the other German states to send representatives to a Union Parliament at Erfurt; the lesser princes did not dare to refuse, but the more important ones abstained.

By this point the Habsburgs had reestablished their authority in their provinces and they now moved to defend their power in Germany. Countering both the Frankfurt and Prussian proposals, they summoned a session of the defunct Diet of the German Confederation, in which Austria had always been the dominant power, and at the same time they sent troops to aid a minor prince against his liberal parliament. These actions left Frederick William with the alternative of defending his new Prussian Union by force or submitting to Habsburg threat and hegemony. Having neither the inclination nor the means to resist, he capitulated by signing an agreement at Olmütz (November 1850) which revived the old German Confederation and served as a bitter reminder of their military impotence for subsequent Prussian leaders.

Thus in three years the revolutionary conflagration ignited by the sparks from Paris had swept through Germany, the Habsburg Empire and much of Italy. The overall results seemed to be that virtually every state involved had granted at least one liberal constitution under duress, and that both Prussia and the Habsburg Empire had come out with stronger, more efficient governments. In general, manhood suffrage came to be recognized as a basis for political authority, but it was by no means fully implemented. Even more important was the dissemination of, and growing popular enthusiasm for, the principle of national unification on the basis of linguistic and ethnic identity. In the Habsburg provinces this sense of nationality had a divisive influence which all but broke the empire apart, and was only contained by widespread and repeated military action, including Russian intervention. In Germany and Italy, however, the idea would eventually serve to bring together disparate political units in a new form of national union.

Why a revolutionary tidal wave should have swept across so much of Europe at this time is not entirely clear. The evidence suggests that simple defiance of authority spread as a contagion, but those who caught the infection had the most varied motives and objectives. In Paris a wide spectrum of the population became involved in the demonstrations, but the dominant element in the revolution was the workers, and their insistence on their right to work. Little similar influence is to be found across the Rhine. In both Germany and Austria the leaders of the movement for change were almost always intellectuals – usually students or former students – and members of the professions, including lawyers, bureaucrats and politicians. In Berlin large numbers of artisans swelled the mobs, but they fought no June Days; in Vienna the railroad workers were courted by the student leaders and paraded as mascots, but actually played only a minor part in the demonstrations. Elsewhere the working class was even less in evidence; the movements for national self-determination in Italy and

Hungary were led by the nobility, who proposed only the most cautiously liberal changes in the form of government with which they would replace imperial Habsburg rule.

EUROPE AFTER THE REVOLUTIONS

Napoleon III

While the electoral success of Louis Napoleon demonstrated that France was still predominantly rural and peasant, the revolution of 1848 also revealed that the nation was developing a new urban dimension, and the Second Empire would see unprecedented economic growth and prosperity in the cities – particularly Paris. Although there was nothing in the administration of Louis Napoleon to bear out his lifelong claim that he was a socialist, he helped to foster an economic boom which provided ample employment for the urban poor as well as great wealth for the well-placed and ambitious. Many in the emperor's entourage had been active Saint-Simonians, and they encouraged him to use the powers of the state to develop the national industrial economy, particularly by completing the railroad network that had been projected in the early 1840s. This Louis Napoleon moved to do, mobilizing all the resources of the state to build a national system of main lines which was essentially completed in a decade, bringing with it a wave of prosperity and a new level of national integration. The sheer size of the undertaking provided employment for the surplus manpower of both the cities and provinces, stimulated business and facilitated the continuing urban growth. Further, the much more rapid communications strengthened the administrative hold of the authoritarian government on the country and laid the base for the industrialization of France along the same centralized lines of organization. Taken all together, these changes contributed greatly to the transformation and integration of the old territorial monarchy into a modern nation state.

After the railroads, the most important project undertaken by Louis Napoleon was the massive rebuilding of Paris, quite possibly the most ambitious and successful example of urban reconstruction in the history of the West. Although planned cities had been built in the seventeenth and eighteenth centuries – Washington, DC being a major example – no ruler had had the resources or audacity to impose a geometric plan on the crowded maze of a major medieval city. Perhaps the nearest anyone had come was in the preliminary efforts of the Bourbons to create vistas along the north–south and east–west axes of Paris. Napoleon I manifested an interest in continuing this project, but his military activities left him too little time to accomplish much. Thus in a sense Napoleon III inherited the project, but he also totally transformed it. Virtually all of the great avenues and boulevards in the center of today's city were imposed on a tangle of streets and alleys by Louis Napoleon's architects. Not only did this enterprise open new arteries for traffic in the city (focused in part on the five new railroad stations for the five major lines), but it also established standards for construction and architectural style, even requiring private owners to maintain a uniform façade for long stretches of the new roads. By no means the least important part of this undertaking was its financing; the cost was divided between the imperial government and the City of Paris, which meant that it bore heavily on the city's property owners. They mounted bitter protests, which were only partly blunted by the official explanation that the broad avenues would be much easier for the army to control in case of revolution.

Once he had firmly consolidated his regime in France, Louis Napoleon turned his attention to his position in Europe. Although the English government recognized him at once, the major Continental rulers were slow to follow suit and the Russian tsar, after crushing the Hungarian revolt, refused to accord this upstart ruler even the minimal courtesy of recognizing him as a fellow monarch. Apparently this slight was enough to decide Napoleon on a course of war, and he found an excuse in Russia's apparent preparations to move against a vulnerable Turkey. With Great Britain as his ally – the British had long opposed Russian influence in the Black Sea area – he declared war on Russia, besieging the Russian naval base on the Crimean peninsula in the Black Sea. When Tsar Nicholas I died suddenly in the midst of the war, the Russian commanders conceded defeat, and Napoleon obtained his chief objective: a general peace conference over which he could preside in Paris. Clearly this event was intended to mark the end of the period inaugurated at Vienna in 1815 and to replace it with a new community of popular national states. It failed in this grand design, but the Paris Congress did reinforce Turkey's independence, and the neutralization of the Black Sea, with international guarantees.

Developments in Italy

This conference also marked the entry onto the European diplomatic stage of Italy's kingdom of Piedmont and its remarkable statesman, Count Camillo de Cavour. Cavour had sent a military contingent to the Black Sea to aid the allies with just this end in mind, as a brilliant first move in his campaign to unite all of Italy around his young king, Victor Emmanuel II. A sophisticated man of affairs, Cavour admired the economic progress and political reforms he had witnessed in visits to Britain and France, and hoped to institute similar measures in Piedmont. Before any of his hopes could be realized, however, the occupying troops of the Habsburg Empire would have to be driven out of Italy. What Cavour sought to do was to get Britain or France to undertake this task, since it could be accomplished only by a major power. When Britain disappointed Cavour, by declining to reward his assistance in the Crimean War with a campaign against the Habsburgs, his only hope was the new emperor of France. Not only did Louis Napoleon have an army and the authority to use it, but he also seemed to have retained from his boyhood exile a warm sympathy for the cause of Italian liberty and unity. Playing on this sentiment, Cavour succeeded in winning Bonaparte's commitment to military support if the Habsburgs should open hostilities against the Italians; but Napoleon's price was the province of Savoy and the city of Nice. To set the plot in motion Cavour mounted a press campaign calling for rebellion in the Habsburgs' Italian provinces; in short order Vienna fell into the trap and declared war against Piedmont.

Moving his troops by rail, Napoleon launched a rapid attack against the Austrians that was capped by victories at Magenta and Solferino, and then suddenly withdrew his forces from the conflict, apparently because of his revulsion at the horrors of the battlefield (which he saw for the first time following Solferino), and his fear that the war might spread to other Italian states and possibly provoke Prussian intervention. The Habsburg emperor and Napoleon quickly agreed to terms by which the Austrians would give up Lombardy but retain Venetia. To Cavour's great disgust Napoleon not only failed to fulfill his commitment to Piedmont but also insisted on collecting his reward of Nice and Savoy. Even so, the war stirred up such nationalistic fervor in northern and central Italy that a series of popular uprisings drove out the Habsburg rulers, and the newly liberated peoples promptly declared their allegiance to the kingdom of Piedmont. To legitimate these wholesale annexations by Piedmont, Cavour arranged plebiscites in all of its new territories, where without exception the populace voted total approval of their amalgamation within a unified Italy under Victor Emmanuel II. This popular excitement next spread to the Papal States around Rome and then to the kingdom of Naples in the south. In Sicily local revolutionary committees assumed control in town after town, prompting Cavour to send an expedition to the island under the dashing nationalist and republican agitator Garibaldi, to assure its annexation to his growing Italian kingdom. (By sponsoring Garibaldi in this action Cavour also shrewdly assured the loyalty of a potential rival to Victor Emmanuel.) Garibaldi and his "thousand volunteers" received a wild welcome in Sicily, from where they pushed on to Naples to find that the reactionary king had fled, leaving them in complete control and with visions of marching on to Rome and Venice. Fearing that Garibaldi's forces would threaten the pope in Rome and hence bring Catholic France to his aid, Cavour rushed Piedmontese troops to the Papal States, both to preserve the status quo in Rome itself and to claim the rest of these territories for his king. When Cavour died in 1861, essentially all of Italy, with the exception of Rome and Austrian Venetia, was united. Then as a result of Prussia's victorious war against Austria in 1866, in which Italy had sided with Prussia, Venetia was ceded to Italy by the Habsburgs. In 1870 France's defeat by Prussia in the Franco-Prussian War put an end to the French occupation of Rome, leaving the city to the kingdom of Italy. Rome was promptly made the capital of the newly united nation, though the small enclave of the Vatican was officially left to the pope.

Rivalry between Prussia and Austria

While Napoleon III was busy establishing his position in Europe and Cavour was plotting the unification of Italy, Austria and Prussia were contending for leadership within the German Confederation. The balance of power would finally shift decisively in favor of Prussia, beginning with the accession of King William I in 1861. Until he became regent, in 1859, William had spent his entire life in the army, and knew little else. Not surprisingly, his chief advisor was his minister of war, General von Roon, and their primary objective was to reform the Prussian army. Since 1815 the population of Prussia had increased by some 50 percent while its army had remained the same size. Roon's program was to bring the army back to strength by more rigorous use of universal service, and in the process to strengthen the role of the Prussian nobles, called "Junkers," in the officer corps. An increase in the size of the army, however, required a corresponding increase in the military appropriation, which the lower house of the Prussian legislature voted down. To resolve this crisis the king turned to a brilliant and ambitious career diplomat named Otto von Bismarck. Appointed chancellor in 1862, Bismarck not only succeeded in raising the needed revenues (by simply ignoring the legal requirement that they be approved by the legislature), but also set German history on a new and fateful course.

Like his friend Roon and the other leading military officers, Bismarck was eager to enhance the position and prerogatives of the Junker class in Prussia, but far more than his parochial colleagues he saw this goal in the context of the larger one of the unification of Germany under Prussian leadership. The reorganization of the Prussian army would present Bismarck with the perfect base for the diplomatic program he now unfolded.

Theoretically, a system of universal training and conscription had been adopted in Prussia during the Napoleonic Wars, but now the development of a flourishing iron and steel industry in the Ruhr valley, and the establishment of a rail system, gave the generals the means to mobilize and equip virtually all Prussian men of combat age. Further, they found that the rapidly growing urban population provided conscripts and reserve officers whose superior education made them far easier to train during their three years of service. Going well beyond their original intent, Roon and his fellow generals, with the full backing of Bismarck and the king, transformed the Prussian army into the first prototype of the modern mass army).

Bismarck hardly waited for the completion of the process to put his powerful new instrument to the test. In 1864 the Danes tried to transform their dynastic rights in the largely German-populated provinces of Schleswig and Holstein into outright acquisition; this move inflamed nationalist sentiment in Germany and offered Bismarck the opportunity he needed to flex his military muscle. With the ultimate aim of provoking a confrontation with Austria, the Prussian chancellor proposed joint military intervention to the Habsburgs, an invitation which they could hardly refuse without relinquishing their leadership in Germany to Prussia. The ensuing campaign was as brief as it was successful, with the result that Denmark ceded the provinces of Schleswig, Holstein, and Lauenburg to Prussia and Austria. Bismarck then maneuvered Austria into occupying Holstein while Prussia took responsibility for Schleswig (and annexed Lauenburg in exchange for a cash payment to Austria). As the chancellor had calculated, this arrangement proved totally unworkable, and led to the desired confrontation between the two German states in 1866.

Ever the professional diplomat, Bismarck carefully prepared the way for his intended triumph. First he won a promise of neutrality from Napoleon III with the implied promise of compensation for France, then concluded an alliance with the new Italian kingdom by offering the prize of Venetia in exchange for military aid against Austria. He then challenged Austria with a series of hostile moves at a meeting of the German Confederation, charging it with violations of the Confederation's constitution, and finally he moved Prussian troops into Holstein. Austria countered by persuading the Confederation to censure Prussia for violating federal territory with this mobilization) at which rebuff Prussia proceeded to declare the Confederation dissolved, and opened hostilities with a successful attack on Hanover. The Italians, who had long sought an ally to help them evict the Austrians, now quickly moved against their old enemy on sea and land, but were defeated on both. Meanwhile the main Prussian forces, making effective use of the new railroads and telegraph communications, converged on the Bohemian town of Königgrätz where they met and totally destroyed the Austrians, thereby leaving Vienna itself open to the Prussians. Although the Habsburgs were now at his mercy, Bismarck was interested only in establishing Prussian hegemony in Germany, and offered terms which left the Habsburgs secure in their empire with the exception of Venetia, which was handed over to the Italians.

Prussia now annexed Hanover and several smaller north German states that had joined Austria in the war, while establishing a tight military alliance with the principal southern states that effectively reduced them to satellites. Napoleon had demanded Luxemburg and some Belgian territory as the price for his neutrality, but this secret deal was now leaked to the press, providing Bismarck with an excuse to discredit the French and denounce the bargain. Finally Bismarck's reorganization of Germany was completed with the formation of the North German Confederation, which united all of Germany north of the Main under a constitution that was similar to that of the original German Confederation but which was actually subverted by the overwhelming influence in the new government of Prussia's ultra-conservative monarchy. Thus just four years after he came to the aid of his frustrated monarch, Bismarck had enabled Prussia's generals to make the kingdom the dominant power in central Europe, and had proceeded to unite all of Germany under Prussia's hegemony. (In gratitude for this accomplishment the Prussian parliament promptly passed a bill giving retroactive sanction to Bismarck's unconstitutional acts in raising and spending vast sums for the military without parliamentary consent.)

At this juncture the defeated Habsburgs recognized the need for a major reform of their cumbersome imperial government. The centralized administration which had been developed after 1848 – known as the "Bach System" – had won approval in Austria but was opposed throughout the rest of the empire. After Austria's defeat in Italy, and as the other subject nationalities renewed their demands for autonomy, the imperial government finally abandoned this last attempt to create an efficient bureaucratic rule; in 1867 the empire was reorganized as a Dual Monarchy, in which Hungary and Austria became equal, independent states united by a single Habsburg monarch. They shared a common foreign and military policy, supported by equal financial contributions, and they divided the other subject provinces between them – a measure that only exacerbated the discontent of the national minorities that were seeking self-rule.

The decline of Napoleon III

Jealous of Bismarck's dazzling success, Napoleon III now began a campaign of diplomatic intrigue against his rival. This proved to be a fatally unequal contest for the emperor, who had neither the wit nor strength – not to mention luck – to match the chancellor. Bismarck now turned his attention and formidable skills to establishing Prussian superiority over France, and Napoleon repeatedly played into the hands of his enemy. The first mistake of the French ruler was a clumsy renewed effort to acquire the duchy of Luxemburg from the king of Holland. Skillfully exploited in the press by Bismarck, this led to an international conference at which Luxemburg was neutralized, to the humiliation of Napoleon, who was also now beginning to be pressed by a national opposition at home.

It was at this juncture that a vacancy on the throne of Spain suddenly dominated European affairs. After the Spanish queen was expelled by a revolution (1869), the provisional government that took power began shopping around for candidates among unemployed minor royalty in Portugal, Italy, and eventually Germany. Bismarck came up with a distant relative of Prussia's William I whom he persuaded the Spanish to choose. In retrospect it is difficult to believe that this possible succession was worth anyone's serious consideration, but the French press treated it as a threat to French security, forcing Napoleon to protest to William I. The candidacy was now withdrawn by the father of the young prince, but Napoleon allowed himself to be maneuvered by both supporters and opponents in France into a gratuitous demand for guarantees against its being renewed, together with an apology from William I. This impertinence gave Bismarck just what he needed to inflame public opinion in both Germany and France beyond the combustion point; using the press once again, Bismarck released an edited version of the French demand which made it appear that Napoleon had deliberately provoked the king, and had been completely snubbed in response. The emperor saw no choice but to declare war.

French defeat

The war between France and Prussia was an unequal contest from the beginning, not because Prussia was bigger or stronger but because Bismarck had a clear objective and the personal force to impose it on his military commanders. In fact the French army was larger than the Prussian, and quite as experienced and well equipped; what it lacked was a plan of action. The Prussians not only had a meticulously detailed schedule of operations, but also, by making the maximum use of the railways, they were able to mobilize much faster and impose their plan on the French, who never succeeded in coordinating the efforts of their several armies. Six weeks after the declaration of war, with two French armies shut up in frontier fortresses, the main unit, together with the emperor, surrendered at Sedan, on September 2, 1870. Napoleon was taken prisoner by the Prussians, and in Paris, never the base of his support, republicans seized the opportunity to proclaim the end of his empire and the birth of the Third Republic. This Napoleon would not reappear on the French stage: he returned to the exile in England from which he had emerged, and died three years after his defeat.

The Parisians who were so eager to see Napoleon go, however, were also the most determined group in the nation to hold out against the Prussians, and they continued resistance until a Prussian siege starved the capital into surrender in January 1871. At this point Bismarck offered a truce to permit the election of a provisional government to negotiate a peace. This election returned a National Assembly that was both conservative and in favor of peace, thanks to the combined efforts of the peasants and the property owners. Avoiding embattled Paris, the new assembly met in Bordeaux and voted to accede to Prussian demands for a huge indemnity and the cession of the border provinces of Alsace and Lorraine.

In Paris, however, a passionate minority continued to foment resistance. The long siege had had the effect of polarizing political opinion in the city, particularly because the wealthier inhabitants had mostly sought safer and more comfortable surroundings, leaving the rigors of the siege to the less affluent. When the siege was finally lifted, the Prussians arranged a triumphal entry into the city, which further inflamed Parisian sensibilities and led to a confused series of events in which groups of citizens moved some cannon from the center of the city to workers' districts. Alarmed at what appeared to be a radical challenge to its authority, the provisional government moved from Bordeaux to Versailles and sent troops into Paris to reclaim the guns. The results were the opposite of those intended. Instead of taking control of the city, the troops fraternized with the rapidly-forming mob, which refused to relinquish the guns, and in the confusion two generals were murdered. At this point the government at Versailles began organizing a new army, and the leaders of the Paris mob formed a revolutionary government which they called the Commune, which also began to arm itself to defend the city.

Once again Paris was under siege, this time by a rival French government; fighting continued from early March to the end of May, when in what became known as the "Bloody Week," the Versailles troops finally crushed the resistance. During the fighting the government treated all prisoners as deserters from the French army and executed them without trial; the *communards* retaliated by shooting hostages. In the end, some twenty thousand people were killed, and thousands more were imprisoned or transported to penal colonies. To many observers this violent struggle appeared to be a larger-scale installment of the June Days, but in one important respect it was quite different. Although the Commune is often treated by Marxists as an early example of "proletarian" rebellion, it was in fact almost entirely Jacobin in character; despite its name, most of its participants were actually small business and property owners, who fought for republican government and a continued resistance to the Prussians, not for socialist or communist ends. Not only was Paris itself still without industry, but because of the siege it had been cut off from the provincial factories which had supplied the industrial workers who fought in the June Days.

Germany united

Once Napoleon had surrendered at Sedan and his government had collapsed in Paris, there was no power left on the Continent with the strength or desire to challenge Prussian hegemony. If the Habsburgs had reasons to resent Bismarck's triumph, they fully realized the risks they would run if they challenged him, while the tsar saw no conflict of interest with Prussia and had already been completely won over by Bismarck's flattery and favor.

In January 1871 Bismarck proclaimed the formation of the German Empire, with William I as emperor. Formally, this amounted to bringing the south German states into the North German Confederation by a series of individual treaties with each new member. The result was a federation of 25 states, very uneven in size and power, and all totally dominated by the largest and most conservative – that is, Prussia.

Thus by the 1870s the principal goals of 1848 had been realized, though in an ironic and ominous fashion. Germany was united and possessed a constitution ostensibly based in universal suffrage. Italy was freed from Habsburg hegemony and united in a constitutional monarchy. The Hungarians had achieved autonomy within the Dual Monarchy, and the Austrians had a constitution. Even France, defeated by Prussia and torn by civil war, would finally emerge with a republican form of government as well as a constitution based in universal manhood suffrage. But the picture of Europe that had now emerged was hardly the one that the revolutionaries of 1848 had envisioned. Much later, nostalgic veterans of 1848 would look back at their uprisings as the "springtime of the peoples." In March and April and May of 1848 the weather had been superb and the revolutionaries had been young and generous. They had fought for a world in which all people would be free both to develop their personal talents and to work for a more just society. But the world they wanted was already out of date.

The revolutions of 1848 were the combined product of the new urban populations and the restless young and educated members of society whose ideal was still the rational society of the Enlightenment and whose ambition was a career in the new national and liberal states they hoped to form or at least reform. Unfortunately they had been educated for the past, not the future, and the new states would be shaped by forces they did not understand. While almost all the revolutionaries of 1848 were sentimental about "workers," they had little contact with, and less understanding of, the actual industrial proletariat. To a surprising degree the earliest factory industry on the Continent was in the provinces, beyond the reach of the rail lines that brought in English goods, while the burgeoning capital cities where the revolutions had broken out had few if any industrial workers.

What they did have was a swollen population of poor immigrants from the countryside. This was a direct consequence of the new railroads, which not only brought the people to the cities but also brought in the food and commerce that supported them – or that at least made it possible for them to expect to be able to survive in the cities. This new demographic and economic shape of the cities, in turn, led them to develop a new form of political organization. First, it became impossible to exclude the urban masses from voting, so that universal manhood suffrage became the general rule. This expansion of the electorate then led to the development of modern political parties, which represented the major interest groups among the voters, gradually coming to include the factory workers as the new industry developed.

Along with universal manhood suffrage came the equally significant new development of a universal manhood obligation to military service. It was the Prussians who had first, rather accidentally, introduced this practice in the course of reforming their army, instituting a system of training all male citizens as soldiers for some three years. Taken together with the new railroads, which facilitated both mobilization and supply of the army, their training program produced such dazzling results that it became the mandatory model for all European powers. To be sure, the French had fought as a nation during the Napoleonic era, but they had not been able to maintain substantially more men in the field than Louis XIV, simply because of the limits of supply. By 1870 these limits no longer existed; the modern nation in arms had become a realizable concept, and with it the bright hopes of the "springtime of the peoples" had turned into the nightmare of an armed camp of nations.

9

The Consolidation and Expansion of Europe

By 1870 the major cities of Europe were all linked by a rail system that made it possible to supply their expanding populations with food, fuel, and cheap – largely British – manufactured goods. As has already been noted, industry developed slowly on the Continent, and mostly in provincial enclaves out of the reach of British competition. This was a situation that would change rapidly in the last quarter of the nineteenth century, however, as Europe developed its own industry, generally located in or near the major cities. A central factor in this transformation was the invention in 1878 of a process for making good-grade iron from low-grade ore. The first effect of this "Thomas–Gilchrist method," as it was called, was to make it possible to use the huge deposits of iron in Lorraine by smelting it with the coal in the Ruhr valley, thereby creating the first base for heavy industry in Europe. Thanks to the same technique a somewhat smaller center of iron production was then created in Bohemia, while in the United States the method was used to unite Lake Superior iron ore and Pennsylvania coal in an operation even larger than that in the Ruhr valley. Together these developments would vastly expand the supply of inexpensive iron and steel in the western world – a development that was to have all but incalculable consequences for the subsequent course of industrialization.

Before the Thomas–Gilchrist process, Britain had a virtual monopoly of heavy industry – that is, the manufacture of machines and equipment. Almost all of the locomotives, rolling stock and rails for the world's railroads had been manufactured in Britain, frequently straining even that country's huge capacity. By the early 1880s, however, there was ample cheap steel on the Continent for the Europeans themselves to fill in the network of main rail lines with a complete system of feeder lines. These new routes extended the industrial market into the Continental hinterland, leading at first to an expansion of Britain's consumer industries, particularly textiles and hardware; but they also served as a stimulus to local industrialization, so that the Continent was soon producing its own consumer goods as well as rails and factory equipment.

At almost the same time, a series of developments in ship design and construction produced a small, efficient type of steamship, called a "tramp steamer," which could move manufactured goods and raw materials from port to port at minimum cost. Thus as the rail feeder lines extended the inland reach of the new national industrial economies, so the tramp steamers allowed their inexpensive extension overseas, both to other industrial countries and to economically undeveloped areas around the shores of the world's oceans. This maritime phase of the West's new economic expansion meant in fact the beginning of a new phase of its overseas empire, this one dependent not on concentrated trade in the special products of plantations but rather on an opportunistic exchange of miscellaneous, often mundane, goods. While the effects of this new commerce were felt around the oceanic world, its impact was particularly marked on Africa. Europeans had earlier established themselves in coastal trading areas, but now they were able to penetrate the African interior through the agency of explorers, missionaries, traders, and military expeditions that could be supported and supplied by the new cargo ships and river boats. In a competitive scramble, the western powers now partitioned most of the African continent among themselves — unsure of what advantages would accrue to them from control of such territories, but unwilling to be left out of the race.

The new abundance of cheap iron and steel also fueled a new level of development of industrialization itself. From the beginning industry had carried the implication of continuing and accelerating improvement in its productive capacity, not merely through quantitative expansion of simple procedures but also through the invention of new applications of industrial power. One of the most important of such developments was the use of iron for constructing bridges and buildings; another was the exploitation of scientific advances that would lead to the birth of the chemical industry. This latter important manifestation of industry began to take shape in the mid-century in Germany, but grew explosively with the general industrial expansion following the Thomas–Gilchrist breakthrough; among its first products were dyes, fertilizers, dynamite, and later synthetic drugs and textiles. In time the introduction of industrially produced fertilizers, together with the manufacture of the first agricultural machines, announced the beginnings of the industrialization of agriculture, which was to yield a historically unprecedented level of efficiency in food production.

Another new industrial development took place in the area of electrical technology. The first, urgently needed, application of electricity was the telegraph, without which railroad scheduling would have been nearly impossible; invented in the 1840s, the telegraph made use of a code of short and long electrical impulses to transmit messages great distances over wires. The further development of the same basic technique also led to the invention of the telephone in 1876. At about this time another series of developments produced an efficient generator of electricity, and numerous applications of centrally produced electric power. The first and most important use was for lighting following the invention of an effective light bulb around 1880; by the turn of the century most cities in Europe and America were amply provided with electric illumination, so that for the first time in history the activities of a significant part of the population were no longer tied to the natural cycle of light and dark. Another important application of the cities' electric power supply was to run the urban trolley – the street-level, elevated, and subway railways that moved commuters from home to work and back. Electric motors could also be used in factory operations for which steam engines were too cumbersome and inflexible. In this same period the invention of the internal combustion engine, together with the rise of the petroleum industry, gave birth to the gasoline-powered automobile by the mid-1880s, diesel-fueled steamships and railroad engines, and even airplanes by 1903.

All of these developments created new industries to produce chemicals, petroleum products, electric light and power, telegraph and telephone equipment, automobiles, etc. The exploding quantity of plants and factories involved in all this industrial production were concentrated in Europe's cities, transforming them into industrial centers that offered employment to a great new wave of peasants from the countryside. For the first time the urban population gained a solid preponderance over the rural one in Europe as a whole, while at the same time the total population continued to increase, and the internal shift in population was more than matched by overseas emigration. All of these changes taken together created a new political situation, not merely on the Continent but throughout the western world. The emergence of heavy industry on the Continent and in North America challenged England's monopoly for the first time, and led to the establishment of high tariffs against British goods in Germany, France, and the United States. In all industrial countries workers began organizing for both union and political action, and politicians began to be concerned about the threat of worker uprisings if employment was slowed – by foreign competition, lack of raw materials, or failure to find markets for the continued outpouring of manufactured goods. This concern led rapidly to a growing European interest in the non-industrial world as a source of materials and markets, as well as a new interest in founding colonies that could relieve the pressure of Europe's exploding population and the threat of worker discontent.

By the end of the nineteenth century most of the elements of our late twentieth-century world were already in place, at least in embryo form, and even if we today would have found its way of life quaint and uncomfortable, we would still have recognized it as unmistakably related to our own.

GERMANY AND FRANCE

Bismarck

After Bismarck had crushed Napoleon III in the Franco-Prussian War and proclaimed the German Empire, he turned his attention to consolidating his position as chancellor of the new German state and ensuring its preponderance in Europe. He carefully contrived the new constitution to leave all ultimate authority in the hands of the emperor and his chancellor, but he still had to contend with political opposition, notably from Germany's Catholics and socialists.

In 1870 Pope Pius IX had convened the first general council of the Catholic Church since the Council of Trent three centuries before. Its purpose was to reaffirm Catholic support for traditional values and the authority of the Church, especially as wielded by the pope. To dramatize this position the new council promulgated the doctrine of Papal Infallibility, which declared that official statements by the pope on questions of faith and morals were infallible. This doctrine was passionately opposed by a minority of the Vatican Council, and it also provoked vigorous reaction from a number of European states that had formal relations with the Vatican, including the German Empire, where a Catholic party in the new Reichstag (parliament) opposed Bismarck's policies. Bismarck used the pope's assertion of authority as an excuse to curb the privileges of the Catholic Church in Germany and to extend state control over its operations. This campaign continued in full force until 1878, when Bismarck began looking for allies against those he took to be a greater threat, the socialists.

In 1878 a socialist congress was held at the German city of Gotha to found a "Socialist Workers' Party." In spite of the fact that this organization turned away from its Marxist and revolutionary origins to adopt a reformist political program, Bismarck took it as a dangerous challenge to the state, and made its suppression a principal issue of the Reichstag elections of 1878. Although he succeeded in passing legislation that outlawed most socialist activity, the Reichstag refused to curb the speech or activities of its own deputies. Finally by 1883 Bismarck felt secure enough from the threat of rebellion by the workers to initiate a program of insurance for them which effectively attached them to the state that provided such handsome benefits. This policy was eventually to serve as a model and standard for the entire European world.

At about the same time (1879) Bismarck initiated another major shift of policy by introducing a protective tariff. Probably his basic motive was need for money to support his rapidly expanding state functions, since tariffs were still the chief source of government revenue. The bill had the added advantage, however, of commanding the support of both the East Prussian estate owners and the Rhineland industrialists, since both groups were feeling the effect of overseas competition. With this added income, and backed up by the political support of these two powerful groups, Bismarck had now consolidated his position sufficiently within Germany to allow him to concentrate his attention on his favorite field, foreign policy.

In the treaty of 1871 that concluded the war with France, Bismarck had forced the cession of Alsace and part of Lorraine, and the payment of a huge indemnity. He assumed that the loss of territory would motivate the French toward a war of revenge, but he counted on the indemnity to weaken the country for some time. To his consternation, France had paid the entire sum by the middle of 1873; moreover the transfer of such a large sum seemed to depress the German economy and stimulate the French one. At this point Bismarck feared the French might be planning to attack, and he staged a war scare to bring international pressure against France to restrain her. Actually the French were horrified at the prospect of another war, and the whole tempest subsided, but Bismarck had launched a successful policy of isolating France. To this end he signed a treaty of alliance with the Dual Monarchy in 1879, then in 1881 arranged the "Alliance of the Three Emperors" between Germany, Austria, and Russia; and finally in 1882 he established the Triple Alliance with Austria and Italy. All of these alliances involved some degree of mutual defense against unprovoked attacks by another power; their net result was to base German policy on a close collaboration with Austria, and to prevent a clash between the Dual Monarchy and Russia that would involve Germany and thus offer France an opportunity to attack.

From the center of his diplomatic web, in Berlin, Bismarck seemed to be controlling the destinies of Europe. But it was a static system he had created, which failed to take into account the forces that were beginning to drive the European world in new directions. Perhaps most importantly, the center of political gravity in Europe was shifting from the plains of the north to the Mediterranean, which thanks to the Suez Canal was coming back to life.

The Turkish Empire

For some three centuries the Mediterranean had stagnated, with two-thirds of its shores encumbered with the disintegrating remains of the once powerful empire of the Ottoman Turks. Most of the North African harbors had become pirate nests, which until the early nineteenth century were tolerated by the European powers only because the Mediterranean was not worth a struggle. On the European mainland the Ottomans had reached the peak of their power in the seventeenth century, with the seige of Vienna, and after that they had been driven back to the Balkans. By the end of the eighteenth century they were losing the northern shores of the Black Sea to the Russians, and by the early nineteenth century the subject peoples of the Balkans were beginning to stir. The Greeks were the first to win independence from their Ottoman rulers, in 1829, thanks chiefly to their terrain, which protected them from massive land attack and gave them easy access to the sea and British support.

By this time the Turkish sultan had undertaken to reform his anachronistic army, but he was already being viewed as the "sick man of Europe," and the powers were positioning themselves to prevent a total collapse of the empire from putting Constantinople and control of its Straits in Russian hands. In the middle of the century Britain and France had shored up the staggering empire against Russian advances in the Crimean War (1854–6), but this was only a token effort compared to what was to come. The British were instinctively opposed to allowing the Russians any nearer India, but at this time the stakes in the Mediterranean area still had more to do with prestige than with critical material interests. Serious interest in maintaining control over the eastern Mediterranean awaited the opening of the Suez Canal in 1869.

Strange as it may seem, the construction of a canal between the Red Sea and the Mediterranean was undertaken not by any government but by a private company, based in France and headed by an entrepreneur named Ferdinand de Lesseps. While it was a very large feat of engineering, it was not a difficult one and could easily have been achieved before. That the British had not made the attempt was probably due to the fact that its usefulness would depend on the development of cheap, efficient steamboats, something that seemed inevitable but that would not actually take place until the 1880s. Once the canal was built, however, Britain immediately recognized its value, and when Egypt's spendthrift ruler offered to sell his shares in 1875, Britain's prime minister, Benjamin Disraeli, rushed to buy them for his government.

At about this same time uprisings against Turkish rule occurred in the Balkans. In spite of some Russian support the rebels were defeated, but in 1877 Russia officially declared war on Turkey in support of her fellow Slavs. Britain promptly warned Russia against any attempt to change the status of Constantinople, the Straits or the Canal. What the British had realized was that Suez was becoming their principal and essential route to India, and that even a modest naval force (such as Russia's) controlling the Straits of the Dardanelles would also effectively control access to the Canal. Thus when the Russians defeated the Turks, in 1878, and imposed a treaty largely liberating the Balkans from Turkish rule, Britain threatened to send its fleet to intervene, and an international Congress was quickly convened in Berlin. The terms of the treaty were modified, but the Turks lost all their European territory except for a narrow strip around Constantinople and the Straits. England then guaranteed the Ottomans continued control over their Asian provinces in return for the right to garrison Cyprus and to administer Egypt in a joint protectorate with France. The result was to give Britain a strategic base in the eastern Mediterranean, while the removal of the Ottomans from Europe left Russia and Austria as rivals for hegemony over the Balkans.

The joint British–French protectorate in Egypt was short-lived; in 1882 a nationalist uprising gave Britain an excuse to establish full control over the country. This action did not lead to a crisis, however, because the French were busy consolidating their own protectorate in Tunis (today Tunisia), which they had seized in 1881 from the remnants of the old imperial government just as Italy was about to move in that direction. To the Italians, who were in urgent need of finding an outlet for their excess population, the French offered Tripoli (now Libya) instead – a great desert which was hardly useful for their purposes. Further west, the French had already done their best to develop Algeria into a stable version of provincial France, at least in the fertile strip along the coast. Only Morocco was still independent, but it too, except for a small Spanish coastal enclave, would become a French protectorate in 1912.

The Third Republic in France

The full impact of the Suez Canal would not be felt until the European economy reached its next level of development in the 1880s. Meanwhile France was chiefly occupied in adjusting to the emergence of a unified and militarily superior German Empire. The first necessary step was to pay Bismarck's indemnity, an action which he ensured would take place by quartering troops of occupation in France until the payment was made. At the same time a new regime had to be established to replace the Second Empire which had collapsed with Napoleon's defeat. The National Assembly that was elected after the defeat was war-weary and conservative, and serious consideration was given to a restoration of the Bourbon monarchy. Ultimately the republicans triumphed, however, and in 1875 a constitution was passed that provided for a government based on a bicameral parliament. This Third Republic, as it was called, followed closely the lines of a revised constitution promulgated by Napoleon III in the spring of 1870, when he realized that his son was too young and weak to succeed him, and his wife too inflexible and unpopular to head a regency.

The first task of the new republic was to replace the totally discredited French armed forces with a new army, based like the Prussian one on universal conscription. It was this effort that alarmed Bismarck in 1875, but French intentions in rearming were purely defensive. Also in imitation of the Prussian military example, the French government undertook to reform and extend its system of public education, since it was generally thought that France owed its defeat to Prussia's schoolteachers as much as to her generals. This impression was created by the Prussian reserve officers, who came largely from the educated urban classes, and who did bring a new intellectual dimension into military affairs.

Another legacy from the upheavals of 1871 was the mass of those who had been arrested for participation in the commune and were still languishing in prisons or penal colonies. Although the general public had been terrified of this threat to law and order, the brutality of its repression was sufficiently troubling to the French conscience to bring the government by 1879 to a vote for amnesty and a repeal of anti-socialist legislation. This policy of liberalization did not go as far in France as it did even in conservative Germany, however, since there was still no attempt to deal with the grievances of the poor through a program of social legislation.

With the advent of the 1880s, France emerged from her post-war problems and undertook ambitious programs of building up the national transportation and education systems. Feeder rail lines were laid which brought every market town into communication with the rest of the nation, while the national school system was extended to make education universal, free, and compulsory to the age of thirteen. It was these developments, together with universal manhood suffrage and military service, that turned "peasants into Frenchmen," and thus completed the structure of the modern nation state.

The economic muscle that made this transformation possible was provided by France's share of the new Lorraine–Ruhr iron and steel complex. Although Germany owned more than half of its production, it still gave France a base of heavy industry that allowed her to produce capital equipment as well as consumer goods, finally pushing the country into the industrial age. Factories began to proliferate, and a genuine if still small urban working class, or "proletariat," began to form and play a role in French politics.

With its rail system complete and its own heavy industry in operation, France was beginning to develop a surprisingly self-sufficient national economy. As different segments of the population came to be involved in this economy, they voted for their interests in national elections. The first major example of such participation in politics was the passage in 1892 of the Méline Tariff, which established high protection for agricultural products and most manufactured goods – thus shielding France's still inefficient peasant farms and small factories from their much larger English or German competitors. This alliance between industry and agriculture was to dominate the politics of the Third Republic for half a century, thanks to the peasants' continuing electoral strength. The victims of this conservative policy were the factory workers, who had to pay high prices for peasant-grown food but still had too little leverage to negotiate comparable wages from their employers, especially since the protected industries were without pressure to compete and expand, and hence remained essentially stagnant.

The Dreyfus affair

On the surface, French politics of the 1880s and 1890s were dominated by challenges to the parliamentary government from both the right and the left. "Monarchists," mostly country gentry, hated the Republic because it had devalued their pretensions, while provincial (Jacobin) republicans, as well as socialists and Bonapartists, all despised the parliamentary government which they saw as primarily serving business interests. While none of these factions constituted a serious threat to the regime, they succeeded in seizing national attention by combining their forces around a political adventurer and former general named Boulanger. In 1889 Boulanger won election to the Chamber from Paris, but he failed to fulfill the hopes of his followers that he would stage a coup and proclaim a dictatorship. The plot became known, however, and when the government attempted to try him for treason he fled to Brussels and finally committed suicide.

A far more serious crisis to shake the early Republic was the political battle that developed around the Dreyfus affair. In 1894 the French secret service turned up hard evidence that critical military documents were being delivered to the German embassy in Paris. Since the documents apparently came from the French general staff, the culprit was sought among that body, and on the basis of strong similarity of handwriting, a Captain Dreyfus was accused, convicted, and sentenced to life in a penal colony. From the start the case attracted considerable attention, and it was widely noted that the captain was the first Jew to serve on the general staff. In 1896 an intelligence officer, Colonel Picquart, discovered that the incriminating handwriting was actually a forgery, and that the real culprit was a disreputable major named Esterhazy. In an attempt to prevent a scandal, the army promptly sent Picquart to serve in North Africa and exonerated Esterhazy in an obviously rigged court martial. Instead of resolving the case, however, the army's obvious attempt to bury it turned it into a national crisis of conscience, and provoked the novelist Emile Zola to publish his still famous letter "J'accuse" in which he charged the army with the deliberate perversion of justice. The gathering storm of public emotion finally broke in a fury, dividing most of France and much of the western world between those who would sacrifice an individual to the safety of the state (in the form of the authority and reputation of the army) and those who put justice first. Dreyfus was tried again by another military court, which attempted to avoid complete retraction of the original verdict by finding him guilty, but with "extenuating circumstances." By this time no one believed the army, however, and in 1899 Dreyfus was pardoned by the president; in 1906 he was finally given a fair trial, cleared of all charges, and returned to the army with the higher rank of major.

Anti-Semitism

Why the army acted as it did has never been fully explained, nor why the affair provoked such vigorous public reaction on both sides of the debate. Certainly one important element in the wave of feeling that arose was the issue of anti-Semitism. Jews had always suffered disabilities in the Christian west, but in France these had been largely eliminated by Napoleon, and his lead had been followed in much of the rest of Europe west of Russia. In the spirit of the Enlightenment some Jews began to shift their allegiance from their own religious and ethnic group to the new nation states, and they came to play increasingly important roles in the urban society that was taking shape in Europe. In this they were clearly aided by their traditional commitment to literacy and education, as well as by the fact that they had long been city-dwellers in a Europe that generally forbade them to own land. Their facility in adapting to the new urban conditions of the nineteenth century certainly created envy and distrust in others, but this can be only a partial explanation of a particularly virulent new strain of anti-Semitism which gained momentum in the European world in the late nineteenth and early twentieth centuries. In a sense the Dreyfus affair announced the onset of this plague, and it was read as a warning against assimilation by a number of far-sighted Jews, some of whom now began turning to Zionism as their only hope of escaping persecution by their Christian neighbors.

Although passions in France were aroused by the Dreyfus case, the affair only indirectly affected electoral politics. Instead, the critical political confrontation of the 1890s was over the imposition of a graduated income tax, which was voted by the lower house of the parliament in 1895 and promptly defeated by the senate. This division raised the constitutional question of whether or not the upper house could force the dissolution of a ministry; in this case the moderate cabinet that was behind the tax proposal finally decided it could not withstand the combined forces of wealth and property, and resigned. The result was the abandonment of the program of social reform that was to have been financed by the income tax – one that would have paralleled Bismarck's social legislation, and with the same purpose of reducing class conflict. Frustrated on that front, the leftists shifted their attack to the army – an easy target after the Dreyfus affair – and the Church, which had supported the army against Dreyfus and thus aroused a new wave of anti-clericalism on the left.

ITALY AND EASTERN EUROPE

Italy

While France and Germany were developing their new heavy industry and consolidating the organization of their nation states, the Italians were attempting to establish a government on a peninsula that had no important deposits of coal or iron and therefore no base for heavy industry. They managed to import enough coal and iron to expand their rail network and develop a major cargo fleet, but they had serious difficulty in producing goods to pay for their essential imports. This basic weakness of their economy was compounded by the difficulties of communication between the north – Piedmont plus the former Habsburg territories, and the south – the former Bourbon kingdom of Naples. While the economy of the north was relatively modernized, with commercial farming in the Po valley and labor-intensive industry in the cities, the south languished in desperate poverty, with its growing population rapidly exceeding the limits of its subsistence agriculture. There seemed to be no remedy for the situation in the south except the palliative of finding some outlet for emigration.

From the beginning the unified Italian nation state was a shaky institution in which nationalist ambitions rather than social and economic development were put forth as political goals. These included the occupation of Rome as the national capital (in 1870) and demands for contested border areas in the north and colonies overseas. The government was a constitutional monarchy in form, but it had a narrow electoral base that excluded the poor. Like the French government, it was chiefly occupied at this time in creating a Prussian-style army based on universal service; it also voted for social legislation and the establishment of a system of public education, but these measures were not effectively implemented because of lack of funds.

Nationalism in the Austrian Empire

North of the Alps, the Habsburg regime was trying to turn the Dual Monarchy of Austria and Hungary into a viable institution. In the aftermath of their defeat by Prussia (in 1866), the Habsburgs had granted the Hungarians nearly full autonomy. The Habsburg emperor Franz Joseph remained as a somewhat limited constitutional ruler of both Austria and Hungary, and the two realms were also joined in a customs union and shared common ministries of Foreign Affairs, War, and Finance. All matters of local government, however, were left to the two separate parliaments that met in Vienna and Budapest.

Given the intense nationalism that had infused virtually all European politics since 1848, it is perhaps surprising that the Habsburg lands did not disintegrate into a welter of ethnic enclaves. Hungary, however, was held together by the vigorous grasp of the Magyar landowners, who controlled the parliamentary government through Hungary's very limited suffrage and who refused to grant any rights to the Romanians, Slovaks, Croats, and various southern Slavs who lived within their boundaries. With the economy still largely agricultural, and half the farmland in vast Magyar estates, this repressive policy worked.

In the Austrian kingdom the emperor tried a more liberal approach, with a constitution that provided for a wide suffrage base and relative freedom of political action. This satisfied the German majority and many of the minorities, but not the Czechs, who wanted the same autonomy for their province of Bohemia as that granted to the Hungarians. Franz Joseph tried to comply with the Czech demand but met such implacable resistance from both the Austrian Germans and the Magyars that he ended by giving the Czechs special rights only in their local government (particularly the right to use the Czech language).

Although the Czechs maintained a vigorous opposition to their position in the Austrian monarchy, the other minorities included in it – Ruthenes, Poles, and various groups of Slavs – more or less acquiesced in their status. The Austrian constitution provided for broad (eventually universal manhood) representation in a bicameral parliament that operated with considerable freedom, even though the emperor had the final authority, with the right to rule by decree when the parliament was not in session. The various ethnic groups were represented in the parliament, but none of their delegations was large enough to impose its particular demands on the rest. Instead, policy was influenced primarily by two conventional parties, the Christian Socialists and the Social Democrats. Both favored social legislation and neither had revolutionary intentions, but the Christian Socialists were responsible for injecting an ugly anti-Semitism into their campaigns.

During the last two decades of the century the Dual Monarchy developed a base of heavy industry in Bohemia. With this almost unlimited source of cheap iron and steel it was possible to fill in the rail system that created a single well-balanced and highly productive economy within the customs union of the Habsburg lands. While Hungary remained largely agricultural, with only some light industry such as textiles, Austria produced coal, iron, heavy machinery and an advanced communications system. Ultimately this economy would enable Austria to build up a Prussian-style army that would mobilize the military manpower of the entire Dual Monarchy. As the capital of Austria, Vienna benefited enormously from this rapid economic expansion. The city suddenly grew far beyond its traditional bounds, providing employment for a flood of immigrants that poured in, especially from the east, and the character of the city was completely transformed from that of the residential seat of a feudal empire to that of the administrative and financial center of a new multinational state. This economic and military consolidation of the Dual Monarchy produced a powerful governmental unit, but at the cost of imposing a master language (German or Magyar) on the subject minorities – something which had not been necessary in the old feudal affiliation of nationalities under the Habsburg emperor. Ultimately the multilingual nature of the Dual Monarchy would subject its social structure to what would prove to be fatal strains.

The growth of Russia

To the north and east of the Habsburg territories stretched the vast reaches of the Russian Empire. Less touched by the French Revolution than the rest of Europe, Russia had not followed the pattern of political and social protest that led to 1848. In the final quarter of the nineteenth century, however, it was beginning to respond to some of the influences affecting the rest of the Continent – including the movements for social and political reform, the intensification of nationalism, and the development of modern industry and a national economy.

Without question the greatest single social reform accomplished in Russia during the nineteenth century was the liberation of the serfs by Alexander II in 1861. While there had been a gradual awakening in some circles to the injustice and inefficiency of serfdom, Alexander's decision to act was precipitated by the failure of Russian troops in the Crimean War to measure up to their better-educated and more advanced opponents. This consideration was reinforced by the unsuitability of serf labor for Russia's expanding commercial agriculture, particularly in the Ukraine, which was increasingly supplying Europe's growing cities with grain.

The liberation, however, meant more than social and economic reform; it involved the complete reconstitution of local government. To a significant degree serfdom had been the product of an imperial decision to make the landowning nobility responsible for the collection of taxes and the preservation of law and order on their estates. Freeing the serfs from their masters also meant depriving them of the administrative and judicial framework of their lives. To replace these functions the government turned to the traditional village organization (the *mir*), which was made responsible for collecting not only the taxes due to the national government but also the rents which the peasants now owed to the nobles for the land they received under the terms of the liberation. In addition, local councils (or *zemstvos*), elected by most of the adult males, were to collect local taxes and use them to maintain roads, schools and other public services. While this arrangement gave the peasants a voice in their own affairs, and a new sense of personal dignity, it also left them almost as closely bound by the authority of the *mir* and *zemstvos* as they had been to that of the nobles. (Not until 1906 was there a program to assist ambitious peasants to buy land and secure their economic independence.)

Although Russia did not experience the paroxysms of nationalism that had swept through Germany, Italy and the Habsburg Empire, it did respond to the stirrings of some of its ethnic minorities – notably the Poles, who revolted in 1863–4 – as well as to the aspirations of fellow Slavs still under Turkish rule in the Balkan peninsula. As in the western countries, nationalism in Russia was generated largely by the ambitions of the young, who aspired to careers or adventure; given the structure of Russian society (still far behind the west in urbanization), this meant primarily junior officers in the army. This tendency was probably reinforced by the transformation (in 1874) of Russia's traditional long-service military force into a modern organization based again on the Prussian model.

In 1877 the tsar used his new army with overwhelming success to support the rebellion of Slavic Christians against their Turkish rulers. In the treaty of San Stefano that followed, the Turks recognized an autonomous Bulgarian state that was to be sponsored by Russia. This undertaking by the tsar signaled the return of the government to an aggressive policy in the area of the Black Sea, especially since it followed a denunciation of the disarmament clauses of the treaty that had been dictated to Russia after her defeat in the Crimean War (1856), which forbade her to maintain coastal fortifications or armed ships in the region. Russia's move into Bulgaria alarmed the Dual Monarchy, however, and the emperor called for a great-power congress to meet in Berlin, to resolve what was rapidly developing into a serious conflict of interests. As a result of this congress Russia's gains were largely nullified; Bulgaria was divided into three parts by the powers, only one of which they recognized as an independent state, while another was returned to Turkish rule. Russia received some minor territories, but the British were the major beneficiaries of the conference, arranging with the sultan to guarantee his Asian provinces against Russian attack in exchange for the island of Cyprus, which they occupied. All of this left the Russian and Pan-Slav nationalists deeply frustrated.

Although Russia was developing into a modern nation state, her progress was slower than that of the western powers, chiefly because she lacked a national industrial economy, and particularly a mechanized system of communications. Railroad building was begun very early in Russia, but made little headway at first because of the huge distances involved, as well as the country's lack of capital and metallurgical production. By the 1880s, however, even though she still had little indigenous industry, Russia enjoyed a boom in rail building that was largely financed and supplied from the west. Just as in western Europe, the establishment of a rail system made coal fields accessible to cities and thus provided a basis for industrialization. Thus while Russia still lagged behind most of the rest of Europe in economic, political and social development, she was clearly on the same path.

THE SCRAMBLE FOR EMPIRE

The powers that emerged as dominant in the European world in the 1870s were all products of the industrial revolution to some degree. Only Great Britain, however, was fully industrialized at this time; the others were still more or less dependent on British capital and steel to build the growing rail systems that were integrating their political, economic, and military organization. In the 1880s and 1890s, the proliferation of heavy industry and new abundance of cheap steel brought this process of internal integration to new levels of intensity in the emergent nation states. The economic base of Europe was expanded and extended by completing rail systems with feeder lines, by developing consumer indus-

Canada

United
States

P A C I F I C

O C E A N

New Zealand

A T L A N T I C

O C E A N

Puerto Rico
(US)

Guiana

Br.

Dut.

Fr.

Sp.
Morocco

Morocco

Rio de Oro
(Sp.)

Gambia

Port. Guinea

French

West

Sierra Leone

Gold
Coast

Togoland
(Ger.)

Rio Muni
(Sp.)

German
S.W. Africa

Colonial Empires

British

Portuguese

French

MAP 5 *The colonial empires on the eve of the First World War*

tries, and by creating a huge new merchant marine. Although the participation of the various states in this transformation was most uneven, the process did create general problems which would affect all of them in different ways and measures.

Germany, France, the United States, and to a lesser extent Italy now began producing their own rails, and their own consumer goods, which were then distributed to their hinterlands by their feeder lines. The ultimate result would be largely self-sufficient national economies within which British goods would face shrinking markets. For a century, since the beginning of the industrial revolution, the British had never had to worry about markets, except briefly during the heyday of Napoleon's Continental blockade. All of Europe that was accessible to rail or water transport was open to and eager for their goods. Now suddenly that market began to close. But the British also had the oceanic world to turn to, and they now did so with a new sense of urgency, because unlike the other powers Britain was in no sense self-sufficient, most critically in food for her rapidly growing population. She had to import not only her staple foods but also the raw materials to supply her factories that produced the exports to pay for her imports. As a result of her need for new trading partners, Britain now began looking with renewed interest at the concept of "empire," which had fallen into disrepute in the middle of the nineteenth century. The title of Empress of India, which was added to the others of Queen Victoria in 1876, was no mere idle flourish, but rather a signal of England's current economic and political status. For no matter how ethnically homogeneous or politically coherent, Britain was less a nation state in the Continental sense than the operating center of an oceanic trading empire upon which she now genuinely depended for survival.

As their own industrialization proceeded, the nation states of the Continent were also discovering that such progress produced problems along with wealth. At first the new industries provided sufficient employment for the rapidly growing urban population, but as the ranks of factory workers expanded the various governments became increasingly aware of the political threat posed by the potential for mass unemployment, of the kind that had led to the June Days of 1848 in Paris. They also came to recognize that an industrial economy – to a far greater extent than its commercial predecessor – could be sustained only by continued growth. Thus it required ever more raw materials and ever larger markets, but without providing equal growth in the demand for labor, because of its increasing efficiency. One response to these problems was to ensure that the home country would remain a market for its own products by imposing high tariffs; this was done by all five of the Continental powers, and the United States as well, at the end of the 1880s or early 1890s. The other principal reaction was to look to the preindustrial world for markets, sources of raw materials, or territory that could absorb surplus – that is, unemployable – population.

It was the combination of these drives with revolutionary new techniques of marine construction and propulsion that brought the industrial powers (including Great Britain, the United States, and Japan) into the relationship with the non-industrialized world that is generally referred to by the term imperialism. In previous eras of expansion the European powers had established colonies in the New World, but in Asia and Africa they had tended to remain in the ports and trading posts on the coast. With this new phase, however, European adventurers, traders and troops – often accompanied by Christian missionaries – began to move inland from these coastal footholds, staking claims for territory or influence in an endless variety of ways. This expansion began as a tentative probing by European powers of the new possibilities of profiting from their industrialization; it turned into a headlong rush for political and military control when the powers began competing with each other for territory.

Africa

That this late nineteenth-century rush for empire began in Africa seems to be quite accidental. In 1870 there were only two European settlements on the African continent which extended from the coast into the interior, and clearly neither of them had previously been viewed as a base for territorial expansion. The Cape Colony, on the southern tip of the continent, had originally been established by Dutch settlers, but was ceded to Britain by the Congress of Vienna in 1814 to serve as a way-station on the route to India. The other European colony was Algeria, on the North

African coast, which had been occupied by the French in their effort to clean out a pirate's nest there in 1830.

In their new Cape Colony the British found a deeply entrenched population of "Boers" (Dutch for "farmers") – descendants of the Dutch settlers of the seventeenth century – who were unalterably committed to a fundamentalist Christianity and not prepared to accept British interference in what they considered their God-given way of life, including their practice of subjecting their black neighbors to forced labor. When Great Britain outlawed slavery in 1833, the Boers organized a mass migration to the north, where they established two independent states (1835–7), which the British could never decide either to recognize or to try to control. At best relations between the British and the Boers were uneasy and at worst they flared into sporadic armed clashes. A showdown finally became inevitable when diamonds were discovered in the colony in 1871, and gold in 1886. Hordes of prospectors and speculators were attracted to the region from all corners of Europe, and a contest developed between the Boers and British over whether or not the new immigrants were to be granted political rights and power. Ultimately the struggle led to a bitter, bloody war (1899–1902), which the British finally won. A long effort at reconstruction finally produced the Union of South Africa (1910), in which the rights of all white settlers were equally protected.

The story of the French in Algeria was very different. Their original attack on the pirate port and city of Algiers in 1830 had been a success, but their attempt to maintain a continuing military presence in the area thereafter had met with violent resistance from Algeria's native Berbers and Arabs, who fought a classic guerrilla war against the foreigners, staging intermittent raids and ambushes which were followed by swift retreats into the desert or across neighboring borders. This resistance was largely brought under control by the Second Empire, but the defeat of Napoleon in the Franco-Prussian War shattered French prestige and invited the rebels back to the attack. By this time (1870), however, there was a substantial European population (as much Spanish and Italian as French) along the Algerian coastal plain, which the new French Third Republic decided to recognize as an "extension of France" across the Mediterranean. To provide effective protection to the settlers the Republic discovered it would have to prevent Tunis and Morocco from providing safe havens for the rebels and serving as bases for the resistance; as a result French policy in North Africa came to be oriented toward the establishment of "protectorates" (i.e. military control) over these two neighboring states.

Originally Britain's problems in the south of Africa and those of the French in the north had no relation to one another, and the two European nations would probably have remained separated in Africa by the enormous land mass on whose periphery they impinged if it had not been for still another development at another extremity of that continent. When the construction of the Suez Canal was first undertaken by the French, the British had manifested more concern for the naval threat it might offer to their Indian interests than appreciation of its potential for increasing their Indian trade. In part, at least, this was because the world's ocean shipping was still predominantly propelled by sail, which was not suited to the Suez route. By 1875, however, when the bankrupt khedive of Egypt was forced to sell his shares in the canal, its potential was more obvious, and Britain's prime minister, Disraeli, promptly bought the lot for his government. This transaction did not make the Egyptian ruler solvent, and the principal European powers now seized upon his financial weakness as an excuse to establish control over his government and thereby the canal. Originally this control took the form of a commission – under a British and a French controller – to oversee the finances of the khedive. Egyptian popular reaction against this foreign intervention eventually led to open hostilities against the commission, however, at which point the French withdrew from the enterprise. The British now seized this opportunity to mount a military expedition against Egypt which occupied Cairo, took over the canal, and eventually took command of the Egyptian army; thus by 1883 Egypt had become a British colony in everything but name.

Although it was a French company that had built the Suez Canal, the British had a far greater interest in controlling it because of their increasingly vital involvement with India and trading partners farther east. French interests lay in the other direction, and the French withdrawal from Egypt was motivated chiefly by a desire to take advantage of the distraction provided by the crisis to establish themselves in Tunis – a move that had been generally opposed by the other powers. With the British busy in Egypt the French were now able to occupy Tunis, and despite continuing local resistance they gradually extended their control to most of northwest Africa, from Tunis through Morocco, and southward across the Sahara to their holdings on the African west coast. By 1914 this vast area would appear on European maps as French West Africa.

Meanwhile the Italians were actively seeking overseas territory on which to settle some of their excess population, and Tunis – the nearest point to Italy on the North African coast – was clearly their first choice. They did not dare to challenge the French, however, and turned instead to the African shore of the Red Sea, where they established colonies in the desert outposts of Eritrea and Somaliland as a base from which they hoped to conquer Abyssinia (Ethiopia). That ancient and impoverished kingdom was located on a mountainous plateau that had remained isolated by its inaccessibility and visited by few Europeans; nevertheless it seemed to offer the would-be conquerors some relatively fertile land and the prestige of an easily acquired "empire." When they launched their projected invasion, however, the Italians were promptly met and defeated by a larger army under the Ethiopian emperor Menelik, who – though unknown to Europeans – was himself a formidable conqueror who had just doubled the size of his realm by providing his troops with modern rifles purchased from French arms dealers. Deeply humiliated by this unprecedented native victory, the Italians finally settled for a protectorate over Libya (1912) – a worthless piece of desert between Tunis and Egypt which would do little to alleviate either their overpopulation or their appetite for prestige. (In 1935, long after the other European nations had lost interest in such ventures, Mussolini would dispatch Italy's armies to Ethiopia again in order to avenge their old defeat. This time the invaders would have planes and bombs while the defenders were still relying on Menelik's original imported firearms, with the result that there was no contest, and the Italians would occupy the country for several years until ousted by the Allies during the Second World War.)

While Britain and France were focusing their chief interest on Africa's northern and southern coasts, the two nations were also staking out competing spheres of influence in West Africa, based upon coastal settlements they had established there in the era of the slave trade. Gradually European control was expanded into Africa's vast interior as the great rivers were followed up from the coast, first by explorers and missionaries, then by government military expeditions. The French moved inland from their bases in Senegal, Guinea and the Ivory Coast, while the British laid claim to large territories lying inland from the Gold Coast and the mouth of the Niger River, finally establishing the large colony and protectorate of Nigeria in 1914. In the 1890s the British also moved toward the interior from Egypt, with their decision to establish control over the kingdom of the Sudan, located directly south of Egypt on the Nile River. This move was prompted by a Sudanese revolt against Egyptian hegemony, which at first the British accepted; they soon reversed this policy, however, when they found evidence of a considerable slave trade through the Sudan, and began to fear that France would use this as an excuse to seize the area. Mounting a major expedition into the Sudan, the British took it in 1898, which was in fact barely in time to prevent its conquest by a French expedition that had been dispatched there from West Africa. Having penetrated southward to the upper Nile and northward from Cape Colony through the establishment of Rhodesia and the conquest of the Boer territories, the British had thus nearly fulfilled the dream of the South African imperialist Cecil Rhodes that the British presence in Africa should extend from "the Cape to Cairo."

Finally, and purely for reasons of prestige, the Germans entered the competition in the mid-1880s with claims to three areas that had been neglected by the British and French: a piece of the equatorial west coast, the desert region of Southwest Africa, and a highland region of East Africa on the shore of the Indian Ocean. These acquisitions, taken together with the old Portuguese colonies of Angola and Mozambique, meant that all of Africa's coastal territory was now under the control of European nations with the exception of the tiny republic of Liberia, on the west coast, which had been established by American abolitionists under the mistaken impression that it would serve as a homeland for freed American slaves. All of the interior of Africa had been at least officially claimed by European governments as well, except for independent Abyssinia and the great interior of the Congo valley, at the heart of the continent. This latter oversight provided an opportunity that was seized by Belgium's King Leopold II, an enterprising promoter and speculator who had invested part of his personal fortune in this region. In 1878 he set up an "International Association of the Congo" to administer the territory – officially to assure free navigation of the Niger and Congo rivers, and to bring an end to slavery and the Arab slave trade that still operated across central Africa. In fact the association was a private company, under the personal authority of Leopold, that had as its only purpose the ruthless economic exploitation of the territory and its inhabitants. As the abuses of his rule were exposed and condemned in Europe, Leopold finally responded by transferring administration of the Congo to the Belgian government, a process that was completed in 1908, when the territory was given the name of the Belgian Congo. For practical purposes all of Africa had now been partitioned among the European powers, a process that had been completed in about two decades.

India

During the same period a wholly different but comparable development was taking place in Asia. This huge land mass had been the object of European colonizing efforts since the arrival of the Portuguese in the Indian Ocean at the end of the fifteenth century. Originally these took the form of securing, by force or treaty, trading ports from which the traditional luxuries of spices and silks could be shipped to Europe. In this trade the Portuguese were the European pioneers, but they were soon joined and challenged by the English, French, and Dutch. For the most part, the Asian shores they touched were densely populated and did not invite either conquest or settlement. Nevertheless European imperialism made inroads where it could, notably in Indonesia, where the Dutch established extensive colonies, and in India, where the French and British fought for control in the middle of the eighteenth century. Having expelled the French from India in 1763, the British found themselves protecting friendly local rulers from hostile neighbors, and in the process occupying territories that produced rents and revenues. By this means the nature of the British enterprise in India was gradually transformed from luxury trade to a governmental administration that was progressively extended in varying degrees to the entire subcontinent.

Although the British finally controlled a huge expanse of territory in India, this possession never provided space for the settlement of significant numbers of emigrants. Great Britain did maintain a large number of civil servants in India, as well as a smaller body of military personnel, but few of these became permanent residents and their number was never more than a fraction of a percent of the total population.

In the middle of the nineteenth century the Indian Mutiny nearly destroyed the imperial regime. When the British had finally reestablished firm control, the government in London took a number of steps to make their administration more organized and efficient. One indirect result of this reform was the improvement of internal communications in India, including the building of railroads (first begun in 1853) and telegraph lines. This step was to have an enormous impact on a country with hundreds of ethnic groups, and almost as many languages, which had never before been unified under one government. The first effect was to streamline British administration, but it also had increasingly significant economic consequences. British industrial products, especially cheap textiles, had found an outlet in Indian ports from the beginning of their export, but the opening of the Suez Canal route, combined with the building of railroads into the Indian interior, turned India into a truly major market for British industry late in the nineteenth century.

China

This demonstrated potential of a densely populated Asian country as an outlet for manufactured goods was not lost on any of the industrial powers. China, of course, remained by far the most important untapped market. Although known to Europe since the Middle Ages, China had carefully controlled the access of European traders and missionaries to the country, and at the beginning of the nineteenth century virtually excluded them. This policy was based primarily on a conviction of superiority; for the Chinese rulers the West had nothing of interest to offer, either commercially or culturally, and they saw no reason to permit contacts that would therefore be of benefit only to the foreigners.

The first direct challenge to China's isolation was mounted by the British in the shameful Opium War (1841–2), in which Britain's colonial forces were sent into China to protect their profitable sales of opium to the Chinese against attempts by the Chinese government to stamp out this drug traffic. Britain's victory exposed the administrative and military weakness of China's imperial regime, and resulted in the first of many concessions that would be seized by European nations from the tottering Manchu dynasty. In the treaty that concluded the war, Britain gained possession of the port city of Hong Kong, as well as the right to trade in five other major Chinese ports. This defeat of the Manchu regime by the foreigners gave encouragement to a revolutionary movement that was taking shape within China. In 1850 a massive peasant uprising (known as the T'ai P'ing rebellion) took place; it was not fully suppressed until fourteen years later. It succeeded not only in throwing off the established administration but also in seizing and redistributing land. Although the revolt eventually collapsed, it further weakened the empire and also advertised its sorry condition to the West.

During this same period the British fought three wars with India's eastern neighbor Burma (1824–6, 1852–3, and 1885), which finally reduced that country to the status of a British Crown Colony. Moving farther east, Britain also sent a squadron to Siam (1855) to persuade that country to open its ports to British trade; the commercial treaty that resulted was followed by similar Siamese agreements with the other principal European powers.

It was the French who made the next move in this eastward progression of European imperialism, going beyond Britain's sphere of influence to the still independent states of southeast Asia. In 1858 the French fleet was sent to the empire of Annam, roughly today's Vietnam, ostensibly to put an end to the persecution of European missionaries. Taking the port of Saigon, they forced the emperor to cede three southern provinces to France, thus initiating a process which would bring all of Indochina under French control by the end of the nineteenth century.

With their new possessions in the Far East, Britain and France were now in a position to make greater demands on China's government, which was still struggling to contain the T'ai P'ing rebellion. First the westerners used the confusion to gain special rights for their traders and missionaries, then in 1863 the British simply took over the administration of foreign trade in China, setting up a customs service that supervised not only the collection of customs but also the dispersal of the proceeds in the maintenance of ports and waterways. At this time Russia joined the list of foreign nations eager to gain from China's weakness, and in 1861 was formally ceded China's maritime province on the northern shore of the Sea of Japan; on the southern tip of this territory the Russians would build Vladivostok, their first major Pacific port.

During the next three decades, western influence and activity increased in China, provoking popular resentment and violence, but also motivating some feeble efforts by the government at reform and modernization. The first rail line was not built until 1888, and although unimportant in itself it was followed by the opening of coal and iron mines and the construction of a steel mill to make further rail development possible. In the mean time, however, China was faced by yet another foreign adversary, when Japan challenged China's traditional hegemony over Korea. In 1876 the Japanese began by formally recognizing Korea's independence and opening direct diplomatic relations with her government, while also sending troops to reinforce it against the Chinese. In 1885 China and Japan agreed to a mutual withdrawal of troops from Korea, but in 1894, when a nationalist Korean revolt threatened their interests, the Japanese replaced the existing government with a puppet regime, and fired on a Chinese troopship bringing reinforcements. With this excuse, and with every prospect of success, Japan now openly declared war on China. In a few months the Japanese destroyed the Chinese army and navy; in the Treaty of Shimonoseki that concluded the débâcle China formally recognized the independence of Korea and gave Japan the island of Formosa, the Pescadores Island, and the Liaotung Peninsula, as well as a large indemnity.

This war of Japanese aggression and conquest had an enormous impact both on China and on the western imperialist powers. It finally shocked the Chinese into a full understanding of their helpless inferiority in the modern world, while Japan's unabashed seizure of territory stimulated the interested European powers to step up their own scramble for concessions from the fallen giant. Russia had an interest in the Liaotung Peninsula as a possible eastern terminal of its Trans-Siberian railroad, which was then under construction, and Germany was ready to support Russia's intervention in order to gain backing for her own project of occupying Tsingtao on Kiaochow Bay. Ultimately the German government extracted a 99-year lease on Tsingtao with rights to develop its resources, while Russia gained a lease of the southern Liaotung Peninsula, including Port Arthur, to use as the eastern terminal of her railroad. Not to be outdone in the Chinese arena, the British seized this opportunity to obtain rights in the Yangtze valley. All these and a number of other such exactions imposed on China provoked a violent reaction against the foreigners by the Chinese.

In 1889 the emperor attempted to inaugurate sweeping reforms aimed at making China able to stand up to foreign pressure, but the chief result of this program was a wave of anti-modern sentiment that was added to a traditional anti-foreign phobia. Finally this hatred of the foreigners and all they represented came to a head in the "Boxer Rebellion" of 1900, led by the dowager empress and a conservative faction at the court, who imprisoned the emperor and encouraged the formation of a nationalist military society called the Boxers (because it posed as an athletic club). The rebellion began with the murder of the German minister in Peking, and then took the form of a siege of all the European legations, which were barely rescued by an international military force. Outbursts elsewhere led to barbarities by both sides and ended in the deaths of about two hundred Europeans, most of them missionaries and other civilians. The European troops finally put down the Boxers in 1901, then forced the Manchu government to sign a treaty which established measures to protect foreigners and a huge indemnity to be paid over a period of 40 years by an independent customs service.

Russo–Japanese rivalry

Just before the Boxer crisis broke, the United States government had secured assurances from the concerned powers that each would maintain "open door" access to the others in its spheres of influence or control. Two of the concerned nation states, however, were not satisfied with general and equal access to the largest potential market in the world. Both Russia and Japan had specific, urgent, and conflicting ambitions in Manchuria and Korea. Russia alone of the great powers aimed at direct territorial conquest in China. Drawing on her European experience of the importance of warm-water ports, she was determined to seize Manchuria and Korea as the eastern end of her Trans-Siberian railway, while the Japanese intended to use these same areas for emigration and as a source of coal and iron. Thus the two powers were set on a collision course from which neither would swerve.

When it became clear, in 1904, that the Russians were consolidating their positions in Korea and Manchuria, the Japanese launched a surprise destroyer attack on Port Arthur which disabled Russia's eastern fleet. The ensuing war – which lasted a year and a half – was hardly an equal contest. The Japanese navy established its total superiority over Russia by annihilating her Baltic fleet when it finally made its appearance; but the decisive battle had already been fought on land, at the head of the Liaotung Peninsula, where the Russians were at the end of a 5,000-mile, single-track rail line and the Japanese were only a few hundred miles from their main bases. The treaty of peace restored Manchuria to China, but transferred Russia's lease on the Liaotung Peninsula to Japan, as well as recognizing Japan's hegemony over Korea and thus preparing the way for her outright annexation of that territory in 1910.

Among European nations the chief concern had previously been over Russia's threat to their balance of power in China; now Japan's victory raised for the first time a fear that a non-western nation might pose a threat to European hegemony in the Far East. This fear was still premature, however; Japan had defeated Russia not only because she had a modern military force, but more decisively because she had it at hand. The Russian army, even had it been thoroughly modernized, was dependent on the railroad for supplies, and could hardly have pushed the Japanese back to their waiting ships. Japan's victory was impressive, but she owed it as much to her geography as to her much advertised modernization.

What the Europeans should have recognized at this point – as the Japanese clearly did – was that Japan would never be a viable nation state until it controlled its own industrial resources, especially coal and iron, and that therefore the acquisition of these necessities by conquest would form the core of Japanese policy in the future.

US expansion

The final acquisition of territory by a modern power in this period occurred not in China, but off her southern coast in the Philippines, which the United States seized from Spain in 1898. This story began in the Caribbean in 1895, when the Cubans revolted against their Spanish rulers; the brutality of Spain's repression shocked Americans, and when an American warship (the Maine) was blown up in Havana harbor, the press coverage of the incident produced war fever in the United States. War was declared in 1898, and American victory followed swiftly. An American naval unit in the Pacific destroyed one Spanish squadron in Manila Bay, while other American ships blockaded Cuba and annihilated the main Spanish fleet off Santiago. Cut off from reinforcement, the Spanish land forces in Cuba were quickly defeated, and peace was made by Spain's cession to the United States of Puerto Rico, Guam and the Philippines, and its recognition of Cuban independence. Thus, although the United States had traditionally opposed all forms of colonialism (supposedly because of her own early experience), the Spanish–American War established her as an imperial power, and announced her intention of intervening in the affairs of her Latin neighbors when necessary.

At the same time (1897), the Hawaiian Islands were annexed by the United States after American settlers there had staged a coup against the native monarchy. Although the American government had not promoted this development, the incorporation of the islands in some way into the European world system at about this time was probably unavoidable. Since the early nineteenth century the French and British had been establishing colonial outposts in the myriad islands of the South Pacific, and by the 1880s the Germans and Americans had joined and intensified the game. This "opening of the Pacific" was stimulated by a number of factors, including the competition for concessions in China and the development of ports on the west coast of the United States. It was also during this period (1870–1900) that the world's cargo and naval shipping was gradually transformed from wooden sailing ships to steel and steam-propelled vessels which required frequent stops at coaling stations, and many of the islands seized by one or another power at this time were developed for this purpose. Finally, behind all the considerations influencing action in the Pacific lurked the assumption that it was only a matter of time – and not much of that – before the Isthmus of Panama would be pierced by a canal that would bring the Pacific into practical range of Atlantic commerce.

Emigration from Europe

One important motivation for imperial expansion in the late nineteenth century was to provide land for Europe's exploding population, and for that purpose most of Asia was unsuited because it was already densely populated. The western hemisphere had always been the principal haven for European emigrants, who came increasingly to the United States in the nineteenth century, while at the same time the British colonies of Canada, Australia and New Zealand also began to attract substantial numbers. The early overseas emigration to these territories had been largely British, but in the second half of the nineteenth century it included a growing contingent from the Continent – first Germans and Scandinavians, then Italians, and finally eastern Europeans. At first glance this massive transfer of population might not seem an integral part of the "scramble for empire," but it does come at exactly the same time and involves some of the same factors. If its driving force was the population explosion in Europe, it was made practical by the improvement and expansion of overseas transportation, together with the railroads that opened the interior of the host countries.

This phase of European expansion did not involve the acquisition of new territory, but consisted rather of a revived interest in more or less neglected possessions, as Europe's concern grew to find an outlet for its rapidly growing excess population. By mid-century Great Britain had established claim to four of the half-dozen or so best areas of emigration, but she had developed them

slowly, almost reluctantly. The first was Canada, which had originally been settled by the French in the seventeenth century, then
conquered by the British during the Seven Years War, after which
it was used as a refuge for displaced Loyalists at the end of the
American Revolution. No attempt was made to unite the several
separate Canadian colonies until 1840, and the first federal constitution was given to the country in 1867 with the British North
American Act, which also gave Canada the official status of a
self-governing dominion of Great Britain. It was not until the
early 1880s, however, that the Canadian government brought
the first transcontinental railroad into operation, for the first
time effectively integrating the western and eastern sections of the
country.

In parallel developments, two other self-governing British
Dominions were taking shape in the South Pacific. Australia, the
world's largest island or smallest continent, received its first British
settlers in 1788 in the form of convicts who established a penal
colony. Other shipments of convicts followed until the practice
was finally stopped in 1850 as the result of strenuous public
protest; by this time, however, the convicts were far outnumbered
by private settlers, whose immigration was accelerated by the
discovery of gold in 1851. New Zealand, made up of two islands
lying farther out in the South Pacific, was settled more slowly and
was not claimed by the British government until 1840. In 1852 it
was given a self-governing constitution, but the final step of colonial independence, the granting of dominion status, did not occur
until 1901 for Australia and 1907 for New Zealand. Finally the
other colony to be significantly settled by the British, the Union of
South Africa (the former Cape Colony), became Britain's fourth
self-governing dominion in 1910.

All four dominions were basically extensions of British civilization overseas, in spite of an important French minority in Canada
and a Boer one in South Africa. Further, they developed as extensions of Britain's economy, providing the mother country with
both markets and raw materials. As her rail lines pushed west,
Canada sent more and more wheat to Britain, while Australia and
New Zealand – best suited to herding – sent wool, and with the
advent of refrigerated shipping in 1882, meat and dairy products.

At this point, however, it is important to note that the United

States served Britain's colonial needs better than her own colonies throughout the nineteenth century. It was closer than the colonies, and its advanced and rapid economic growth meant that it was better able than the less developed regions to provide England with markets, food, and especially employment for emigrants. Just as industrialization had began in Great Britain, so too did the phenomenal growth of population that was brought about by industrialization in all of Europe in the nineteenth century; the result was a massive emigration from the British Isles, which poured into the United States in the first half of the century.

Indeed it was this immigration, followed by that from other parts of Europe, which permitted the opening of the American West, for to begin to realize the wealth of its land the United States needed a capable, motivated and fast-growing population. During the eighteenth century the British colonists had hardly settled the coastal plain, let alone crossed the Appalachians (except for raids and explorations). What was needed to develop and settle the country – and what occurred in the nineteenth century – was a large and sustained influx of immigrants, in conjunction with the development of transportation into the interior. At first canals proliferated, but the real impetus to westward movement was the railroad. By 1850 rail lines had connected the eastern slope of the Appalachians with the Mississippi River system, thus effectively opening the interior to intensive settlement for the first time. At about this time, too, the famine caused by a potato blight in northern Europe and Ireland, and the revolutions of 1848 in many parts of the Continent, greatly increased the already growing influx of Europeans into the United States. The flow abated slightly in the 1860s, recovered in the 1870s and then took another jump in the 1880s, coinciding with the new spurt of European imperialism. The final and largest outpouring of Europeans into the United States occurred between 1900 and 1914. Undoubtedly the greatest sustained, long-distance transfer of population in history, this exodus to the United States was the product of both the demographic revolution that more than doubled Europe's population, and the industrial revolution that created rail transport as well as mechanized production. It can properly, therefore, be considered a most important part of the expansion of Europe, which dominated its history in the final quarter of the nineteenth century.

THE OCEANIC POWERS: GREAT BRITAIN,
THE UNITED STATES AND JAPAN

Britain

While the five powers on the Continent were consolidating their political, military and industrial bases in the creation of new nation states, three other countries – England, the United States, and Japan – were responding to the same challenges in very different ways.

Although normally considered a European power, Britain was still effectively divided from the Continent by the Channel, which had stemmed the progress of the Napoleonic armies and to some extent the ideas of the Enlightenment as well. It had also contained the Continental conflagration of 1848, in part precisely because no significant segment of the British population – in spite of a widespread desire for reform – ever adopted the revolutionary agenda of 1789. In Britain there was no large body of unused talents and energies seeking an outlet in "careers open to talent," like that which added such force to the European revolutions of the nineteenth century: this was largely because the industrial revolution, in its indirect as well as direct efforts, provided previously unheard-of opportunities for advancement.

The movement for social reform in Britain led to modest advances that aided the prevention of widespread discontent. With the passage of the Second Reform Bill, in 1867, the suffrage was considerably extended for adult males, although there was no attempt to make it universal for them. In a parallel development, in 1870, an education bill provided public support for enough primary schools to bring basic education within the reach of most children, although Britain's public education system was not up to the best standards of the Continent. Finally in 1871 an army reform bill completely reorganized that service to bring it into line with the modern military establishments of Europe, with the striking difference that recruitment was wholly voluntary and the army small.

During this period, however, Britain easily maintained her industrial and financial preeminence in the European world. She supplied it not only with large quantities of consumer goods, especially textiles, but also with much of the heavy machinery, rails, and trains used by the Continent in its drive toward industrialization, not to mention the capital to pay for these imports. It was a system that contributed greatly to Britain's wealth for at least half a century, and benefited Europe as well, until it came to an abrupt end with the sudden development of heavy industry on the Continent in the 1880s.

When the major European countries crossed the threshold into full industrialization, they rapidly began to contend with English imports in their own national markets, and usually finding themselves at a disadvantage, turned sooner or later to protective tariffs. With the whole oceanic world open to them, the British were not critically threatened by this sudden narrowing of their Continental markets, but the trend clearly announced a radically new orientation of world trade. While the European powers were all still largely supplied with staple foods by their own peasant agriculture, Britain was almost wholly dependent for food on overseas imports, principally from the United States, Canada, Argentina, and Australia. This meant that the Continental states were more or less self-sufficient – with the major exception of Italy, which lacked coal and iron – while England most decidedly was not. In this sense, as well as in her lack of a conscript army, she did not qualify as a "nation state" comparable to the Continental model, but rather as the center of a vast oceanic empire in which her formal relations with the many parts ran the gamut from simple trading partner to sovereign ruler.

During the middle of the nineteenth century, Queen Victoria's government not only avoided European entanglements as far as possible, but also viewed England's colonial commitments with considerable skepticism. With the opening of the Suez Canal, however, English policy began to change. From an astonishing indifference to the construction of the Canal (1859–69), the government moved to purchase a controlling interest in the Canal Company in 1875, and then in 1878 vigorously supported the calling of the Congress of Berlin to keep Russia out of the eastern Mediterranean. The change of mood in England at this time was clearly indicated by the act of Parliament secured by the prime minister, Benjamin Disraeli) that conferred on Queen Victoria the additional title of Empress of India. With the reawakening of public interest in empire and the opening of the Mediterranean route to India and the Far East, England became concerned with the politics of the Balkans and the fate of the Ottoman Empire, especially Constantinople and its potential threat to the Suez route.

To reinforce these strategic interests as well as to maintain her presence in the world ocean, Britain had to convert her naval fleet from wood and sail to steel and steam. Notice of her vulnerability had been given her by Napoleon III's small but efficient modern fleet, the first of its kind, and she now began building her own version of a steam-powered, armored navy – only to find that other European powers, including Russia, were on the same course. This led by 1889 to the passage of a Naval Defence Act authorizing the maintenance of a fleet equal in strength to the combined forces of the two largest navies on the Continent. Without secure access to her empire for markets and supplies, England could not survive.

The United States

Finally there were two more countries currently in the process of becoming industrial powers, the United States and Japan. While the potential wealth and power of the United States was coming to be recognized in the 1870s, the Americans were only just beginning to realize this promise. The long and difficult period of "reconstruction" following the Civil War did not come to a formal end until 1877, with the official readmission of all rebel states into the Union, and their full integration into the life of the nation took longer. At the same time, however, the development of east–west communications progressed rapidly, with the first transcontinental rail line completed in 1869, to be followed by four more in the next two decades. This meant that the undeveloped half of the richest continent in the world was suddenly open to intensive settlement and exploitation. With the new rail lines providing transport, cattle raising and commercial farming expanded in the west and midwest on an unprecedented scale, while spectacular discoveries were made of deposits of gold, silver, and a range of lesser metals, principally in California. All of this provided a powerful stimulus for the emerging national economy, and for the new heavy industry that would combine Lake Superior iron ore and Pennsylvania coal to produce the steel rails and bridges, farm machines, and factories that would transform the United States into the greatest economic power in the world by the end of the century.

In some ways these developments in the United States could be compared with the national unification taking place in Germany. Although the areas involved were quite disparate, a similar role was played by rails in unifying the territory. It could even be said that sectional resistance to unification had had to be resolved by force in both countries. Here the resemblance ends, however, for the constitutions that organized the unification in the two cases were quite different, with the American being more democratic in every aspect. In the United States the suffrage base was technically nearly universal for males (although in fact the emancipated slaves in the South would be disenfranchised by intimidation), while the burden of the central government was far less in taxes and military service, neither of which would become obligatory until the First World War.

Finally it is necessary to consider the role of "nationalism" in the United States. While there was a strong sense of national identification among most Americans, it was not based on ethnic or linguistic distinctions as it was in Europe. With the exception of the native American populations, all Americans were immigrants, and at the end of the century, with the tide of immigration rising rapidly, there was a widely accepted understanding that all new arrivals became "American" by the voluntary act of arriving. Clearly the process of cultural assimilation had been easier in the early years of the nation, when most immigrants came from English-speaking countries, and troubles multiplied when the newcomers spoke other languages and had other ways; but whatever the difficulties and shameful lapses, the basic concept of nationality in the United States was that of a "new nation brought forth upon this continent," in Lincoln's words, in which peoples of all ethnic backgrounds would be united.

Japan

The last of the new industrialized nation states to make its appearance on the world stage was utterly improbable. Not only was it located on the opposite side of the globe from Europe but it had also vigorously resisted any contact with the industrial nations of the West. The first change in this policy came when an American naval squadron induced the Japanese government to establish diplomatic relations with the United States in 1853. The American motivation at the time was principally a desire to gain humane treatment for shipwrecked seamen, but commercial interests soon took advantage of this opening, which also inevitably led to Japanese contact with other seagoing nations.

The Japanese regime with which the westerners had to deal was an astonishing anachronism which had survived from the seventeenth century, thanks to Japan's insular isolation. Europeans saw it as an exotic form of feudalism, based in a rice economy, and managed by great landlords who were held in check by forced attendance at the court of a war-lord ruler (Shogun). The small rural gentry (samurai) managed the land and served as armed retainers of the lords, equipped with weapons that the Europeans found more appropriate to museums than to a field of battle. In theory this social system was presided over by a shadowy emperor, who was confined to a palace in the holy city of Kyoto.

The opening of Japan to outside contacts provoked a violent anti-foreign reaction in the country that divided the ruling classes and led to some armed clashes with ships from the British, French, Dutch, and American navies. Although these European naval forces were very limited, their technical superiority was so overwhelming that the Japanese were finally persuaded that the only way to defend themselves against the West was to adopt its methods. With the country in turmoil and the feudal regime incapable of resolving the crisis, a vigorous young emperor by the name of Mutsuhito came to the throne in 1867, took direct personal control of the government and launched an extraordinary program for the modernization of Japan. The resistance of the great lords collapsed, and their prerogatives in local government were transferred to prefects of a centrally administered system modeled on that of the French. At the same time a program of universal education was undertaken, and a year later universal military service was instituted as the base for a European-style army, trained originally by French, then German, officers. The navy, predictably, was organized along British lines. To support these developments the government guided and supported the development of industry; the critical fact was, however, that the country's deposits of coal and iron were meager, and these necessities would always have to be supplied from abroad.

Whatever their deficiencies as a modern power, the Japanese had no industrial rivals within the eastern hemisphere, and they also had nothing to learn from the West in the sphere of nationalism. Because of their long near-total isolation on their islands, they had become one of the most highly integrated societies of comparable size known to history. Thus when the emperor took genuine control of the country and undertook its modernization, there was a minimum of open resistance to him, and in two decades he was able single-handedly to transform the government from a feudal system to a parliamentary regime based on European models. The first constitution granted by the emperor provided for two deliberative bodies whose members were appointed and whose powers were purely advisory, in a pattern that suggested Napoleon's Consulate. This government was rapidly liberalized, however, and the constitution of 1889 finally established a partially representative lower house based on limited suffrage, though decisive powers were still reserved for the emperor, much as in the German model on which it had been based.

INDUSTRIAL SOCIETY

The same factors that sent Europeans around the world in quest of empire at the end of the nineteenth century also served to transform European society at home. The establishment of a base of heavy industry in Europe and America, and the rapid acceleration of the production of cheap iron and steel, led not only to the extension of established institutions, such as railroads (which were now pushed into the remote corners of the hinterland), but also to the introduction and application of new techniques which were to affect nearly every aspect of modern life.

The new technology

Chemistry as the first laboratory science to be systematically exploited for industrial purposes, in the mass production of dyes, medicines, fertilizers, and explosives. Next, an efficient means of generating and transmitting electricity, developed in the 1880s, together with the perfection of a practical incandescent light bulb, made possible the widespread urban use of electricity for domestic and public illumination. At the same time a new electric motor was applied to a wide variety of uses; it gave new flexibility to many light industrial processes, and also made possible the creation of street railways, which proliferated through the cities of Europe in the 1890s, followed closely by subway systems in Paris and Berlin. As these extended the horizontal dimensions of urban development, the electric motor was also used to power elevators, which in turn, together with the use of structural iron or steel for building skeletons, would make possible the skyscraper. Although this spectacular form of building became an American specialty, the first iron structure of unusual height was the Eiffel Tower, built in Paris in 1889 to demonstrate the possibilities of this form of construction for the international exposition of that year.

Still another decisive innovation was the telephone, invented in 1876 and in limited but growing use in major cities by the 1890s. Together with the telegraph, which already linked most cities of the Continent (and crossed the Atlantic by oceanic cables), this development marked the start of our global system of instant communications.

It was also in the last decade of the nineteenth century that the first practical internal combustion engine was produced. Originally used in small boats, it was rapidly adapted to land use by numerous ingenious mechanics intent on building forerunners of our automobiles. By 1895 several experimental models were actually functioning, at least one of which would be put into limited production for sale. Even more astonishing, it was quickly recognized that the gasoline motor could fulfill a previously impossible dream by enabling a vehicle to fly in the air. Experiments with this application of the engine began almost as early as those adapting it to sea and land use, even if no single machine actually flew until 1903.

Urban civilization

The material changes that took place at the end of the nineteenth century, together with the rapid growth of the cities and the large shifts of population to the cities from the countryside, led to the emergence of a new urban way of life throughout the industrialized world. The inhabitants of the cities increasingly fell into new categories; except in a few industrial centers factory workers were usually outnumbered by the workers in endless small shops and unskilled occupations – that is, more were involved in supplying the wants of the city-dwellers as tradesmen and servants than in tending machines. In addition there was a dramatically growing segment of the population that worked in the offices of the new large enterprises – not only the industries but also the banks, commercial institutions, public utilities, and government agencies. All of these office functions required a secondary education, thus creating a demand for more schools and the expansion of the education system to include more than the small elite it had previously served. University facilities also had to grow in order to provide the managerial staff of this rapidly growing category of "white collar workers," as they came to be called. By the same token, ambitious, intelligent youth, if they could secure the necessary education, could usually find openings in the new occupations; thus the process created a new urban upper class of people who through work rather than inheritance were enabled to gain sufficient wealth to buy property and employ servants.

One result of this new selection procedure was that it enabled Jews to make their way in significant numbers into the expanding urban elite, through their traditional commitment to education and experience with urban occupations. Their assimilation into the society of the dominant group was accepted or resisted to a varying extent in different parts of Europe, but even where there was little overt opposition to their social rise there was often an underlying current of resentment and hostility, especially among the less successful, which was to have serious and eventually horrifying consequences. In the mean time, however, Jews were to contribute significantly to the development of urban culture.

By the end of the nineteenth century the new upper class had developed a characteristic style of living, which was similar but not identical in the cities of the Continent and those of Britain and America. Central to this way of life was the family, which served to educate the young and to accumulate and transmit property. On the Continent these affluent families normally lived in large and beautifully appointed urban apartments, while in Britain and

America they tended to prefer private houses in the suburbs; in either setting they were attended by domestic servants – at least one maid, and usually two or three. During the summer, if they could manage the expense, they vacationed in the mountains or on the seashore in summer hotels. Work, thrift, and achievement were all considered virtues. While some of this class became wealthy, most aimed at solid independence and comfortable prosperity; once this was established, the leisure it permitted was generally used to pursue the liberal professions, including the law, medicine, science and scholarship, journalism, politics, and arts and letters. The result was a series of remarkable developments in all of these fields.

It was in the disparate areas of painting and the sciences that the late nineteenth century saw the greatest achievements, which together would bring about a fundamental transformation of both the intellectual and aesthetic worlds that the educated westerner inhabited. In the 1860s even those who assimilated Darwin's shattering thesis could still think of the natural world as stable and comprehensible, and subject to eternal laws of cause and effect that could be discerned through diligent observation. In a similar vein, the visual arts at that time (along with literature) aimed at faithful representation of a reality which was confidently held to be sufficiently simple and unambiguous to be grasped by the senses and by common sense. But by the first decade of the twentieth century such assumptions about the bounds of both reality and art were no longer tenable. Scientists had learned of levels of existence that had previously been unseen and unsuspected, and that even defied rational understanding, while the arts reflected this new understanding of the complexity of man's inner and outer worlds, as well as radical new ideas about what art could be.

Impressionist painting

The extraordinary explosion of creativity in painting that took place in the last quarter of the nineteenth century was known as the Impressionist and Post-Impressionist movements. This artistic renaissance represented a revolutionary break with past tradition in painting, and opened the path that would lead eventually to the avant-garde abstract and expressionist art of the twentieth century. All but one of the leading painters in this movement were French (Van Gogh was born in Holland), and the phenomenon was originally part of a general flowering of culture that took place in Paris at this time. After the Franco-Prussian War and the Paris Commune clash were put behind it, this city had entered on a period of peace, prosperity and great vitality that was given the name of *la belle époque*; the gay and spirited life of the city in this period no doubt played a large part in inspiring the artistic out-pouring of the Impressionists, just as it served as an important subject of their work.

The romantic painters had forged a new path to some extent in admitting drama and movement, and even some experimental effects, to their canvases, but the Impressionists would turn their backs decisively on all of the conventions that were still held sacred by the powerful French Academy of Fine Arts: the smooth finish of photographic realism, subdued tones and dark back-grounds, formal and posed subjects, classical models and themes, symmetrical composition. The Impressionists were interested above all in light – the brilliant and changing effects of sunlight – and color as the creation of light. They also tried in their paintings to capture the immediate impression of a natural scene or spon-taneous human moment, and they focused on the everyday life around them rather than on exotic or idealized subjects. Technical innovations played an important part in this shift of artistic em-phasis, for it was only recent improvements in the manufacture of paints that made it truly practical for the artist to leave his studio and produce a whole painting on location.

The Impressionist movement also derived important aesthetic inspiration from Japanese prints, which – along with many other things Japanese – became widely known and admired in the West after the Japanese had "opened their doors" to Europeans in 1868. The most influential features of Japanese art were its bold asymmetry and use of empty space, as well as its flat, two-dimensional figures, seen as elements of design rather than objects of realistic portraiture.

Although all of the great painters of the late nineteenth century are sometimes called Impressionists, the title is more accurately reserved for the founders of the movement and those who adhered most closely to representational norms – Degas, Manet, Monet,

Pissarro, and Renoir. The later and more extreme innovators are then called the Post-Impressionists, a category which usually includes Cézanne, Gauguin, Seurat, Toulouse-Lautrec, and Van Gogh. In turning away ever more boldly from the tradition of reproducing visual reality, the Post-Impressionists focused increasingly not only on the expression of feeling and "inner" reality, but also on the painting as an object in itself, deriving its significance from pure color, texture and design. From this path there would finally be no turning back, and the twentieth century would see varieties of artistic expression in the West that would have been simply inconceivable only decades before.

Advances in Science

Meanwhile another, and in a way similar, revolution was taking place in man's understanding of reality itself, as a consequence of a gathering momentum of discovery in the sciences during the last decades of the nineteenth century – most importantly in the fields of physics and chemistry. Partly as a result of their work with electricity, scientists were able to learn that atoms were not the smallest particles of matter, as had been thought, but rather were composed of still smaller particles. Most of these subatomic particles were identified by the end of the century, though the solar model of atomic structure would not be formulated for another ten years. In the last decade of the nineteenth century the French chemists Pierre and Marie Curie made their important discovery that a few of the supposedly "immutable" elements were radioactive, meaning that they spontaneously discharged subatomic particles, thus changing themselves into other elements. In this process, moreover, considerable quantities of energy were released, a finding that suggested the startlingly new idea that matter and energy were not distinct but rather somehow interchangeable.

On the basis of these and related findings of the late nineteenth century (including the demonstration that the speed of light was constant), the German physicists Albert Einstein and Max Planck formulated the theories upon which all of twentieth-century physics would be based. Planck's quantum theory, published in 1900, set forth as an equation the discontinuous manner in which energy was exchanged between mass and radiation, while Einstein's first publication, in 1905, contained not only his "special theory of relativity" (dealing with all phenomena except gravity) but also his famous formula ($E=mc^2$) defining the relationship between mass and energy. Mass is only latent energy, he proposed, and the quantity of energy (E) contained within a given mass was enormously greater than the mass, being equivalent to the mass (m) times the square of the speed of light (c^2). This theory would be proved in the 1930s when it was found that splitting the nucleus of an atom would release this vast amount of energy – a finding that led in short order to the birth of both the atom bomb and the "nuclear age" in which mankind has lived uneasily ever since this awesome power came into his hands.

Less unsettling were the advances made in this period that led to the birth of modern medicine. It was not until the third quarter of the nineteenth century that biological research revealed the microscopic organisms (bacteria and viruses) that were responsible for causing infectious diseases, and the nature of the body's immunological defenses against these invaders. Armed with this understanding, scientists were then able to make rapid strides not only in discovering the particular organisms responsible for specific diseases but also in controlling diseases through preventive measures. Major contributions in this field were made by the French chemist Louis Pasteur, a pioneer in developing the process of vaccination, who gained fame particularly for producing a vaccine for rabies which could be effective even after the disease had been contracted, and for demonstrating the importance of sterilizing milk (in a process ever since called pasteurization) to prevent it from transmitting disease. The German biologist Robert Koch also advanced the science of immunology by discovering the bacteria responsible for the deadly scourges of tuberculosis and cholera. The American doctor Walter Reed found that the virus responsible for causing yellow fever was transmitted by the mosquito and thus could be controlled by eliminating the stagnant water where mosquitoes bred. Finally the English surgeon Joseph Lister observed that bacteria caused the often-fatal infections that followed wounds and surgery, and hence that such infections could be prevented and fought with simple antiseptic procedures; these were already understood, although the discovery of antibiotic drugs lay some decades in the future.

The publication of Sigmund Freud's *The Interpretation of Dreams* in 1900 signaled another revolution in thought that can be seen as a distant relative of the development of medical science. Freud's main theory of the reality of unconscious, mental life originated during his years as a medical student in Vienna. Experimenting with hypnosis as a therapy for mental illness, he found that it seemed to reveal a hidden level of the personality – a repository of powerful feelings and memories – of which the conscious mind was totally unaware. Further, in patients suffering from "hysteria" – a common disorder among Freud's patients, generally involving psychosomatic symptoms – he discovered that confronting the conscious person with what he had said under hypnosis could lead to spectacular cures. These findings led Freud to construct the theory that the mind protects itself from frighteningly painful and unacceptable feelings by "repressing" them – that is, banishing them from consciousness – but that this way of dealing with them paradoxically allows them to retain all of their original power to terrify, which can be dispelled if they are brought into the light of reason, accepted, and integrated into the conscious personality. The therapeutic process for Freud involved efforts of the conscious mind to penetrate the unconscious, not through passive yielding to hypnosis but through active self-analysis and the investigation of the meaning of feelings, associations and particularly dreams, which Freud regarded as a window to the unconscious.

The response to Freud's propositions varied from enthusiastic acceptance as revelations upon which a new religion would be based, to rejection as utterly unprovable nonsense. In the middle ground were various followers who would proceed to elaborate their own rival versions of the psyche's topography – the most influential of whom was the Swiss Carl Jung, who posited the existence of a "collective unconscious" which is part of the inheritance of all mankind and is expressed in universal symbols. In any event Freud's work focused attention on possible "unseen" levels of the mind, much as physics and chemistry and microbiology were probing previously invisible levels of organization in life and all matter, thereby contributing in a similar way to expanding the universe of man's understanding.

10

Peace or War

In 1898 a Russian industrialist and financier, I. S. Bloch, published a seven-volume work entitled *On Future War and its Consequences*. Although it was issued in a French translation, and abridged versions appeared in several other languages, it did not provoke any wide public response. Shortly after its publication the tsar issued a formal invitation to the governments of all the powers to send delegations to a conference on peace to be held at The Hague in 1899. Whether the tsar was moved to this action by the argument of the book, as Bloch contended, or by Russia's inability to keep up with the then current arms race, as a number of both Russian and foreign statesmen believed, is impossible to know. But either way, in view of what was to follow, it is certainly of interest to look at Bloch's analysis.

Together with a team of scholars working in his own privately maintained institute, Bloch had undertaken to study the current industrialization of arms production, assess its impact on recent battle situations, and project its implications for future combatants. The conclusions at which the study arrived were simple and unambiguous. It began with the startling pronouncement that the firepower of new infantry weapons and field artillery would give the defense an overwhelming advantage, particularly if it were dug into trenches. These conditions would render victory virtually impossible on the field, thereby reducing any war to one of position and siege, which would be decided only by the question of which side had the will and resources to resist the longer. Because of the altogether unprecedented size and cost of contemporary armies, however, no national economy would be able to bear the

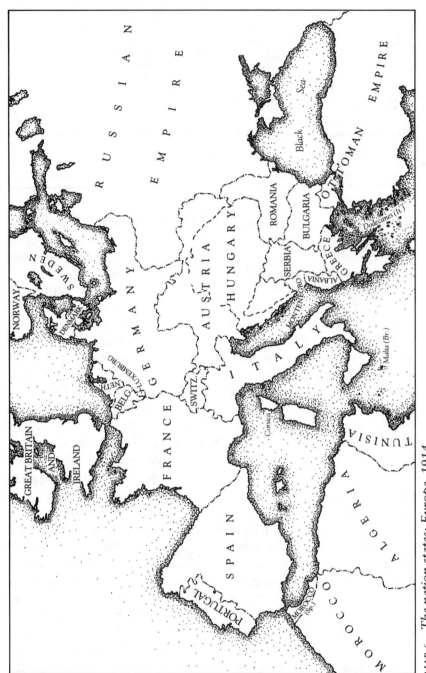

MAP 6   *The nation states: Europe, 1914*

financial strain of such warfare for more than a few months, nor would most economies be able to supply either their armed forces or their civilian populations with food for much longer under wartime conditions. The ultimate result of the attempt to fight and win a modern war, Bloch asserted, would probably be the complete social disintegration of one or all of the participating states within a year or two – certainly a sobering message for the precariously placed and well-intentioned Tsar Nicholas II.

Twenty-six countries accepted the tsar's invitation and sent delegations to the conference, none with much show of enthusiasm and most probably only to avoid the opprobrium of a public refusal. Each mission was headed by a senior statesman or diplomat and supported by military and legal experts. The principal delegates from Russia, Britain, France, and the United States were at least publicly committed to the idea of arbitration of international disputes, although several of their military and naval experts did not share their views. But the Germans opened the conference by rejecting the idea of arbitration and arms limitations altogether, on the grounds that it would deprive them of the military advantage they had been working to achieve for at least a decade: the capacity for rapid mobilization.

After this disastrous début the conference finally settled down to negotiating a modest convention on the conduct of war. The participants agreed to ban the use of poison gas and dumdum bullets (designed to expand on hitting the body), and for five years to prohibit the dropping of bombs from balloons. They also extended the existing rules governing the treatment of prisoners and the wounded. Finally the members turned to the matter of establishing a court of international arbitration. Any consideration of mandatory arbitration was out of the question because of German opposition, but the Germans were finally persuaded, in part by pressure from the international press, to agree to the establishment of a permanent Court of Arbitration that would not be given any powers of enforcement. With this unspectacular achievement the conference was adjourned.

The general estimate of this exercise in organizing peace was undoubtedly expressed by the American ambassador to Germany, Andrew D. White, when he wrote that "Probably . . . never has so large a body come together in a spirit of more hopeless skepticism." And the tsar expressed his reaction to its failure by ordering a fifteen-year program of industrial development in Russia to manufacture modern field artillery in massive quantities. Significantly, his creation of a heavy arms industry was undertaken with no specific opponent or objective in view, beyond the belief that it was essential if Russia was to remain a member of the councils of Europe. But why? No clear issues divided the powers — and certainly none was worth even a fraction of the apparent risk of modern war. The latest "crisis" had been the confrontation (1898) of French and British expeditions in the African Sudan, south of Egypt, and in spite of efforts by the press to stir up hysteria over the incident, the governments of Britain and France had taken that occasion not only to resolve the immediate problem but also to improve their relations. Their clear conclusion was that colonial differences were not worth a European war, a belief that was generally shared in Europe, if not always openly proclaimed.

In fact Europe's current imperialist rivalries played almost no part in the relations among the powers. The failure of the Hague Conference and the growing tensions among its member states really derived from the experience of the revolutions of 1848 and their consequences. The Habsburgs had dealt with the uprisings that had occurred in their empire by simply bombarding the capital city of each of their major provinces into submission — a response to nationalist stirrings that was unlikely to suppress them for very long. In Germany at the same time the Prussian kaiser's great servant Bismarck had used the birth of German nationalism to unify the many separate German states under Prussia, and then to make this Prussia the preeminent power in Europe, primarily by creating Europe's first version of universal military service and an industrially supplied fighting force.

Bismarck himself seemed to be satisfied with the ascendancy he thus gained for his nation, reinforced with the defeat of France in 1871 and the shifting alliances he constructed thereafter to keep the European balance of power in Germany's favor. But Bismarck's effective power came to an end with the death of William I in 1888, and the new Kaiser William II seemed to raise his sights to incorporating all of Europe as his realm. With the enthusiastic support of his industrialists and generals, the new ruler worked energetically and successfully to make Germany the overwhelming military power on the Continent – and then began openly seeking opportunities to prove this superiority in an armed contest with Germany's major rivals.

As Germany's military preparations became apparent, the other European governments and their leaders became convinced of the necessity of keeping pace – an undertaking that was certainly not discouraged by the arms manufacturers in each of the competing countries. Contemporary critics of this arms race made much of the criminal cupidity of these "merchants of cannon," but undoubtedly the mere existence of heavy industry made its eventual application to military ends inevitable. The industrialization of warfare was taking place along with the industrialization of all other aspects of life in the modern world, and just as Bloch had warned, this change was occurring faster than a corresponding shift in understanding and social institutions. Most of Europe's generals and admirals were quickly becoming obsolete; with few exceptions they knew little of industry and its implications for modern combat, and talked instead of such things as the "moral tonic" of war. One of Bloch's most accurate prophecies, as it turned out, was that virtually none of the existing commanding officers would be capable of directing a modern battle, and that as a result the junior officers would be killed faster than they could be replaced, leaving the troops engaged in purposeless mutual annihilation. Europe's political leaders were equally unprepared for the devastating effects of the new industrial warfare, and for its inconclusive nature. Like the generals, they were still thinking in terms of the "last war," at the same time that they were busily increasing their stockpile of the new weapons and moving inexorably toward the employment of these weapons in the most terrible war the world had yet seen.

ALLIANCES AND ALIGNMENTS

Bismarck's diplomacy

When Bismarck proclaimed the German Empire in 1871, at the conclusion of the Franco-Prussian War, he was announcing not only a new power but also the dominant power on the Continent;

and from that point on, his every effort was directed to the maintenance of that position. Hence four years later when the French unveiled their new universal-service army, based on the Prussian model, the chancellor raised the specter of a French war of revenge. In fact, the French action had been purely defensive, for no one in France wanted a war of revenge or of any other sort. But the myth he had created served Bismarck's purpose, and he built his future policies around the principle of keeping France in diplomatic isolation. To this end he created a system of alliances with the other Continental powers, the basic element of which was his treaty with Austria, which was signed in 1879 and would last until 1918. This was reinforced in 1881 with the Three Emperors' Alliance. By attaching Russia to Germany and reducing tensions between Russia and Austria, Bismarck was acting primarily to prevent France from gaining a diplomatic partner. Finally in 1882 the Chancellor signed the Triple Alliance with Austria and Italy, with a similar purpose of reducing friction between these two hostile powers. This agreement was renewed in 1887 and remained in force until 1915. Bismarck's diplomatic structure was now in place, and seemed to secure Germany from any serious threat by a hostile power.

In 1887, however, the Alliance of the Three Emperors came up for renewal, and this time the tsar declined to continue this commitment to peace with his Habsburg rivals. Instead, he accepted a "Reinsurance Treaty" with Bismarck, which pledged Germany's support of the status quo in the Balkans; this compromise appeared to protect the balance of power that Bismarck had tried to establish, but actually it marked the beginning of the end of peace in Europe.

Shifting alliances

In 1888 the old Kaiser William I died, to be succeeded in quick succession by his dying son Frederick III and his headstrong grandson William II. The new Kaiser, impatient to exercise his powers and unsympathetic with Bismarck's cautious policies, dismissed the aging chancellor in 1890. Shortly afterwards he refused to renew the Reinsurance Treaty with Russia, on the grounds that it conflicted with his allegiance to the Habsburg Emperor Franz Joseph.

With this action he effectively removed the keystone of Bismarck's diplomatic arch – since the chancellor had foreseen that much the most likely cause of a major confrontation in Europe would be the rivalry between Russia and the Dual Monarchy in the Balkans. As the power of the Ottoman Empire ebbed and the nationalist aspirations of the indigenous Slavic populations rose, Russian ambitions were encouraged and Habsburg anxieties aroused. Only Germany's weighty presence in the area, and her refusal to take sides with either rival, had prevented the outbreak of hostilities. Now that the Kaiser had spurned Russia and proclaimed his loyalty to the Habsburgs, the Russians immediately began negotiating a rapprochement with France, Germany's major opponent, that culminated in a military alliance in 1894. Considering that the French Third Republic was the most liberal regime on the Continent, and the Russian Empire the most absolutist and reactionary, this diplomatic arrangement was no small tribute to the impact of the Kaiser's blundering foreign policy.

With the Franco-Russian Alliance came the first crack that would ultimately divide Europe into two armed camps, although this implication was not immediately apparent. Governments and the newspaper-reading public of the various countries were occupied and distracted by a variety of events and crises, both domestic and foreign, that began to take place at an ever-quickening pace. Chance events in Africa, imperial ambitions in Asia, and political tempests in Europe competed for the headlines of the new mass-circulation press; but behind this confusion the division of Europe was being forced by irresponsible actions and reactions in a seemingly inexorable march toward disaster.

New threats to stability

In 1898 the German Reichstag passed a bill authorizing the construction of a fleet intended to be so large that no other navy (i.e. the British) would dare attack it. Such an undertaking was made possible by Germany's rapidly expanding steel production and growing industrial wealth, but it was hardly justified by any existing threat to her interests, and it was taken as a hostile act in Great Britain. At about the same time another German project took on a symbolic significance that further alienated not only the British but also the Russians. For ten years the Germans had been building a rail line from Constantinople to Ankara, with the intention of carrying it on to Baghdad and the Persian Gulf. While this construction was conceived of by the Germans as having economic rather than military value, it provoked increasing suspicion and diplomatic resistance from the two powers with interests in this area, Russia and Great Britain.

When the Chinese "Boxers" attempted to drive foreigners out of their country in 1900, a new arena of conflict was opened. An international expeditionary force was rushed to Peking to rescue the foreign embassies, and at first it appeared that these troops might well be kept on for the final partitioning of China. Instead, the European powers seemed content to retire after the crisis — with the exception of Russia, which used its Trans-Siberian railroad to move troops into Manchuria with no apparent intention of withdrawing them. The significance of Manchuria for the Russians is easy to see in a glance at the map; control of this area would not only give them direct access to their own Pacific port of Vladivostok, but also offered the possibility of a rail line to China's "warm water" harbor at Port Arthur, which they had already marked out for occupation. All of this maneuvering served to emphasize the fact that with the construction of the Trans-Siberian railroad Russia was no longer a mere colonial power in the Far East but rather an Asian power in her own right. And this brought her into direct confrontation with that other Asian power, Japan.

The Japanese, painfully aware of their lack of coal and iron, had long since staked out claims to Korea and Manchuria as their sources of these two essential raw materials. While Japan was not committed to outright annexation of these territories, it obviously could not tolerate their occupation by another power. The first major reaction to Russia's move was the Anglo-Japanese alliance, signed in 1902. This treaty marked a dramatic reversal of Britain's previous policy of staying aloof from the diplomatic maneuvering that was engaging all the other powers, and in an unspecific way it provided the Japanese with the moral support they needed to face a major confrontation with the Russians. In 1896 the Russians had begun the penetration of North Korea from their base in Manchuria; the Japanese attempted negotiations at this point but received no satisfaction, and ended by breaking off diplomatic relations with Russia. For the next ten years the Japanese prepared for war with their rival. Then in early 1904, Japanese naval units attacked Port Arthur without warning, disabling the Russian Asiatic fleet. The ensuing war lasted a year; the Japanese laid siege to and captured the city of Port Arthur and won a major victory at Mukden, at the junction of Russian rail communications between Port Arthur and the Korean peninsula. In a final vindictive action, after the outcome of the war had been decided at Mukden, the Japanese annihilated Russia's Baltic fleet, which had barely been able to make its way to Asian waters. The peace treaty, signed in 1905, restored Manchuria to China, transferred to Japan Russia's lease of Port Arthur and its rail connection with the Trans-Siberian railroad, and recognized Japan's dominance in Korea. The Japanese then reinforced their position in a "treaty" with Korea, by which Korea gave Japan control of its foreign policy.

As the news of Russian defeats reached St Petersburg, it gave hope to the opponents of the tsar's absolutist government. There were large public demonstrations and widespread demands for the establishment of constitutional, representative government. When the tsar temporized, the opposition organized a general strike that forced him to issue the "October Manifesto," a limited constitution which was accepted by the liberals but only served to reinforce the belief of the more radical political elements that the tsar's government had to be overthrown by full-scale revolution. The government, by now backed up with the troops who had returned from Siberia, moved to suppress the radical movements, and although it succeeded in reestablishing control, it also provoked more support for the radical opposition. In 1906 the first Duma (assembly) was elected, by universal suffrage, but the radicals rejected its purely consultative role, forcing its dissolution. Although a series of Dumas followed, the tsar was never willing to allow a truly representative government to evolve, and public opinion came to be increasingly polarized between an ineffective liberal position and an intransigent revolutionary one.

Anglo-French cooperation

At the beginning of the Russo-Japanese conflict it seemed possible that Britain and France might become involved in it as allies of the opposing sides. Instead, the two governments were moved by the war to come to a quick resolution of their outstanding differences, recognizing the right of free passage through the Suez Canal as well as Britain's interests in Egypt and those of France in Morocco. In addition they agreed to hold talks to coordinate their mutual defenses in Europe.

The Germans, correctly sensing that this "entente" was actually aimed at them, decided to put it to an early test. Their first opportunity came when France negotiated arrangements with the sultan of Morocco which amounted to making the country a French protectorate. The German government responded by sending the Kaiser on a surprise visit to Tangier, where in a belligerent speech he proclaimed the complete independence of Morocco; this challenge provoked a panic in Paris, where there was no interest in taking on the Germans. It was the sultan who finally saved the situation, by inviting all the European powers to an international conference which met in Algeciras (1906). Although the principle of Moroccan independence was reaffirmed, all delegations except those of Germany and the Dual Monarchy supported France, which retained rights to patrol the Algerian–Moroccan border and, with Spain, to supervise Morocco's internal police. The Germans deeply resented this rebuff.

It was actually during this conference that Great Britain launched the epoch-making battleship, the *Dreadnought*, which with its ten twelve-inch guns completely outclassed every other fighting craft in the world. Paradoxically, this development reduced all existing navies to an equal starting level, thereby giving Germany new hope of achieving parity with Britain and thus setting off a furious naval arms race between the two countries. With this rivalry as a stimulus, the British then moved to resolve their differences with Russia, concluding an agreement that was similar to, though less extensive than, the one they had recently signed with France. With the conclusion of this negotiation the three imperial rivals – Britain, France and Russia – were aligned in what was called the "Triple Entente," united by a common distrust of Germany and her "Triple Alliance" with the Dual Monarchy and Italy. Europe was now divided into two armed camps, with Great Britain fully involved and the diplomatic reach of the participants retracted to the Continent and its near environs – that is, first to Morocco and then, most importantly, to the Balkans.

A second Moroccan crisis developed in 1911, when the French moved troops into Fez to restore order after an anti-foreign uprising. Seeking every opportunity for a confrontation, the Germans objected that France had thus violated the terms of the Algeciras settleement, and they backed up their protest by sending a gunboat to the Moroccan port of Agadir. Once again the French reacted to this sabre-rattling with horror and the Germans offered to close the matter in return for the entire French Congo. At this point the British objected to Germany's threatening of their ally. Eventually the French did concede part of the Congo and some other territories to Germany, and the Germans agreed to a French protectorate over Morocco. The peace had not yet been shattered, but the diplomatic atmosphere was growing increasingly stormy.

The Balkans

The situation in the Balkans was far more complex than that in Morocco and infinitely more dangerous to European stability. The Ottoman regime in the Balkans had been disintegrating for well over a century, and in 1878 the Congress of Berlin had recognized the autonomy of a number of the former Ottoman provinces – notably Serbia, Montenegro, Bulgaria and Romania – while it had put Bosnia under Habsburg administration. For all the European powers the real prize was control of Constantinople and the Straits (the Bosporus and Dardanelles), which for Russia would provide access to the Mediterranean and for any power would give control over the Suez Canal. But the Ottoman collapse never went so far as to encourage European rivalry in this arena. The Russians persisted in their attempt to gain the right of free passage through the Straits from the Ottomans for both their naval craft and their merchant shipping (most of the latter carrying grain from the Ukraine), but for various reasons the other powers all opposed this aim and the Russians would not obtain such rights until the Second World War.

Besides Russia, the other power with a direct interest in the Balkans was the Dual Monarchy, which feared that the emergence of the new large Slav state of Serbia would both arouse nationalistic sentiments in her own Slavic subjects and offer a military threat. The Habsburgs annexed Bosnia in 1908 in order to forestall any move by Serbia to acquire it, winning Russian support for the annexation by promising Habsburg support of Russia's use of the Straits. After the annexation was accomplished, however, the Austrians reneged on their part of the bargain, provoking deep resentment among the Russians. In this and all other diplomatic confrontations in the Balkans, the Germans firmly supported the Dual Monarchy (sometimes against their better judgement), mainly in order to preserve their alliance, but also to protect their own economic interests in the region, which were symbolized by the projected Berlin-to-Baghdad railway.

In 1912 Serbia, Bulgaria, and Greece joined forces to expel the Ottomans from Europe once and for all. Backed by Russia, they attacked Turkey with surprising success, and the Bulgarians actually threatened Constantinople until warned off by the Russians. This "First Balkan War" was terminated by a Treaty of London in which Turkey ceded most of her remaining European territory to the three victors. Dissatisfied with the division of the spoils, Serbia and Greece then formed an alliance against Bulgaria, and were joined by Romania and by the Turks — who saw a hope of recovering some of their lost territory at the expense of Bulgaria. The ensuing "Second Balkan War" was brief, resulting in the defeat of the Bulgarians and some minor territorial adjustments. The significance of these wars was that they had threatened to involve all of the major powers by impinging on the interests of Russia and Austria, and thereby on their allies, now arrayed against each other in two uneasy camps. No longer very concerned about Russian designs on the Straits, the Austrians now focused their fears on the growing strength of Serbia, convinced that she posed a threat to their vital interests. With the Russians committed to the defense of this Slavic neighbor, any change in Serbia's status clearly risked a confrontation that would have far-reaching reverberations. The impending crisis was not long in coming.

War approaches

On June 28, 1914, the heir-apparent to the Habsburg throne, Archduke Franz Ferdinand, paid an official visit to Sarajevo, capital of the Habsburgs' recently annexed province of Bosnia. Serbian nationalists, who had intended to make Bosnia part of their own new state, had not forgiven their Austrian enemy for this annexation, and the archduke made his appearance in Bosnia despite warnings of possible terrorist retaliation. Ignoring all caution, the archduke and his wife were riding through the city in an open car when a young fanatic rushed up and shot them both. That the Serbian government was in some way implicated in the assassination was widely – and probably correctly – suspected. As a result the Austrian government assumed it must teach Serbia a lesson, and soon learned that Germany's Kaiser and his advisors agreed, even if it meant risking a general war.

On July 23 Austria delivered an altogether unacceptable ultimatum to Serbia demanding humiliating concessions and a virtual surrender of sovereignty. While rejecting outright submission, the Serbs, with Russian encouragement, sent a conciliatory reply but at the same time ordered a general mobilization. This expected response served the Austrians' purpose, which was to conduct a short punitive campaign against the Serbs without involving the other powers. On July 28, therefore, Austria declared war on Serbia and shelled Belgrade. The following day, the tsar ordered mobilization of Russia's southern military districts, wishing to warn Austria but without threatening Germany. Then on the next day the tsar changed his mind and took the fateful first step toward European war by ordering a general mobilization. The Germans took this as the provocation for which they had long been preparing: they immediately mobilized their own forces and declared war on Russia (August 1). France decided to mobilize against Germany in defense of her Russian ally, and Germany immediately declared war on France (August 3). On August 4, Great Britain declared war on Germany, whose troops had meanwhile invaded Belgium. Finally on August 6, Austria declared war on Russia. The European world was at war.

The question of what really caused this catastrophe has been discussed and debated ever since, yet no clear answer has emerged. Of the hundred or so principal actors in the drama – the statesmen, diplomats and officers – few, if any, clearly wanted a general war, but almost all had something they feared more than the risk of war. The Austrians feared that unchecked Serbian nationalism would infect their Slavic subjects and lead to the disintegration of their state. The Germans feared the loss of their one sure ally, Austria, if they did not back her to the hilt. The Russians feared that Austria intended to block their ambitions in the Balkans, and the French feared that they would lose Russia as an ally against Germany if she were forced to back down in the confrontation with Austria over Serbia. Finally the British feared Germany's growing navy and her habitual belligerence in her dealings with other powers. At bottom each government was so afraid of finding itself confronted by a superior force that it dared not weaken its position by concessions, even to avert war.

To seek the origins of this morbid contagion it is probably necessary to go back again to the ferment that swept through much of Europe in 1848 and the response of the Habsburg and Prussian governments, which in both cases – though for different ends – was a resort to force of arms. The Habsburg Empire suppressed its nationalist revolts, then lost its Italian provinces, by force of arms. Meanwhile its Prussian rival was containing and organizing the new German state also by force of arms; the Kaiser and his government seemed to have no idea of how to achieve Germany's "place in the sun" except by the threat of military force. In the course of this birth of a nation the new German power persuaded its neighbors that their only hope of security lay in matching its military might. Only such a fear could explain the action of the three great imperial rivals (Britain, France, and Russia) in setting aside their differences to undertake a mutual defense against the German menace.

THE FIRST WORLD WAR

The invasion of France

The war began according to plan – the Schlieffen Plan. Formulated some ten years before, when Schlieffen was chief of the German General Staff, it had been designed to meet the challenge of a two-front war. It called for a massive attack on France's northern frontier that would envelop her main forces and encircle Paris before the slow-moving Russians could seriously threaten Germany's eastern border. To have any hope of success this daring maneuver would have to be launched immediately after the declaration of war. The right wing of the German forces would have to have an overwhelming preponderance of force, and swing wide to the west through Belgium (and perhaps the edge of Holland as well) to avoid the French forts in the east. The plan estimated that the Germans would have about a month to accomplish the conquest of Paris before having to deal with their other major rival, the Russians.

The German mobilization was ordered August 1, 1914, and was completed on schedule. The first German troops crossed the Belgian border on the night of August 4, but already it was apparent that the Schlieffen plan was fatally flawed. The High Command had been forced to withhold some units from the right wing to block an anticipated French attack on Alsace, and the Belgians declined to behave as the German plan had assumed they would. Not only did they refuse the German demand for free passage through their country, but they also mobilized their army and fought. Although their heroic resistance hardly affected the German timetable, the Belgians would later destroy most of their main railroad bridges and thereby create serious problems of supply for the invaders. But the most important unanticipated event was that Great Britain suddenly made Belgian neutrality a *casus belli*. In the 1830s the Belgians had successfully freed themselves from Dutch rule, and in 1839 their independence and neutrality had been officially guaranteed by all the principal European powers, including Prussia. Britain's decision to be alarmed by Germany's violation of this agreement brought the British into the war at the very outset; they declared war on Germany on August 4, and sent a small but professional expeditionary force to help the French try to stem the German advance. Although they were not yet prepared to offer much help to the French, their participation would of course have incalculable long-range implications for the war.

With a million and a half men under arms, the German advance was by far the largest offensive action in recorded history. Although the French had a million defenders (with some 90,000 British), they were too few and too poorly positioned even to slow the pace of the German army. In the third week of the war, however, the Russians appeared to be moving toward East Prussia and the German command withdrew a few more divisions from their right wing in order to meet this threat. This decision decisively weakened the German onslaught, as their right wing suddenly did not have enough men to sweep around Paris and began to turn east too soon.

Sensing their new opportunity to check the German avalanche, the French prepared to make a stand on the Marne River, the last barrier before Paris. French troops were brought to the Marne from the east, and even the garrison of Paris was rushed out to the field of battle, by a fleet of taxi cabs. After a week of furious fighting, the French and British finally got the upper hand. However the Germans retreated only a short way (no more than fifty miles) before they began digging earthwork fortifications, which they held when the French arrived in pursuit. Unable to force the Germans from their position, the French concentrated on establishing a parallel defensive line that would at least prevent any further German advance. With the momentum of the attack now broken, both sides had time to fortify their positions with all the military hardware that the industrial revolution had put at their disposal – improved rifles, machine guns and rapid-firing artillery. As Bloch had predicted in his study, On Future War, the defensive power of the new weaponry now took over, and the war became a seemingly unwinnable mutual siege. The double line of trenches was quickly extended to the Swiss border in the south and the Belgian coast in the north, with a total length of well over the 300 miles between the two ends. Through nearly four years of fighting, hundreds of thousands of soldiers occupied the trenches, engaging regularly in massive attacks and counterattacks that would never shift the battle line more than ten miles in either direction. The Schlieffen Plan had failed by a mere fifty miles, and with its collapse the Germans had lost all reasonable chance of winning the war. They had no plan for recognizing or dealing with this eventuality, however, and by doggedly proceeding toward their original objectives they effectively condemned themselves and their adversaries to a suicidal struggle.

War in the east

While the German offensive in the west was still rolling through France, another struggle of comparable magnitude was developing in the east. Starting with Austria's punitive action against Serbia (which proved far more difficult than expected), it was followed by an Austrian attack on Russia along the Hungarian frontier, and finally by a Russian response in the form of two of their armies lurching into East Prussia. To meet this threat the Germans used troops rushed from the western front, under generals Hindenburg and Ludendorff, who stopped the Russian advance at Tannenberg. This victory made the generals heroes in Germany, and would eventually catapult both of them to virtually dictatorial powers in later crises. By the end of the year, when the winter made further campaigning impractical, a continuous front – similar to that in the west – was established from the Baltic mouth of the Niemen River to the Romanian border. If this line was never as complete or fixed as that in the west, it was a product of the same powerful defensive weapons that would dominate all battlefields of the war.

War at sea

Having given no thought to the possibility of fighting the British, the Germans had made no provision for a battle for the sea. It began, however, when four German cruisers, too far at sea to return home when the war began, attempted to join forces and raid British shipping. They succeeded in destroying the first British squadron that was sent to the rescue, but were then destroyed in turn by a superior British force. During the same period, German cruisers shelled a few towns on England's North Sea coast and German submarines sank a few old British cruisers. In spite of these minor successes, however, the major result of the war at sea was to cut Germany off from the outside world, including her colonies. Before the end of the first year, almost all of Germany's western colonial possessions were taken over by British or French forces, while those in the Far East were seized by the Japanese, who had declared war on Germany for that purpose.

A final consequence of Germany's overseas activity was the involvement of Turkey in the war on Germany's side. This peculiar alliance was achieved by the decision to "sell" to the Turkish government two powerful German cruisers (complete with their crews) that had been caught by the British in the Mediterranean and had sought refuge in the Dardanelles. These German ships were then sent by Turkey on a raid against Russian ports on the

Black Sea, an action which led not only Russia but also France and Britain to declare war on Turkey.

A protracted war

As 1914 drew to an end the fighting tended to subside, partly because of the weather, partly from the exhaustion and frustration of all participants, and most of all because both sides were running out of arms and ammunition. With the declaration of war both France and Germany had drafted their workers and closed their armaments factories, expecting to fight the whole war with existing stocks of military supplies, but by the end of the year these were dwindling and both sides were forced to resume production with desperate urgency. For France the problem was compounded by the loss of her industrial areas in the northeast, and for the Germans by the fact that they were cut off from all outside sources of raw materials by the British navy.

Just as I. S. Bloch had predicted, the firepower of the new weapons had established the superiority of the defense, and the senior officers of all armies were unprepared to cope with this problem. As he had also predicted, the casualties on both fronts had been unprecedented. (In France the postal and telegraph service broke down under the weight of notices to next-of-kin.) The losses in money had been stupendous too, but Bloch's conclusion that these developments would lead to bankruptcy and social disintegration was not borne out by events. Despite the staggering costs of the war, the fighting capacity of the powerful nation states was unimpaired, and neither side showed signs of failure of morale or loss of will.

Heavy fighting resumed early in 1915 on the western front and continued through the summer, with no appreciable results on either side except further appalling casualties. On the eastern front new offensives produced more movement, but in the context of the large distances involved, and the huge numbers of the Russian troops, these failed to prove decisive.

Behind the battle lines, the governments of the warring powers worked to improve their production of military supplies, and to find strategic alternatives to the increasingly massive and murderous clashes that were taking place on both fronts. For Britain and

France this meant primarily attempting to join forces with Russia through the Mediterranean, outflanking the Central Powers (Germany and Austria) to the south, while for Germany it meant either breaking out of the British blockade or imposing a similar blockade on Britain. These objectives were pursued in several ways.

The Mediterranean and Middle East

Italy, although a member of the Triple Alliance with Germany and Austria, had remained neutral in 1914. Early in 1915, however, both sides made diplomatic moves to gain her support in the war. As the price of their participation the Italians set the acquisition from Austria of the borderlands of the Trentino and the harbor of Trieste. Germany tried to persuade the Austrians to comply with these demands but they refused, at which point the Allies (Britain and France) signed a secret treaty with Italy promising to give her all she sought when they had won the war. As a result Italy declared war against Austria (though not against Germany until over a year later), and fighting began on the Austro-Italian border. Italy's military impact on the war was negligible, however, at least at this stage.

A similar quest for allies was conducted by both sides in the Balkans, where the principal states (Romania, Bulgaria, and Greece) were initially inclined to neutrality. The first to enter the war was Bulgaria, which joined the Central Powers after they promised her substantial territorial concessions from Turkey as well as gains at the expense of Greece and Serbia. The Greeks could not bring themselves to join the Allies but agreed in a secret treaty to permit a British and French landing at Salonika. Here the Allies established their only base in the Balkans; they were too weak to go to the aid of Serbia, which Austria finally crushed with German help, but they hoped their presence in Greece could at least impede Germany's communications with Turkey.

For Britain and France the two ultimate military objectives in this theater of the war were to establish contact with Russia through the Balkans or the Black Sea, and to prevent the Germans from pushing across Turkey to attack British forces in Mesopotamia and threaten Britain's control of the Suez Canal. Both of these objectives would be achieved if the Allies could win control of

Constantinople and the Dardanelles; accordingly the British and French planned an attack on Turkey in the European arm of the Dardanelles, called the Gallipoli Peninsula. The execution of this campaign was less impressive than its conception, and left Turkey more than ample time to fortify its position on the peninsula; the result was a limited disaster for the Allies in which they lost three battleships and were forced to abandon the attack on Constantinople for the rest of the war. As it turned out, the Germans did not attempt to exploit their land route to the Middle East by seizing the Suez Canal, so that the Allied defeat in Turkey did not have the serious consequences that the British had feared. (An incidental consequence of the failure, however, was to discredit the chief author and backer of the plan, Britain's young First Lord of the Admiralty, Winston Churchill.)

Naval blockade

Germany meanwhile was pursuing its naval war against Britain with its newly developed submarine, which had just established its credibility by successful attacks on British cruisers. In February 1915 the German government announced the blockade of Britain, and without warning its submarines began sinking ships of all kinds that were going to or from Britain. By May not only had an American merchant ship had been sunk but also the British passenger liner, the *Lusitania*, with heavy loss of life including over a hundred Americans. The public reaction in the United States was so violent that America's entry in the war seemed imminent, and this threat finally forced the German government to back away from its attempt to cut Britain's sea lines.

All-out offensives, 1916

The Germans now had only one chance left to avoid strangulation by the British blockade and that was a land victory in the West. Accordingly in 1916 the German High Command planned to gamble on ultimate victory by an even greater offensive on the western front than had yet been tried. In February the Germans added to their western forces half a million men from the eastern front, then attacked a fort (Verdun) on France's eastern border –

which they correctly believed the French would defend at all costs, for symbolic reasons, even though it was nearly surrounded by German lines. The battle lasted five months, with joint casualties running over half a million. The French held the fort but at a disastrous price, which included the serious weakening of their contribution to the attack they were preparing with the British along the Somme.

This Allied counteroffensive was on an even greater scale than Verdun. Before it finally ended in November, both the British and Germans had suffered over 400,000 casualties and the French half that number. Even with their surprise introduction of tanks (which were not effectively used), the British were unable to drive the Germans back for more than half a dozen miles. All three armies were devastated by this senseless slaughter, yet even this failed to convince the generals of the murderous futility of their stubborn reliance on ever larger numbers of guns and men.

In the spring of the same year the Germans made one other spectacular attempt to break out of their isolation. While they had been deterred by the American warning from using submarines against neutral shipping, they finally decided to challenge the British fleet in the North Sea in a full-scale battle of "Dreadnoughts." In the course of a few hours of the battle of Jutland, each fleet lost six ships, and the outcome was as indecisive as that of the battles on land. The German crews and ships generally showed themselves superior to the British ones, but in spite of their serious losses the British pressed the attack, until nightfall gave the Germans cover to return to base.

For the Germans the logic of the fighting on land and sea in 1916 was clear: they must either break the Allied blockade or gradually starve. The failure of their offensives brought on a governmental crisis that ended with the total subordination of civilian authority to the military High Command, under the direction of General von Ludendorff. Although all governments involved in the war had been forced to exert some measure of control over transportation and military supply, Germany's siege situation forced her to move further and faster than the others toward a largely state-directed economy.

When the German generals took over, in the fall of 1916, they quickly came to the decision to open an unlimited submarine attack on Britain's supply lines, even though this would unquestionably bring the United States into the war on the Allied side. With Britain reduced to a food reserve sufficient for only a few weeks (or months, at best), it seemed possible to force her submission before the United States could raise – let alone train and transport to Europe – an effective military force.

Peace moves

Even though they had just made this drastic decision to push for victory, the Germans paradoxically opened the year 1917 with an announcement that they were ready to negotiate a peace, asking the American President Woodrow Wilson to be their liaison with the Allies. Wilson requested both sides to state their terms. The Central Powers declined, saying they preferred negotiation, but the Allies drew up a long list, including the reorganization of Europe along lines of national self-determination – a proposal that seemed highly revolutionary to powers that conceived of their states (or hoped to) as multinational European empires. Another, and probably more genuine, peace initiative came from the new Habsburg Emperor Charles, who had succeeded the ancient Franz Joseph on the throne at the end of 1916. Seeing nothing more to gain from continued war, he made contact with the French government and found a favorable response; the talks came to nothing in the end, however, because of the inability of the two governments to agree on the details of a settlement, especially on the question of Italy's acquisition of Trieste. In the mean time President Wilson proposed a formula of "peace without victory" as a basis for negotiating an end to the war, which elicited a marked lack of enthusiasm all around.

American involvement

Renewed warfare began in earnest on the western front with Germany's planned withdrawal to a carefully prepared, heavily fortified line – named for Hindenburg – while the French were preparing still another and even greater mass attack. Thanks in part to their new position, the Germans were able to inflict terrible punishment on the French. The French offensive collapsed, its commander (General Nivelle) was dismissed, and several French units mutinied against the senseless slaughter. By this time, however, the United States had declared war on Germany (April 6, 1917) and begun a program of mobilizing its industry and manpower that would astonish the world.

Russian defeat

Meanwhile on the eastern front the Russian armies were preparing to take the offensive in spite of staggering problems of supply and transport. After the failure of the Hague Peace Conference in 1899, Russia had undertaken an ambitious program for creating an arms industry but this had by no means reached its goal. The troops were now seriously short of weapons, and the army had drafted factory and transport workers indiscriminately, leaving the civilian population as well as the armed forces short of basic necessities. The weak Tsar Nicholas II was not only utterly incapable of remedying this situation, but also appeared to be allowing most of the powers of government to fall into the hands of his fanatically reactionary wife and her favorite, the infamous monk and adventurer nicknamed Rasputin, "the dissolute." Strikes and riots broke out in the capital, Petrograd (as St Petersburg was now called), and in March of 1917 the troops mutinied, bringing down the government and forcing the tsar to abdicate.

The Duma, Russia's consultative assembly, now assumed power, establishing a provisional government that was made up largely of intellectuals who were favorably disposed to western political ideas. Their announced purpose was to continue the war, to recognize the virtual independence of Finland, Poland, and Estonia, and to call an assembly that would write a constitution and establish a democratic government. Unfortunately the members of the provisional government had neither practical experience in governing nor any democratic constituency in Russian society. Almost from the start they found themselves in conflict with a rival organization that the socialists had set up in Petrograd, called a Workers' and Soldiers' Council, or soviet. The socialists' main objective was to negotiate a peace with Russia's enemies in the war, and to replace the authority of army officers with that of elected soldiers' committees. Into this confused situation the

Germans deliberately injected a number of exiled Russian revolutionaries who had sought refuge in the West, most importantly Vladimir Lenin, whom they carefully transported from Switzerland to Russia in a sealed railway car. It was their hope – which Lenin would more than fulfill – that the radicals would gain control of the government and take Russia out of the war.

At the end of June 1917 the provisional government launched the Russian army on what was to be its last offensive against the Germans. It made some headway before it collapsed, but this failure was followed by the general disintegration of the armed forces. The revolutionaries (Bolsheviks) in the capital seized this opportunity to attempt a coup, which the provisional government put down, arresting a number of leaders including Leon Trotsky, who had recently returned from exile in the United States.

By October, however, the Soviet was in control of Petrograd, the army was in revolt, and the peasants were killing their landlords; I. S. Bloch's prediction that modern war would lead to social disintegration seems to have been borne out in his native Russia. In November the Bolsheviks, under Lenin and Trotsky, were able to stage a successful coup, and they immediately took steps to bring about Russia's disengagement from the war. Lenin fully understood that to win and consolidate power within Russia he had to make peace at any price with Russia's foreign adversaries; the military struggle he had to prepare for was an inevitable civil war.

As "foreign commissar" of the revolutionary government, Trotsky proposed a general armistice in November 1917, on the basis of a return by both sides to their prewar territorial boundaries. The Allies evaded a direct response, while the Germans accurately read this suit for peace as an indication that the new government was willing to pay almost any price for peace. Accordingly the Germans proposed terms that amounted to a Russian surrender of all but her heartland; she was to turn over to the Central Powers control of the entire Ukraine, as well as her provinces and territories in the Baltic (Finland, Latvia, Lithuania, and Estonia), in Poland, and in parts of the Caucasus. At first the Bolsheviks rejected these conditions, whereupon the Germans resumed their offensive, recognizing the "independence" of the Ukraine and even threatening Petrograd. Realizing that he could not continue both the war and the revolution, Lenin finally agreed to the German terms in the Treaty of Brest-Litovsk (March 1918). This brutal amputation of Russian territory appeared to constitute a spectacular victory for the Germans; by ironic justice, however, it actually robbed them of their last chance for victory in the West, by tying down a million men – that could otherwise have been moved to France – in the occupation of the conquered lands. The treaty also made a mockery of Germany's later demands for a just peace, when she was forced to accept the terms dictated by the Allies.

Beating the submarines

In the west, the German submarine campaign had reached a peak in March of 1917, when it succeeded in nearly strangling Great Britain. In their desperation the British tried organizing their shipping in convoys that were accompanied by destroyers and lesser armed craft, and the results were as encouraging as their previous losses were threatening. By the end of that year both Britain and the United States were building more ships than they were losing, while the American troops were arriving in France in rapidly increasing numbers (that would reach a total of two million before the end of the war).

As 1917 drew to a close the character of the war had changed dramatically for the first time since early 1915. The United States had entered the war and Russia had collapsed. The German submarine campaign still applied pressure to Britain's sea lines, but the Central Powers were being even more seriously threatened with starvation by the British blockade. Clearly, the stalemate that had gone on so long could not continue much longer, and yet the outcome of the war was as undecided as ever, dependent primarily on the question of which side could move faster. The Allies had to break the German submarine offensive and establish the Americans as a major force on the western front before the Germans liquidated their eastern front and shifted their armies west to deliver a final fatal blow to the Allies.

War aims

As the war continued, the morale of the troops and the civilians on both sides finally began to deteriorate decisively. It was this problem which had motivated Germany's first tentative peace proposals in 1917, and it now resulted in the first clear statements of war aims by Allied powers, which were issued at the beginning of 1918. The Allies were by no means assured of victory at this point, but it became essential to look forward to the successful conclusion of the war in order to continue the effort. On January 5 the British Prime Minister, David Lloyd George, made a major speech in which he outlined Britain's objectives, and three days later the American President Woodrow Wilson delivered the most important oration of his career, spelling out America's objectives in his famous Fourteen Points. Although the style of the two pronouncements was different, their essential thrust was very similar. Wilson's fourteen points would play the largest role in the final settlement, partly because of America's great prestige and partly because of their contractual ring.

Wilson's points were: (1) that peace should be established by open negotiations and agreements; (2) that freedom of the seas be respected in war and peace; (3) that all trade be as free as possible; (4) that arms be reduced; (5) that colonial disputes be resolved with the interests of local populations considered; (6) that Russia be freed of all intervention to develop her own institutions; (7) that Belgian independence be restored; (8) that Alsace-Lorraine be returned to France; (9) that Italian frontiers be adjusted along lines of nationality; (10) that the various ethnic groups in the Habsburg Empire be allowed autonomous development; (11) that the conquered Balkan states be liberated and restored; (12) that the sovereignty of the Turkish parts of the Ottoman Empire be recognized and other parts be granted autonomy, but that the Dardanelles be open to all shipping under international auspices; (13) that Polish independence be established with free access to the sea; and (14) that an association of nations be formed to provide mutual guarantees of integrity for great and small states alike.

Decision in France

By the spring of 1918 the Allies were transporting far more goods and troops past the German blockade than had seemed possible a few months before, while the Germans were shifting far fewer troops west from the Russian front than had been expected. The

Germans really had only one more chance to break the western front and win a military victory, and this they attempted to do in their long-planned offensive of 1918. In March of 1918 Ludendorff launched an attack that broke the British lines and gained as much as forty miles. The situation was stabilized by the addition of French reinforcements, but the shock was sufficient to induce the Allies to establish a joint command, under the French General Foch. Before Foch could organize a counterattack, Ludendorff won another series of major victories that brought him to the Marne, where the Allies (including an important segment of Americans) finally stopped the German advance. By mid-July, however, Foch had finally assumed the offensive, and in August the British were attacking in the north, using tanks for the second time. The tide of battle had turned. Although the Allies still could not achieve a military breakthrough, the German Command knew that they no longer had any real hope of winning the war, and decided to sue for peace before the Allies could mount an invasion of Germany and force an unconditional surrender. On September 29 General Ludendorff demanded that the German government ask for an armistice, and a new ministry was formed which began an exchange with President Wilson over armistice terms. Wilson insisted that Germany return all occupied territory and form a democratic government. At this point Ludendorff resigned his command, the crews of the German fleet mutinied at their Kiel base, and a revolution broke out in Munich. On November 9 the Kaiser abdicated, and a German armistice commission was sent to meet General Foch at his headquarters, a railroad car at Compiègne.

Though less drastic than Wilson's, the armistice terms now offered by the Allies were certainly those of the victor to the vanquished. Their main object was to make it impossible for the Germans to resume the conflict. All German-held territory west of the Rhine was to be evacuated, Germany's treaties with Russia and Romania (which had entered the war and been defeated earlier in the year) were to be revoked, and finally German troops were to be withdrawn from occupied areas in eastern Europe. In addition, most of Germany's railroad cars and locomotives, trucks, submarines, and other ships were to be surrendered to the Allies. The Germans, who had hoped for some simple cessation of hostilities, were horrified but helpless. They signed, and the greatest war the world had yet seen came to an end on November 11, 1918. The social disintegration attendant on this war, however, had only begun.

THE PEACE

At the beginning of 1918 Germany appeared to have won a near-total victory in the east. Russia, in the throes of revolution, had withdrawn from the war on German terms, abandoning to German rule not only their border domains (Finland, Latvia, Lithuania, Estonia, and Poland) but the important province of the Ukraine as well. In addition, Romania had collapsed, while Italy had suffered a crushing defeat by Austrian and German forces, and was barely able to continue resistance with British and French help. In the west at this point German prospects were less bright but still impressive. The submarine campaign had failed to cut British communications and American forces were arriving in ever-increasing numbers, but the German armies were poised for one more offensive which in fact nearly achieved a final victory. By mid-summer this offensive had failed, and with it German hopes of winning a victory in the west, and yet overall they were still in a strong position and very far from conceding defeat.

In October their position was weakened as their main ally, the Habsburg Empire, suddenly fell apart. The Italians, with French and British help, won a final decisive victory over the Austrians, capturing both Trieste and Fiume. Then in early November separate Hungarian, Czechoslovak and Polish republics were proclaimed, followed by a "United Kingdom" of Serbs, Croats and Slovenes. The Habsburg emperor abdicated, and the new republic of Austria was announced. At about this same time the army of the Ottoman Empire disintegrated, forcing the government to capitulate to the Allies and accept their occupation of Constantinople.

It was at this point that the German armistice commission finally met with the Allies to work out the terms of a halt in the fighting. Despite all these developments in the east and the failure of their offensive in the west, the Germans were completely unprepared for, and incapable of accepting, the defeat that was formalized by the armistice. Their profound, instinctive and virtually universal rejection of the reality of their military failure would dominate not only German politics but all of European affairs for the next quarter-century.

The Allies were now determined to put an end to German military ambition for all time. The French were all too aware of how close they had come to collapse from sheer exhaustion, and they read in the terms of the Brest-Litovsk treaty what would have been their own fate had the Germans won the war in the West. They wanted a peace, above all, that would prevent another onslaught by their ancient enemy, whom they fully expected to be back on the offensive in twenty years. The British, profoundly relieved to have the slaughter ended, were also reassured by the surrender of the German fleet, including the submarines that had brought them within weeks of starvation and capitulation. They wanted a swift return to normal prewar conditions, in the form of a peace that would not have to be enforced. Meanwhile the Americans, who had found themselves deeply involved in a war they had not wanted any part of, demanded nothing less than that their painful participation in the defeat of Germany be for the ultimate purpose of ending all such wars forever. They had entered the fray to "make the world safe for democracy," they announced, assuming that free and democratic nations would never voluntarily start wars, and now they wished only to go home and leave their moral formula to work its political magic.

The Peace Conference

The Peace Conference opened in suburban Paris in January 1919. All governments that had declared war on the Central Powers were invited to send delegations. Twenty-seven responded, but of these only the five principal combatants – France, Britain, Italy, the United States, and Japan – were to participate in the actual drafting of treaty terms. Even this select company was quickly reduced to the principal delegate of each of the three major powers: France, Britain, and the United States.

As host, the French prime minister, Georges Clemenceau, presided over the sessions with the British prime minister, David Lloyd

George, and the American president, Woodrow Wilson. It was an extraordinary meeting of strong but divergent personalities. Clemenceau, a savage parliamentary debater who was hated and feared by his colleagues, had been brought to power only as a last resort because of his furious energy and his implacable passion for France. Lloyd George, by contrast, was a consummate political manipulator who had maneuvered his way from obscure Welsh origins to Britain's highest political office. Finally Wilson, formerly a professor and college president, had exploited his considerable academic talents (especially for phrase-making with a high moral tone) to take him to a governor's mansion and the White House. As rigidly self-righteous as Lloyd George was supple and Clemenceau cynical, Wilson assumed he could instruct his allies as he would wayward students. In exasperation, Clemenceau once asked him why he insisted so doggedly on his Fourteen Points, when the good Lord made do with only ten.

The Conference met in full session only a few times, but its members with their aides served on a large number of committees dealing with special problems. The main business was drafting treaties between the Allied governments and each of the Central Powers. By far the most important treaty, needless to say, was that with Germany, and this absorbed most of the attention of the "Big Three." Clemenceau was obsessed with the problem of French security, which he saw as requiring the annexation of the west bank of the Rhine (the Rhineland), while Wilson refused to consider any such flagrant violation of his sacred principle of self-determination. Lloyd George was forced to exercise his considerable negotiating skills to prevent an irreparable break between the other two leaders, and he finally persuaded Clemenceau that seizing German territory on that scale would involve an unacceptable risk of future trouble. Wilson, in the mean time, refused to discuss final terms for Germany until a covenant (constitution) for his projected League of Nations was drafted as the treaty's first article.

The purpose of Wilson's League was to contain and resolve international disputes before they ignited armed conflict. An extension of the Vienna Congress System, it would be a formal organization of two representative bodies: an Assembly in which each member had one vote, and a Council in which the great powers would be permanent members and to which a number of others would be elected for a term. These bodies were to meet once a year to resolve, or refer to an International Court of Justice, any disputes that threatened the peace. Any state failing to comply with the decisions of the League would be judged an aggressor and be subject to a complete embargo by all the member states. To the French this project seemed a hopelessly flimsy defense against a revived Germany, while to the United States Senate it represented an undesired degree of permanent involvement in European affairs. To Wilson, however, it was humanity's ticket of admission to the Promised Land.

With the League Covenant finally in place, the negotiations returned to the question of French security. France was offered a fifteen-year occupation of the Rhineland, but Clemenceau regarded this as worthless because it provided no protection against the expected revival of German militarism in twenty years. To reassure him, Wilson and Lloyd George offered treaties guaranteeing France against German aggression (though the American version was never ratified by the United States Senate), and finally Clemenceau agreed to the Anglo-American terms, convinced that British and American support were more important to French security than a longer French presence in the Rhineland.

The Treaty of Versailles

The final terms of the treaty with Germany included the return of Alsace-Lorraine (seized by the Germans in 1871) to France, some corrections of the Belgian border with Germany, and international control of the Saar (with its coal going to France) for fifteen years, after which a local plebiscite would determine if the area would belong to France or Germany. Much more extensive territorial changes were made in eastern Germany in order to reconstitute a viable Polish state. Germany was forced to cede parts of Silesia in order to assure Poland of a coal supply, and a substantial piece of East Prussia (which had a large Polish population) to serve as Poland's corridor to the Baltic Sea. East Prussia was now separated from the rest of Germany by this "Polish Corridor," an arrangement which was seen as a particularly outrageous affront by all subsequent German leaders, whatever their other differences in attitude toward the war and the peace.

In addition the treaty called for the drastic limitation of German arms, to an army of 100,000 troops and a navy of six warships and no submarines. The Germans were required to surrender most of their merchant ships to the Allies, and even to build new ones for them, supposedly in reparation for the ships they had sunk. Finally the Germans were required to supply France, Belgium, and Italy with large quantities of coal for ten years, and to pay an as-yet unspecified sum of money to the victors, in order to cover the "costs" of the war. The clause specifying these reparations invoked Germany's responsibility for the war, thereby focusing German resentment against the treaty more as a symbol of defeat than for its specific terms.

As a matter of fact the treaty was remarkably moderate in its terms, considering the magnitude of the war and the losses sustained by the victors, and it was also surprisingly true to the non-vindictive spirit of Wilson's Fourteen Points. Clearly, however, it was a serious tactical error to force the Germans to accept responsibility for unspecified reparations, particularly when the Allies had no concrete measure of damages owed, or of Germany's capacity to pay. This point was raised by a young British economist, John Maynard Keynes, who had served on the staff of the British delegation until he resigned in protest at this economic settlement. He then published a devastating attack on the treaty entitled *The Economic Consequences of the Peace*, in which he argued that the Germans could not possibly pay the great sums that were being proposed by the victors. Needless to say, the Germans seized on this document to support their denunciation of the treaty and their refusal to pay the reparations. Moderates on the Allied side also found Keynes's argument convincing, and it helped to create the widespread impression that the terms of the treaty were unreasonably severe. (Today there is less certainty that Keynes was right, given the enormous "reparation" payments the Germans were able to extract from the countries they conquered in the Second World War.)

The treaty was signed on June 28, 1919, five years to the day after a Serbian nationalist had assassinated the Habsburg heir in

Sarajevo, leading to the first outbreak of hostilities. The palace of Versailles was chosen as the scene for the signing of the treaty, since it was here that the Prussians had proclaimed the German Empire after their defeat of France in 1871 – a blow that was still vividly and bitterly remembered by the French.

Intended to establish a base for peace, the Treaty of Versailles actually served primarily to provoke German resentment and sustain German belligerence, while failing to provide for any means of enforcing its terms and preventing a revival of German military power. With the treaty on paper and signed, both the British and Americans withdrew from the Continent, psychologically as well as physically, while Russia, wholly absorbed in its own revolution, had ceased to exert any influence on Germany after its capitulation a year earlier in the Brest-Litovsk Treaty. As a result, France was left alone to enforce the treaty terms on Germany. This proved an impossibility, since France was not only weaker than Germany to begin with, in both population and resources, but had also suffered much greater damage from the war, losing a larger percentage of its men of combat age than had any other participating state. Germany was wholly unreconciled to the idea of defeat, and even with her borders trimmed would have no rival for the industrial and military dominance of the Continent in the postwar period.

The other peace treaties

While the terms of the Versailles treaty were being worked out, the successor states of the disintegrated Habsburg monarchy, and the border states of the former Russian Empire, were setting up provisional governments and rounding out boundaries. The main contribution of the Peace Conference to this process was the drafting of treaties between the victors and the defeated German allies in eastern Europe: Austria and Hungary (now separate republics), Bulgaria, and Turkey.

In the Treaty of St Germain, Austria recognized the new states of Czechoslovakia, Yugoslavia, Poland, and Hungary, ceding territory to all but Hungary, and also to Italy, in the name of self-determination. Actually the new states all contained captive minorities, which they promised to respect – including the

German-speaking former Austrians of a region called the Sudeten-land, which was now assigned to Czechoslovakia, providing Hitler with an excuse to dismember this nation twenty years later. Finally Austria also agreed to pay reparations and limit her army, and she was forbidden to merge politically with Germany, at least without permission from the Council of the League of Nations.

While the Austrians were signing the treaty in which the Allies defined the borders of Poland, the Poles themselves were busy trying to establish much more extensive ones, fighting first against Czechoslovakia and then Russia. In the spring of 1920 they almost captured Kiev and much of the Ukraine, then were driven back by the Russians all the way to Warsaw; finally they rallied and recovered part of their original advance at Russia's expense.

By the Treaty of Trianon, Hungary lost three-quarters of her prewar territory and two-thirds of her population to her neighbors, and she was also required to pay reparations and drastically reduce her armed forces. By this time a Communist-dominated republican government had established itself in Hungary, and it refused to accept the punitive treaty. Neighboring Romania, which had been given the Hungarian province of Transylvania in the Allies' treaty, now went to war against the new regime and overthrew it; in its place a quasi-monarchical government was established which signed the treaty.

In 1920 the sultan of Turkey, helpless before the Allied occupation of Constantinople, signed the severely punitive Treaty of Sèvres, by the terms of which he renounced all claims to non-Turkish territory, which meant in effect abandoning everything but Anatolia and Constantinople. The Straits were to be internationalized and demilitarized, Armenia was granted independence, Mesopotamia and Palestine were mandated to Britain, the Turkish islands were divided between Italy and Greece, important territory on the Aegean coast was awarded to Greece, and also Smyrna (on the Anatolian coast) was to be occupied by Greece until a plebiscite was held. The crisis of the Ottoman defeat, however, had given force and opportunity to a nationalist revolution in Turkey, led by military hero Mustapha Kemal, which in two years would overthrow the sultanate and establish a republican regime. The nationalists had denounced the treaty signed by the sultan, and the new government now negotiated a new one with the Allies which modified the terms in Turkey's favor. In particular Turkey gained the region of eastern Thrace, and the Greek gains were omitted from the new agreement. With the departure of the Allied forces from Constantinople, Mustapha Kemal formally proclaimed the Turkish Republic and became its first president, then launched the country on an unprecedented program of reform and modernization.

The statesmen meeting in Paris had no forces to impose order, let alone an overall settlement, on the turbulent new states of eastern Europe. In addition they feared that intervention might provoke a revolutionary response, giving communism a foothold in the long territory that separated Russia from western Europe. The new revolutionary regime in Russia was regarded at best with distaste by most government leaders in the west, and although they were not prepared to go to war against it, they were concerned to prevent any contamination of the West by the infection of communism, particularly in the new German Republic. In the disorder following Germany's defeat both Berlin and Munich had been taken over briefly by communist insurrections, and a full-scale revolution in Germany seemed a frightening possibility.

In eastern Europe the formerly subject peoples who constituted the new or enlarged successor states had in every case liberated themselves, and the treaties drawn up by the Peace Conference did little more than exert some influence on the drawing of boundaries. (In the most extreme case of Allied intervention, they brought about the withdrawal of Romanian troops from Hungary.) While the boundaries that were finally established were far from satisfactory to all the parties concerned, disputes were worked out locally and did not involve the Allied powers.

German resentment

Right from the start, however, the Versailles Treaty became a bitterly contested issue between Germany and the Allies. To begin with, the Germans vigorously protested their exclusion from the Paris meetings. They regarded the end-product as a "Diktat" rather than the negotiated settlement they felt they deserved, since they had not surrendered unconditionally. Further, they charged that the terms of the treaty were vindictive and violated the Fourteen Points which they had invoked in requesting the armistice.

It is easier than it was at the time to see that the specific

German objections to the treaty were more excuses than reasons for their resentment. There is every reason to believe that if the Germans had been victorious they would have produced a far more punitive document, as they did in the Treaty of Brest-Litovsk with defeated Russia; To a remarkable degree, furthermore, the treaty was faithful to the intent of the Fourteen Points. As an example, the much-protested "Polish Corridor" was in fact specified in the Fourteen Points, and the particular selection of territory made for this purpose had the justification that the last prewar German census showed its inhabitants to be predominantly Polish; the establishment of the corridor, in short, was an imperfect but not unreasonable way to meet what the Allies perceived to be a legitimate requirement of the new Polish state. It clearly outraged most Germans, however, who were hardly concerned with the needs of Poland. To them the treaty was only the sign and symbol of a defeat which few Germans could bring themselves to accept.

Instead of dismissing the German allegations of injustice, however, the Allies gave them a sympathetic hearing from the start, using them to begin backing away from a treaty they did not want to have to enforce. As a result, the treaty was to be a major subject of debate in both Europe and America for twenty years after it was signed, with the German cause gaining ever-increasing public support in Britain and the United States, and even to a lesser degree in France. This conversion of the victors can probably be attributed to their revulsion against the war they had just fought, and to a consequent determination to avoid any commitment which might lead to their having to fight the Germans again. Blindly, they hoped to assume Germany's defeat, as carefully defined on paper, without imposing it by force. Thus they ultimately left Germany potentially the dominant power on the Continent, with its population both unrepentant and unsubdued. It was a formula for disaster.

THE RUSSIAN REVOLUTION

The provisional government

In Russia the postwar era began when the Bolsheviks seized the government in November 1917 and took Russia out of the war with the Treaty of Brest-Litovsk in March 1918. From the beginning of the war public opinion in the cities had been increasingly hostile to the imperial regime, initially because of its incompetence and then because of widespread and probably accurate suspicions of treason in high places, notably in the entourage of the empress.

By the spring of 1917, Russia's armies were disintegrating and the imperial government was in extreme disarray, while the railroads were unable to transport adequate supplies either to the armed forces or to the cities. Food shortages led to riots and strikes in the capital, Petrograd, and when the tsar ordered the garrison troops to fire on the demonstrators, they mutinied and joined the rioters instead. The Duma, Russia's consultative assembly, now constituted itself a provisional government and refused to dissolve itself at the order of the tsar. Stripped of all power by this spontaneous revolution, the tsar abdicated in favor of a brother, who promptly abdicated in turn, leaving official government in the hands of the Duma.

This body now called for the election of a constituent assembly (one that would draw up a constitution), and in the mean time, as a provisional government, announced democratic reforms and took what steps it could to revive army morale and continue the war. In general the provisional government represented an admirable but unrealistic attempt to implement western liberal ideals, which few Russians – beyond the intellectual elite in the Duma itself – understood, or would have supported if they had. Technically the Duma was made up of representatives of the entire country, but in practice the members represented only themselves. This unhappy fact was rapidly brought home to them by a "soviet" – a council of workers and soldiers – which leftists had organized from the seething mass of strikers and mutineers, and which soon came to constitute a rival government. Although it did not control the government's administrative centers in the provinces, the Petrograd soviet physically dominated the capital in a way that would ultimately prove decisive.

Significantly, Petrograd was not only the seat of government in Russia but also much the largest city in the nation, as well as its most important center of heavy industry – particularly arms production. In striking contrast to the backward agricultural character of most of the country, Petrograd had some of the Continent's largest and most modern factories; and as a consequence the city contained a concentration of industrial workers that could not be matched in any of the other cities in Europe.

The issues that divided the provisional government and the soviet were complex. While the government advocated a major program of social reforms, it favored continuing the war on the side of the Allies, and it reserved all major decisions for the coming constituent assembly. The soviet leaders were mostly radical socialists who favored disengagement from the war and ultimately a government based on numerous local, elected soviets of workers, soldiers, and peasants. These objectives were given powerful formulation by a number of exiled revolutionaries – most importantly Lenin – whom the Germans now deliberately transported back to Russia (and would also provide with liberal amounts of money) for the purpose of destabilizing the provisional government and removing Russia from the war.

Lenin's program was more radical than that of the other soviet leaders; he demanded all power for the soviets, an immediate end to the war on Germany's terms, the seizure of land by the peasants, and control of the factories by the workers. Lenin and his followers (known as the Bolsheviks, while the more moderate revolutionaries were called the Mensheviks) provoked opposition in the Petrograd soviet, and were quickly suppressed when they tried to displace the provisional government in July of 1917. Some of the Bolsheviks were imprisoned, but Lenin escaped to Finland.

A moderate named Alexander Kerensky now assumed leadership of the provisional government, which immediately faced a new threat, this time from the right. Kerensky's appointed commander-in-chief of the armies, General Kornilov, became the center of a right-wing plot to put an end to the power of the Petrograd soviet, and probably the radicals in the provisional government as well. Refusing Kerensky's dismissal, Kornilov prepared to march on the capital in September, but his intended coup was undermined by the defection of large numbers of troops and the mobilization of the city's Bolsheviks – whose cause was greatly strengthened by this development. Seizing the opportunity to discredit Kerensky, Leon Trotsky (with Lenin, the other major Bolshevik leader) managed to persuade the populace in Petrograd that Kerensky had been untrustworthy in the affair, and was moreover intending to surrender the city to the Germans. To defend the city,

Trotsky organized a "Military Revolutionary Committee," which was actually intended to coordinate the brewing Bolshevik revolution. Lenin now returned to Petrograd (in October) to play his part in the long-awaited event.

The Bolsheviks seize power

Mounting disorder in both cities and the countryside finally gave the Bolshevik leaders their chance, and on November 7, 1917, the Military Revolutionary Committee seized the principal government offices and arrested most members of the provisional government. Kerensky fled and attempted to organize resistance, but finding that endeavor futile he finally went into exile (in the United States). Trotsky and Lenin now convened a congress of soviets from all over Russia; seeing that the Bolsheviks were in full command of this body, its more moderate and conservative members walked out in protest. The congress then gave its stamp of approval to the coup and established a new government (called a Council of People's Commissars) under the leadership of Lenin as president, Trotsky as foreign minister, and a younger party organizer named Joseph Stalin as minister of minority nationalities.

While this drama was being played out in Petrograd, the rest of the country – including the army – was in chaos. Rail communications were irregular at best, cities were running out of supplies, and the troops were making their way home as best they could. The new government controlled Petrograd and little else, but it was led by one of the greatest revolutionary geniuses of all time. Lenin, like many European socialists of the time, was a student of Karl Marx and a believer in the class struggle. Unlike many Marxists, however, he rejected any democratic implications of Marx's work, and concentrated all his energies on creating a dictatorship of the ideologically "most advanced" element of the society – namely the Bolshevik party – under the direction of an elite governed ultimately by himself. Curiously, once he had seized power in Petrograd, Lenin went ahead with the national election for a constituent assembly that had been planned by the original provisional government – presumably because he expected it to yield an overwhelming vote of confidence for his takeover of power. Instead, in the only free election ever held in Russia, the voters returned an assembly that was only a quarter Bolshevik, while over half the members were of the more moderate socialist parties favored by the peasantry. Lenin permitted this parliament to meet once (January 1918), then sent armed guards to dissolve it, in an action that his opponents were powerless to resist.

Early years of Bolshevik rule

The Bolsheviks now began to work quickly, both to implement their own program and to co-opt the local revolutions that were taking place in the army and the countryside, as the soldiers were turning on their officers and the peasants on their landlords. They nationalized the banks, repudiated the tsar's foreign debt, turned factories over to their workers and large landholdings to their peasants. Meanwhile they called for peace and made no move to prevent the mutinous soldiers from returning home to claim their share of the redistributed land. These popular moves were followed by increasingly repressive measures which clearly indicated the real direction that the Bolsheviks intended to go – which was away from the decentralization of power and ownership and toward ever tighter control by the ruling clique of all aspects of the economy and society.

Nationalization of all industry was undertaken first, a process that was relatively easy to accomplish given the concentration of factories in the capital, their recent origin, and their orientation toward fulfilling the requirements of the tsar's government. Workers were organized into state-controlled "unions" that were forbidden to strike. More gradually, the new government also worked toward the nationalization of land and the collectivization of agricultural labor, beginning this policy with forced levies of food, and a campaign to displace peasant resentment from the government on to the class of small landholding farmers called *kulaks*.

To implement such a radical program, Lenin recognized that it was essential to disengage from the war at any price, which meant accepting Germany's highly punitive treaty of Brest-Litovsk (March 1918). With the conclusion of this treaty the Bolsheviks moved the Russian capital from Petrograd to Moscow, primarily to increase the distance between themselves and their enemies –

not only the Germans but also the anti-Bolshevik factions within Russia who were organizing armed revolts and rival regimes all along the western border.

Between 1918 and 1920 the Bolshevik government had to fight these counter-revolutionary forces on half a dozen fronts, originally with no army at its disposal. Trotsky now proved himself a military organizer of the first order, mobilizing an all-volunteer force which he then developed into a highly effective conscript army, equipped with the artillery produced by the tsar's arms industry. Favored by their interior position, and the failure of the counter-revolutionaries to coordinate their efforts, the new "Red" (Bolshevik) Army was able to deal successfully with most of the "White" (anti-Bolshevik) forces that were organized by local opponents of their regime.

An alarming challenge to the Bolsheviks came when the Allies landed troops at Vladivostok and Archangel to protect large quantities of military stores which they had shipped to their tsarist ally, but which the imperial government had not succeeded in distributing to its armies before it was overthrown. Once in Russia, these British, French, American and Japanese forces inevitably lent support to the anti-Bolshevik cause, in the hope of regaining Russia as an ally against Germany. Since the Bolsheviks expected "capitalist" opposition, they saw this intervention as evidence that their regime was being threatened from all sides. In fact, however, the western allies had been motivated originally by the fear that the arms stockpiles might fall into German hands, and when Germany was defeated they had no further interest in remaining in Russia. (The Japanese, by contrast, had joined in this Allied intervention in order to pursue their own territorial goals in the Far East; they seized Vladivostok and were not driven out by the Russians until 1922.) After the Armistice only Clemenceau expressed unmitigated hostility to the Soviet regime, and even if he had wanted to undertake a new war against it the French army was in no position to do so.

Ultimately the greatest impact the Allies had on Russian affairs was by defeating Germany and thereby forcing abrogation of the Breat-Litovsk Treaty. Even though the Baltic territories that had been surrendered to Germany by this pact became independent states, the Red Army did succeed in recovering the Ukraine from local forces once the Germans had withdrawn from it – no trivial gain for the new regime.

Perhaps the most serious threat that the Red Army had to deal with came from the Poles, who attacked and overran the Ukraine in 1920. The Soviet forces counterattacked with such vigor that within two months they were threatening Warsaw, but then the Polish army again took the offensive, with the help of French officers, and reconquered all of Poland, together with a fringe of Russian territory, establishing a border that would last for nineteen years. This struggle essentially marked the end of the civil war into which the Bolsheviks had been plunged, and which they finally had won, firmly establishing their authority within all of Russia proper. From this point on, the main concern of the new regime would shift to the desperate plight of the Russian economy.

In the midst of all this military turmoil the Soviet constitution had been promulgated (July 1918). Almost simultaneously the tsar and his family were murdered by the soviet that was holding them prisoner, in a small town on the edge of Siberia, to prevent their rescue by a local anti-Bolshevik army. Although the two events were unconnected, together they symbolized the consolidation of the Bolshevik regime. The new constitution provided for a hierarchy of local and provincial congresses of soviets, leading up to the national congress in Moscow. This congress, the Supreme Soviet, would then elect a Central Executive Committee, which in turn would ultimately direct the government. In actuality all this "soviet domocracy" was completely dominated byBolshevik part – now renamed the Communist party – which in itself was controlled by a Central Committee ruled by a vry small group of part leaders called the Politburo. It was a totally centralized and authoritarian regime, and acknowledged as such by its authors, although they described it as a "dictatorship of the proletariat."

Although this machinery of government was set up in the name and vocabulary of Karl Marx, its faithfulness to Marxist theory would be questioned – and often rejected – by western European Marxists. As its chief designer, Lenin was undoubtedly guided less by his interpretation of Marx than by the exigencies of his particular situation, using whatever tactics would work best to gain control in the midst of Russia's chaos. By taking command of the Petrograd workers' soviets, he was able to use their tightly organized support to seize the government's administrative centers and thus inherit control over what remained of the army and the old imperial bureaucracy. It was Trotsky, as minister of war, who was chiefly responsible for building up a new "Red" army, which he forged into a highly disciplined, surprisingly well-equipped and effective fighting force. Since the troops were chiefly of peasant origin, Lenin's promise of "all land to the peasants" gave them something to fight for and established a level of commitment and morale which could not be matched in any of the various counterrevolutionary forces that sought the restoration of the old order.

Having drawn on the hate of the peasants for their landlords, as well as on the frustrations of minor bureaucrats and junior army officers, Lenin and Trotsky created the basic elements of a disciplined military-administrative regime which had little resemblance to its proletarian origins in the Petrograd soviet. In fact the Russian Revolution was more a replay of the French Revolution of 1789 than a forerunner of Marx's anticipated proletarian revolution. Like the French prototype it drew its original energy from the peasants' hunger for the land, and its leaders consolidated their position through the development of a political party and a powerful army. There were, however, significant differences. The Bolsheviks and their Politburo established a level of dictatorial control that made the Jacobins and their Committee of Public Safety look amateurish, and of course the French had attempted nothing comparable to the nationalization of Russia's economy.

Undoubtedly the Bolsheviks owed their triumph to the ruthless authoritarianism of their rule, but it was also that aspect of the Russian Revolution which separated them from the large majority of European socialists and alienated even many of those committed to armed revolution and militant communism. Clearly the Bolsheviks misjudged this situation in the rest of Europe, for they fully expected other European socialists to follow their example and carry out socialist revolutions that would ultimately create Marx's international socialist society. The lack of response to their seizure of power in Russia left Bolshevik theorists facing a question that Marx had never considered, of whether or not real socialism was possible in a single country. Events soon settled the matter by eliminating any hope of extending the revolution beyond Russia, but not before the Russian leadership had been seriously divided by the issue. It was this issue which would ultimately determine who would inherit Lenin's supreme power at his death in 1924. Trotsky, who continued to think of socialism primarily as an international European movement, would ultimately give way to the less sophisticated Stalin, who cared only about defending the socialist revolution, and the regime it established, in Russia.

A World Safe for Democracy

The Peace drafted by the Paris Conference was in some ways an epilogue to the drama of 1848. The most obvious example is its confirmation of the Dual Monarchy's disintegration into its residual ethnic units. This disposition of the formerly subject territories was largely realized by the time the Conference met, having been accomplished by spontaneous local responses to the collapse of the Habsburg armies. As expressions of national self-determination, the new governments of the successor states enjoyed massive popular support; despite this fact, however, they were not – with the exception of Czechoslovakia's parliamentary regime – democratic in a conventional western sense, but rather administered by centralized authority based on military power.

This seeming contradiction is actually in keeping with the rhetoric of 1848, which was far more nationalist than democratic. Contemporary demands for constitutions and universal suffrage, in fact, were undoubtedly aimed at assuring national self-determination rather than at establishing parliamentary government. In general, aside from occasional members of a prosperous and well-educated urban elite, few inhabitants of central and eastern Europe had any knowledge of, let alone interest in, Britain's type of parliamentary democracy. And when those who did attempted to implement their views – as for example in the Russian Duma and provisional government in 1917 – their impact was usually trivial and their fate often tragic. This dichotomy ultimately reflects the fundamental ambiguity inherent in the concept of "democracy" which had been formulated for the modern world in the eighteenth century: the Continental version envisioned a perfect government perfectly administered by an "enlightened" ruler or elite with the mass approval of the population, while the English version took the form of equitable compromise negotiated among equals through parliamentary institutions.

In the former German Empire, the legacy of 1848 was more complex. In 1849 the Frankfurt Assembly had drafted a liberal constitution for a German federal government, which under different circumstances might have been able to win the support of a significant portion of the German people. But the Prussian king had finally scotched this project by refusing to serve as the constitutional ruler of the "bastard" republic. With his defeat in the 1914–18 war the Kaiser was finally forced to abdicate in favor of a republic, but it was the victorious Allies who had required this move toward "democracy" and not the German people. The result was that the consequent "Weimar" Republic had no popular support in Germany and was viewed instead as a humiliating symbol of national defeat. The new regime enjoyed a model constitution, skillfully drafted by political scientists who were inspired by the work of the Frankfurt Assembly, but it never represented the German national will. In a more subtle but far more critical way than the Allies' minor amputations of German territory, their imposition of the Republic on their defeated enemy violated the deepest German instincts for self-determination.

In a quite different manner, France too now reaped a harvest from 1848. In their June Days of that year the French had fought a brief but savage class war, which left them with a politically conscious proletariat, complete with a revolutionary tradition, that was unique in Europe. This represented the beginning of a polarization of European politics which was to have the gravest consequences for the future, and which also had its roots in 1848 since Marx's *Communist Manifesto* was published in that year. Although at the time its claim that the "specter of communism was haunting Europe" was pure hyperbole, by 1918 most of the European world did indeed feel threatened, not only by the version of Marxist revolution that Lenin had brought about in Russia but also by the unshaken faith of the Russian Communist party in Marx's theory that this revolution must and would eventually engulf the rest of the industrialized world. In 1920 a majority of the country's large Socialist party voted to accept the proffered leadership of the Russian Bolshevik party in the struggle to bring about international communist revolution. This major defection from nationalism was in direct opposition to the prevailing sentiment in the other western European states, even among the most radical groups, but as it would turn out, Lenin's greatest threat to the parliamentary democracies would come from this very fear of his promised international communist revolution – a fear which would do much to enable right-wing dictators to come to power and overthrow struggling democratic regimes in the name of saving them from communism.

THE ECONOMIC CONSEQUENCES OF THE WAR

Economic reconstruction

Once the main lines of the peace had been established, by far the most ominous problem facing the European world was the collapse of its economy. By the end of 1918 much of the Continent was cold and hungry; a terrible winter compounded by a murderous epidemic of influenza had turned an already desperate situation into a deadly crisis. In Germany the Allied blockade had reduced food supplies to a level that threatened serious malnutrition, and severe hardship continued even when the blockade was lifted since the German government refused to use its final reserves of gold and ships to import food. The Belgians were on the brink of mass starvation thanks to German depredations, and were saved only by American aid. The French were desperately short of fuel, since their coal mines had been wantonly destroyed by the retreating Germans. Even the British had serious difficulty supplying their basic needs with the remnants of their merchant fleet. Finally in much of eastern Europe, including Russia, similar shortages were further aggravated by a near total breakdown of transportation.

Although a vast amount of work needed to be done in all these countries to produce and distribute the basic necessities of life, their economies had been so exclusively devoted to wartime needs that they were no longer capable of using the energies – human and industrial – that were liberated when the fighting stopped.

Food was in desperately short supply, primarily because so many of the farm workers had been drafted into the armies, and the few who now returned from the war found little with which to work. Animal stocks, machinery, seeds, even the fields, were all exhausted. Similarly in the areas of industry and transport a huge program of reorientation and renewal was necessary to restore a peacetime economy. Much of the old plant had been converted to war use, and all factory and rail equipment had been badly run down or worn out.

When the war industries ground to a halt, large numbers of workers were thrown out of jobs just as the demobilized troops were streaming back home to look for work. Those who had left established jobs to join the armed forces had a legal right in virtually every country to reclaim them on their return, but many of the jobs no longer existed. Young men who had entered the army directly from school were in an even worse situation and would not find regular employment for years. In Germany some of these uprooted returnees formed themselves into loosely organized groups that were allowed to live in military camps, or worked as lumberers on large estates, especially in East Prussia. Known as "Free Corps," these paramilitary bands were made up primarily of young men who were bitter about Germany's defeat and their own loss of purpose, and eager for a chance to renew the war against all the forces they blamed for their predicament. They were looked upon by reactionary politicians and generals as reserve troops to be drawn on in a revolutionary crisis, and in fact some were used to destroy separatist and left-wing movements in several German states. Most importantly, they would later provide many of the recruits for Hitler's private army of storm troopers.

Reparations

The unlimited demands of the war had had the ultimate effect of expanding and developing the basic industrial capacity of all the major powers, so that once retooled for peace, the factories would be able to produce vastly greater quantities of goods with far fewer hands. This essential reorganization, however, would require a huge investment, and − except in the United States − capital was in desperately short supply. In Britain and France the financial situation was dependent on the reparations settlement which was due to be announced in 1921. The Peace Conference had decided in principle that Germany and her allies were responsible for all the material loss and damage suffered by the victors; but it had also declined to draw up the actual reparations bill that would be presented to the losers. The fact that the commission was given such a long time for its deliberations probably seemed at the time to be a concession to reason and justice, but the consequences were most unfortunate. Not only did this delay prevent a speedy restoration of the economy in Britain and France, but it also invited rumors and polemic that poisoned the atmosphere and contributed to the deterioration of the peace.

The debate over the reparations bill had begun during the Peace Conference (see above, p. 270) but the question no one seemed to consider was not how much Germany would be able to pay but how she was to be made to pay anything at all. Blithely ignoring this basic problem, Britain and France proceeded to base their postwar financial planning entirely upon the assumption that large reparations payments would be made.

All the main participants in the war, except the United States, had financed their effort at least in part by borrowing. The French, with the richest part of their country overrun by the Germans, had seen no alternative to borrowing, first from Britain, then from America. The British, although they began by trying to pay their way through taxes, were gradually driven to liquidating overseas investments and then finally to borrowing from the United States. The Germans also depended heavily on borrowing, but they turned to their own investors, guaranteeing the loans with the indemnities they intended to extract from the vanquished after their coming victory. Finally the imperial government of Russia had borrowed heavily in the Paris financial market in order to pay for the war, but the Bolsheviks had promptly repudiated these loans, thus adding greatly to France's problems. In all of this financial puzzle the reparation payments fit like a key. If the Germans paid the French, they in turn could pay the British and both could pay the Americans, who simply could not or would not understand the British suggestion that the European world – including the Americans – would be infinitely better off if they would forgive their war-related debts.

German difficulties

On both sides, in short, an unprecedentedly costly war had been paid for by government borrowing on the promise of expected exactions from the defeated enemy. When the Allies won, the bottom promptly fell out of Germany's financial structure, and with her consequent failure to pay the expected reparations a similar if less drastic financial collapse took place in France. It soon became abundantly clear that the promises and guarantees that all the governments had held out would not be fulfilled, whereupon public confidence in the value of all related currencies and government bonds plunged to the level of reality, precipitating the most extreme inflation the world has ever known. The French franc swiftly fell to a tenth of its wartime value, while the German mark dropped even lower with the signing of the armistice, and would be virtually valueless by the end of 1923.

The social impact of this inflation was profound, and in the long run disastrous. For the moderate investor, i.e. the bulk of the bourgeoisie, the inflation meant financial ruin, including the loss of that freedom of action and conscience that had given its members their unique place in European culture. For the very rich, however, especially the factory owners (who had made gross profits during the war), inflation made it possible to wipe out corporate indebtedness with worthless currency. In all countries involved in the war, a new class of "war profiteers" emerged to flaunt their unedifying gains before the unemployed ex-soldiers and ruined middle classes. It was against this economic backdrop that Europe's postwar political drama would be played out.

In 1921 the reparations commission announced its final figure for Germany's indebtedness (132 billion gold marks), which was to be paid over the course of thirty years. At the same time the commission, finding Germany in arrears with the interim payments of five billion marks per year that had been specified by the Paris Conference, gave her a deadline for meeting this obligation, backed up by a threat to occupy the Ruhr valley, Germany's center of heavy industry. The Germans managed to borrow enough in London to meet the deadline, but of course this action only continued the wartime pattern of "paying" for the war on paper while postponing the inevitable showdown. By the end of 1922

Germany was again in default of its scheduled payments and showed no sign of even attempting to meet this obligation. Without the German cash, the French were unable to meet their own war-debt installments, so they now prepared to take action to seize the Ruhr. Consultation with the other principal beneficiaries produced a British refusal and a Belgian agreement to participate. French and Belgian troops began moving into the region in January 1923. In order to get something of value from Germany in lieu of the unpaid reparations, the French planned to operate the mines and factories (which were manned by German workers) and ship the products home. It was a cumbersome scheme at best, and it was ultimately sabotaged by the German government, which began paying the workers not to work. This passive resistance successfully denied any benefits to the French, but it also proved extremely costly to the Germans, since their government simply printed the money to support the workers. The result was the final explosive inflation that totally destroyed the mark.

In September 1923 a new German cabinet, formed under Gustav Stresemann as chancellor, began taking the painful measures necessary to restore the value of the mark. The workers' resistance in the Ruhr was called off and reparations payments were resumed. Taxes were increased and government expenses were sharply curtailed. The exhausted currency was then replaced by a "new mark" which was given the value of the preinflationary one and was backed by the real wealth of of the nation – that is, the value of all land and industries in Germany. To everyone's surprised relief, the new mark was accepted at this assigned value, both in Germany and in the international market.

In the mean time the Allies set up an international commission, under an American banker named Charles Dawes, to work out a practical schedule of reparations payments. The "Dawes Plan" was issued in April 1924: essentially it reduced the amount due each year, and provided for a large loan to Germany, about half of which would be raised in the United States. It also set up a mechanism to facilitate the transfer of such huge sums, by establishing that all foreign exchange (dollars or pounds) destined for Germany would be paid to a special bank which would forward an equivalent sum in marks to the proper recipient; the dollars or pounds would then be used by the German government to meet its foreign obligations, including reparations. The plan was generally greeted as a great success, although in point of fact it did not so much make it possible for the Germans to pay reparations as provide a method by which France could be paid indirectly with American loans. Germany readily participated in this sleight-of-hand, which not only resolved her confrontation with France but also appeared to open up to her a new and unlimited source of credit in the United States.

Fascism in Italy

During these half-dozen years following the armistice, the victorious powers were struggling with internal problems almost as serious as those which afflicted Germany. Italy had emerged from the war a badly shaken and deeply frustrated country. The Italians had entered the war on the Allied side only because they were offered important territorial gains at Austrian expense, but the Paris treaty-makers had reneged on this commitment. Moreover the Italian troops had been humiliated on the battlefield and large numbers had been killed, while the country's ramshackle economy was in total disarray, with unemployment rife and food scarce. The social disintegration that Bloch had promised as a consequence of modern war was experienced in Italy almost as much as in Germany and Russia.

Just as in Germany and Russia, these conditions of confusion and hardship spawned prophets of revolution and reaction. For a brief time in 1920 workers and peasants seized factories and estates, but this spontaneous uprising did not elicit any serious political response. Instead it generated a morbid fear of revolution among the property-owning classes, and thus contributed significantly to their growing support of a new movement called fascism which promised to end disorder and the "Bolshevik" threat. Its founder and leader was an opportunistic demagogue named Benito Mussolini, who had previously agitated for causes at all points on the political spectrum. Having led the fight against Italy's entry into the war, when national sentiment began to shift in its favor he had totally reversed direction. After the war he seized the opportunity presented by the masses of unemployed veterans, whom he began organizing in disciplined gangs of street fighters. Dedicated to a violent doctrine of nationalism, anti-Bolshevism and total allegiance to their leader, these "fascisti" as Mussolini called his followers (after the bundle of sticks that had served as the symbol of government office in ancient Rome) constituted a private army which Mussolini intended to use to seize power. From 1920 to 1922 they fought socialists and communists in the streets, and as they grew in power unleashed a campaign of terror against all their political opponents, which was tacitly if not openly supported by both the government and the army. In the elections of 1921 Mussolini and forty-four of his followers won parliamentary seats and the way seemed open for him to make a quasi-legal bid for dictatorial power. By the fall of the following year the fascists clearly had enough power to proceed with the coup that Mussolini had been preparing. A huge political rally, advertised as a "march on Rome" forced the king to choose between calling out the army to disperse the fascists or giving them control of the government by making Mussolini the prime minister. Assuming that the pro-fascist army would not fight against Mussolini, the king accepted what he considered to be inevitable.

As prime minister Mussolini now demanded and got from the parliament the power to rule by decree for a year. This was all he needed to turn the government into a fascist dictatorship. In early 1923 the fascist gangs were merged into a militia, and the troops in the regular army were also required to swear allegiance to the "Duce" (leader) as Mussolini was called. Parliament remained technically in existence, but it was turned into an entirely fascist body through the combined effects of new "laws" (such as the one that abolished all other political parties) and the open intimidation, exile, and even murder of Mussolini's opponents.

Mussolini's takeover the Italian government gave the European world a new political term, "fascist," that would be applied to a wide range of policies, practices and regimes, without ever being rigorously defined. Some characteristics of Italian fascism are particularly noteworthy, however, because they would be found again in the German case. First of all the regime was a response to the failure of democratic government to master postwar problems. It was anti-communist and also anti-democratic, but at the same time it called itself socialist and did in fact enjoy wide popular support, which it gained particularly by its extreme nationalism.

Its values were openly opposed to those of traditional Judeo-Christian morality, being based upon an equally traditional suspension of that morality in time of war – when all means are considered justified for the end of defeating the enemy and saving the homeland. The basic organization of Italian fascism, as of Bolshevism, was the party, that extra-governmental system of communication and coordination first introduced in European history by the Jacobins in the French Revolution.

A common but confusing characterization of fascism has been its description as a movement of the "right" as opposed to the communist "left" according to the traditional scheme for indicating the political orientation of a group or party in the parliamentary spectrum. Under close scrutiny this distinction seems of little use, since both movements called themselves "socialist" and denounced democracy and capitalism equally. Similarly fascism is sometimes seen as a nationalist movement and communism as international, but obviously communism became nationalistic in Russia, and the fascists established transnational connections. Perhaps a more illuminating perspective is one in which both fascism and communism are seen as reflexive reactions against a parliamentary liberalism that had only recently been imported to the Continent from Britain and the rest of the Atlantic community. Parliamentary institutions had enjoyed great prestige in the nineteenth century as a result of the current wealth and power of Britain and the United States, but this form of democracy was still basically foreign to the traditions and experience of Continental Europe. In Italy, parliamentary government had been imposed on the newly created nation in the mid-nineteenth century only because the country had been united under the kingdom of Piedmont, which happened to have adopted Great Britain's parliamentary governmental forms. There was little experience of self-government in the rest of Italy, and the new regime had generally proved ineffective in governing that turbulent and deeply divided society.

Britain in the 1920s

Although its parliamentary regime had not been brought into question, Great Britain emerged from the war with other problems. For one thing the British had put aside their attempt to resolve the Irish problem during the war, but the Irish independence movement had continued in full force, gaining in strength and violence until by the end of the war it amounted to a full-blown revolution. Nor was resolution of the conflict a simple matter of granting what the Irish nationalists demanded, since they were opposed by the Protestant majority in the northern province of Ulster. These privileged landowners had originally come to Ireland in the sixteenth and seventeenth centuries as colonists from England and Scotland, and they had no intention of becoming subject to what they considered to be Ireland's Catholic peasant "natives." In 1920 the British Parliament passed a compromise bill, the Government of Ireland Act, which effectively separated the northern province from Southern Ireland, giving each sub-state its own parliament as well as representation in the House of Commons. The North accepted this arrangement but the South did not, and the troubles continued. In the following year, however, the compromise was essentially agreed to by representatives of the more moderate wing of the independence movement, whose leaders signed a treaty with the British creating a completely self-governing Irish Free State in the south. The new state did not, however, include the Protestant province of Ulster, which as "Northern Ireland" would remain part of the United Kingdom, even though it established its own capital and parliament in Belfast. This exclusion of Ulster from the independent state of Ireland was immediately denounced by the more extreme Irish nationalists, who continued to fight for unification by means of a campaign of terror against the "loyalists" in Northern Ireland.

In Britain itself, politics were largely dominated by economic problems, especially rising unemployment and an outdated industrial plant that made it increasingly difficult for British goods to compete on the world market. To give immediate relief to the jobless the government increased unemployment payments, which became a way of life for a large segment of the working classes, while to deal with the problem of growing competition from the other industrial nations the Conservatives proposed resorting to a protective tariff against foreign goods, as well as arrangements with British dominions and colonies to preserve their markets and raw materials for British trade. These measures were opposed by the Labour party, which held that nationalization of industry would provide a better solution to Britain's economic problems. In 1923 the controversial tariff proposal led to an electoral defeat for its Conservative sponsors and the formation of Britain's first Labour government in 1924. Although it lasted less than a year and was too weak to attempt any nationalization of industry, it did establish the precedent of socialist participation in the parliamentary government of the country.

In foreign affairs the British were most concerned with restoring the European trade that had been cut off by the war, and consequently were opposed to France's hard line with Germany, which they felt only delayed the return to prewar trading relations. At the same time they recognized that the Germans had left the French little choice, and as a result were inclined to offer France some guarantee of security. To this end they backed a proposal for what was called the "Geneva Protocol," which would have committed the members of the League of Nations to submit their disputes to its arbitration, and to enforce its judgements. Because of the objections of the dominions, Britain finally withdrew its support of this measure, but then considered reviving the original treaty of mutual guarantee which the British and Americans had offered France in 1919 but which had lapsed with America's failure to ratify it.

The United States after the war

In the United States the postwar period began with the Senate's rejection of the Versailles Treaty and membership in the League of Nations. The reasons for this aberration were largely political, and even personal, since it was prompted in part by the clash of personalities between President Wilson and Senator Henry Cabot Lodge of Massachusetts. But the decision also reflected a widespread American antipathy to any further "foreign entanglements." On the domestic scene Congress passed a National Prohibition Act, implementing the Eighteenth Amendment to the Constitution (1918) which outlawed the production and sale of alcoholic beverages, while in 1920, following Britain's lead of 1918, the Nineteenth Amendment gave the vote to women.

In 1921 Warren Harding succeeded Woodrow Wilson as President, announcing a sharp break with the high-minded purpose that had motivated America's war effort. The Senate's refusal to ratify the Versailles Treaty was now followed by other measures expressing the country's reaction against foreign involvement and a desire to put "America first." One early act of the new administration established extremely high tariffs against foreign imports, and another stringently limited immigration for the first time in America's history. Quotas were now established for admitting immigrants which clearly reflected a racist reaction against the massive Catholic and Jewish influx from eastern and southern Europe that had poured in since the turn of the century. By limiting the numbers to be accepted from each country to a percentage of the residents from that country living in the United States in 1890, it effectively restricted immigration from all but northern Europe, and in a 1924 version of the law the Japanese were completely excluded. These highly discriminatory regulations caused deep resentment, particularly in Japan, and two decades later would have the grim consequence of almost completely barring any Jewish immigration from Hitler's Europe.

In a more enlightened effort to reduce America's international commitments, President Harding, at the end of his first year in office, convened the Washington Conference to discuss the limitation of naval armaments and the regulation of Pacific and Far Eastern affairs. Britain, France, Italy, Japan and the United States agreed to a ten-year moratorium on new naval construction, some restrictions on the size of various types of ships, and a limit on overall fleet tonnage according to the approximate ratio of 5 to 3 to 1 – the United States and Britain to be in the highest category, Japan in the middle, and France and Italy in the lowest. The powers also guaranteed each other's possessions in the Pacific, and agreed to respect China's territorial and administrative integrity as well as its "open door" in trading relations. The Conference clearly indicated in which part of the world Americans believed their current interests lay. With respect to Europe their only concern now seemed to be in organizing repayment schedules for the war loans made to France and Britain, while in the Pacific they sensed, although greatly underestimated, a growing threat.

During the war Japan had taken over Germany's colonial interests and possessions in the Far East, notably her Pacific islands and her concession in Shantung. In Russia, moreover, Japan had joined the Allies in occupying Vladivostok, and had maintained her forces there well after the others had withdrawn. Clearly she was probing for imperial toe-holds, though without openly challenging the western imperial powers in the area – Britain and America. Japan's new strength and position were recognized by the League of Nations mandate for the German islands north of the equator, and by her participation in the Washington Conference. What occurred to very few was that the naval agreement would provide Japan with a screen behind which it could begin a vast building program that would eventually challenge the United States in the Pacific.

Eastern Europe

In central and eastern Europe postwar adjustments were more radical than in the west, largely because the breakup of the Habsburg Empire and the withdrawal of Russia from her border provinces had created ten new states. Of these only one – Czechoslovakia – possessed heavy industry; the rest were predominantly agricultural, with largely peasant populations. The half-dozen that had comprised the Dual Monarchy had previously formed a single viable economic unit, but as independent states were seriously injured by the tariff walls that their governments rapidly established. This tendency to economic fragmentation was abetted by a virulent nationalism which in turn contributed to the transformation of several of the governments into authoritarian regimes. The striking exception again was Czechoslovakia, which retained a vigorously democratic government.

One characteristic shared by virtually all of these "successor states" (not to mention some of their neighbors) was the determination to acquire border territories assigned to neighbor states, but which they claimed were inhabited by their fellow nationals. Instead of resolving such disputes, Wilson's formula of "self-determination" created endless insoluble problems. No matter how many maps were drawn there were always minorities left in each new governmental unit. (To take the most striking example, even before they had properly established their new states, the Czechs and Poles had gone to war over a territory, Teschen, which each claimed. In spite of these tensions, however, the new nations of eastern Europe felt the need of collective arrangements to guard them against Russian and German ambitions. The most famous of these, known as the "Little Entente," bound Czechoslovakia, Romania, and Yugoslavia in a military alliance backed by France, which in turn was allied with Poland.

In the mean time, things were not going smoothly for the revolutionary regime in Russia. Although the Bolsheviks managed to master the half-dozen counter-revolutionary uprisings that had challenged them, they barely escaped a major disaster in their war with Poland (1920), and did suffer a serious loss of territory. Their continuing military struggle against the various "White" armies not only weakened the central administration, but took a damaging economic toll by disrupting the transportation system. As the railroads proved incapable of getting the necessary food to the cities, or manufactured goods to the country, the peasants began to hoard their crops. This created shortages in the cities which rapidly deteriorated into famine, producing the inevitable demonstrations which often turned into riots, until one, at the naval port of Kronstadt (near Petrograd), developed into a full-scale insurrection, involving the very garrison which had played the decisive part in the November revolution. Faced with this mortal challenge by their own heroes, the Bolsheviks responded with overwhelming force and a major policy capitulation, first smashing the uprising, and then – almost simultaneously – announcing a radically new economic policy.

In the years 1921 to 1927, under this program (the New Economic Policy or NEP), the Bolsheviks largely restored private enterprise in agriculture and the manufacture and sale of consumer goods, while retaining tight control of heavy industry, banking, foreign trade, communications, and transport. This new policy quickly eased the worst consumer shortages and thus brought the protest to an end, but it also led to a new threat to the socialist character of the regime, as classes of prosperous small merchants and landowning peasants (kulaks) began to gain wealth and power. Lenin's purpose in instituting the NEP had clearly been to buy time while he gathered his political forces for a new campaign to socialize the economy. But in 1922 he suffered the first of several strokes, with the last and fatal one coming in 1924. As a result, the period of the the NEP was dominated by the inevitable struggle for the succession to his dictatorial power. The principal rivals were Trotsky, who as minister of war was largely responsible for the Bolsheviks' victory in the civil war, and Joseph Stalin, minister for minorities and secretary of the party. Although Lenin had expressed growing doubts about Stalin, he had made no move to install Trotsky as his successor, and after Lenin's death Stalin quickly proved himself master of the party infighting which ensued. Thoroughly entrenched in power by 1927, Stalin brought the NEP to a speedy end and launched a new socialist offensive in the form of a series of "Five-Year Plans" for economic development. In the mean time Trotsky was exiled and eventually murdered, probably by Stalin's agents.

Germany after the war

The central factor in postwar Europe, however, was Germany. Before the war it had been only one – even if the strongest – of five great powers on the Continent. Now with the Russian and Habsburg empires destroyed and Italy in turmoil, only France was left to counter Germany's inherent power. Even if the French army was probably stronger than its just-defeated rival, Germany was potentially far superior both in population and in industrial capacity. It was the clear recognition of this painful prospect that made French leaders so obsessed with their country's security in the postwar period, and in retrospect it is hard to blame them for not liking what they saw across the Rhine.

Because the Allies had refused to deal with the Kaiser's imperial regime, the Germans had been forced to improvise a republic to negotiate the armistice and peace. This measure proved to be a fatal error on the part of the Allies, because it relieved the imperial government of the onus of the defeat which the German people were not prepared to accept, and placed it on the new Republic. Largely for this reason the parliamentary government established by the Weimar constitution never had the real support of the German people, nor a clear political majority with a firm electoral base. All its ministries were coalitions, and few of its deputies were convinced democrats. Both communists and ultra-nationalists made repeated attempts to overthrow it by force, so that during its first half-dozen years the Republic had to depend on the army to put down a series of such revolutionary challenges; this the generals were willing to do not because they loved the Republic but because they needed the state to support the army.

The army was unquestionably the strongest institution in the country. Even though it had been drastically reduced to a mere 100,000 men by the Versailles Treaty, it retained its wartime organization and discipline, with the troops remaining loyal to their commanders amid the dissolution of all other authority. The generals were basically monarchist in spirit, but most remained loyal to the legally constituted government for as long as it continued to function. In return, the Weimar regime readily gave huge appropriations to the army, and connived in clandestine rearmament beyond the Treaty limits.

While the established order survived in this precarious manner, extremist political activity grew more frenzied on both the left and the right. Local communist organizations staged repeated strikes and uprisings in various German cities, while a number of right-wing parties formed gangs and private "armies" intending to take over the state by force. Like Mussolini's fascists these armed bands engaged with increasing openness and frequency in acts of violence and terror against any and all they took to be their political enemies. The objects of their attacks included not only communists, socialists, and democrats, but also Jews, as the strain of anti-Semitism that had been perennial in Europe now flared into virulent new life in postwar Germany.

While the Weimar government resisted attempts at subversion from all quarters, both national and local authorities tended to look upon the communists as by far the greatest danger, especially since they owed allegiance to the Russian communist regime, and hence tolerated and sometimes even subsidized the right-wing groups as a form of defense against the left. Moreover the judiciary like the army was essentially carried over intact from the empire and its sympathies definitely lay with the ultranationalists; communist agitators who were brought to trial were harshly dealt with, while right-wing extremists received only token reprimands.

The rise of Hitler

It was in this turbulent political atmosphere that Adolf Hitler's Nazi party first appeared as one of numerous right-wing organizations to take shape in Munich, which was becoming the center of the reactionary movement. An Austrian by birth, Hitler was an unsuccessful artist and impoverished drifter in prewar Vienna who had found purpose in life only when he enlisted in the German army at the beginning of the war. As a soldier he had been decorated for courage under fire, but he failed to earn a commission because he was considered too "hysterical" to be capable of leadership. Full of rage over his personal failures and rejections, Hitler had eagerly seized on current right-wing theories that allowed him to lay the blame for his own humiliations, as well as those of Germany, at the door of particular groups of people he could hate and fight. Among these were the liberals and moderates associated with the Weimar government's "betrayal" of Germany, but Hitler reserved his most violent hatred for communists and Jews, both groups that had been particularly prominent in the cosmopolitan life of Vienna.

It was in Vienna that Hitler had imbibed the virulent racism that informed all of his political views. In Austria, Germans were in closer contact with "foreigners" than they were in Germany proper, and because they felt threatened they were apt to take refuge in a defensive prejudice that justified their mingled fear of and contempt for the outsiders in their midst – primarily the Jews and the Slavic groups of eastern Europe. In this setting the pseudo-scientific doctrine of German racial supremacy which was born around the turn of the century found a particularly warm reception. A wholly fanciful extrapolation of the scientific theory of evolution, this doctrine was given its most influential formulation by an expatriate Englishman living in Germany, Houston Stewart Chamberlain, whose rambling philosophizing on the subject had been a great success throughout Germany when it was published in 1899.

According to Chamberlain's racial theory the human species had evolved as a hierarchy of separate subspecies, which were caught in a perpetual struggle for supremacy in which the fittest would inevitably displace the less fit. Highest on the evolutionary ladder in this formulation was the "Germanic race" (also called Teutonic, Nordic, or Aryan), defined as the descendants of the German-speaking tribes that had settled northern Europe. On the lowest rung of the ladder was an inferior "Slavic race," while the "Jewish race" was seen as beneath human dignity altogether – a subhuman strain that was both despicable and dangerous. Jews, it was thought, sought to undo their biological superiors in every possible way; they were therefore the enemies of the German people as much as any military antagonist, and should be similarly dealt with – by all-out war.

Significantly, this theory focused German resentment not only on the particular ethnic groups about which the Austrian Germans had traditionally felt the most anxiety, but also on groups that happened to be far more convenient scapegoats (especially the Jews) than the more powerful non-German peoples of western Europe – who were granted some respect in racist theory on the basis of their "Germanic" heritage from the barbarian invasions. The whole construction was entirely without scientific basis, and represented only a pathological response to stress by seriously disturbed minds, but it drew on deep and ancient strains of xenophobia and anti-Semitism in central Europe, and found growing numbers of fanatic adherents among the distressed and displaced victims of great social upheaval.

There is no doubt that Hitler believed the racial and political theories he expounded, but like Mussolini he was also a completely nihilistic opportunist whose first goal was to gain personal power by whatever means worked best. After the war he began his political career as a rabble-rouser in the beer halls of Munich, discovering his route to power in an exceptional ability to move crowds with his impassioned oratory. His passion was genuine, in the sense that he was seething with the hatreds he so effectively evoked in his listeners, but at the same time the specific content of his speeches was clearly calculated to win a fanatical following for himself. As it happened, the idea of belonging to a master race was as strongly appealing to his desperate audiences as it had been to Hitler himself, and most of his related ideas proved similarly seductive. But he did not hesitate to change his program and pronouncements to suit different situations at different times, and he made no secret of his Machiavellian approach to gaining his ends – nor of the contempt he felt for all those he was able to manipulate by these means.

In the early 1920s few could have guessed what phenomenal success at manipulating others Hitler was to enjoy a short decade later. In 1919, when he became its leader, the Nazi party was a small ultra-nationalist group that had been given a subsidy by the army as an anti-communist investment. The official name of the party was the National Socialist German Workers' Party ("Nazi" being an abbreviation of the German word "National"). Its members were unemployed veterans and workers, who although they saw themselves as socialists were violently opposed to both the communists and the Social Democrats. In 1920 Hitler published an official Nazi party platform, which stated many of the goals that he was actually to achieve in the next quarter-century. While this was intended to win as many converts as possible by appealing to the prejudices of all classes of German society, Hitler also began to lay another power base by organizing the party along military lines, with the armed and uniformed Storm Troops as its backbone. This private army surrounded its commander-in-chief at political rallies, staged demonstrations of its military muscle in the streets, and engaged in attacks on both armed and unarmed political opponents.

In 1923, when Stresemann took the unpopular step of calling off German resistance to the French occupation of the Ruhr, Hitler decided the time was ripe for a Nazi takeover of the tottering republic. Starting from a Munich beer hall, a couple of hundred Nazis marched out behind Hitler and General Ludendorff (the recent military hero, now incredibly decked forth in Wagnerian costume), calling for the populace to rise in their wake and march on Berlin. A small contingent of government troops, and one volley that left a few marchers dead and wounded, ended the incident, but the courts failed to follow through by condemning the leaders. Ludendorff was acquitted altogether of the charge of treason, and while Hitler was convicted, he was given a mild sentence of five years' imprisonment, and was released after only one. This year of comfortable confinement had the ultimate effect of supporting him while he wrote the blueprint for his intended conquest of the world, *Mein Kampf* (My Battle). The failure of his attempted coup had led Hitler to reassess not his ambitions but his tactics. Next time, he concluded – and announced openly to anyone who cared to listen – the Nazis would gain absolute power the way Mussolini, Lenin and Napoleon III had gained it – by exploiting the democratic process against itself.

THE POLICY OF FULFILLMENT AND THE ERA OF
GOOD FEELING

Locarno

When the Germans realized that France intended to maintain her
occupation of the Ruhr despite their resistance, they formed a new
government dedicated to "fulfillment" – presumably of the peace
terms, and initiated a more conciliatory policy. First they called off
the campaign of passive resistance in the Ruhr, then took the
necessary drastic measures to bring Germany's inflation to a
sudden halt. These moves were met by the American Dawes
Plan, which provided loans to facilitate scaled-down reparations
payments and stimulate Europe's strangled economy. It looked
as if an "era of good feeling" was beginning, in which Germany
would assume a more normal place among Europe's nations.

The architect and manager of Germany's new policy was its
foreign minister Gustav Stresemann, a nationalist politician with a
particular flair for foreign policy. He recognized that the popular
mood in western Europe and America had shifted away from
wartime emotions of suspicion and hate to an overwhelming desire
for peace and reconciliation, and he adjusted his strategy accordingly. With a benign countenance and gently rounded shape he
embodied the stereotype of the affable beer-quaffing German,
which most Britons and Americans found reassuring; but beneath
that pleasant exterior was a heart and mind of a Bismarck.

At the Paris Conference the British and Americans had agreed
to guarantee the French border against future German invasions,
but this guarantee became a dead letter when the Americans failed
to ratify the treaty. Apparently suspecting that the British were
now considering such a commitment to France even without
American participation, Stresemann moved to counter this reinforcement of the hated Versailles Treaty by proposing a mutual
guarantee of the Franco-German border. This took the form of a
non-aggression treaty among France, Belgium and Germany to be
guaranteed by Britain and Italy. At the same time Germany offered
Poland and Czechoslovakia commitments to submit all border
disputes to arbitration before resorting to action. Unlike the Versailles Treaty, these agreements, which were signed at Locarno

in December 1925, were freely accepted – indeed proposed – by Germany, and thus appeared to offer a new base for peaceful relations in Europe. A close reading of the texts, however, revealed another possible interpretation. With the non-aggression treaty Stresemann had made it impossible for France to honor its commitments to Poland and Czechoslovakia: if Germany attacked them, France could not defend them without obligating Britain and Italy to come to Germany's aid. No one wanted to believe that Germany harbored any such intentions, but close observers of Weimar politics would have had to know that all high government officials issued regular ritual denunciations of the Polish Corridor. In retrospect the central themes of German foreign policy following the war can be seen as the separation of France first from Britain and then from her east European allies. Locarno contributed to both of these goals.

Another important part of Stresemann's policy involved his use of the Dawes Plan machinery to finance the reconstruction of Germany's economy, and in the process to strengthen political ties between Germany and the United States. Stresemann argued that it was America's war loans to Britain and France that had played the major role in bringing the United States into the war on the Allied side, and he boasted that if he could borrow enough from the United States he would bind it to Germany instead.

The Dawes Plan amounted to a ready-made mechanism for the implementation of this policy, although officially it had provided only for an "international" loan to Germany to facilitate reparations payments. Stresemann's policy evoked an enthusiastic response from American investors, moreover, since they were struggling with an excess of capital because of their unprecedented wartime profits: the United States, which had entered the war heavily indebted to British bankers for financing American railroads and industry, had emerged after the Armistice as the world's principal creditor, and Americans were eager to find ways of investing their money. Thus they readily gave their backing to Stresemann's projects, whether to finance reparations or to pay for the endless public works that he encouraged. This process was to fuel a sudden and brief economic boom in both Germany and the United States, which soon expanded to Britain, France, and most of the European world.

Investment in Germany

With credit readily available, manufacturers in the United States as well as Europe expanded recklessly – particularly in the new industries like automobiles and radios that had been developed by the war – without making sure of adequate markets in advance. In this atmosphere of heady optimism, bankers and borrowers alike became lax and dangerously overextended, while speculation on the stock exchanges drove stock prices far beyond any conceivable intrinsic value. Although credit was abundantly supplied to the Germans, they were forced to service this new debt by short-term, high-rate loans – a procedure normally regarded as criminal when practiced by an individual. The spectacular inflation caused by Germany's reckless wartime borrowing had been brought under control, but this new round of borrowing, by nations and individuals alike, was clearly setting the stage for a financial collapse of the international economy that would make the postwar plight of all the combatants pale by comparison.

Stresemann's predictions about the effects of loans on the lender's political outlook were more than justified by events. As the Dawes Plan went into effect, Germany's image was transformed in both Britain and America, and usually at the expense of France. From having been mortal enemies, popularly endowed with sinister traits of character, the Germans were increasingly pictured in the Anglo-American popular culture as an admirable, industrious, and "cleanly" people, with whom it was a privilege to do business. At one level this was undoubtedly a healthy change; the intense wartime emotions were largely spent by now, and the proper business of the survivors was to make a better world. But the "good feeling" fostered by Stresemann, like the prosperity of the stock market, contained a dangerously large element of wishful thinking.

A logical consequence of the Locarno settlement had been an invitation to Germany to join the League of Nations. Her sponsors connived at covering up all the awkward evidence that would argue against her membership in good standing in this concert of nations, including the final report of the Disarmament Control Commission. This body had been created to monitor Germany's compliance with the disarmament clauses of the Versailles Treaty, and the publication of its final report made clear that Germany had deliberately and systematically violated both the letter and the spirit of these provisions. This report was as vigorously suppressed by Allied authorities as if its contents were the actual danger; in fact what was dangerous was the intention it revealed on Germany's part to evade the treaty and restore her military base, and on the Allies' side the determination to avoid facing the implications of the thinly veiled rearmament. A fitting climax to this excursion into fantasy was provided in 1928 by the American Secretary of State and the French Foreign Minister, who invited all states to sign a treaty renouncing recourse to aggressive war: the Kellogg–Briand pact, as it came to be known, attracted some sixty signatories but few if any true believers.

By their excessive loans, American and British bankers soon made themselves dependent on Germany's economic well-being, just as Stresemann had foreseen, and they now proposed a further reduction in reparations, primarily to safeguard their investments. A new international commission, presided over by another American banker, Owen Young, met and agreed that all Allied supervision of reparation procedures should end, and the total payments should be reduced by about a third. To celebrate the signing of this agreement, Briand announced the early withdrawal of the remaining occupation troops in the Rhineland (originally due to leave in 1935).

In five years Stresemann had brought Germany from economic collapse to a significant economic revival, and from partial military occupation (in the Ruhr) to full and equal membership in the European community. This ambitious program, moreover, had been accomplished with the eager assistance of Germany's former enemies. In early October of 1929 Stresemann suffered a stroke and died. Two weeks later the New York Stock Exchange, having reached unprecedented heights, suddenly crashed, in the worst débâcle in its history. The flood of fictitious wealth which had inundated the financial world suddenly evaporated. Loans to Germany ceased just as rapidly, and as a result so did Germany's interest payments to her creditors. That was enough to end the fragile "era of good feeling," and the western world began its swift, sickening slide into the Great Depression.

The business boom that had reached its climax in 1929 had not restored the affluent economy of prewar Europe. Even though many members of the middle class managed to earn salaries that reestablished their comfortable way of life, inflation had destroyed the value of their investments and thereby eroded their financial security. Further, although unemployment had been reduced it had not been eliminated, primarily because the war had stimulated the mechanization of industrial processes, thereby reducing the need for labor. At this time few employers in either Europe or the United States recognized the need to pay their workers enough to make them consumers of the goods which they produced (a notable exception being Henry Ford), and markets were further limited by the increasing trend toward tariffs and currency controls in most national economies.

In short, the burst of financial activity that led up to 1929 had represented the frenzy of fever rather than the restoration of robust health. The whole structure of the apparent boom was built upon recklessly overextended credit – in the stock market, in loans to Germany, and in the financing of speculative investments and the installment purchases of new homes, cars and appliances. When the crash came, every financial failure, personal or corporate, brought on a series of others, with the process spreading ever faster and further, until the principal industrial economies were all reduced to near chaos. Millions of workers lost their jobs and joined the already large number of the postwar unemployed; the impoverished had no source of assistance, and many died of hunger and cold. The two countries that were worst hit by this depression were precisely the two that had briefly enjoyed the greatest boom: Germany and the United States.

THE GREAT DEPRESSION AND THE COLLAPSE OF THE WORLD ORDER

The US Depression

The Depression hit the United States and Germany the hardest for the very reason that their economies had expanded the most since the war. In Britain, where unemployment was endemic, and in France and Italy where industry was less developed, the shock was less brutal.

The American president, Herbert Hoover, had been elected by a landslide two years before (1928) on a platform of continuing prosperity. Though an able and humane man, he was psychologically quite unprepared to deal with the desperate situation that now confronted him, in particular because he was deeply imbued with the pervasive American prejudice against direct government relief for even the most deserving of the unemployed. His attempts to alleviate the situation were limited to such indirect measures as public works to provide employment and government credit agencies to save financial institutions (such as insurance companies) from bankruptcy. Although he was undoubtedly headed in the right direction with this program, it proved wholly inadequate to cope with an economic crisis in which ten million Americans were out of work.

With unemployment hitting veterans along with everyone else, the demand spread for an immediate cash settlement of the "bonuses" that Congress had promised to those who had served in the recent war. To encourage Congressional implementation of this controversial measure, veterans began assembling from all over the country for a "march on Washington" that would demonstrate both their strength and their desperation. By mid-June of 1932, 17,000 had arrived in Washington, most of whom camped in a shanty town on the edge of the city. The Senate refused to join the House in voting the bonus appropriation, but – in a classic move to defuse the situation – did allocate the funds to pay for the veterans' travel home. At this rebuff most of the demonstrators gave up and departed, but some 2,000 remained, causing the president to panic and order the army to disperse them with a show of force. If this response would have been appropriate in a European confrontation such as Mussolini's march on Rome, it was grossly excessive in these circumstances, and contributed significantly to Hoover's defeat in the presidential election of November 1932, by the challenger, Franklin Roosevelt. Although Roosevelt evoked no great enthusiasm at this time, the incumbent regime had so patently exhausted its ideas and energies that any change was welcome.

The Nazis in power

Meanwhile in Germany the flow of American credit had ceased with the stock market crash of 1929, and the previous American loans began to be recalled. The precarious economic revival that Stresemann had orchestrated came to a sudden end, and a new period of desperation began in which Germany's economic and social distress would exceed even that of the immediate postwar years. The catastrophe of the Depression was international in scope, but the German people naturally looked first to their own government in assessing responsibility for their misery, and began to listen again to the radical explanations and prescriptions of the communist and Nazi parties, both of which had gone into partial eclipse during the years of relative prosperity.

It was the Nazis who became the major beneficiaries of the crisis. Hitler and his party had gained a significant popular following in the early 1920s, but had lost it in the general prosperity of the second half of the decade. In 1924 the Nazis held thirty-two seats in the Reichstag, while in 1928 they retained a mere twelve. Hitler, however, had never lost confidence that he would ultimately triumph, and had continued his political campaigning unabated, adding important recruits to his inner circle. Those who would play the largest roles in the party's future were Fritz Goebbels, who as a propagandist for the Nazi cause was as able and cynical as Hitler himself, and the sadistic Heinrich Himmler, who would become head of the Nazi police forces – the SS and Gestapo. After the ridiculous failure of his attempted Munich coup in 1923, Hitler had determined that his best hope lay in the ballot box; like Mussolini, Napoleon III, and Lenin, he would come to power by almost legal means, then abolish the democratic process he had thus exploited. The national emergency that followed 1929 presented him with the opportunity for which he had been waiting, and he released a new storm of propaganda aimed at all segments of the German people, playing endlessly on their fear of communism and hatred of the Jews.

The legislative election of 1930 dramatically revealed the impact of the Depression on the voters. All moderate parties suffered severe losses and all extremists gained. The Nazis won 107 seats, thereby becoming the second largest party in the Reichstag (after the Social Democrats) and the center of a growing coalition of right-wing parties whose leaders and backers began to see Hitler as their best hope for coming to power. Their opposition, meanwhile, was deeply split; although the Social Democrats constituted the largest party, they had no chance of winning an outright majority or of forming an effective coalition because the communists systematically voted with the Nazis, in what would prove to be a successful but suicidal campaign to destroy the republic. Under these circumstances the only counterweight to Hitler was the reactionary war hero Marshal von Hindenburg, who in March 1932 easily won reelection to the presidency in spite of his eighty-four years. His nearest competitor, however, was Hitler.

In the hope of securing a conservative majority Hindenburg called new Reichstag elections; instead the Nazis made massive gains, receiving 230 seats and thereby becoming the most powerful party in the parliament. Although they did not themselves constitute a majority, they could paralyze the government by refusing to enter into any coalition, and the price they now demanded for their cooperation was Hindenburg's appointment of Hitler as chancellor. Hindenburg refused, and called still another election in the hope of getting a better hand, but the results were roughly the same, except that the communists made a significant gain, thus frightening the conservatives into a more conciliatory attitude toward Hitler. Post-electoral negotiations next led certain conservative leaders to believe that he would be a moderate, constitutional leader, ready to share power with them, so that when the current chancellor lost a vote of confidence and resigned (January 28, 1933), they persuaded Hindenburg to appoint Hitler to the post.

Once in power Hitler moved rapidly to consolidate his hold on the government and establish his long-planned dictatorship. He dissolved the Reichstag once again and called for new elections, confident that with the resources of the state under his control he could entirely eliminate his opposition. During the campaign storm troopers openly patrolled the streets, attacking and intimidating opponents, while the radio and newspapers were compelled to serve as organs for the Nazi party. The message was drummed into the electorate: the Nazis were Germany's glorious new future; it was pointless as well as dangerous to try to stand against this tide, and in the future all rewards would go to those who worked with the new power that was now in charge of the state.

Despite these tactics the Nazis did not achieve the overwhelming success they expected. Instead they received only enough –

with the support of their Nationalist party allies – to constitute a bare majority in the parliament. Hitler then resorted to more extreme measures to establish his rule. During the elections a fire had broken out in the Reichstag building, and although it was almost certainly set by the Nazis themselves Hitler blamed it on the communists and charged them with planning a revolution in which the fire was the first step. The communists were so widely feared that this outrageous fabrication caused a panic, and drove the weary and frightened populace to surrender themselves to Hitler's vigorous, confident leadership.

Hitler's dictatorship

Proclaiming a national emergency, Hitler now proceeded to "suspend" the constitution and all civil liberties, with the full cooperation of Hindenburg and the conservatives, and with very little objection from anyone. The Communist party was outlawed and its leaders were arrested, including members of the Reichstag, while the Social Democrats and other opponents of the Nazis were threatened with the same fate. On March 23, 1933, what remained of the Reichstag voted itself out of existence as a legislative body with the fateful "Enabling Act," which vested all power in Hitler's government. Hitler had thus acquired absolute power in Germany, using essentially the same quasi-"legal" means that Mussolini had used to acquire dictatorial power in Italy over ten years before. When Hindenburg died the following year, Hitler assumed the title of president and retained that of chancellor as well, but such technicalities had long ceased to matter. The title that Hitler preferred, as did Mussolini, was simply "Leader" (*Führer* in German, *Duce* in Italian).

Within a few months after becoming chancellor Hitler had completely transformed Germany into a totalitarian dictatorship. Formerly the nation had been a federation of states, each with its own governor and legislature; all these and other independent authorities were now replaced by Hitler's lieutenants. All political parties, trade unions, and other associations were outlawed and dissolved, leaving only the Nazi party which, like the Fascist party in Italy and the Communist party in Russia, was now transformed from a political movement into an administrative apparatus.

In Germany the civil service included not only the usual state functionaries but also university professors, secondary school teachers and even some doctors and musicians, all of whom were directly vulnerable to the new regime. Almost immediately thousands in all categories were dismissed, on the grounds of being either "non-Aryan" or less than wholehearted in their enthusiasm for the Nazi state. From the start, of course, the persecution of the Jews had the highest priority on the Nazi agenda: not only were Jews forbidden to hold government jobs but they were also subjected to boycotts and harassment aimed at depriving them of their livelihood, as a first step toward their total physical elimination.

Finally Hitler developed the chief mechanisms for carrying out his decrees. From his original bodyguard, the SS (Schutzstaffel or "security forces"), composed of the most ruthless of his followers, he created an elite corps within the army. He also established a secret state police called the Gestapo, and particularly charged it with eliminating all enemies of the state, especially Jews, a mandate which rapidly led to the construction of concentration camps. At the same time the various governments of the federal states were dissolved and all functionaries were brought directly under the authority of the central administration – that is, the Nazi party.

Few observers in or outside Germany read Hitler's preliminary moves for what they actually portended. The obvious logical conclusions to be drawn from his ranting speeches were simply too preposterous to be believed by rational people. This incredulity was further nourished by the fact that the only existing model of a fascist dictator was disastrously misleading. For a decade Mussolini had been spewing forth a sulfurous rhetoric that far exceeded his deeds in violence; if he had violated civil liberties ostentatiously, the actual crimes he had committed were trivial compared with what Hitler would unleash. Often American and European visitors to Italy took away the impression of a well-ordered society in which, they reported approvingly, the "trains now ran on time." As a result it hardly occurred to anyone that Hitler's even more vicious threats and imprecations would prove to be understatements. But undoubtedly the main reason that the Nazi menace was so misjudged was that few people, in Germany or in any other country, had their minds on anything but their own immediate economic woes.

Hitler and Roosevelt

In the United States, Franklin Roosevelt was inaugurated as president on March 4, 1933 – one month after Hitler took office as chancellor of Germany. Until they died, within two weeks of each other in the spring of 1945, these two leaders would personify two radically different responses to the greatest social crisis of the European world in modern times. While Hitler based his hypnotic appeal in morbid fear and hate, Roosevelt countered with his challenge to the American people that they had "nothing to fear but fear itself." Unlike as the two men were, however, they did have in common the need to consolidate their power before implementing their revolutionary aims. At the same time that the Reichstag was passing the Enabling Act, Roosevelt was launching his "New Deal" program, with a massive reorganization of the American economy, beginning with the banks and running through industry, agriculture, transportation, housing and labor relations. In the spring of 1933, needless to say, most Americans were far too preoccupied with the extraordinary measures being taken by their own government to take much note of, let alone understand, the counterdrama being played out in Germany.

Japanese moves

In Japan, meanwhile, the military was gaining increasing power at the expense of the fragile new parliamentary democracy. During the year before Hitler and Roosevelt came to power, Japanese army and navy commanders took advantage of the economic troubles of their own nation as well as those of other powers to move their troops from Korea into the Chinese province of Manchuria. The American secretary of state immediately issued a formal protest against this violation of Chinese sovereignty, but this action neither deterred the Japanese nor elicited support from any of China's European guarantors. The Chinese themselves, however, organized a boycott of Japanese goods, which hurt Japan sufficiently to provoke her to occupy the port of Shanghai until the boycott was called off. In the mean time the Japanese set up an "independent" regime in the three eastern provinces of Manchuria, under a Chinese puppet ruler subject to close Japanese supervision. In a sense this was a return to Japan's old policy of securing essential markets and resources – especially coal and iron – on the Asiatic mainland by military means. She had seized control of Manchuria originally when she had driven the Russians from the province in the Russo-Japanese War of 1904–5, only to be deprived of it by the great powers at the ensuing peace conference.

At the end of 1932 the League of Nations appointed a commission to "investigate" China's charges of Japanese aggression in Manchuria. The subsequent report blamed the Japanese, but stopped short of ordering them out of Manchuria – and in fact recognized their "special interests" in the area. In spite of this supine response, the Japanese used it as an excuse to withdraw from the League and repudiate the moral obligations it theoretically imposed. Their move in Manchuria was the first example of naked conquest, without excuse or apology, that had occurred since the First World War, and it would not be the last. All those with expansionist designs could take heart from the incident, which clearly demonstrated the paralysis of the democracies and the impotence of the League of Nations when confronted by aggression in this time of worldwide economic crisis.

International efforts

Further deterioration of the postwar international settlement was clearly registered in the proceedings of two major conferences, one on disarmament held in Geneva, the other on the world economy in London. The efforts of the British to reduce arms foundered on French concerns for security and German insistence on immediate military equality. In the absence of any international agreement the British proceeded with their own disarmament, while the French were barely maintaining a large but long-obsolete military establishment, and the Germans were preparing for a major rearmament program. Recognizing the obvious fact that no reaction would be forthcoming from either Britain or France, Hitler saw no point in continuing the charade presented by both the disarmament conference and the League of Nations, and in October of 1933 he simply withdrew Germany from participation in both bodies.

At about the same time the International Economic Conference met briefly in London to attempt to stabilize the major currencies. Since the Depression had undoubtedly been triggered by a financial crisis, the conference was intended to hold out some final hope of reviving the international economy – until President Roosevelt made it clear through his delegate's opening remarks that the United States would not cooperate, thereby robbing the affair of any possible chance of success. While it would be difficult to argue that the conference was actually on the point of resolving the world's troubles, it is hard to understand in retrospect why the American president would take such a hostile attitude toward international cooperation. The answer appears to be that Roosevelt was forced to sacrifice his foreign policy to the rigid prejudices of a bloc of western senators whose support was essential for his New Deal legislation.

Isolationism in the United States

The roots of the isolationism in the American West were deep and varied, but included resentment of British and east coast financiers as owners of the railroads that had opened the West, as well as the presence of large blocs of voters of German and Irish (and thus anti-British) origin. But isolationist sentiment did not begin or end with Western populism: it had played the key role in the failure of the United States Senate to ratify the Versailles Treaty, chiefly because of the articles concerning the League of Nations and the Anglo-American guarantee of French security, and during the following decades it spread until it permeated all of American public opinion. As we have seen, moreover, Americans were not the only people who saw their own national interests as distinct from the common good; in fact this public reaction would become all but universal in the democracies, and the general postwar tendency for political leaders to turn inward was greatly accelerated as the Depression deepened. The dictatorial and aggressive rulers did not fail to take advantage of this phenomenon, and exploit the opportunities it presented.

European troubles

After Germany's withdrawal from the League, France and the principal eastern European countries made some efforts to revive their collective security agreements, but without any striking success. Early in 1934 the French government was implicated in a major financial scandal, indicating to many frightened citizens of that country that democracy was no longer a viable form of government. Both communists and right-wing extremists saw an opportunity to seize power in the course of the subsequent disorders, and it even looked for a while as if France was on the point of following Italy and Germany into an authoritarian regime. Although nothing of that sort ever materialized, the Third Republic never fully regained its credibility.

Later in the same year (June 1934), Nazi Germany startled the European community with a massive "blood purge" of the more radically socialist elements that remained in the party, particularly among the Storm Troops, as well as of a wide range of enemies of the regime. Hitler himself reported that seventy-four people had been killed, but the real death toll was probably much higher – possibly as many as a thousand. Hitler's power was now uncontested in Germany, and the openness and savagery of this act gave adequate warning to anyone who cared to take note of what his methods of rule would be in the future.

Stalin

In Russia, meanwhile, Joseph Stalin had gathered all power into his own hands by 1927, and the following year had launched the first of his three Five-Year Plans, the object of which was nothing less than the transformation of the Russian economy from one that was still based almost entirely on peasant agriculture to that of a self-sufficient modern industrial power that would be equal – at least militarily – to any in the West. Whereas in the West this profound change had taken close to a century, Stalin intended to bring it about in Russia in a decade, whatever the social cost, for he feared that the failure to catch up with the industrialized nations would put Russia at a fatal military disadvantage in the life and death contest that he sensed was in the offing. As it turned out he was right in his presentiment about the imminent military threat, and in one way it was perhaps fortunate for Russia, and for the democracies as well, that he succeeded in his desperate crash program. This success, however, was achieved at a staggering cost: the lives of millions of peasants, who were sacrificed to Stalin's determination to transform the traditional agriculture into large mechanized collective units.

The focus of the Five-Year Plans was on creating a heavy industry – that is, the production of coal, iron and steel, electric power, oil, cement chemicals, machinery and railroads. The required effort would be immense, for Russia had virtually no heavy industry on which to build and no surplus wealth to invest in such development. In particular she did not have the huge surplus of food necessary to fuel a monumental construction undertaking. Stalin's solution to this problem was, characteristically, military. In a program euphemistically called "collectivization," he used the army to reorganize agricultural production under the authority of the state. Food necessary for the industrial centers would be commandeered through the imposition of quotas. Russia's peasant farmers, most of whom had only emerged from serfdom in the middle of the nineteenth century and had only been given land by the revolution, were now once again reduced to the status of serfs, this time on large "collective" farms that were owned and operated by the state. Each farm was milked of its quota, and if there was not a sufficient surplus left over to feed the farm workers, it was they who starved.

Most of the peasants – particularly the well-to-do *kulaks* -- reacted to collectivization as if it were an invasion and occupation by a foreign military power. Villages fought armed battles with Stalin's soldiers, and farmers resorted to the traditional Russian "black earth" practice of destroying their crops and animals rather than surrender them to the enemy. But it was an unequal contest, for Stalin was ready to destroy as many peasants as necessary to quell the resistance; he declared the kulaks "enemies of the people", who were to be "liquidated as a class." At the end of this virtual civil war at least ten million peasants had been killed outright or sent to labor camps – the figure is Stalin's own guess – while more millions died during the famine (1932–3) that followed the disruption of agricultural production. The state, however, got its quotas and Stalin's "miracle" of industrialization proceeded on schedule.

In addition to turning Russia into a major industrial and military power, Stalin's other major objective was to consolidate his own position as absolute ruler of this mighty juggernaut. As in Hitler's case, what this involved primarily was a purge of the party that had brought about his rise in order to eliminate any possible challenge to his leadership. Stalin's purge, however, was considerably more extensive than Hitler's, because the Russian ruler had to wipe out the whole generation of Bolsheviks who had worked with Lenin to bring about the revolution and to govern Russia for the ensuing decade. Stalin's only serious rival as Lenin's heir had been Trotsky, who had already been expelled from the party and country in 1927, but at the first opportunity Stalin determined to get rid of everyone who had had any connection with Lenin or Trotsky, had publicly voiced any opinions about Russia's government, or had served in any position of responsibility in the party, army, or bureaucracy. This wholesale terror began in 1936 and had achieved its objective by 1938. Stalin's secret police arrested and executed many thousands of accused "traitors" and "conspirators" (including two of its own chiefs), until quite literally no one was left alive in the Russian leadership except Stalin and the functionaries he chose for their total dependence on his favor. All surviving members of Lenin's Politburo were killed, as well as fifty of the seventy-one members of the current Central Committee of the Communist party and all of the top commanders of the Red Army, along with thousands – and perhaps millions – of lesser Bolsheviks and anti-Bolsheviks, intellectuals, trade union leaders, army officers, and petty state officials. To legitimize his actions Stalin staged a series of highly publicized show trials, at which the best-known and most admired of the doomed Bolshevik leaders were induced (probably by torture) to "confess" plotting against the revolution and Russia, after which they were condemned and executed for their "crimes."

Stalin had little interest in the world revolution promised by Marxist theory, and little knowledge of conditions in the European countries where local communist parties still saw themselves as brigades in the army of that revolution, and saw Russia as their fatherland. The instructions that Stalin issued to these willing troops at first expressed chiefly his antagonism toward socialists and liberals, whom he declared to be more dangerous enemies of communism than were the fascists. He even held that a fascist government was preferable to a democracy because it would lead more quickly to a communist revolution, an attitude that had fateful consequences in Germany where the communists in the Reichstag contributed decisively to Hitler's takeover by refusing to vote with his opposition.

The Popular Front

Because of this parochial orientation Stalin did not begin to see the military threat that Nazi Germany posed to Russia until Hitler had been in power for over a year. In 1934 Stalin took Russia into the League of Nations, which he had previously scorned, and as Hitler's intentions became ever clearer Stalin began negotiations with the West aimed specifically at containing Germany. In 1935 he concluded agreements with France and Czechoslovakia providing for mutual aid in the event of aggression. Then in 1936 came a wholly new directive from Moscow to European communists to cooperate with all left-oriented parties in an international "Popular Front" against fascism. This seeming conversion of Soviet Russia to the democratic cause came much too late to stem the fascist tide, and Europe's enthusiasm for Russia's leadership in this cause was soon cooled by the purge trials. For a time, however, the concept of the Popular Front captured the imagination of beleagured democrats in a number of countries and it had a dramatic impact on the legislative elections of 1936 in France and Spain.

In both countries, the main issues in the elections were long-overdue social and economic reforms, but there the similarity ends. In France the financial scandal that had rocked the government in 1934 had brought a huge mob into the center of Paris, where it appeared to threaten not only the government but the Republican regime as well. Although it proved to be no more than a spontaneous demonstration of frustration and disgust, the parties of the left feared it was a forerunner of the sort of anti-democratic subversion that had already occurred in Italy and Germany. To meet this threat, they tried to organize an electoral alliance of all democratic parties, and to everyone's surprise found the communists eager to participate. This French Popular Front was given its first test in the general election of 1936, in which it won a clear victory. The socialist leader Léon Blum now became prime minister, and immediately introduced a sweeping program of social and economic reforms, similar in intent to the American New Deal; the body of legislation drafted by this government still serves as the basis of France's welfare program. At the time, however, it met with bitter opposition, which crumbled the Popular Front alliance barely a year after its electoral success.

The Spanish Civil War

A few months before the French elections of 1936 a Popular Front alliance had also come to power in Spain. Ever since the Napoleonic period Spain had existed in remarkable isolation from the rest of Europe. Unaffected by the political and economic tides that had swept the Continent from the turmoil of 1848 through the First World War, Spain's internal politics had long been marked by instability and extremism as well as by chronic separatist movements in Catalonia and the Basque region.

Although Spain had played no military part in the First World War, her industry had expanded in response to the general wartime boom and suffered from the postwar depression, during which revolutionary communist and anarchist doctrines made great headway among the chronically impoverished workers and peasants. In 1923 a military coup established General Primo de Rivera as dictator, under King Alfonso XIII. The general managed to maintain order but finally was forced to resign in 1930 by widespread popular opposition to Spain's absolutist monarchy. With his defeat Alfonso fled the country, and elections were held for a constituent assembly, which promulgated a radical republican constitution in 1931.

This new Republic represented a victory by middle-class moderates and working-class socialists, but it faced violent hostility from the reactionary elements that had supported the monarchy — the Catholic Church, the landowning aristocracy, and most significantly the army. Moreover it never gained the support of the numerous and violent anarchists, who demanded aggressive pursuit of agrarian reform. As a result, the election of 1933 produced a victory for the extreme right, which in turn provoked greater unity on the left and a decisive victory by a Popular Front Alliance in the election of 1936. This government promised a number of revolutionary projects, including land reform and the expropriation of Church property.

Faced with this prospect, the forces on the right regrouped and prepared another military coup. Its leader was General Francisco Franco, who had been minister of war in the rightist government of 1933, and its political wing was the "Falange" (phalanx), a nationalist party that had been organized originally in 1932. Franco's troops invaded Spain from Morocco, where they had been stationed, and were joined by garrisons in Spanish towns as they advanced on Madrid. Because they failed to take the capital, however, what had been intended as one more coup turned into a long, vicious civil war which rapidly involved the major European powers.

From the beginning Franco's forces were given planes, tanks, and troops by Mussolini and Hitler, both of whom used this battleground (as the Italians had used Ethiopia) to test the advanced new weapons and strategies they were developing. The Russians sent some aid to the beleaguered Republican government, but Britain and France confined themselves to support of the principles of neutrality and non-intervention, which meant that they refused to sell weapons to the Republic while doing nothing to prevent Germany and Italy from supplying the other side with everything it needed. Given this arrangement, the outcome of the war could hardly be in doubt, but it proved to be a surprisingly long and bitterly fought struggle. Franco and his allies finally won in 1939 with the capture of the Republican strongholds of Barcelona and Madrid.

The Axis

As it burst upon the consciousness of the European world the Spanish Civil War seemed to polarize internal as well as international politics. The Popular Front formulation of Franco's opposition carried the implication that the democratic parties and the communists had a common interest and objective in fighting against the challenge from the dictators, and were thus natural allies. It was at this time also that the word "fascist" came into common use as a generic term to describe the dictatorships in Germany, Italy, and Spain, with the implication that they had a common purpose, which was generally defined as anti-communism by defenders of the dictatorial regimes and as anti-democratic totalitarianism by their foes. Moreover the actions of Hitler and Mussolini in Spain demonstrated that they saw themselves as united in their aims, which they proceeded to cement in the fall of 1936 by signing a pact which came to be known as the "Rome–Berlin Axis." (Indeed it was not until Mussolini went to Franco's aid that the democracies were forced to give up hopes of reviving their former alliance with Italy against Germany.) Shortly afterwards, Germany opened negotiations with Japan which led to a treaty supposedly directed against the International Communist Party; Italy also signed the agreement the following year, and the fascist coalition was formally established.

The democracies proved utterly incapable of providing an effective response to the fascist challenge, chiefly because a large segment of those who opposed fascism was still not ready to join in an alliance with the communists. Indeed most conservative democrats in France and Britain – and in the United States as well – tended to see fascism as a comparatively welcome bulwark against the communism they feared above all else. This reaction was encouraged by the difficulty of deciding just what fascism did portend. Within Italy and Germany the fascists had obviously established one-party dictatorships, but on the other hand they obviously enjoyed wide popular support, and they did appear to be using their monopoly of power to strengthen their desperately failing economies. If they were also using it to strengthen their armed forces, which they brandished as a general threat, they carefully refrained from any direct challenge to the major democratic powers that would have provoked them to active opposition. So far, the fascists had confined their armed conflicts to internal struggles or to such remote areas as Ethiopia and Spain, which allowed the democracies to justify their inaction as "non-intervention," or refusal to become involved in distant quarrels.

Behind these evasions lay the perfectly rational horror of war felt by people of all political stripes in the democracies. Above all else they continued to hope they would not have to go to war again, and they seized on every explanation of the fascists' aggression that would make it appear limited or not threatening to them. Conservatives were eager to believe that the fascists' actions were necessary to counter the communist menace, while liberals were often quite as eager to regard the dictators' demands as reasonable on the grounds of self-preservation or as the righting of past wrongs – notably the Versailles Treaty, which liberals now vied with the Nazis in defaming. In effect, the weapon of terror which the fascists had used so effectively to quell opposition in their own countries also worked toward the same end in the outside world, as opponents recoiled from the threat of violence. In general it was only the communists who realized the necessity of using the methods of the fascists – that it, war – to defeat them, and the failure of the Popular Front experiments in both Spain and France was due chiefly to the pervasive reluctance of the non-communists, even on the left, to join with the communists in taking this stand.

In 1937 a British diplomat, sent to inquire into Hitler's objectives, brought back a disquieting report of intended "territorial adjustments" to bring all German-speaking areas into a new, greater, Third Reich ("third empire" after the Holy Roman and Hohenzollern ones). This was a nightmarish projection of the old democratic doctrine of self-determination, to which the British responded by treating the German demands as reasonable and trying to meet them with reasonable concessions. The result was a British policy, proudly dubbed "appeasement" by its authors, which gave Hitler a perfect point of departure for his escalating demands. In the fall of 1937 he began open preparations to revise Germany's eastern boundaries, and in 1938 he unleashed the campaign of German military conquest that would shortly engulf the world in war.

ON THE BRINK

The annexation of Austria

Although Hitler's ambitions were unlimited, his particular military moves were made (as his political ones had been in his seizure of power in Germany) largely in response to specific perceived opportunities. The first such openings were provided by the geopolitical situation in central Europe that had emerged from the First World War. The republic of Austria was a particularly troubled state: formerly only a province of the old Habsburg Empire, it was a wholly inadequate economic base for Vienna, the former imperial capital of the Habsburgs. The obvious solution of merging Austria with Germany had been rejected by the Paris Peace Conference, and even a customs union of the two states that was proposed in 1931 was blocked by the French, who remembered the role played by the earlier one in the consolidation of Bismarck's empire.

The population of Austria was almost entirely German-speaking, but it was deeply divided politically between Marxists and Christian Socialists (Catholics). Both parties maintained paramilitary organizations, which fought a pitched battle in 1934, in which the Catholic forces actually shelled a workers' housing project in Vienna. There was also a small Austrian Nazi party, which agitated for union with Germany and sought its opportunity in the division between the communists and Catholics; the street battle of 1934 provided these troublemakers with the occasion to attempt a coup, in the confident expectation of help from Germany. This time, however, Hitler held his fire, since both Italy and Yugoslavia had responded to the disorder by moving troops to their Austrian borders. A new Christian Socialist government was then formed, which now turned its attentions from the communist to the growing Nazi threat. In 1936 Mussolini signed the pact that formally established his alliance with Hitler, thus effectively eliminating Italy as a restraining influence, and Hitler began inundating Austria with propaganda aimed at undermining the government, while the Austrian Nazis also greatly increased their activities.

In early 1938 Hitler felt ready to move. First he presented a number of demands to the Austrian chancellor, which he followed up by calling for his resignation when the chancellor reaffirmed Austria's independence and refused to make concessions. The next day German troops crossed the border and occupied the country without resistance. Hitler now proclaimed Germany's annexation of Austria, and launched a reign of terror that wiped out all opposition to Nazi rule. The whole operation was conducted with such ruthless expedition that there was hardly time for any international reaction, beyond routine protests from France and Britain. Most people in the democracies were made uneasy by this blatant aggression, but most also tended to take refuge in the supposedly extenuating circumstance that the Austrians were "Germans," and in the massive approval that Austrians gave to their union with Hitler's Germany in a plebiscite called after the fact.

Czechoslovakia

In a major speech just preceding the annexation of Austria, Hitler had promised "protection" to all Germans living outside the Reich. After the Austrians the next people on this list were the three and a half million German-speaking Czechs living along the western boundary of Czechoslovakia, in what was called the Sudetenland. Unlike Austria, Czechoslovakia was a vigorous and viable state, as well as the only functioning democracy in eastern Europe. It was also much the strongest and richest of the east European nations because it contained Europe's second largest base of heavy industry after Germany's Ruhr valley. Its army was well equipped and trained, as well as highly motivated, but Czech defense was based primarily in a system of fortifications located in the same Sudeten borderlands that Hitler was now proposing to annex.

Pro-Nazi elements in the Sudetenland had been challenging Czech authority since 1933, and even anti-Nazi Sudetens tended to favor the idea of union with Germany. In early 1938 Hitler turned his attention to promoting violent disorders in the Sudetenland, which were capped by demands from the Sudeten Nazis for complete independence from Czechoslovakia. The Czech government made major efforts to arrive at a compromise acceptable to the secessionists, but to no avail, and Hitler had the pretext he sought for his next aggressive move. Here, however, he proceeded with more caution than he had with Austria, because the Czechs were clearly willing and able to fight, as well as formally allied with France and Russia. Hitler therefore had to find out how far the Czechs were willing to go to defend their borders, and how much help they could expect to receive from their allies.

At first it looked as if Hitler would be stopped this time.

Preliminary German troop movements brought a partial Czech mobilization, while the French responded to Hitler's threat of war by calling up large numbers of reservists and the British mobilized their fleet. Both France and Russia reaffirmed their commitments to the Czechs, and the Czechs prepared to fight, confident that help would be forthcoming at least from France and Britain in the event of a German invasion.

As we know now, Hitler did not intend to take on France and Britain at that point since the German army was not yet ready, but he was convinced that they would not finally go to war in defense of principle or a third country. Events bore him out dramatically. In September of 1938, just as war seemed inevitable, the British revealed that they were not willing to fight Hitler after all, and in fact were determined to prevent the outbreak of war in Europe at almost any cost. The British prime minister, Neville Chamberlain, with little previous experience in foreign affairs, had great confidence in his ability to arrive at reasonable solutions to difficult problems. In addition he had an absolute horror of war, bred of the destructiveness and futility of the war Europe had concluded two decades before, and he was convinced that his task was to find a way of "resolving" Hitler's grievances that would spare Britain and the rest of Europe from the new war that Hitler was threatening.

In the summer of 1938 he saw no reason why the Sudetenland, with its German-speaking population, should not be ceded to Hitler's Reich, especially if the consequent new boundaries of the Czech Republic were guaranteed by all concerned. Clearly he was hoping despite all evidence to the contrary that Hitler's expansionist ambitions would be fully satisfied once all of Europe's Germans were in his fold. In retrospect it is hard to understand how anyone could honestly have hoped to arrive at such an accommodation with Hitler, but the evidence is strong that Chamberlain did – as much because of his overwhelming desire for peace as because of a total failure to take Hitler's measure. This is not to say that he did not find the Führer trying in the extreme, but he discounted this aberrant behavior because he did not really expect much of "foreigners" in any case. Apparently it did not occur to Chamberlain, or anyone else who wished to accede to Hitler's claim on the

Sudetenland, that Czechoslovakia would be defenseless against Germany if she lost this border region with its superb fortifications.

In mid-September of 1938 Hitler felt confident enough to proceed with the seizure of Czechoslovakia. He demanded immediate "self-determination" for the Sudetenland and promised armed intervention to achieve it. The Czechs mobilized, and Chamberlain feared that the French would honor their obligation to go to the Czechs' aid, thereby precipitating a general war. To head off this disaster he offered to fly to Germany to meet Hitler, in history's first example of "shuttle" diplomacy. Hitler agreed to meet him, and to wait a week before opening his attack, in order to give Chamberlain time to consult his government and the French, as well as make it clear to the Czechs that they would be abandoned.

In eight days Chamberlain was back in Germany to draft an accord, only to find that Hitler had raised the ante to include immediate cession of the Sudetenland to Germany, and satisfaction of all claims on Czech territory by the Poles, Hungarians, and Slovaks as well. In other words, Czechoslovakia was to be completely dismembered and thus put out of effective existence as a state. With no mandate to accept such terms, but still determined to save the peace, Chamberlain next called on Mussolini to arrange a conference of heads of state from Italy, Germany, France, and Britain. Delighted to be included in the negotiations and desperately eager to avoid having to go to war as Hitler's ally, Mussolini persuaded Hitler to meet with him, Chamberlain and the French premier, Edouard Daladier, the next day in Munich (September 29, 1938). At this conference the other heads of state agreed immediately to all of Hitler's demands, and the Czechs were handed their fate without any pretense of consultation. In return, Hitler agreed to make no further territorial claims, in Czechoslovakia or elsewhere in Europe.

Chamberlain returned triumphant to a grateful nation, waving his copy of the agreement and boasting that he had ensured "peace for our time." Daladier was met on the Paris airfield by an immense mob that he assumed was there to lynch him – until he was greeted by a roar of approbation as he emerged from his plane. Within a year the very name of Munich would become synonymous with craven treachery and surrender, and "appeasement" would become a term of moral reproach, but there is no doubt that in the early fall of 1938, the democracies – the United States included – were overwhelmingly relieved that war had been averted.

The Munich Conference was the last time Hitler bothered to give the democracies assurance of his future peaceful intentions as an excuse for their inaction. The whole affair served to confirm his conviction of complete superiority to his opponents, and he made no further effort to cloak his aims in euphemisms that would be acceptable to them. It now became impossible for even the most anti-war elements among them to deny the truth about the Nazis – that they were from their origin a party of violence, dedicated to the victorious completion of the First World War. In March of 1939, the German army rolled into Czechoslovakia – Hitler himself actually entering Prague in a tank. Deprived of their border fortifications and abandoned by their allies, the Czechs could offer no resistance.

The Second World War

When the British and French leaders signed the Munich agreement with Hitler, on September 29, 1938, they acceded to his demand that Czechoslovakia be dismembered but they hoped that his acquisition of the Sudetenland would mark the end of German territorial expansion. By the following March, however, when the Germans rolled into Prague and took over all of Czechoslovakia, this violation of the Munich terms came as no surprise to the British and French, who had already begun reluctant preparations for war. Nor was there any surprise in the West when Hitler followed his occupation of Czechoslovakia with demands on Poland to surrender the long-resented Polish corridor. This time the disabused Chamberlain responded with a guarantee to Poland, and the French followed suit. By this time Hitler was probably confident that the British and French would back down if directly challenged, but in any case he was prepared to take the risk. Indeed it was unclear what the British or French intended to do to implement their pledge of assistance to Poland, since they were unprepared for an offensive on the Continent – and in fact had no plans for offensive action of any sort.

This lack of foresight was the logical result of a widespread assumption that the defense would be as dominant in any new conflict as it had been in the last war. In pursuit of their security the British had focused military interest on the development of an ultra-secret radar warning system that was being installed along the island's east coast, together with the truly remarkable Spitfire fighter plane that had been designed to take maximum advantage of the radar. At the cost of a very short flying time, the Spitfire was capable of climbing rapidly to great height and delivering a blast from eight guns that would bring down any targeted bomber with near certainty; at the time of Munich, however, the plane existed only as a prototype, and it was barely in production by the next spring. In any event its qualities were highly specific to the defense of Britain and therefore of no use in support of Poland.

The French had a large army but it too was wholly oriented toward the defense, being organized around elaborate fortifications known as the Maginot Line, which had been erected during the 1930s along the German frontier. Such an excessive reliance on static fortifications would come to be known derisively as the "Maginot mentality," and accounts for much of the failure of both the French and British to stop the Germans when it would have been easiest.

One obvious approach to the German menace would have been for the western democracies to find allies in the east. Unfortunately they had thrown away their first and best opportunity when Chamberlain had sacrificed Czechoslovakia – with its tough modern army, heavy industry, and vigorous democratic state – in his vain quest for peace. Moreover in doing this they had alienated the Soviet Union, both by failing to invite the Russians to the Munich conference and by a capitulation that made the Russians very doubtful about the democracies' value as allies. By the time the British and French were forced to acknowledge that they needed Russia's help, their efforts were too little and too late; the Germans had already applied themselves to winning Russia's participation in their next venture by promising to divide a defeated Poland with its eastern neighbor.

Russia could hardly be expected to be interested in the independence of Poland for its own sake. Relations between the two countries had never recovered from the war in 1920 when the Poles had stopped the Red Army before Warsaw and driven it back well into Russia, finally establishing an eastern border that included significant sections of White Russia and the Ukraine. Under these circumstances the Poles did not look to the Russians for disinterested aid against German aggression, and in fact refused to permit Russian troops to set foot in Poland, even to fight invading Germany. In short, both Russia and Poland, like Britain and France, were still busy refighting the last war, or at least reacting to it, and all four nations were therefore unable to cope effectively with their current predicament. This collective short-sightedness was to cost all of Hitler's adversaries what was doubtless their last chance to join forces and stop him without a major war.

Perhaps the worst miscalculation of the democratic leaders was to accept the Nazi–Soviet ideological antagonism as an immutable factor in international relations, and to indulge the hope that the Nazi and Communist regimes would transform their violent denunciations of each other into mutual destruction. Instead both Hitler and Stalin readily sacrificed their "principles" to their strategic interests, and after swift secret negotiations, staggered the West by announcing a non-aggression pact, on August 23, 1939. Easily the most stunning of Hitler's string of diplomatic coups, this pact protected him from a two-front war, gave him access to vital raw materials in Russia, and left Poland at his mercy. One week later, on September 1, 1939, the German armies struck the helpless Poles from the west, the north, and even the south, in a superbly planned and executed attack, incorporating the newest arms and tactics. As the German invasion began, the British and French governments sent an ultimatum to Hitler, which he answered with a tirade of abuse; in response, they declared war on Germany.

Considering all the blame Chamberlain has since received for his Munich agreement, it is well to remember that he was the first head of state to voluntarily declare war against Hitler on moral grounds and before his own country had been directly threatened. France followed immediately, as did Canada and the other Commonwealth countries, but their action depended on Britain's lead. The Soviet Union and the United States did not enter the conflict until they were attacked, some two years later. Roosevelt did what he could to rally American support for Hitler's victims during the intervening period, but Stalin loyally aided his German ally until the Nazi attack on Russia demonstrated how disastrous his cynical gamble had been.

PHASE ONE

Poland

The German attack on Poland began before dawn on September 1, 1939. Two days later the prime minister Neville Chamberlain,

This map shows the theater of combat between Germany and her allies and Great Britain and her allies from September 1939 to May 1945.

MAP 7 *War in Europe, 1939–45*

THE RHINE

NETHERLANDS

Rhine Arnhem
Nijmegen   Munster   Ems
                          Lippe   Hamm
                  Wesel
              Duisburg Essen Dortmund
Eindhoven   Ruhr
        Venlo   Düsseldorf
              Krefeld   Wuppertal

                      Cologne
              Aachen   Sieg
        Liège   Bonn Remagen
Namur   Lahn
      Eupen
        Malmédy   Coblenz   Frankfurt

Sedan   Eifel   Bingen   Mainz

                              Moselle
        Bastogne   Mannheim
                              SAAR
          Luxemburg   Saarbruken
F R A N C E   Karlsr
      Metz   Vosges   Rhine
      Verdun   Black
                  Saverne   Forest
            Nancy Strasbourg

0   50 miles
0   80 km

Petsamo
Murmansk

White
Sea
          Archangel

Leningrad
Tikhvin
Novgorod
Kalinin
          Moscow

UNION OF
        SOVIET
SOCIALIST
      REPUBLICS

Katyn   Kuibyshev
  Smolensk Tula
Bryansk
  Orel
Gomel   Kursk

Kiev
  Kremenchug   Kharkov
          Voroshilovgrad   Stalingrad
      Dnepropetrovsk
Krivoi Rog Taganrog Rostov
Odessa   Bataisk
    Perekop
  Yalta   Krasnodar
Sebastopol Novorossilsk Maikop
                      Grozny

Caspian

Black   Sea   Batum
          Caucasus Mts.   Baku   Sea

Ankara
T U R K E Y

Cyprus   SYRIA   Tehran
          Mosul
                  I R A N   AFGHANISTAN

Beirut
LEBANON Damascus   Habbaniya
PALESTINE   Baghdad
Jerusalem   I R A Q   Abadan
      Trans-   Basra
      Jordan   Persian
                  Gulf
Cairo Port
      Said
      Suez

Suez Canal

T

━━━ Furthest advance of Axis
      military power

0   450 miles

- - - Boundary of unoccupied
      France, June 1940–Nov. 1942

0   725 km

-·-·- Prewar national boundaries

told the British people that they were once again at war with
Germany:

> I have to tell you now that ... this country is at war with Germany
> ... You can imagine what a bitter blow it is to me that all
> my long struggle to win peace has failed. Yet I cannot believe that
> there is anything more, or anything different, that I could have
> done, and that would have been more successful ... We have a clear
> conscience, we have done all that any country could do to establish
> peace, but a situation in which no word given by Germany's ruler
> could be trusted, and no people or country could feel themselves
> safe, had become intolerable ... It is evil things that we shall be
> fighting against, brute force, bad faith, injustice, oppression, and
> persecution. And against them I am certain the right will prevail.

The public response was sober but solid, and the French and
Commonwealth governments followed Britain into war. Immediately this combination resumed the old World War I nomenclature of the "Allies," which was continued by the changing cast
of Hitler's enemies throughout the war, in spite of an official
attempt in 1942 to change its name to the "United Nations." With
Britain's declaration the Americans were forced to accept the in-
evitability of the war in Europe, but they remained adamantly
isolationist and confident that they could avoid involvement in this
war simply by choosing not to participate.

The conquest of Poland was accomplished in three weeks, in a
textbook demonstration of the Germans' new strategy, called
"blitzkrieg" (lightning war). Because it became the basis of all
subsequent modern warfare, it is hard to realize how new and
terrifying this form of attack was at the time, when most military
experts still thought in terms of the defensive strategy employed
throughout the First World War. Instead of marching their troops
overland and digging in to hold their territorial gains, the Germans
now put their divisions in tanks and armored vehicles, which with
close air support, would blast through the enemy's lines, surround
them in a surprise offensive, and sweep on to destroy all bases for
continued resistance, including industry, transportation, and civilian morale.

Poland provided the first test of this strategy. Her military
resources were no match for the Germans; her army, which con-

sisted primarily of infantry, was large and courageous, but it was primitively equipped, with transport still mainly dependent on horses. In the first few hours of combat the German air force (Luftwaffe) struck all of Poland's military airfields at once and destroyed the entire Polish air force in a single blow. Although the Luftwaffe was far from the level of equipment and sophistication it would later reach, its superiority in this situation was total. Further, it followed its initial attack by strafing roads and rail-roads, thoroughly disrupting all communications and military transport. Then as the columns of German tanks poured into Poland their way was prepared by terrifying dive bombers (Stukas) that wiped out all anti-tank resistance. In six days the Polish army had simply ceased to exist as a military organization, and the Germans had arrived at the suburbs of Warsaw.

After a furious siege the city surrendered, on September 27. Meanwhile the Russians, assured that they would meet no resis-tance, moved quickly from the east to occupy the eastern third of the country, disarming the Polish units that were fleeing from the Germans and imprisoning their officers (many of whom they later executed). At the same time Soviet troops occupied Estonia, Latvia and Lithuania; these former provinces of imperial Russia had established their independence in the course of the First World War and Russian Revolution. Now on the military offensive for the first time since 1920, the Soviets imposed treaties on these small and helpless states giving Russia possession of, or access to, their principal military and naval bases. Six weeks later, Finland resisted a similar capitulation, and held off a large-scale Russian attack for three months before finally surrendering some border territories to overwhelming force. The Soviet Union was expelled from the League of Nations for this aggression.

The "phoney war"

In spite of their unhesitating declaration of war on Germany, neither Britain nor France provided any military support for their Polish ally. Short of a major attack on Germany's western frontier – for which they were wholly unprepared – there was nothing they could have done that would have saved the Poles for more than a few days at most. Instead they concentrated on building up their own military forces, basically resuming the defensive tactics of the last war. The French brought their Maginot defenses up to full strength, simply hoping to keep the Germans out of France with a minimum of casualties, while the British reinstituted their naval blockade of Germany. Considering that the Maginot Line did not cover the Belgian frontier, which had provided the invasion route of 1914, and that the Germans now had access to Russia's resources (which were plentifully supplied by Stalin), this overall strategy seemed at best an exercise in wishful thinking.

The British did make other preparations for war, but these proceeded slowly. Even before the attack on Poland, they had passed the first peacetime conscription law in their history, and now they began to strengthen their war industries, especially their naval building program and the production of their Spitfire fighter plane. Together with Canadians they also built airfields and schools across Canada that now began the training of thousands of British and Commonwealth air force personnel. But Hitler made no move to attack his declared enemies in the west, and an atmosphere of uneasy calm pervaded Europe throughout the fall and winter of 1939–40. This standoff came to be called the "phoney war" in Britain ("drôle de guerre" in France), or jokingly, the "sitzkrieg" – sitting war, in derisive comparison with Germany's deadly "blitzkrieg."

Norway

Then in early 1940 British forces seized a German ship in Norwegian waters, and a few weeks later announced that they had mined the area to cut off German shipping. Determined to avoid a repetition of the last war's blockade, the Germans had clearly planned an offensive to secure control of the North Sea, and they now moved with overwhelming dispatch to occupy Denmark and invade Norway by sea and air. The Danes had no time to resist as the Germans rolled across the border, but the Norwegians fought, with some hastily improvised French and British aid. It was an unequal contest, however, with the Germans far better organized and supplied than the unprepared Allies. By the end of April Denmark and Norway were completely occupied.

Incredibly, the British public seemed not to have grasped the significance of this German thrust. Chamberlain, with his gift for memorable statements of his miscalculations, blurted out that Hitler had "missed the bus," expressing the general opinion that the conquest of Norway had been a pointless diversion for the Germans. In fact, it was a major coup. Instead of fighting a submarine campaign from a few North Sea ports, as in the previous war; Germany could now survey the main North Atlantic shipping lanes by sea or air from Norway's coasts.

Blitzkrieg in the West

Two weeks after they had consolidated their hold on Norway, the Germans finally launched their thoroughly prepared and brilliantly conceived onslaught against the West. On May 10, 1940, the German army and air force swept into Holland, Belgium, and Luxemburg, in a blitzkrieg attack vastly larger than the one that had overwhelmed Poland. These countries had hoped to protect themselves from German aggression by remaining neutral; they had not joined the alliance with France and Britain, therefore, and by themselves they could offer no resistance. When the Dutch refused to surrender, the Germans smashed Rotterdam to rubble in the first demonstration of saturation bombing, and then strafed its fleeing inhabitants, killing forty thousand.

This awesome attack on the Low Countries was actually a mere diversionary tactic to pull the French and British forces out of their prepared positions. Just as the Germans had planned, France and Britain rushed their troops to meet the German attack in Belgium, but at this point the Germans – who had kept their main forces in reserve – launched a powerful assault on the point where the Maginot Line stopped. Although the French were well aware that their Belgian border was not fortified, they had supposed this hilly, forested region to be a barrier in itself to troop movement; thus the motorized German units rolled through it virtually unopposed, and then cut through northern France to the Channel, thereby surrounding the French and British forces in Belgium. Under different circumstances the Germans might then have found themselves caught between the attacking French and British units and the main French army; but the Allies were totally unprepared for the German maneuver, which therefore succeeded in trapping the Allied units, totalling over a quarter of a million men, leaving them entirely at the Germans' mercy. Hitler's purpose in this maneuver, however, was not the destruction of these forces, but the conquest of France. Ignoring the isolated British and French forces, the German tank columns rushed south toward Paris. Meeting almost no resistance from the disorganized and demoralized enemy, they entered the undefended capital on June 13, 1940. Meanwhile the Allied troops behind the German lines made their way to the coast at Dunkirk, where they were evacuated across the Channel by an astonishing collaboration of the British navy with private commercial craft and yachts. This heroic rescue mission provided one heartening moment in what was an otherwise utterly crushing disaster.

The picture darkened further as the surrender of Paris was followed by the total collapse of the French army and government. On June 16 the Germans replaced the French premier with the aged World War I hero Marshal Pétain as their puppet head of state, and on June 22 Pétain proceeded to sign an "armistice" with the conquerors which gave them full control of the entire country and its North African colonies (Morocco, Algeria, and Tunisia) as well. By the terms dictated to the French, the Germans were to occupy the northern two-thirds of the country (giving them both its Channel and Atlantic coasts), while Pétain would serve as chief of a collaborationist government set up in the southern resort town of Vichy, which would officially administer the unoccupied portion of the country and its North African possessions.

At this point, with most of the French convinced that further resistance was inconceivable, the day after the armistice was signed a young general, Charles de Gaulle, escaped to London and with British help broadcast an appeal to the French nation to continue the struggle. He established a headquarters in London for what would be called the Free French forces, and was joined immediately by Frenchmen who had been at Dunkirk, and later by others who had been at sea during the German takeover or had managed to escape from occupied France. Although the Free French could do little to aid the actual military effort of the British, the very existence of such an organization, together with the radio broadcasts it directed across the Channel, provided essential encouragement and a focus to the underground resistance movement that gradually began to take shape in France.

The Battle of Britain

With the fall of France, Canada effectively became Britain's major ally; this Commonwealth partner now threw its full efforts into the task of serving as Britain's arsenal and supply base, as well as preparing its own armed forces for the heavy burden they would take on in the fighting to come. Even with this support, however, Britain faced a bleak prospect. With Germany in control of the Atlantic coast from the North Cape to the Pyrenees, and Spain as a non-belligerent German ally, the British were completely sealed off from the Continent. Further, Stalin's active cooperation with the Germans assured them an adequate source of critical raw materials. Moreover the overwhelming magnitude of the German advance that had taken place in a mere three months (April to June, 1940) confirmed British fears that Germany possessed a uniquely powerful army. Hopes that the Polish campaign had been a demonstration more of Polish weakness than of German strength were now dashed by Germany's success in the west. Although Britain's mobilization had been proceeding, she was in no military posture to take on the most powerful war machine the world had ever seen. By any reasonable measure her situation was hopeless. But she did have a few factors in her favor.

Very important among these was the leadership of the new prime minister, Winston Churchill. Long recognized as a gifted parliamentary debater, he now emerged as a magnificent orator, with matchless ability to rally the British people and imbue them with his own courage and conviction that they would ultimately triumph. Churchill's outspoken insistence on warning against the growing danger of the dictators, and his constant demand for more arms during the 1930s, had kept him politically isolated in Britain during the days of appeasement; but when that false hope of peace finally gave way to reality with the fall of France, Chamberlain was ousted and replaced by Churchill, as the Commons resolutely made ready for war. The sentiment in Parliament reflected that in the nation; once it was clear that they were in danger, the British people prepared to resist, in Churchill's words, "if necessary for years, if necessary alone."

In this desperate situation Britain may have been saved by the very speed of Germany's subjugation of the Continent. It was evident that the Germans were surprised by the French collapse, and although they were now installed as the masters of Europe they had not yet given thought to the question of how to handle Britain. Hitler apparently expected that the British would sue for peace, and that they would be more than happy to accept the liberal terms with which he tried to woo them: he would not challenge their independence (or their rule of their colonial empire) if only they would not challenge his rule of Europe. Britain's outright rejection of this compromise drove Hitler into a frenzy of preparation to force her submission. Yet a cross-Channel invasion could not be hastily improvised. The Continent had been won by tanks, which were useless in this situation, and so far the German air force had been used only for ground support. Although they had a formidable submarine fleet with which to sink British ships, the Germans did not have sufficient ships of their own to stage a successful invasion by sea, as a trial attempt demonstrated when it was easily crushed by British planes. Finally in August 1940 Hitler decided that the Battle of Britain could be fought only in the air. By this time the Germans had bombers in production, but not in sufficient numbers. At first the Luftwaffe tried to attack the Royal Air Force directly with massed raids on its airfields. This produced aerial battles in which Britain's new radar – together with the remarkable abilities of the British planes and pilots – proved their worth by finally deciding the battle in Britain's favor. By mid-September the Germans shifted their air attack to London and other urban centers, hoping to cripple British industry and crush civilian morale, but in spite of the dreadful damage they wreaked on the population they were not able to break Britain's will or ability to resist. Finally, with the coming of winter and mounting losses to their aircraft, the Germans gave up their offensive, conceding what amounted to a limited but decisive victory for the British. For the first time in the war a German attack had failed.

American support

The courage that the British displayed under the German assault made a deep impression on Americans. While they were not yet ready to go to war on Britain's behalf, they now began to support the idea of giving assistance to their former ally in her brave and lonely struggle. In 1940 the American government provided Britain with fifty destroyers. Although an attempt was made to make this gesture seem less than a commitment to the war, by describing the ships as "over-age," and by making the arrangement "reciprocal" (with Britain leasing naval bases in her western colonies to the United States in exchange), it was, as its opponents warned, a major step toward war. Two weeks later the Congress instituted universal military service, as a "defensive measure" to "keep us out of war." Later that fall the United States and Britain agreed to standardize design and dimensions of much of their military matériel, and the United States began using its navy to protect ships carrying American arms to Britain. In March of 1941 Congress passed the famous Lend-Lease Act, which made it possible to continue and increase shipments of arms and food, without promise of payment, to Britain or any country designated by the president as contributing to the security of the United States.

While this new Anglo-American cooperation against Germany was beginning to take the shape of an alliance, Hitler's boasted "new order" was being established in occupied Europe. Poland and Czechoslovakia, both utterly crushed and wholly inaccessible, had sunk from international view, leaving hardly a trace. In the west the populations of Denmark, Norway, Holland, Belgium and France, reeling under the trauma of defeat and occupation, had each been divided, with some ready to collaborate with the conquerors and a very few determined to resist. This split poisoned the atmosphere in the occupied countries, and the prospect that the occupied peoples would form a united front against the foreign masters grew increasingly remote as the Germans bled the conquered territories of their resources, reducing the inhabitants to a desperate individual struggle for mere survival. Among the French, mutual recrimination was aggravated by the existence of the puppet regime formed around Marshal Pétain, which pretended to rule the unoccupied rump of France while engaging in efforts to curry German favor. The picture of life in conquered Europe as it emerged to the British and Americans could only contribute to their realization that no accommodation with the Germans would be possible.

THE EXPANSION OF THE WAR

Fighting in North Africa and Greece

After the Germans had called off the aerial assault on Britain, and the coming winter weather had made a cross-Channel invasion impractical, there was a brief lull in the war as Hitler pondered ways of attacking his enemy indirectly through her empire, or alternatively of seizing the opportunity to focus all of Germany's efforts on the eastern front — meaning ultimately the invasion of Russia. Hitler had never lost sight of Russia as a primary object of conquest, nor changed his view that the Russians were his natural enemies, both as "Slavs" and as communists. The non-aggression pact that he and Stalin had signed in 1939 had served the short-term interests of both leaders but it had done nothing to alter their mutual distrust or the essential conflict of their interests.

The next theater of the war, however, was determined not by Hitler but Mussolini. With the collapse of France and the imminent defeat of Britain, Mussolini felt it safe to declare war on the Allies and gather in some easy imperial spoils. In so doing, however, the Duce brought the war to what Churchill referred to as "Europe's soft underbelly," that is, the Mediterranean basin. After occupying the southeastern corner of France, the Italians captured Britain's colonial garrison of Somaliland in East Africa and then launched a large attack from Libya on the British forces in Egypt. After six weeks of defensive action the British commander launched a limited counterattack which led to a major rout, breaking the Italian offensive capability in North Africa.

In the mean time (late October), the Italians invaded Greece from Albania (which they had seized in 1939 when it was — like Ethiopia — virtually defenseless). The Greeks fought off the invasion, while the British attempted to come to their aid, dispatching part of their North African force to Crete and other Greek islands, and reinforcing their naval position in the eastern Mediterranean. A brilliant British victory off Taranto put half the Italian fleet out of action, and shortly afterwards (early December) the Greeks inflicted a serious defeat on the Italian army. These Italian losses on both sides of the Mediterranean, together with the ferment in the Balkans caused by the German victories in the west, now produced a critical situation which required Hitler to take action on Italy's behalf, even though he had not been consulted by Mussolini about the Greek adventure and there is no evidence that he had previously contemplated such a move. In April of 1941 German troops moved in force into Yugoslavia, which they occupied as a base for the conquest of Greece, while German air units were moved into Italy to combat the British navy. Simultaneously a combined German and Italian army, commanded by the renowned German general Rommel, launched a powerful attack against the depleted British forces in Libya, forcing them back to the Egyptian frontier. By June of 1941 the Germans had driven the British out of Greece, after which they captured Crete, in the first paratroop invasion ever attempted. Although both Yugoslavs and Greeks continued to offer some guerrilla resistance to the Germans, the defeat of the British really meant that Germany now appeared to be within reach of seizing effective control of the eastern Mediterranean. If Hitler had been seriously interested in this area, one would have expected him to take advantage of his position and gain access to the petroleum in Iraq and Iran; during the spring the British had been able to take over the French-mandated territory of Syria, thus giving themselves a base from which to occupy Iraq and influence Iran, but the Germans made no move to drive them out of this region. One explanation for German caution was undoubtedly the presence of Russian troops in the Black Sea area; but the main reason was that Hitler's interest lay elsewhere.

The invasion of Russia

On June 22, 1941, Hitler launched his long-planned invasion of Russia. The Balkan campaign had required two months of spring weather and may thereby have cost him the conquest of Russia, for like Napoleon before him, he was to meet a formidable enemy in the Russian winter. Comparison of Hitler's Russian campaign with that of Napoleon yields other striking similarities as well. In each case Europe's current conqueror, frustrated by his failure to cross the Channel, turned to Russia's steppes to deploy his victorious troops. Each also miscalculated the reactions of the Russian people as well as the vagaries of Russia's climate, and in both cases the attempt to take on Russia transformed the scale of the war to the aggressor's decisive disadvantage. Finally, in each case the offensive served as the decisive turning-point in his fortunes.

The German attack on Russia came as a complete surprise to the Russians in spite of numerous signs and warnings. Although the Red Army had been maintained in force since the revolution, Russia was by no means prepared to meet a major invasion, and this unreadiness undoubtedly contributed to Hitler's decision to seize this occasion to gain one of his major objectives. In addition, Hitler needed to make this move not only before Britain could recover enough strength to go to Russia's aid, but also while the United States was still out of the picture. Finally, it is clear that he expected a blitzkrieg attack to lead to a swift success in Russia just as it had in Poland and France, and he made no provision for winter because he did not expect the fighting to continue that long.

Germany's three principal objectives in Russia were Leningrad to the north, on the Baltic coast, Moscow, deep in the Russian heartland, and Stalingrad, even farther east than Moscow and far to the south near the Black Sea – a sweep that was to require a continuous front of two thousand miles. The territory to be conquered included the wheat fields of the Ukraine, the coal and metals of the Donets Basin and the oil of the Caucasus. With these resources Hitler's German Empire would become invulnerable to threats to its overseas supply routes. Further, Hitler conceived of this territory, along with Poland, as ideal for German settlement, so that his plan also called for the massive slaughter and deportation of its population. (The vast reaches to the east of the Volga River apparently held no interest for Hitler, whose territorial ambitions extended as far as the Middle East and even parts of Africa, but not to Asia.)

The Axis forces invading Russia, including important elements of Italians and Hungarians as well as the Finns and Romanians, numbered some 3,000,000 men, against perhaps two million Russians under arms. Moreover the Germans had reason to expect serious defections from Russia's Ukrainian divisions, and they were not disappointed. As the attack developed, entire units of Ukrainians surrendered, frequently eager to join in the attack. Although the German army accepted and used but the Germans had great success in the south, defeating a large Russian army and taking both the Ukraine and the rich industrial area around Rostov, not far from Stalingrad.

With total victory now within their reach, the Germans turned back toward Moscow in October. But the Russians had been given two months in which to strengthen the defenses of that city, and to rebuild their army with troops from the east. Moreover they had managed to build up their war industries, to the east of the capital. Perhaps most significant, the Russian population had by now been aroused to such a fury of patriotism by the German brutality that the political and ethnic differences that had recently divided them were forgotten as they joined in a bitter struggle to resist the conquerors by any means.

As Russia's defensive assets now began to take their toll, the German drive on Moscow slowed to a standstill. With their supply lines stretched thinner and thinner through a deeply hostile population that harassed them without respite, the Germans were suddenly caught by the Russian winter arriving three weeks before its normal time (exactly as it had for Napoleon). Totally unprepared for the ordeal ahead, the German soldiers froze for lack of warm uniforms, while their tanks were immobilized by lack of antifreeze, and the snow left the roads impassable. With the German army mired outside Moscow, the Russians were able to mount limited counterthrusts, which by the middle of January, 1942, succeeded in driving the Germans back a hundred miles, their first retreat of the war. Even so the Russian situation remained desperate, as the Germans dug in and began making preparations to renew their attack in the spring.

Stalin's diplomatic maneuvering before the war had ensured that Russia would have to fight alone, at least at first. As soon as Hitler opened his attack, however, Britain had offered Russia an alliance, and the United States Congress voted to extend Lend-

Lease to Russia. Despite the tensions that had existed between Russia and the democracies, Hitler was now generally recognized by Americans as representing by far the greater danger, and while they were not yet ready to send troops themselves, most were ready to send anything else they could to aid anyone already fighting. In October of 1941, the United States and Britain signed a protocol in Moscow by which they agreed to ship large quantities of supplies to Russia over the hazardous northern route. This agreement constituted the first formulation of the triple alliance that would finally defeat Hitler.

The United States drawn into the war

Earlier (in August 1941), Roosevelt and Churchill had drafted the Atlantic Charter, setting forth their joint war aims (although the United States was not yet formally at war), which was intended to serve as the philosophical base of the anti-Axis alliance. In this document the two leaders asserted that they sought no territorial gains, but only to restore self-government to people who had been deprived of it by force, and to disarm all aggressors. The Charter was rapidly subscribed to by fifteen other states and governments-in-exile, who were to lend what aid they could to the three major undefeated powers in the struggle against Hitler and his partners.

The fall of France had occurred in June of 1940, the Battle of Britain had been fought in the autumn of that year, and Germany's opening offensive in Russia had followed in June of the next year, continuing through the end of 1941. The United States had been slow to react, but by March of 1941, with the Lend-Lease bill, she was deeply involved in the war effort. Roosevelt did everything in his power to mobilize American industry as the "arsenal of democracy," and to deliver the needed supplies to Britain and Russia, even though transporting the goods to Russia meant providing American naval escorts for merchant ships as far as Iceland, which involved a number of shooting incidents with German submarines that led to the crippling of one American destroyer and the loss of another.

Despite these developments, however, isolationist sentiment remained so strong in the United States that even at this late date virtually no one advocated or supported direct American intervention in the war. In the 1940 presidential campaign both Roosevelt and his Republican rival, Wendell Wilkie, had promised to keep the country out of the war, and in the summer of 1941 the House of Representatives was so evenly divided on the question of mobilization that a bill to extend the draft passed by only a single vote. Even the Lend-Lease program was offered and justified by its supporters as a means of ensuring that Americans themselves would not have to fight.

But the United States would not be permitted to stand on the sidelines much longer. On December 7, 1941, the Japanese bombed Pearl Harbor, America's principal naval base in the Pacific, sinking two battleships and crippling five others – thus destroying the main American battle fleet. (Only the aircraft carriers escaped, since they happened to be at sea.) At the same time the Japanese also attacked the American base at Manila and British installations in Singapore and Malaya, following these actions with an amphibious offensive through the islands of the South and Central Pacific that rivaled the speed and efficiency of the German blitzkrieg.

The origins of this violent outburst can be traced back as far as the middle of the nineteenth century, when Japan began her spectacularly rapid transformation from a feudal agricultural society into a modern industrial and military power. Imperial expansion was part of the European model that Japan imitated, and even before the turn of the century the militaristic oligarchy that had directed Japan's industrialization was also seeking an empire that would provide her with land, food, and the essential raw materials she lacked.

In 1894 the Japanese attacked the decaying Chinese Empire and gained the island of Formosa, and a decade later they successfully fought the Russians for control of Korea and dominance in the northeastern Chinese province of Manchuria. During the First World War they tried to take over the Chinese possessions and concessions of the warring European powers, but were finally restrained by the Allies – particularly the United States – who forced them to sign a treaty in 1922 that recognized China's independence.

This move did more to establish the United States as an enemy in the Japanese view than to protect China from further aggression. In 1931 Japan attacked and seized Manchuria, which she had long coveted for its coal and iron supply, and finally in 1937 she launched a major invasion designed to make her master of all the rest of China. By this time the western nations were too caught up in their own troubles to offer effective support to the Chinese, whose own government had disintegrated in a power struggle among nationalists, communists and provincial war-lords. The Japanese advanced from victory to victory in China, and as Hitler conveniently removed Holland, France and Britain from the Far East they also moved quickly to fill the resulting power vacuums in the European colonies. When the German invasion put Russia out of action as well, the United States remained the only power capable of opposing Japan's imperial ambitions.

Nevertheless trade between the two countries continued uninterrupted until the summer of 1941. At that point the United States called for Japanese withdrawal from China and French Indochina, and placed an embargo on American trade with the Japanese until they had met these conditions. Negotiations followed throughout the autumn of 1941, until in November the adamant refusal of the United States to moderate its demands led the Japanese to decide on war. What they hoped to do was eliminate the threat posed to them by the American Pacific fleet – by destroying it in a surprise attack – and then to reopen negotiations with the objective of obtaining American recognition of their hegemony in the Far East. The attack on Pearl Harbor was ordered on December 1 and carried out six days later.

Although the bombing did greatly reduce American power in the Pacific, it fell far short of the desired effect of bringing a chastened United States to the conference table to offer concessions to the Japanese. Indeed in hindsight it might be considered the worst tactical mistake of the entire war, for it instantly brought the full force of the United States on to the Allied side. The American people, previously wavering and divided in their commitment to the war, responded to Pearl Harbor with outrage, which Roosevelt encouraged as much as possible in a speech declaring that December 7 would be remembered as a "day of infamy." On December 8 the Congress declared war on Japan with a single dissenting vote, and three days later Germany and Italy joined their eastern ally by declaring war on the United

States, thereby further fulfilling the hopes of those who wanted total American involvement in the war. The United States responded by recognizing a state of war with the whole Axis coalition.

The speed and certainty with which Americans reacted to direct provocation suggests that many besides Roosevelt seized upon it almost with relief, as an opportunity to do what they had long wanted to do. Perhaps the United States would have entered the war even without Pearl Harbor but there is no way of knowing, and certainly the longer the country remained officially neutral the better from the point of view of the Axis powers. Even though the United States was not yet fully prepared for war her potential military power was enormous, and would ultimately prove decisive in determining the outcome of the struggle. The readiness of the Axis nations so casually to add the United States to the roster of their enemies at the end of 1941 is a mark of the overwhelming success their aggression had met with up to this time, and the contempt in which they held the hitherto tardy and insufficient efforts of all who had resisted.

THE WORLD AT WAR

Japanese gains

At the beginning of 1942 Axis confidence seemed well justified: the immediate prospect for the Allies was grim indeed. Both the British and the Russians were fighting for their lives, with the British apparently losing the battle to keep their sea lanes open and the most populous and productive part of Russia already behind the German lines. Now the Japanese, having disposed of America's main battle fleet, were scoring one success after another in the Pacific. In conjunction with their attack on Pearl Harbor they had launched an overwhelming offensive against the unprepared American forces on the Philippines, after which they went on to take Guam and Wake Island from the United States. At the same time they seized Hong Kong and Malaya from Britain, sinking two of Britain's most powerful battleships off Singapore. With the Netherlands unable to offer any defense to her colonies, the

C H I N A

OUTER
MONGOLIA

U S S R

Aleutian

Attu
Kiska

INDIA

NEPAL

Vladivostok

MANCHURIA

Nanking

Hiroshima

Honshu

JAPAN

Tokyo
Sagami Bay
Yokohama

N O R T H

P A C I

Calcutta

Chungking

Changsha

YUNNAN

Kweilin

Yellow Sea

Shanghai

Nagasaki

Ryukyu Is.

Okinawa

Inland Sea

Mandalay

Bay
of
Bengal

BURMA

Rangoon

SIAM

Hong
Kong (Br.)

Formosa

Bonin Is.

Iwo Jima

Midway I.

Isthmus
of Kra

Gulf
of
Siam

FRENCH INDO-CHINA

Saigon

Luzon

Bataan
Corregidor
Mindoro

Manila

Philippine
Islands

Leyte

Marianas Is.

Saipan

Guam

Wake I.

Eniwetok I.

Kwajalein

Marshall Is.

MALAYA

Singapore

BR.
BORNEO

Mindanao

Celebes

BORNEO

Caroline

Yap

Truk I.

Islands

Angaur (US)

Tarawa

Gilbert
Islands

Sumatra

NETHERLANDS EAST INDIES

Java Sea

(Port)

Java

Bali

Timor

Hollandia

New
Guinea

Bismarck
Arch.

Rabaul

Buna

Solomon
Islands

Guadalcanal

Nanumea

Port
Moresby

Coral
Sea

Samoa

Fiji Is.

INDIAN OCEAN

Port
Darwin

A U S T R A L I A

New Caledonia (Fr.)

Sydney

Melbourne

NEW ZEALAND

Wellington

——— Furthest advance of Japanese
military power

■ Japanese territory in 1931

■ Dutch possessions

■ British Commonwealth and possessions

Distances in Nautical Miles
Panama to Honolulu   4,700
San Francisco to Honolulu 2,100
San Francisco to Manila   6,200
San Francisco to Shanghai 5,500
Singapore to Honolulu   5,900
Sydney to Honolulu   4,400
Yokohama to Honolulu   3,400

MAP 8   *War in the Pacific, 1941–5*

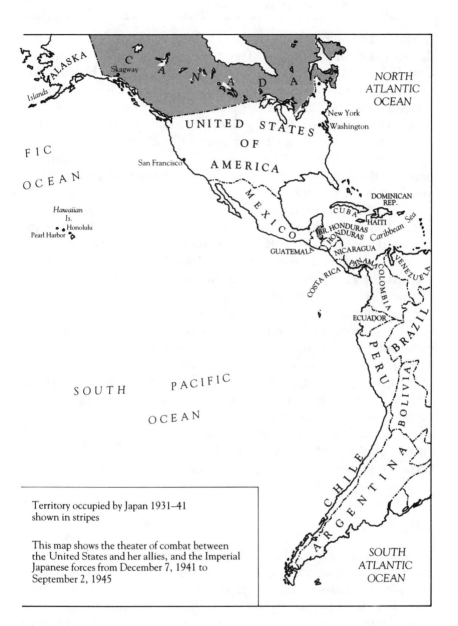

NORTH
ATLANTIC
OCEAN

FIC

OCEAN

*Hawaiian
Is.*
Honolulu
Pearl Harbor

SOUTH   PACIFIC

OCEAN

Territory occupied by Japan 1931–41
shown in stripes

This map shows the theater of combat between
the United States and her allies, and the Imperial
Japanese forces from December 7, 1941 to
September 2, 1945

Japanese next moved systematically into the Java Sea, and after defeating an American naval force occupied the bulk of the Dutch East Indies (Indonesia). The fall of France in 1940 had already provided Japan with the opportunity to seize Indochina, and no one was able to contest the extension of Japanese control over Thailand and Burma. Thus by May of 1942 Japan had established an enormous empire, including essentially all territory (with the exception of an area of China inland from Hong Kong) that lay between the borders of India on the west, Australia to the south, and Russia on the north.

Wake Island represented Japan's farthest reach in the direction of the United States, and clearly if she were to protect these gains she would have to drive the Americans from their other islands in the eastern Pacific as well – the Aleutians in the north, and Midway Island as a base for a final attack on Hawaii. Morever the Japanese were also contemplating an assault on Australia to prevent its falling into American hands. Thus although their territorial ambitions might seem largely fulfilled by this first explosive expansion, the Japanese found themselves forced to continue their offensive, just as the Germans had, in order not to lose the advantage of being the aggressor. In particular they had to strike at the United States while it was still unprepared for the struggle, just as Hitler had sought to take on Russia at the earliest opportunity. There is no indication that Japan got as far as planning an invasion of the United States, but in the spring of 1942 she was certainly poised to seize the remaining American outposts in the Pacific.

Allied successes

It was at this point, however, that the military tide finally began to turn against the aggressors. In the spring of 1942 the United States seized the initiative from the Japanese, later in the fall the British won a decisive battle against the Germans and Italians in North Africa, and finally at the end of the year the Russians launched an overwhelming counteroffensive against the Germans at Stalingrad. By the beginning of 1943, therefore, the Axis powers were on the defensive in every theater of the war. They had spent the advantage of surprise, and they had done so without destroying the capacity of Britain, Russia, and the United States to rally and retaliate. In each case, moreover, the invaders had pushed beyond their own lines of supply just as their opponents were beginning to produce or receive reinforcements that would enable them to take advantage of this overextension. In 1943 the Allied giants were fully mobilized, and that year saw them begin the slow and painful process of retaking conquered territory which two years later would finally drive the Axis forces to surrender.

The first victory for the Allies in the Pacific occurred on May 7, 1942, when American air and naval forces in the Coral Sea broke up a Japanese expedition that was probably heading for Australia. A month later the Japanese launched a major offensive against the Americans on Midway Island, hoping to destroy the aircraft carriers they had missed in Pearl Harbor and to cut the sea route between the United States and Australia. Having broken Japan's naval code, the Americans were prepared for the attack and won a decisive victory, sinking all four of the Japanese aircraft carriers while losing only one. This left the Japanese with only two carriers and no plans to replace their losses, while the Americans still had four, with thirteen more under construction. From this time onward (June 1942) the United States was on the attack in the Pacific, and the Japanese were reduced to a tenacious defense of their widespread conquests. Then within a few weeks there were signs that the tide was also turning against the Japanese on land, as an army of the Chinese Republic won an important battle in Kiangsi. In August of 1942, American marines landed on Guadalcanal in the Solomon Islands (on the southern perimeter of Japanese power), to begin the long and costly counteroffensive that would finally lead to Japan itself.

Stalingrad

For the Germans in Russia, as for the Japanese, the spring of 1942 saw success that hardly presaged the impending turning point in their fortunes. In spite of the setback they had suffered during the preceding winter, the Germans were still a dangerous threat to Russia; they had conquered the richest industrial and agricultural areas of the country, and had inflicted staggering losses on the Russian army and people. Both Moscow and Leningrad lay within their reach, but again Hitler decided to concentrate his forces in the south, intending to take Stalingrad and push on to the rich oil fields of the Caucasus.

A powerful new offensive carried them a thousand miles into Russia. First they took Sebastopol (in the Crimea) and then Rostov; but in early September desperate Russian resistance stopped them at Stalingrad, well before they reached the oil fields but not before their supply lines had been stretched to the breaking point. Had they been able to bypass Stalingrad they might yet have avoided disaster and reached their destination, but the city had become a symbol for Hitler as much as it was for Stalin, and he insisted on its capture. With both sides fully committed to the battle, the fighting was fierce and the losses on both sides horrendous. Finally on November 19 the Russians mustered the reserves to open a new attack, and succeeded in surrounding the entire German army. Forbidden to retreat by Hitler, the Germans continued a now suicidal fight until the remnants of their army surrendered in January of 1943. The Germans would never recover from this blow, although Hitler's reaction was to order "total war," and attempt yet another offensive in July of 1943. By that time, however, the Russians had grown stronger than their adversary. With massive shipments of food and weapons from the British and Americans, as well as an important infusion of fresh troops and the tanks and vehicles they had captured from the Germans at Stalingrad, they now outnumbered the Germans two to one. No longer a match for this enemy, the Germans suffered still another defeat in July, then began the long retreat before the advancing Russian army that would finally end in Berlin.

El Alamein and Algeria

Developments in North Africa during 1942 were no less dramatic and decisive. While the Russians were turning the tide on the eastern front, the Allies established the first front against Hitler in the west. Still unable to mount a direct invasion of Hitler's Europe, Britain and America landed a large expeditionary force in Algeria and Morocco in November 1942 and moved eastward to terminate the long struggle that had been going on between Axis and British forces in Egypt. That front had been opened two years earlier when the Italians had attacked the British in Egypt from their base in Libya; after some initial success, things went from bad to worse for the Italians, until Hitler sent an elite army and one of his best generals, Rommel, who succeeded in pushing the British back from Libya to El Alamein in Egypt. There in June of 1942 the British won a victory that stopped Rommel and ultimately spelled the end of German power in North Africa. For several months the British had rested at El Alamein, apparently just waiting for Rommel to prepare his final attack on the Suez Canal. Actually the new British commander, General Montgomery, was carefully accumulating supplies and organizing troops that were arriving in increasing numbers by way of the Red Sea, until with massive superiority he opened an attack (October 1942) that sent Rommel reeling back across the desert. In November the huge Anglo-American amphibious expedition, under General Eisenhower, had landed in Morocco and Algeria, and although the Germans rushed reinforcements to Rommel through Tunisia, he was now in a hopeless situation, caught between two powerful Allied armies. It is a mark of his military genius that he managed to hold off defeat for another six months, even winning one brilliant if limited victory in the process. In May of 1943, however, the 300,000 Axis troops in North Africa were finally forced to surrender to the Allies. The whole of North Africa had become an Allied base, which meant that the entire Mediterranean coast of Hitler's Europe now lay open to attack.

War production and the atom bomb

The year that saw these first three crucial Allied victories (at Midway, Stalingrad and El Alamein) also saw the full mobilization of America's vast industrial and agricultural resources in a war economy of undreamed-of capacity. It was the flood of weapons, tanks, planes and ships that issued from this "arsenal of democracy" that would give the Allies the decisive edge over the Axis in the end. Such a total use of the American economy also represented a logical extension of the New Deal politics that had been designed to combat the Depression, and one enormously important consequence of America's war production was her complete recovery from the economic collapse she had suffered during the preceding decade.

Along with this mobilization program the United States government undertook a special project that would radically alter the prospects of the human race. On the eve of the war Albert Einstein, the most famous living physicist, had written a letter to President Roosevelt at the instigation of a group of distinguished scientists stating their opinion that it was highly probable that atoms could be split, releasing a fantastic quantity of energy, and that there was no reason the process could not be harnessed as a weapon. Since that time Hitler had made references to the development of secret weapons that would win the war for Germany – a threat which American scientists, including many recent refugees from Germany, did not dare to take lightly, since Germany had led the world in developing the new atomic physics. In fact, it was only Hitler's vicious anti-Semitism, which had driven most of Germany's best scientists abroad, that gave the United States the necessary pool of talent to undertake the task.

In 1942 the American government created a secret agency, called the "Manhattan Project," to design and produce atomic weapons. It was a huge enterprise involving enormous expenditures and a large number of highly trained scientists. The whole undertaking was conducted as a race against what was believed to be the impending appearance of a German atom bomb. Actually, Hitler never gave his depleted corps of physicists anywhere near the necessary support to move toward actual production of such a bomb. Instead the Germans pushed the development of rockets, a project that held out the prospect of much quicker results. They did succeed in producing the first ballistic rocket, the V-2, which they used to bomb London in September 1944, but by then this "secret weapon" was not enough to enable Hitler to snatch victory from the jaws of defeat.

THE TURNING OF THE TIDE

Supplies for Europe

By the end of 1942 the Allies had checked the Axis advance in all five of the principal combat areas of the global struggle: the North Atlantic, the Mediterranean, the Russian front, the South Pacific, and Europe's skies. In each case what tipped the scales of battle in favor of the Allies was the mounting flood of supplies and matériel that was pouring out of the American "arsenal of democracy." The ability to produce and deliver huge quantities of arms and ammunition had first become a decisive military factor in the First World War, but in the Second World War industrial capacity had become all-important. Military power was no longer measured by the quantities of men or weapons a country could mobilize at the start of the conflict but over the long haul by the numbers of tanks, planes, and ships it could produce each month.

When the war began, in 1939, the American economy had not yet emerged from the Depression in spite of Roosevelt's massive New Deal program, but its resources in labor, land and raw materials (including petroleum) were much the richest in the world. By that time all of the other major industrial powers (Britain, Germany, Russia and Japan) were in some phase of war mobilization while the United States was not; but although it was behind, America was in a position to outstrip them all. By the end of 1942 it was just beginning to reach its full capacity, at the same time that the Germans and British were crippling each other's factories in air attacks, and Russia's principal industries had been overrun.

By early 1942 German submarines were stalking America's east coast with impunity, threatening to isolate Britain and prevent the United States from delivering any of its desperately needed matériel to its allies. A year later, however, that problem was being resolved by a huge American shipbuilding program, which simply launched far more tons of shipping than the Germans could sink, while also providing sufficient naval escort craft to drastically curtail the submarine menace. Although this battle would continue throughout the war, American convoys would cross the Atlantic in ever greater numbers, and with an ever-declining rate of loss.

America's first priority in the European theater was to supply the British Isles and build up reserves at home in preparation for an eventual Allied offensive on the European mainland. But in 1942 there were also two other urgent American objectives, which were to assist the British in North Africa and to get equipment to the besieged Russians in Stalingrad. In North Africa, Rommel's brilliant offensive had finally been stopped at the end of June by the desperate British stand at El Alamein, but the Suez Canal still appeared to be in danger. At this point the outnumbered British were saved from disaster primarily by Hitler's decision to shift some of Rommel's reserves to the Russian front, so that by late October when Montgomery launched his counteroffensive he was in command of vastly superior forces. These had been built up by a huge supply and reinforcement effort on the part of Britain and the Commonwealth nations, with a considerable indirect contribution from the United States.

Italy defeated

Montgomery's victorious drive from the east was timed to meet a huge Anglo-American invasion of Morocco and Algeria in the west that would complete the Allies' conquest of North Africa and establish their domination of the Mediterranean by the summer of 1943. This operation also depended on a massive superiority in men and matériel, much of which had come from the United States. Once the two Allied forces had met in Tunisia they were merged under General Eisenhower, who turned north to invade Sicily (in July) and conquered that island in a month. With this invasion, the king of Italy reasserted his authority, dismissed Mussolini from power, arrested him, and appointed as prime minister the leading Italian general, Marshall Bagdoglio. Bagdoglio then dissolved the Fascist party, and when the Allies began their invasion of the mainland from Sicily, he requested peace terms and accepted unconditional surrender. At this point the Germans moved south to check the Allied advance, meeting the invading forces in Naples. A German commando raid rescued Mussolini from an Italian prison and propped him up again as leader of a fascist regime in the German-occupied north of Italy. Allied progress against the Germans was very slow because of the mountainous terrain, complicated by the near total lack of roads and the severe winter weather. Clearly a toehold on the "boot" of Italy did not automatically throw open an invasion route to central Europe; but it did secure the Allies' control of the central Mediterranean.

Aid for Russia

When Hitler attacked Russia, the immediate offers of support to the victim from both Churchill and Roosevelt, though difficult to implement, would rapidly assume major importance as the German drive completely overran Russia's principal industrial and food-producing areas. When the arrival of winter in November 1941 made it possible for the Russians to halt the German onslaught and mount a counterattack, their need for supplies of all kinds became extremely urgent. During 1942 Britain made heroic and extremely costly efforts to get convoys of supply ships around the occupied Norwegian coast to Murmansk and Archangel, and in spite of desperate losses succeeded in delivering the matériel that made possible the Russian victory at Stalingrad. Then when the Germans returned to the offensive, in the summer of 1943, they found Russia better equipped and supplied in most respects than they were themselves, especially in the air, where the Soviet air force was now reinforced with several thousand American planes. The German attack took the classic blitzkrieg form, with seventeen armored divisions launched against Russian defenses near Kursk; in history's greatest tank battle, the Russians defeated the German forces, then drove them back two hundred miles. From this time onward the Germans were on the retreat in the east, although they would force their pursuers to fight for every mile gained, and for good measure left a swath of great destruction in their wake. With their ever-growing advantage in weapons and equipment, however, the Russians were able to maintain unrelenting pressure on the Germans over the huge distance of a drive that would take them to the borders of Poland by the spring of 1944, and to Berlin a year later.

Toward a second front in Europe

From early in 1942 the Russians had demanded that the British and Americans mount an attack across the Channel to relieve German pressure on the eastern front. At that time both the American and British high commands were painfully aware of their lack of preparation for such an undertaking, but they agreed with the strategic necessity of a second front. Originally the Allied air force commanders had been convinced that Germany could be defeated by saturation bombing alone; the British had opened this campaign in the spring of 1942, with the first thousand-plane raids over German cities, and the Americans soon joined in the attack.

By 1943, however, although this bombing had reduced significant areas of Germany to rubble, it had not succeeded in significantly reducing German productivity and military might, making clear the necessity of the cross-Channel land invasion to destroy German power.

At the same time the Allies had conducted a number of commando raids on the European coast and had learned at great cost the difficulty of such amphibious attacks. Although Churchill still preferred the idea of a flank attack through the eastern Mediterranean — as he did in the First World War — and warned of the catastrophic effects of a failed invasion, he finally agreed to the cross-Channel campaign if an overwhelming superiority could be established. This condition effectively delayed the European invasion for a full year, causing the Russians to charge the Americans and British with bad faith. But although 1943 passed without a second front being opened in western Europe, and without any decisive results from the mounting Allied air war against Germany, behind this apparent stalemate the Anglo-American forces were piling up weapons and training men in Britain on a wholly unprecedented scale for the ultimate test of the entire war.

The Japanese halted

During the same period (1942–3), on the other side of the globe, the Americans (with aid from the Australians and British) were struggling to halt the Japanese advance and establish bases from which to launch a counteroffensive in the South Pacific. In early 1942 the Americans suffered a serious naval defeat in the Java Sea, which allowed the Japanese to complete their conquest of the East Indies and land on New Guinea, in what looked like preparation for an attack on Australia. But any such plans were frustrated by an American victory in the Coral Sea, in the first naval battle fought entirely by carrier-based planes. This made it possible for the Americans to land marines on the island of Guadalcanal and seize the airfields, in what would become the starting-point of the American counteroffensive. Almost immediately, however, the Japanese scored a major naval victory over an American and

Australian task force, cutting off the marines in Guadalcanal and leaving them in desperate straits. For the rest of the year (1942) the two navies fought a series of engagements in the adjacent waters, in a continuing struggle for control of the key islands. Gradually the American ships established their superiority, forcing the Japanese to withdraw their land troops and thus leaving the Americans in full possession of Guadalcanal. This was the turning-point of the Pacific war.

In early June of 1942, the Japanese had sent a major task force against the American outpost on Midway Island in the central Pacific, to the east of the Hawaiian Islands. In some ways it was an attempt to repeat their original strike against Pearl Harbor, but this time the Americans were ready, and caught the Japanese force as soon as it came into range with a devastating attack by land-based planes. The Japanese lost four carriers, giving the Americans a decisive naval advantage in the Pacific and ending any Japanese threat to Hawaii.

Although the fighting in the Pacific was different in nature from that in Europe, it too was dominated by America's productive capacity – in this case her ability to outbuild the Japanese navy, although starting from overall inferiority in numbers and weight. Eventually the Americans deployed over a hundred carriers, when Japan had only seventeen, an overwhelming advantage in the long series of naval engagements by which the Americans fought their way back to the Philippines. Virtually all of these battles were decided by carrier-based planes, with the big guns of the battleships and cruisers coming into use only against coastal installations. Behind these fighting ships was an even larger fleet of transport craft that supplied the ever-growing American forces across the vast reaches of the Pacific.

By the end of 1943 there could be no doubt that the tide of victory was running with the Allies. The Americans had begun their successful counteroffensive against the Japanese-held islands in the South Pacific, and on land the Allies had launched a campaign for the reconquest of Burma. Nevertheless, both the distances and the Japanese defenses were so formidable that victory would cost the Allies another year and a half of extremely savage warfare.

THE DEFEAT OF GERMANY

The invasion of France

At the end of November 1943, the three chief Allied heads of state (Roosevelt, Churchill, and Stalin) met in Teheran to coordinate their efforts for the coming cross-Channel invasion of the Continent. For nearly a year the British and Americans had been developing plans and amassing matériel in the south of England, and following the Teheran conference, the final preparations for this enormous and intricate operation were completed.

The plan called for a direct attack across the Channel and a landing in force (a million men in a month) on the coast of France. The Germans were prepared for such a blow but expected it on the Pas de Calais, which had one of the few ports on the French Channel coast. Instead the Allies picked the Normandy beaches, which lacked harbors but provided room for maneuver. To handle the half-million tons of supplies needed in the first month, two artificial harbors, called "mulberries," were organized in England to be towed to France. These consisted of old ships to be sunk as breakwaters, and long floating causeways to take the traffic from the ships to the shore. This proved to be a brilliant solution to a dangerous problem. Even though one of the floating harbors would be destroyed by a storm, the other handled the entire load of supplies without undue trouble, while the Germans easily destroyed the loading facilities of those existing Channel ports which the Allies might have hoped to use.

It is difficult to understand how the main thrust of such plans could have been kept secret, but the Germans were clearly surprised at the direction the invasion took, thus giving the Allies the essential advantage for success. A second and even more important factor was the Allies' control of the air. Even if the bombing offensive over Germany had failed to cripple German industry and morale, it did force the German air force to fight at home and thus effectively prevented any systematic German air attacks on the invasion preparations.

While the buildup for the attack on "Fortress Europe" rushed toward its climax in the spring of 1944, the Russians continued to drive the Germans back along their entire eastern front. Leningrad and Moscow were relieved of pressure in the north and center, and Sebastopol was reconquered in the south, so that by the time the Allied invasion forces had landed in France, the Russians were approaching their own western borders and were preparing to move into East Prussia and Poland.

During the same period the Allied forces in Italy were struggling painfully forward against stubborn German resistance and the formidable terrain. They finally liberated Rome in early June, two days before the Normandy landing, but then were unable to make further progress, and the Germans hung on to northern Italy until Germany itself collapsed.

The cross-Channel invasion had been planned for late May, but an unseasonal storm forced a delay. Then, even though the weather was still poor, the decision was made to go on June 6. The way was prepared by heavy bombing attacks, followed by parachute drops and glider landings, as well as shelling of German installations by hundreds of naval craft cruising offshore. Finally the main body – some 150,000 men with 1,500 tanks and thousands of vehicles – crossed the Channel in 4,000 crafts to land on the Norman shore. In spite of the continued poor weather and the loss of one of the essential "mulberries," and thanks to the Allies' superb organization and their complete control of the adjacent air and sea, the whole operation went off essentially as planned. On land the Germans were still able to offer serious resistance, but incredibly, Hitler soon squandered this strength by insisting that the Normandy landings were a feint, and that the main thrust would still come at the Pas de Calais. With this conviction he refused to allow his field commander, General Rommel of North African fame, to concentrate his reserves against the Allied beachhead in Normandy, thereby giving them a chance to organize their forces and build up supplies.

A week after the invasion, Hitler unveiled one of his vaunted "secret weapons," a flying bomb with a crude jet engine, that was aimed generally at London. These "V-1" rockets, as they were called, might have posed a dangerous threat to the invasion forces if they had been ready a few weeks sooner; but even though they did not prevent the landing, they did influence the British to fight their way up the coast to the V-1 launching sites in the Pas de Calais. Without this diversion of Allied energies from the planned

American breakthrough into central France, it is possible the attack might have been pushed on into Germany, and ended the war then and there.

By early July, however, the success of the invasion was established, and its military implications for Germany were clear to both the Allies and the Germans. At this point the German army mounted a widespread plot against Hitler to save the country from total destruction. A powerful bomb was detonated in Hitler's headquarters, but failed to kill him. Nazi vengeance was swift and characteristic: over a thousand suspects were tortured and murdered. The incident has often been cited as evidence of the existence of anti-Nazi Germans; in fact the conspirators had served Hitler as long as there was any hope of translating his pathological vision into reality, and turned against him only when they realized he intended to drive a defeated Germany to national suicide. Tragically, there is little evidence of any resistance to the Nazi regime among those Germans who were not directly threatened by it, or signs that the German people suffered any moral crisis over the monstrosities it committed. Until the Allied armies' successful invasion of Europe foreshadowed the certain defeat of the Third Reich, German support of the war effort on the battlefield and the home front had been total.

In August the tempo of the war quickened as Allied forces, including a French armored division, moved swiftly up the Rhone valley toward Paris. At the same time the relentless Russian drive was nearing Warsaw. In each case the invading army paused before entering the still occupied capital, but for very different reasons. In both capitals the resistance forces, aware of the approaching armies, rose against the German garrisons. In Warsaw the Germans succeeded in crushing the revolt and destroying the city while the Russians deliberately halted their drive and waited for the enemy to finish the sack of Warsaw before resuming their advance – thereby providing a chilling preview of their postwar plans for eastern Europe. In Paris, by contrast, the Germans fought the uprising only to cover their retreat, but the Americans waited in the environs to allow the French division the honor of entering their capital first.

By September Germany seemed open to attack, but the Allies could not yet transport enough gasoline across the Channel to support a deep thrust on a wide front. Instead the British army under Montgomery, which had been pushing up the coast to the Low Countries with the urgent mission of capturing the German launching pads for the V-1 flying bombs, now also had the desperate need of stopping the new and far more dangerous V-2 rockets which were raining death on London. Once having accomplished that task, Montgomery tried unsuccessfully to capture the bridge across the Rhine at Arnhem by a parachute drop. But in spite of that check, by mid-December Allied forces were arrayed all along the German border from Holland to Switzerland, ready for the final assault on Germany.

Instead of waiting for the blow, Hitler seized the initiative and launched a last desperate offensive in the same wooded area of southern Belgium through which the Germans had swept into France in May of 1940. This move took the Americans so completely by surprise that the Germans came close to breaking through to the Antwerp road and a major petroleum depot, which would have injected new life into their tanks and planes. But although the American lines bent dangerously in this "Battle of the Bulge," they did not break, and relief came rapidly in the form of General Patton's tank divisions and Allied air support. The net result of this last-ditch German effort was only to prolong the war and put off its inevitable conclusion until the spring of 1945.

American gains in the Pacific

At the time of the Normandy landings the American offensive in the Pacific was also reaching its climax. In spite of Japan's powerful fleet the Americans had generally fared well in naval engagements, but had found it extremely difficult and costly to dig the Japanese out of their innumerable island strongholds. Accordingly, their strategy was to take only the key islands that would enable them to extend the range of their air power, first to the Philippines and then to Japan. The first test of this strategy was the Battle of the Philippine Sea, in which the Japanese challenged America's hold on Saipan, an island within bomber reach of the Philippines. Following a decisive victory, the Americans under General Mac-Arthur mounted an amphibious attack on the central Philippine island of Leyte. If the Americans could gain this foothold in the Philippines they could proceed to reconquer the islands and would then be in a position to take the war directly to Japan. The Japanese commanders fully understood the significance of the threat and responded by mustering their entire navy in a final desperate effort to break America's rapidly growing power. The result was the battle of Leyte Gulf, the greatest naval confrontation in history. In three related engagements the powerful Japanese navy was finally destroyed as an offensive force, thus essentially leaving Japan and her far-reaching island empire at the mercy of the Americans. By the end of 1944 Japan's main cities were coming under increasing air attacks, making her situation hopeless; nevertheless Japanese soldiers were still defending the remains of their island outposts with fanatical tenacity, making the prospect of dislodging the Japanese army from mainland China extremely grim. The estimate of the American command was that complete victory over the Japanese would require a full-scale invasion of both China and Japan that would cost the United States another eighteen months and as many as half a million causalties.

The Yalta Conference

In early February of 1945, with the Allied armies poised for the final assault on Hitler's forces, the three principal Allied leaders and their chief advisors met at Yalta, a Russian Black Sea resort, to coordinate their plans for the invasion and occupation of Germany. The Americans were also interested in getting Russia to abandon its neutrality in the war against Japan, particularly to aid in the difficult task of driving the Japanese out of China; Stalin promised to do so in exchange for important territorial concessions in both Asia and Europe. For example Russian "special rights" in Manchuria and North Korea were recognized, while Poland's eastern boundary was moved back to exclude all the Russian territory the Poles had seized from the Red Army in 1920. All three powers renewed their pledge to enforce Germany's unconditional surrender, and issued a declaration promising to support democratic postwar governments constituted by free elections throughout liberated Europe. They also announced an April conference in San Francisco to draft a charter for the United Nations.

The concentration camps

During the spring of 1945 the Russian armies swept into Germany from the east and south while the American and British forces pushed in from the west, crushing all remaining resistance. In the process the Allies overran the Nazi concentration camps and extermination factories, which had ceased operations and been abandoned by the Germans only at the very last minute. They found great piles of emaciated corpses that had been left to rot, and bunks full of equally emaciated prisoners on the point of starvation. Although the existence of the camps had been known to the Allies, the full horror of their reality was not grasped until the American and British soldiers marched in and viewed the apocalyptic scenes. The first photographs and newsreel films flown back to the United States caused widespread shock and shame that Americans had done nothing to combat this crime.

But the whole story of Nazi genocide was yet to emerge. For the Nazis, the deliberate mass murder of civilians had been an integral part of their program from the beginning, not only for the conventional purpose of preventing and punishing resistance, but even more in fulfillment of the goals dictated by their violent hatred of those they considered their "racial" enemies, especially the Jews. Far from merely using anti-Semitism as a demagogic tool, Hitler had been in deadly earnest in his paranoid ravings against the Jews, and after 1939 he and the SS used their ever-widening absolute power to plan and implement increasingly ambitious schemes for ridding the world of Jews, along with the others they deemed genetically inferior to themselves.

The systematic mass murder of Jews began with the invasion and occupation of Poland, where all Jews were imprisoned in ghettos and starved. The invasion of Russia then marked the beginning of direct mass killing, as SS units accompanied German soldiers for the express purpose of rounding up and machine-gunning the Jews in all the towns they overran. Finally in 1942 the decision was made to exterminate the Jews, and the SS-run death camps in Poland began full-scale killing operations soon thereafter: Jews were shipped to these camps by the trainload from all of German-ruled Europe, to be gassed, shot, starved and tortured. In Auschwitz, the largest of these death factories, two and a half million people were slaughtered in two years. By the time the killing was finally stopped by the ending of the war, the Nazis had massacred some six million Jewish men, women, and children – three-quarters of the Jewish population of Europe – as well as an estimated one million non-Jewish victims, including Poles, Russian prisoners of war and gypsies.

Although there were widespread reports about the gas chambers that awaited the survivors of the brutal "deportations" that took place all over Europe, both victims and witnesses tended to cling to the fiction maintained by the Nazis that the Jews were being "resettled in the East" – no doubt in large part because the truth was too monstrous to be believable. But even with full knowledge of the truth, there was almost nothing the Jews could do to save themselves or others could do to help them. German control over the occupied countries was total, and those charged with filling the waiting boxcars were zealous and thorough in carrying out their orders – as were all the police, soldiers, guards, and other functionaries, both German and local, who manned the guns at all stages of the operation. For the most part the Jews who survived were those who had been able to get out of Europe altogether before the Nazis closed the borders as part of their extermination plan. Those who were hidden by courageous non-Jews were usually ferreted out and sent to their deaths, often along with their protectors, in the years remaining before the German defeat.

Although most of the killing was deliberately done out of the sight and knowledge of the general public, the Allies were informed about the death camps, and urged to intervene particularly by bombing the camps and railways when overflying them en route to other targets. Since the Allies were desperately fighting for their own survival and suffering millions of casualties of their own, they took the position that they could not afford any deviation from the straightforward path to victory, and that they were doing the best thing they could for all of Hitler's victims by bringing the war to an end as soon as possible. Unfortunately they were wrong; for the Jews of Europe the Allied victory came too late.

Known as the Holocaust, this massacre has taken its place as the darkest chapter in Western history. Proceeding out of the same pathological passions that led to the most horrifying persecutions of the past, it produced suffering and death on an inconceivably vaster scale, as the persecutors were able to use the full military and industrial resources of a modern nation to accomplish their psychotic purposes. Because it was carried out under cover of the war, it was at first lost to clear view as a part of that war – which had such an unimaginable overall death toll (an estimated 55 million, of whom half were civilians) that even the figure of six million dead hardly stood out for its magnitude alone. As the smoke cleared, however, the Holocaust came to be seen for what it was: a crime unparalleled in history in its proportions, cruelty, and insanity.

THE END OF THE WAR

On April 12, 1945, President Roosevelt died suddenly of a cerebral hemorrhage, and was succeeded by a new, unknown and unprepared American president, Harry Truman, at a time when responsibility weighed heaviest on the office. Within three weeks the Russians had reached Berlin and met the Americans at the Elbe. On the last day of April Hitler committed suicide in a bunker in Berlin, and a provisional German government under Admiral Doenitz offered the unconditional surrender demanded by the Allies. The German armed forces followed suit, its units laying down arms and giving themselves up wherever they were. On May 8, "VE Day," a formal end of the war in Europe was declared by the Allied headquarters, and one month later Germany was divided into four occupation zones and placed under the jurisdiction of the Allied Control Council.

The problems that now faced the Allies, and particularly the Americans, were far more complicated than those of winning the war. Most of Europe was in a state of civil disorder and economic chaos, and only the Americans were in a position to prevent mass starvation, disastrous epidemics and social collapse. The next Allied campaign in Europe would involve shaping the peace and rebuilding the whole society; meanwhile for the Americans the war in the Pacific continued at full intensity, so that their striking forces in Europe were now shifted halfway around the globe to prepare for a landing in China.

The United Nations

From April to June an international conference met in San Francisco to draft a charter for the projected United Nations Organization, which was to replace the discredited and moribund League of
Nations. This charter established two principal organs: a General
Assembly, composed of a representative for each member state,
and a Security Council, made up of five permanent and six elected
members – the permanent members to be the United States, the
Soviet Union, Great Britain, France, and China. The General
Assembly was to serve only as a forum in which members could
present and debate their views, but the Security Council was given
the power to command armed forces as well as to impose lesser
sanctions on the member states. Among the major issues debated
at the conference was the proposal for a veto power for each of
the permanent members of the Security Council, a safeguard that
the Russians insisted upon since they faced the certain prospect of
being regularly outvoted in that body. The veto was finally
accepted by all parties as providing a means to escape from major-
power confrontation, without which the United Nations would
face the same fate as that experienced by the League of Nations –
in which an outvoted power would simply withdraw. As it would
turn out the Organization was indeed saved from speedy dissolution by this measure, but it also meant that Security Council
actions would be limited to the very few issues that could be
jointly undertaken by both the United States and the Soviet Union.
The resulting paralysis later caused many critics to dismiss the
United Nations as a total failure. Yet it was never intended to be a
world government with police powers; rather it was established
primarily to underline the ideals and aspirations that had been set
forth by Roosevelt and Churchill in the Atlantic Charter, and their
other pronouncements about the world the democracies were
fighting to create. Its founders had the relatively modest hope of
providing that world with a more viable version of the League of
Nations – chiefly a permanent communication center where
threats to the general peace or well-being could be identified and
discussed. They also hoped that if there were sufficient consensus,
collective action could be taken that would be in the interests of

all, but in this hope they were as doomed to disappointment as the founders of the League of Nations.

The defeat of Japan

Three weeks after the close of the San Francisco Conference, on July 16, 1945, the United States detonated the first atomic explosion in the New Mexico desert, with implications for the future that completely overshadowed the war. The development of the bomb immediately confronted the new American President Truman with the awesome question of whether or not to use this weapon to cut short the war still raging with Japan. Because the Manhattan Project was still a remarkably well-kept secret, this question was not subject to any general debate; however there seems to have been very little hesitation on the part of the president and his advisors about using the weapon, and word was quickly given to complete the first three atomic bombs and transport two of them to the Pacific front.

It was at this point that the final conference of the Allied heads of state met at Potsdam, outside Berlin, to work out details for the occupation and administration of Germany. The United States was represented by its new president, Harry Truman, and in the middle of the session Winston Churchill was replaced by Clement Attlee, whose Labour party had just been swept into power in Britain's first election since before the war. Stalin alone remained of the original Allied leaders. The Americans seized this occasion to demand Japan's unconditional surrender, and when the Japanese failed to respond, Truman gave the order to drop the first atomic bomb. On August 6, 1945, the bomb was exploded above the city of Hiroshima leaving nine square miles of the target area completely obliterated and 140,000 people killed. A comparable number would die over the next five years as a direct result of the blast, and hundreds of thousands more were severely and permanently injured, while almost all of the survivors would suffer to some extent from the sinister long-range effects of radiation. On August 9, a second atomic bomb was dropped on the city of Nagasaki. The next day the Japanese government officially surrendered on the token condition that the figurehead Emperor Hirohito keep his throne. The Allies agreed, and Japan accepted all of their terms on August 14, with peace declared (VJ Day) on August 15.

Very soon after the first bomb was dropped, questions were raised about the necessity of using atomic weapons against Japan. Critics have charged that there was no need for the haste and secrecy with which the United States proceeded to use the bomb unless the objective was precisely to do so before Japan surrendered. If they sought to demonstrate the power of their new weapon the Americans could have used it in an uninhabited area rather than a city, let alone two. Defenders of the American action have usually argued that there was little reason to expect Japan to surrender for any lesser demonstration, and that the prolongation of the war that was expected as a result of this intransigence would have inflicted far more death and destruction on Japan than did the two atomic bombs – not to mention what it would have cost in American casualties. It is also the case that the Americans themselves did not grasp the vast destructive powers of the bomb until it was used in Japan. Still thinking in terms of conventional bombs, American military planners were anxious to take no chances that the Japanese would be able to build up the defenses of their cities so as to make an atomic bomb attack less likely or effective.

Finally it should be noted that the atomic bombing of Hiroshima and Nagasaki was by no means the only instance of deliberate killing of civilians by the Allies. Previous Allied saturation bombing in both Germany and Japan was aimed at the population of the cities quite as much as at military and industrial targets, in order to reduce enemy strength and morale. Quite comparable to the immediate destruction in Hiroshima was the annihilation of Dresden by British and American incendiary bombs in February of 1945: an estimated 135,000 people died in the resulting firestorm, against which underground shelters were useless. Many other population centers were hard-hit by the Allied bombers and some (like Hamburg) were leveled, while the battering given to Berlin and Tokyo resulted in much higher loss of life than was inflicted by the atomic bombs. None of these attacks, with the possible exception of the one on Dresden, has provoked much soul-searching on the part of the victors, even though most took place when the Allies were very much on the offensive and the surrender of their enemies was not far off. These were an accepted part of a total, savage war which resulted in death and destruction on a catastrophic scale in every arena where it was waged.

Similarly, the peculiar horror of the atomic bombings hardly stood out in a war filled with such endless horrors, and it was really only later that the attention of the world would be focused on what had happened in Hiroshima and Nagasaki. Originally their possession of the atom bomb had given Americans a feeling of relief; it had brought a final conclusion to a terrible war and seemed to promise invulnerability to further military attacks. Only afterwards did it become apparent that the development of the nuclear weapon really meant that no one in the world was safe from the ultimate danger: the annihilation not only of whole populations but possibly of all life on earth. The destructive power that could be unleashed by the nuclear bomb was out of all proportion to any other powers that existed on earth – a cosmic force that was capable of undoing the work of four and a half billion years of evolution, rendering the planet as sterile and hostile to life as it had been at the moment of its formation. Mankind had acquired the power to destroy the complex organizations of matter that constituted his living world and return all to primordial chaos, but not the power to create a single living cell. Thus the atomic bombs that were detonated in Hiroshima and Nagasaki not only concluded the chapter of the history of the European world that we call the Second World War, but at the same time launched a wholly new chapter – distinguished from all preceding ones by its unique possibility of becoming the last – in which we have been living ever since.

13

The Postwar Decade

The postwar decade divides easily into roughly equal halves. The first (1945 to 1950) was a period largely devoted to clearing rubble, restoring basic services and reestablishing administrative government. In the main enemy countries this included war-crime trials and de-Nazification or the equivalent, while in the east European countries the Soviets established military control over what became their satellite states. In the areas of Japanese conquest in Asia, reconstruction involved the liberation of former European colonies and the communists' consolidation of power in China, with the main exceptions to this pattern occurring in Vietnam, where the French fought to prevent a communist national liberation movement from gaining control of the government, and in Korea, which was occupied by the Soviet Union in the North and by the United States in the South.

In Britain and western Europe there was significant political change. In all cases a wide popular base was assumed to be a necessary key to the success of a regime, and viable economic conditions were considered essential to avoiding a communist revolution. In the United Kingdom a Labour government was voted into power to replace Winston Churchill at the moment of his triumph; with Clement Attlee as prime minister, it had a mandate to nationalize the economy and equalize social opportunities. The latter problem was attacked first by sharply graduated taxes on both income and inheritance, and second by opening the country's elite universities to full public competition, backed up with government subsidies to support those who were admitted but could not pay. The most controversial measure of this sort was the establishment of a national system of all-inclusive health care. This wholesale reversal of government tradition in Britain was due in part to a long-standing socialist trend, but even more to the experience of two wars in which the economy had been totally controlled. With everyone's consumption limited through rationing, the government had assumed the obligation of providing each person with the necessary minimum of essential supplies, particularly food. Because the poor received the same quantities as the rich, rationing had the result of improving the nation's diet, and actually the British population as a whole was healthier at the end of the war than it had been at the beginning. This development had the effect of supporting the socialists' claims and hopes, and gave them their first chance to form a government.

Something less complete and much less advertised, but nevertheless effectively similar, occurred in France. Working within the legal framework established by the Popular Front government of 1936–7, the French nationalized as much of their economy as the British had, providing extensive social benefits, including subsidized health care, for those who needed it. Italy followed the same route, somewhat behind France, and Germany in different ways also accepted responsibility for the general public welfare.

Of the major industrial countries of the west, only the United States failed to move in a socialist direction, in part at least because it emerged from the war in far better economic shape than when it had joined the struggle. What could have been an overwhelming problem was the return of its nine million young troops to civilian life, but this transition was eased by the vigor of the American economy, which shifted from war to peace production without any serious loss of pace. This was due in part to the Americans' demand for all the consumer goods, especially cars and household appliances, that they had foregone during the war, and partly to the Marshall Plan, by which the United States advanced huge credits to the European nations to purchase equipment and supplies for their reconstruction. A major part of all war production had been in gasoline engines for planes, tanks, trucks, and jeeps, with the result that the motor vehicle industry would become the most important element of the peacetime economy, not only in the United States but in Europe and Japan as well.

The most significant social legislation passed in the United

States at the time was the so-called "GI Bill of Rights," which provided veterans with financial support to pursue their education. This not only eased their transition to civilian life but also opened the possibility of advanced training to countless young people for whom it would otherwise have been unthinkable. The indirect effect of this measure would be a huge expansion of higher education in the United States in the next twenty years. Even more decisive in the country's development was the impact of the racial desegregation of the armed forces. Although this was far from complete, it was accepted in principle and established desegregation as an irreversible moral principle in American domestic politics.

The second half of the postwar decade (1950 to 1955) saw the consolidation of new regimes in the former enemy countries and the beginning of economic revival in western Europe. In the Soviet world the period was marked by the death of Stalin (1953) and the gradual de-Stalinization of the Soviet Union and its satellite countries in eastern Europe. This led by 1956 to a political crisis in Poland and an armed uprising in Hungary which was brutally suppressed by the Red Army. At the same time the Islamic states of North Africa were in ferment; France renounced its protectorates over Morocco and Tunisia, Libya's independence (de facto since Italy's defeat) was ratified by the United Nations, and the monarchy in Egypt was overthrown in 1952 by a group of army officers who established a republic. From this coup, Gamal Abdel Nasser emerged as the dominant figure and soon president of the new republic (1956). When he began dealing with the Soviets for arms, the Americans withdrew an offer to aid him build a huge dam across the Nile; in retaliation Nasser nationalized the Suez Canal, ostensibly to use the tolls to finance the dam. This move provoked a joint attack by Israel, France, and Britain in which the Israelis overran the Sinai with dispatch but the French and British failed to establish control over the canal before intense pressure from both the United States and the Soviet Union forced them to withdraw. This forced retreat meant the end of European hegemony in all of North Africa except Algeria, where the French were bogged down in a long and bitter struggle to defend the French population from the nationalist guerrilla movement that sought to drive them out.

In Asia the United States held the perimeter against the communists by going to the aid of South Korea – in the name of the United Nations – when it was invaded by North Korea in 1950. This war ended in a stalemate on the original partition line of the 38th Parallel. During the same period the French were defending the Vietnamese regime they had set up against a communist revolt; in 1954 they suffered a decisive defeat, however, and negotiated a peace which divided Vietnam at the 17th Parallel with the northern half going to the communists led by Ho Chi Minh. Until 1956 the French maintained a presence in the South to defend the government against communist guerrilla incursions, and when they withdrew, the Americans moved into the resulting vacuum to strengthen the resistance of the South with economic aid and military advice.

By the end of the decade the political and economic shape of the postwar world was beginning to emerge from the debris of war, much as the shattered cities were taking shape out of their rubble. The countries of western Europe had all reestablished viable economies and responsible political regimes; in addition they had moved significantly toward economic integration and political cooperation, and they were almost all involved in a military alliance with the United States against the Soviet Union. The threat of a Soviet invasion, which had seemed real in the late 1940s, had largely evaporated, but Russia was about to demonstrate in Hungary that she would not tolerate the breakup of her satellite system. Given her newly established (1953) position as a nuclear power, together with her formidable ground forces, she could hardly be challenged in what had become her acknowledged sphere. This left the two superpowers and their respective allies probing to establish themselves on the perimeters of Soviet power and in the still-contested border areas of Greece and North Africa, Korea, and Indochina.

THE RECONSTRUCTION OF EUROPE

Fighting a war, even a global conflict like the Second World War, is a far simpler task to organize than reestablishing the peace. This is because, in the last analysis, war has the single goal of victory, while peace involves all the divergent complexities of daily living. From the beginning of their combined struggle in the war the three principal Allies agreed that the unconditional surrender of Germany and Japan was their sole objective, and they all pursued this end with unwavering commitment. Beyond that they found it difficult to agree, and their prescriptions for a postwar settlement were rhetorical, fragmentary, and imprecise. Admirable as its formulations were, the Atlantic Charter – drafted in August 1940 by Roosevelt and Churchill – was extremely general. Moreover the United Nations Organization, designed to embody the same high principles, would not even begin to function until a year after hostilities had ceased. Even the specific agreements made by the Allied heads of state at conferences (particularly Yalta in 1945) were vague and lacked practical detail.

During the war Roosevelt had repeatedly invoked a Wilsonian vision of "a world safe for democracy," and he may well have intended to call on such principles in formulating a postwar settlement. One can only guess what his success might have been, however, because he died on the eve of victory. Churchill, who had frequently subscribed to the same principles, was voted out of office three months later; and the task of establishing peace fell to the successors of the two great leaders of the war. Harry Truman had been ill-prepared for his job as Roosevelt's successor, while Clement Attlee had been elected in Britain to carry out a major domestic reorganization, so that neither new head of state was in a position to provide the leadership in international affairs that their predecessors would certainly have exercised.

At the Potsdam Conference, in July 1945, Stalin and his two new colleagues agreed on a policy for Germany intended to democratize, demilitarize, decentralize, and de-Nazify the government. In addition they planned to bring Nazi war criminals to trial and to put severe limits on the role of industry in the German economy. But the British and American delegations refused to sanction the territorial changes by which Russia had moved Germany's Polish boundary back to the Oder and Neisse rivers, and they postponed fixing the total amount of reparations (in capital equipment) that Russia should take from Germany until it could be settled by an Allied commission. Finally, it was agreed to establish a Big Four Council of Foreign Ministers to draft treaties with Finland and Germany's other satellites. This Council, which did not complete its assignment until early 1947, was the nearest thing to a peace conference that was held after the war, but it could hardly be compared to the Paris Conference of 1919, or its celebrated predecessors of Vienna, Utrecht or Westphalia.

By far the most pressing problem that confronted the peacemakers was the widespread and often nearly total physical destruction that had occurred in all the areas occupied and pillaged by the Germans, as well as in Germany itself. Many of the larger German cities had been leveled, ports all along Europe's Atlantic coast were smashed, bridges almost everywhere were damaged or destroyed, factories and rail centers (including cars and locomotives) were demolished. As a result, the basic necessities of life were in desperately short supply throughout Europe: shelter was improvised, transport was disorganized, supplies almost non-existent. Further, in the midst of this nightmare setting, millions of refugees were pushing through the debris in one direction or another: slave laborers trying to make their way home from Germany, Germans from eastern Europe fleeing Russian occupation or local revenge, and minorities from the occupied countries seeking haven from nationalist passions uncurbed by authority. In these circumstances political concerns were almost irrelevant. When the Allies attempted to carry out a policy of de-Nazification, they found themselves more urgently involved in the restoration of basic services – water, gas and electricity – and the provision and distribution of food and fuel. But the experts who could operate these services had all been Nazis, and the alternative to putting them back in their old jobs was simply massive death from starvation, cold and disease, and the continuation of the social disintegration that made recovery impossible.

With the Nazi collapse, the Allied powers occupied the zones of Germany agreed upon at Yalta: the Russians in the east, the British and Americans in the west and south, and the French holding two small sections along their frontier. In spite of previous agreements to treat the country as a single economic unit, however, the Russians refused to cooperate from the beginning, making all relations extremely difficult, particularly in the four-power occupation of Berlin, deep inside the Russian zone.

Russian expansion

At the same time, the Soviets began to use their military presence to extend their territorial control all along their western boundary. With the end of hostilities, Finland managed to elude Russian influence and establish an independent regime, at the cost of some minor territorial concessions, but the Baltic states of Estonia, Latvia, and Lithuania were all assimilated into the Soviet Union. Poland presented a more difficult problem. During the war its vigorous government-in-exile had enjoyed wide support, and it fully intended to take over following the country's liberation, but the Russians also had a "Polish" government waiting to be installed. Initially the two were combined, but in such a way that the communist members would quickly dominate the regime. Similar developments took place in Romania, Bulgaria, and Hungary (along with fairly extensive territorial adjustments of their prewar boundaries). Czechoslovakia managed to maintain a small degree of independence from Russia by voluntarily including Czech communist members in its government, while Yugoslavia and Albania, both of which had liberated their own territory by partisan guerrilla efforts, became the only two European states – after Russia – to adopt communism voluntarily. In Greece, too, there had been a significant communist resistance movement during the war, but since the British rather than the Russians occupied the country after the war, the communists did not control the election of 1946 or the government which it established. With the help of their Soviet bloc neighbors, however, the Greek communists then launched a well-organized guerrilla attack against the government which ripened into three years of civil war.

Initially the western Allies had been sympathetic to Russia's concern for the security of her western frontier, but her systematic imposition of dictatorial communist regimes in the liberated east European countries soon caused misgivings. Not surprisingly it was Winston Churchill who first seized on the significance of these developments, when he summed them up in his now-famous phrase, "from Stettin on the Baltic to Trieste on the Adriatic, an iron curtain is descending across Europe." At this time (March 1946) most westerners were still reluctant to accept this gloomy judgement on the postwar world, but American officials were rapidly finding relations with their Russian counterparts in Germany to be more and more difficult. One particularly frustrating example was the Russians' refusal to export food surpluses from their zone of East Germany to the industrial west, where the shortage was acute, while they continued to remove factories from the west as reparations. In response, the Americans finally cut off all reparations shipments to East Germany, and – by the end of 1946 – merged their zone's economy with that of Britain's zone. While this was intended to improve the situation of the West German population, it was also viewed as a necessary step toward general European recovery. In fact the idea was spreading rapidly that effective economic revival would require an international effort, and that Russian resistance to cooperation was based in part at least on a belief that severely repressed living standards would increase the possiblity of social revolution. Such a hypothesis seemed to be confirmed by the strength of the communist parties in France and Italy, where economic recovery was lagging furthest behind.

During the spring of 1947 American policy in Europe began to adjust to the threat posed to the democratic regimes by the combination of economic distress and Soviet-supported communist movements. In March, President Truman delivered a major speech to Congress proclaiming that the United States would support any free peoples threatened by armed minorities or outside pressures, and that such help would be provided primarily as economic aid. This "Truman Doctrine," as it was called, assumed that all communist parties and movements outside of Russia were puppets of the Soviet Union (as the communist regimes of eastern Europe clearly were), and as such represented attempts to extend Soviet influence and control to democratic countries rendered vulnerable by postwar conditions. In response, it announced America's intention to offer aid wherever it was needed to combat such a threat. The implications of this pronouncement would be difficult to exaggerate. In effect it marked the beginning of the Cold War, with its commitment of the United States to "fighting communism" not only in Europe but also in the preindustrial countries that had generally been European colonial possessions before the war and were only on the periphery of the western world that had previously been America's sole concern. Significantly, the doctrine was formulated first for the benefit of Greece and Turkey, both traditionally British clients in the eastern Mediterranean where Britain could no longer play her former imperial role.

The Marshall Plan

By the spring of 1947 political life was beginning to stir again in Europe. The French had ratified the constitution of a new Fourth Republic, which to most people's surprise resembled that of the Third, avoiding both the radical changes (notably the strong presidency) urged by General de Gaulle, and the all-powerful single chamber campaigned for by the communists. The new government, however, was still threatened by the country's weak economy and consequent labor unrest. At about the same time Italy too was drafting a new constitution – also for a republic – and establishing a new government in which a communist bid for power was successfully checked. In Germany, the Americans and British failed to persuade Russia to unify the economy throughout the four occupation zones, and finally announced that they would merge their own in what came to be known as Bizonia. This was followed by monetary and other reforms designed to aid German economic recovery, an end to which the Russians offered opposition, particularly in the form of continuing demands for huge reparations to be taken from current production. Such payments would have defeated American and British plans to make their Bizonia self-supporting, and would also have seriously slowed the recovery of the rest of Europe, which depended increasingly on German steel.

It was against this background that the American government followed the "Truman Doctrine" with the "Marshall Plan," unveiled in a speech in 1947 by George Marshall, former army chief of staff and now Secretary of State. Marshall's plan amounted to an invitation to European countries to draft a joint program for economic recovery and submit it to the United States for funding. Although the invitation was explicitly open to eastern as well as western European countries, the Soviet Union, after some apparent hesitation, rejected the offer and instructed its satellites to do the same. Only Czechoslovakia, still not fully assimilated to the communist system, appeared inclined to participate.

The western states, by contrast, moved directly to form an Organization of European Economic Cooperation, and drafted a plan known as the European Recovery Program, which the United States accepted. Altogether this was probably the most enlightened and effective non-military intervention in the international field ever undertaken, as well as the most generous – over four billion dollars being authorized in the original appropriation. Not only did it offer unprecedented aid to the hard-pressed national economies of Europe, but it did so in a context which encouraged close international coordination and cooperation in Europe.

Following the First World War a number of visionaries had urged the formation of some form of "United States of Europe" to resolve international differences, but the idea never received serious consideration. Under the impact of the Second World War, however, and especially of the occupation, many Europeans – particularly members of the various resistance movements – began to realize that any restoration of a viable society would require the economic integration of the Continent. Immediately after Europe's liberation, various preliminary meetings were held and organizations established to implement one or another unification plan; there was therefore an ample basis for the positive response that Secretary Marshall received.

The Berlin blockade

Unfortunately the reaction behind the "iron curtain" was to reinforce the division of Europe. After their rejection of America's offer, the Soviet Union formed an organization of communist states known as the Cominform, the successor to the former Communist International Party, or Comintern, which the Soviets had dissolved during the war as a gesture of good will to their allies. The main purpose of the new organization, as of the old, was to maintain Soviet control over the communist parties of all countries. Further, under Soviet pressure Czechoslovakia withdrew her original acceptance of the invitation to join the Marshall Plan, and then in February 1948 succumbed to a communist *coup d'état* backed by the threat of Soviet military force. Just as there was little doubt that the Soviet Union and her east European allies would have benefited economically from American aid, the events in Czechoslovakia demonstrated the strength of Russia's commitment to avoiding any form of cooperation with the non-communist world. This point was heavily reinforced by the communist denunciation of the Marshall Plan throughout Europe, and particularly in France, where communist-led labor unions staged a series of political strikes against French participation. This campaign was finally called off, as the workers, recognizing what they stood to gain from the plan, began to defect *en masse*.

In the spring of 1948, following his assimilation of Czechoslovakia, Stalin attempted to eject the western Allies from Berlin by closing the Allied access highway to the city. Because West Berlin was completely surrounded by the Russian zone, it was dependent on western Allied transport through Russian-occupied East Germany for most of its food, all of its fuel and most of its other supplies. Temporary Russian shutdowns of the transport route had been used before for harassment, but this was clearly intended to be a major test of Allied will. The American commander in charge of supplying West Berlin wisely resisted the temptation to force his way through the roadblocks; not only were his troops vastly outnumbered by the Soviet forces in East Germany, but the consequences of such an action would have been impossible to contain. Instead the western Allies began flying in the most urgently needed supplies by air, in what rapidly became an around-the-clock airlift, with improvised cargo planes touching down and taking off every few seconds from the Tempelhof airfield in the American sector of the city. Obviously it had not occurred to the Russians that such a large population could be provisioned entirely by air, and they had made no effort to block this means of access.

If the situation had been less tense, with less catastrophic implications, it would have been ludicrous. Instead it amounted to the first real confrontation of the Cold War, and resulted in a significant, if symbolic, victory for the United States. Although the Americans and their allies barely managed to keep the western sectors of the city supplied, and that at a considerable cost – including numerous casualties, they did succeed, and in the process advertised to the world the effectiveness of American air power. As the contest continued for month after month (eleven all told), the question arose of why the Soviets did not take the next step toward a "hot war" by closing the air corridors with fighter planes. The answer, attributed to Churchill, was that they were deterred by America's atom bomb. In May of 1949 the Russians finally removed the roadblocks, and the stream of supplies for the western sectors of Berlin returned from the skies to the road.

The birth of NATO

While this test of wills was being played out in Germany, a number of other developments suggested that the democracies would weather the postwar transition. As Marshall Plan aid began to arrive, the economies of Western Europe showed signs of significant improvement, and the new postwar political regimes gained confidence and authority. At the same time (1948) the Greek government finally suppressed the communist guerrillas, thus firmly establishing its control of the country. Then to the incredulous surprise of almost everyone, Moscow announced the exclusion of Yugoslavia from the recently established Cominform, revealing that Premier Marshal Tito's original pro-Soviet stance had changed to one of resistance to Moscow's domination. The Soviets responded to this challenge from within their own camp by increasing their control and vigilance over the other satellites to prevent any further defections, but they made no move to impose their discipline on Yugoslavia by force. The United States quickly stepped into this breach with offers of economic aid, which Tito readily accepted, but without making any reciprocal commitments.

In spite of the general improvement of the political climate in western Europe, the United States retained from the Berlin crisis a lively sense of its numerical inferiority to the Red Army. Roosevelt had intended to maintain a large combat force in Europe during the peacemaking process, but with his death and the natural eagerness of Americans to turn away from war, the American army in Europe was rapidly demobilized, while that of the Russians remained at full strength. Although no one expected the Red Army to force its way west, the Berlin blockade seemed to raise the possibility of Russian military intervention in western affairs. In response to this hypothetical challenge, the United States finally reversed its policy of demobilization in 1949, and proposed a treaty that arranged for mutual aid among the western democracies in the case of Russian aggression against any one. The original members of this North Atlantic Treaty Organization were the United States and Canada, Great Britain, France, Italy, Norway, Denmark, Holland, Belgium, Luxemburg, Portugal and Iceland. In 1952 Greece and Turkey joined the alliance, and in 1955 West Germany was admitted. Although officially the treaty provided only for the close coordination of military planning by the member nations, actually the organization was the successor of the western alliance that had defeated and occupied Germany, and thus became a permanent military presence in Europe. As it had during the war, the United States assumed the largest responsibility for providing the alliance with troops and arms, including atomic weapons. The original concept of NATO was primarily as a "tripwire" to turn any local or limited Soviet move against a member state into clearly defined aggression. The fact that NATO was backed by the American atomic stockpile, however, soon established its central function, which was to use the threat of atomic weapons as a deterrent to Russian ambitions. While supporters of NATO policy have credited this nuclear threat with preventing any Soviet attempts at expansion in western Europe, critics have charged that the chief effect of deploying atomic weapons so close to Russia's borders has been to increase the Soviets' insecurity, and consequent determination to keep abreast of the United States in the nuclear arms race.

THE POSTWAR ERA IN THE PACIFIC AND THE COLONIAL WORLD

The end of the war in the Pacific found the Allies even less prepared for the situation that confronted them than they had been after the German collapse in Europe. Even though American planes were subjecting Japan's cities to terrible punishment before the atomic bombs were dropped, the Allied command was still expecting as much as a three-year land war on the Chinese mainland to drive out the Japanese, as well as in Japan itself, where a last-ditch suicidal defense of the homeland was anticipated. Then in less than two weeks following the bombing of Hiroshima and

Nagasaki, the Japanese imperial government capitulated to the Allied commander, General MacArthur, and Japanese troops laid down their arms throughout the empire – usually with no Allied forces to surrender to.

Civil War in China

After Hiroshima, the Russians, who had continually postponed their promised attack on the Japanese, suddenly rushed into Manchuria with all possible speed in an attempt to win a role in the peacemaking and occupation. At this point China was still divided between the government forces of Chiang Kai-shek, the heir of Sun Yat-sen's Nationalist party (Kuomintang), and the rival communist organization of Mao Tse-Tung. Relations between these two groups were complicated; on occasion they had cooperated against the Japanese, although generally they vied for position within China. In 1937, when the Japanese had launched their full-scale invasion of China, Chiang Kai-shek's army and bureaucracy had fled deep into the interior province of Szechwan. Here, having secured Allied recognition and aid, Chiang was able to avoid defeat by the Japanese but accomplished this end largely by avoiding combat. In fact his control of the nationalist forces was shaky; actual command was often exercised by local war-lords, who exploited their individual fiefs and tended to fight only where there was hope of personal gain.

The communist Red Army, developed and led by Mao Tse-Tung, was altogether different. Where the Nationalist forces tended to be based in or near cities, the Red Army was a peasant organization that operated in the countryside, enjoying widespread popular support because of its program of moderate land reforms. Because of their rural base and support, moreover, the communists had frequently been able to operate behind the Japanese lines. By the end of the war they held much of North China and were generally well placed to take over control of many communities when the Japanese laid down their arms. Perceiving the communists as a threat, the Americans tried to prevent this takeover by occupying some of the more important port cities themselves, and by ordering the Japanese to hold other centers until the Nationalists could arrive.

On the day of the Japanese surrender the Nationalist government signed a treaty of alliance and friendship with the Soviet Union agreeing to the independence of Outer Mongolia, to Russian possession of the Manchurian Railway for thirty years, and to the joint development of Port Arthur as a naval base. When efforts to settle differences between the Nationalists and the communists broke down, they opened hostilities for control of Manchuria, which the Soviets had just evacuated. At this point the United States attempted to arrange a truce and form a coalition government, but fighting continued with increasing intensity. At first the Nationalists appeared to be winning, and in the spring of 1947 even captured the communist capital of Yenan; a dramatic reversal followed, however, and by the end of the year the Red Army had taken over most of Manchuria.

During the course of 1948 the fortunes of Chiang Kai-shek declined even further, despite a huge program of aid from the United States. He was either unable or unwilling to effect any of the governmental reforms urged by the Americans that might have strengthened his cause, and in anticipation of his defeat his warlord followers began selling their American-supplied arms to the communists. Not surprisingly the United States now began to cut back its aid to the Nationalists, especially since it also appeared that much of the American money advanced to Chiang was finding its way into his and his family's bank accounts. Finally in 1949 the communists drove out Chiang and the remnants of his army and consolidated their hold on all of China. Since they had no ships they could not pursue him to the island of Taiwan, where he fled and set up a "rival government" which his supporters have claimed to this day is the legitimate government of China.

As soon as the hopelessness of the Nationalist cause was apparent, the United States withdrew from the struggle for China, and simultaneously she also terminated her occupation of Korea. According to wartime agreements, the United States had occupied the southern half of that peninsula and the Soviet Union the northern half following Japan's surrender and withdrawal. As with Germany, it had also been agreed by the two powers that unification of their occupation zones would take place as soon as conditions permitted elections to be held, but also as in Germany it was apparent from the beginning that the Soviets were determined to block the unification of Korea on any terms other than complete communist domination. After a number of futile efforts to overcome this resistance, the United States announced (1948) the Republic of Korea in the south, and the Soviet Union followed by proclaiming the North Korean People's Republic, which it also began arming in preparation for a military takeover of the rest of the peninsula. In 1949 both occupying powers withdrew their own forces, and the United Nations commission established to mediate a settlement between the two regimes warned of the imminent danger of civil war.

On October 1, 1949, Mao Tse-Tung proclaimed the People's Republic of China, with himself as chairman of the central council of the Communist party and Chou En-lai as premier and foreign minister. The new regime was immediately recognized by the Soviet Union and the other communist governments of eastern Europe. The United Nations had been set up originally with the Nationalist Chinese government as one of the five permanent members of the Security Council, and this arrangement was not changed in response to the communists' victory; nevertheless that body essentially recognized the communists as the legitimate choice of the Chinese people. Indeed there was no reason to doubt that the large majority of the population accepted the new regime, which moved quickly to institute needed reforms and reconstruction.

In the United States, however, a vituperative political debate broke out immediately following the communist victory, over alleged responsibility for "losing China." Supporters of the Nationalists treated any wavering from their defense as treason to the democratic cause, although the corruption and incompetence of the Nationalists was clearly beyond possible redemption. At the same time, the view expressed by some enthusiasts that Mao and his followers were "simple agrarian reformers" was at best naïve. Even though Mao won over the peasants by moderate land reforms, his subsequent career leaves little room for doubt that he had far more radical measures in mind from the start. In any case it seems unlikely that Americans could have influenced long-range communist policies in China even if they had backed the communist side, as some critics of American policy were arguing, and certainly there is no reason to think, as the other side insisted, that the United States could have prevented the "loss of China" to the communists by giving more military support to the Nationalists.

Japan after the war

In Japan the sudden end of the war had created an altogether different situation, which put all government authority in the hands of the American occupiers. Although the Allies had not invaded the main islands, they had brought the principal Japanese cities under devastating attack well before the atomic bombings had put an abrupt end to all resistance; as a result, the Japanese had no doubt that they had been defeated, and they accepted the full implications of their unconditional surrender. The American commander of the occupation, Gerneral Douglas MacArthur, wisely proceeded to administer the country through its established bureaucracies even while reforming its institutions. American troops were landed in Japan, but only to establish an official military presence and to take over the weapons and equipment of the Japanese armed services, which were promptly dissolved. From this beginning the demilitarization of the country proceeded without opposition, even to extensive war crime trials, which were presided over by an international tribunal. Next on MacArthur's agenda was the democratization of what had been a traditionally authoritarian society. This included drafting a new constitution closely modeled after that of Britain. The emperor, who had been allowed to retain his throne, had renounced the "divinity" traditionally attributed to him, and the constitution officially transferred sovereignty from him to the people. In addition it instituted a large measure of local government and established universal suffrage, civil liberties, and the right of workers to organize and strike.

MacArthur's most serious problem was the Japanese economy, which for the first two years after the surrender was kept going only by extensive American aid. This plight was due primarily to the war, but it was also greatly aggravated by Japan's loss of the huge empire she had carved out of China and southeast Asia. Suddenly the Japanese were deprived of valuable raw materials they had previously depended upon, as well as the outlet they had exploited for their rapidly expanding population. Those who suffered most from this economic collapse were the poorest classes; to ease their situation MacArthur attempted to break up the huge family trusts that controlled much of Japan's industry and commerce, and to distribute to the peasants some of the land held in the large estates of traditionally absentee landlords. While the former objective proved too ambitious to accomplish abruptly, given the important role of the dominant families in the Japanese economy, MacArthur had greater success in widening the base of land ownership, thereby also reducing the risk of the development of a radical agricultural proletariat in Japan comparable to the one that had given strength to the communist cause in China.

In 1948 the Japanese war crimes tribunal finally rendered its verdicts, sentencing seven of the accused to death and a number of others to life in prison. A year later, reparations were terminated and Japan began moving toward a resumption of normal existence.

Southeast Asia

When the Germans had overrun Holland and France in the spring of 1940, those countries' considerable colonies in southeast Asia were effectively at the mercy of Japan. In the case of France, the Japanese immediately demanded military control of Indochina (including Laos, Cambodia and Vietnam), which France had ruled as a protectorate since the mid-nineteenth century and was now quite incapable of defending. In the case of the Netherlands East Indies, Japan accepted the status quo until Pearl Harbor, but then moved rapidly to occupy the entire archipelago. This displacement of European forces by the Japanese had a decisive psychological effect on the subject peoples in each empire. Ever since the First World War anti-colonial sentiment had been spreading through much of the non-European world, receiving considerable support from movements within the European world as well as from both the United States and the Soviet Union. In addition, a growing number of young men from the colonies attended European universities between the wars, and were drawn almost irresistibly to the dominant revolutionary theory of the time, Marxism.

It is therefore hardly surprising that with the Japanese surrender in 1945, independent republics were proclaimed in Vietnam and in Indonesia by the leaders of nationalist movements in the two colonies – Ho Chi Minh in Vietnam and Achmed Sukarno and Mohammed Hatta in Indonesia. Both the French and the Dutch took up arms to try to regain control of these possessions, and long, bitter colonial wars were fought before the European forces were finally driven out of both territories in 1954. The defeat of the French in Vietnam was followed by an international conference at Geneva which recognized the independence of all three provinces of Indochina – Cambodia and Laos as well as Vietnam – but divided Vietnam along the 17th Parallel, giving the northern portion to the forces of the communist Ho Chi Minh, who had defeated the French, and leaving the southern half in the hands of a French-backed non-communist regime. This arrangement led to only a temporary respite in the fighting for control of Indochina, which would resume in the late 1950s with American instead of French participation.

The other principal states of southeast Asia achieved or maintained their independence without bloodshed. The British colony of Burma was taken from its Japanese conquerors by Allied forces and restored to British rule; unlike the French and Dutch, however, the British were prepared to part with their colonial possessions after the war, and granted independence to Burma in a friendly settlement in 1948. Thailand, which had never experienced colonial rule, had accepted an alliance with Japan and declared war on Britain and the United States; this never involved serious hostilities, however, and in 1946 peaceful relations were quickly restored, especially since Thailand began to manifest anti-communist sympathies. Finally, immediately after the war the United States implemented its promise of granting independence to the Philippines, backed up with considerable economic aid, in exchange for which it retained a 99-year lease on Philippine military and naval bases.

Indian independence

In this same postwar period two other developments were taking place in the colonial world that would have great consequence for the future. The first was the granting of independence to India, and the second the creation of the state of Israel.

Ever since the First World War, in which India had loyally supported Britain, there had been increasing discussion in Britain of granting her independence, at least within the framework of the British Commonwealth, as the empire was called after 1926. The principal opposition came from the British civil servants who lived in India, a large and powerful group who had no wish to be uprooted from their life there, and not coincidentally were convinced that the Indians were incapable of governing themselves. This prejudice was only reinforced by the Bolshevik revolution in Russia and British fears of a conspiracy between the Bolsheviks and the growing Indian independence movement. Even before there was an Indian Communist party (1923) the British began taking measures against conspiracy, their fears leading to a tragic confrontation between demonstrators and British troops at Amritsar, in 1919, in which several hundred Indians were killed. In reaction there was widespread civil disturbance and the formation of a mass National Congress party, devoted to the end of gaining India's independence from Britain. One of the leading advocates of independence, Mahatma Gandhi, emerged as the recognized national leader of the Congress party and began employing a powerful political tactic of civil disobedience against the British which drove them to conceding India ever greater measures of autonomy. The Indian nationalists themselves were divided between those who wanted "dominion" status, which essentially involved a special trade relationship with Britain and "allegiance to the Crown," and those who insisted on severing all ties with their former colonial master. In addition, as the unifying force of British rule receded, the conflict became increasingly acute between India's Hindu majority and Muslim minority (which made up about a quarter of the population). Although the two groups united on occasion in their resistance to the British, the Muslims formed a separate political party (the All-India Muslim League), and it began to appear likely that an independent India would have to take the form of two separate states.

During the Second World War the extreme nationalists in India tended to side with the Japanese against the British, and to retain India as an ally the British were forced to promise a complete emancipation after the war, abandoning their own proposed timetable for more gradual disengagement from the subcontinent.

Their election of a Labor government in 1945 made it certain that they would keep this promise, as did Britain's postwar poverty. In March of 1946 the British government granted full independence to India, which now came under the leadership of its two national parties. The Muslim League insisted on the establishment of separate states for Muslims and Hindus, and when the Congress party finally agreed, the "self-governing dominions" of India and Pakistan were created, in August of 1947, with Pakistan comprising two widely separated areas where the Muslim population was concentrated, on the extreme northwest and northeast borders of Hindu India. The partition was accompanied by massive migrations of Hindus from Pakistan and Muslims from India; the tension between the two religious groups was exacerbated rather than alleviated by this expedient, however, and warfare broke out on both borders that may have cost as many as two million lives. In the midst of this strife Gandhi was murdered by a Hindu fanatic who saw the prophet of national independence as a traitor to India for accepting the partition. In the same year (1948) the leader of the Muslim League also died, and the two nations endured the added hardship of comparatively inexperienced leadership in their struggle to establish themselves in the wake of the British departure.

Unfortunately, the outbreak of hostility between the two religious groups in India would serve only as a preview of similar, and worse, political disintegration that would occur with regularity in the "artifical" states that had been created by European colonial rule, once the imperial masters had withdrawn. Apologists for imperialism tended to see proof in these disorders that the subject populations lacked sufficient political and social maturity to be capable of self-rule, while critics saw such problems as caused at least in part by the experience of being ruled by foreign conquerors. In the case of India, at least, it can be argued that even with the partition and all its accompanying violence, the people of India were better off after the British left than they had been under the anarchy that prevailed before the British took over. As in other cases of colonial rule, moreover, there is no doubt that the English made some contributions to Indian well-being by introducing modern communications and administration, as well as a European language which served both as a route to advanced modern education and as a widespread lingua franca, without which India's many separate linguistic groups would surely have had greater difficulty uniting in a nation.

Israel

The story of Israeli independence in 1948 actually has more in common with the early American struggle for independence from Britain than with the decolonization that took place after the Second World War, for as was originally the case in Britain's American colonies it involved the displacement of an indigenous population by European immigrants seeking refuge from religious persecution. In the middle of the twentieth century, however, the indigenous populations that remained subject to European colonial rule were actively engaged in nationalist movements to drive out their overlords, and the attempt to establish a colony of Europeans on non-European land at this late date met with unequivocal outrage and militant opposition from the original inhabitants that has kept the Middle East in a state of war to this day.

Palestine, the land that had been the home of the Biblical state of Israel, had not had a significant Jewish population since the Romans had destroyed the Jewish state in AD 70 and driven its inhabitants out of the region. A great dispersion of the Jewish people took place at that time which eventually led to the existence of Jewish minorities within most of the societies of the Middle East and North Africa, western and eastern Europe, Russia, and the British Commonwealth countries, as well as in the United States and some countries in Latin America. Throughout the two thousand years of this dispersion many Jews clung to their separate religious and ethnic identity, which was based in part on pride in their ancient history as a nation and on a ritual allegiance to the ideal of rebuilding that nation on its original site.

Although some Jews continued to live in Palestine, there as in the rest of the Middle East and North Africa they constituted only a small enclave within a population which became overwhelmingly Muslim and Arabic-speaking following the conquests of Muhammad and his followers in the seventh century. The native Palestinian Jewish community was not joined by Jewish immigrants from Europe until the Zionist movement was born, in the late nineteenth century. At that time a Hungarian Jewish journalist named Theodor Herzl, who was covering the Dreyfus case, perceived a growing danger to European Jews in the intense nationalism of the period, and organized a number of congresses to discuss the creation of a Jewish homeland in Palestine. A Zionist movement grew out of these efforts, which led to a small but growing migration of European Jews to Palestine, where they bought land and established agricultural communities which they hoped would serve as the nucleus of a new Israel.

At this point Palestine was part of the rapidly decaying Ottoman Empire, but Britain's presence in Egypt made her the closest real power in the area, and when the Ottoman Turks joined the Central Powers in the First World War, it was Britain that drove them out of their Middle Eastern possessions, eventually inheriting control over Palestine and Iraq, although officially only as temporary "mandates" of the League of Nations. The British wre sympathetic to the Zionist goal and in 1917 issued a policy statement, the Balfour Declaration, promising "the establishment in Palestine of a national home for the Jewish people." In 1922 the League of Nations also voted in favor of setting up such a homeland under British protection.

Needless to say, the Arab people of Palestine were horrified by this prospect, which they viewed as nothing less than the establishment of a European colony on their land and at their expense. Until 1933, when the Nazis began their reign of terror in Europe, the Jewish immigration into Palestine was small enough so that the Arab inhabitants were not provoked to armed resistance, but from 1933 to 1939 the flight of Jews to Palestine rapidly increased their proportion of its population from 10 to 30 percent, and the Arabs increasingly tried to stem this invasion with violence and terror. The British government, which wanted to protect the rights of the Arabs in Palestine as well as to avoid an Arab revolt, finally issued a ruling in 1939 which essentially closed the doors to further Jewish immigration into Palestine: only seventy-five thousand more Jews would be admitted over the next five years and then all immigration would stop, the total Jewish population of Palestine would be held to one-third of the Arab population, and further acquisition of land by Jews would be severely restricted. At the time this decision came as a great blow to the desperate Jews of Europe, who had no other hope of refuge, but as it turned out the Nazi dragnet tightened so swiftly after 1939 that in five years only about half the permitted number of Jews managed to get to Palestine. In any event both the Jews and the Arabs now felt betrayed by Britain, and both sides began demanding independence from British rule at the same time that clashes between them were becoming increasingly frequent and deadly.

With the end of the war and the horrifying revelations of the death camps, the World Zionist Congress demanded the immediate admission of one million homeless Jewish survivors into Palestine. When the British rejected this proposal the Jews in Palestine launched a campaign of terrorism to force them out, which finally achieved its objective in 1948. On withdrawing from the fray the British referred the problem to the General Assembly of the United Nations, which proposed a partition of Palestine into two separate states for the Jews and the Arabs. The Arab members refused to accept this plan, but the Jews proceeded to announce their formation of the state of Israel, which was promptly recognized by a majority of United Nations members.

At this rebuff the Arab states of the Middle East (Egypt, Syria, Lebanon, Iraq, Transjordan, Saudi Arabia, and Yemen) joined with the Palestinian Arabs and declared war on Israel. Although greatly outnumbered the Israelis were better organized than their opponents, and they were also fighting with a desperation bred by the Holocaust to preserve Israel as a place were Jews could always be sure of welcome and safety. They won the war decisively, establishing borders for their new state that went beyond those proposed by the United Nations partition. But although the Arabs now retired in defeat they did not sign a treaty with Israel or abandon their objective of expelling the intruders; the state of Israel that was born out of this military struggle would continue to exist only as an embattled fortress, surrounded by enemies whose implacable hostility would break out in regular border incidents and a number of major concerted attacks.

In the course of the war most of the Arab inhabitants of Palestine (approximately one million) had fled from the fighting, taking refuge in the neighboring Arab states but planning to return to their homes once peace was restored. When the Israelis won the

war, however, there was no impulse on either side toward re-
patriation of these refugees. The Israelis were distrustful enough of
the quarter million Arabs who remained within their borders and
had no wish to add to their numbers, while the Palestinian Arabs
were not prepared to give up their hopes of regaining their land
and had no wish to live in a state dominated by the Israelis. The
United Nations assumed responsibility for these refugees, establishing a number of camps that were intended to be temporary
havens but became permanent homes for many of them. Both the
Israelis and the United Nations agency in charge of the refugees
assumed that resolution of the "refugee problem" would come
through resettlement of the Arab Palestinians in the neighboring
Arab states; but this plan, of course, depended on an acceptance of
Israel's permanence in Palestine that neither the Palestinians nor
the Arab states were willing to concede. Although many of the
refugees — especially those of the upper classes — made new lives
for themselves in various Arab capitals, few Palestinian Arabs,
whatever their experience after the war, would become reconciled
to Israel's existence, and some would form the Palestine Liberation
Organization, dedicated to continuing the armed struggle to regain
their land.

This irreconcilable conflict of interests in the Middle East presented a particular problem for the United States, which became
Israel's chief supporter after the war, at the same time that it
became acutely concerned with maintaining access to the world's
largest reserve of petroleum, located in the Arab countries. The
liberation of Nazi death camps by American soldiers and the
publication of photographs taken at these scenes had led to a
widespread public knowledge of the Holocaust in the United
States and a strong desire to aid the survivors: support for the
Zionist project in Palestine seemed to be the only form that such
aid could take, since no one had come up with any alternatives
and since the refugees themselves, along with Jews everywhere,
were generally enthusiastic about the idea. After 1945, moreover,
the only remaining large, prosperous, and influential Jewish community was that in the United States, and not surprisingly it
supported the new state vigorously, with both large-scale financial
aid and well-organized political pressure. Working within the
climate of general good will toward Israel that prevailed in

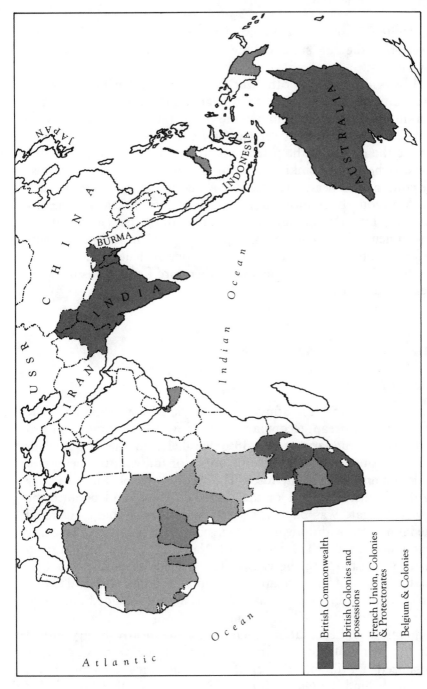

MAP 9   *Africa and the East, 1955*

the United States, the committed pro-Israel forces were able to ensure that the new state had the official backing of the American government.

It was also soon after the war, however, that American government officials concerned with foreign policy and defense began working intensively to cultivate the Arab states, in order to assure an uninterrupted flow of Persian Gulf oil. Although they failed to foresee the nature of the petroleum crisis that began in the 1970s, because they were thinking more in military than economic terms, they did make a persuasive case for America's ultimate dependence on Arab oil. But since no Arab government viewed Israel as anything but a violation and a humiliation, the United States government was caught trying to please both sides in a permanent, bitter dispute, just as the British had done in Palestine, and also like the British the Americans were therefore frequently unable to please either side.

THE ERODING PERIMETER

War in Korea

On June 25, 1950, the army of the People's Democratic Republic of (North) Korea, accompanied by Soviet-built tanks, surged across the boundary of the 38th Parallel into the Republic of (South) Korea, with the obvious intent of unifying the peninsula under communist rule by force. The victims appealed immediately to the Security Council of the United Nations, and because the Soviet delegate was boycotting that body it was able to demand the immediate withdrawal of the invading troops; when this order was ignored, it called on United Nations members to furnish military assistance to the victim. The United States responded by establishing a United Nations command under General Mac-Arthur. His troops were mainly American, but included the South Korean forces as well as token units from a number of anti-communist United Nations members. After nearly being pushed off the peninsula in the first few days of the war, MacArthur organized a brilliant counteroffensive, including an amphibious landing behind the North Korean lines at Inchon, that brought his forces to the 38th parallel in early October. When the North Koreans refused to respond to his demands for the establishment of an independent and democratic Korea, MacArthur pushed toward the Yalu River on the Manchurian border in quest of a total victory. This move was met by a North Korean counteroffensive which obviously had been reinforced by Chinese troops. Nothing daunted, MacArthur tried to drive them back to the Yalu, which only brought more and more Chinese troops, into the field, and he was forced back to the 38th parallel by the end of 1950. The whole of 1951 was taken up with alternating military campaigns and abortive attempts to open armistice negotiations; the result was a stalemate, with the United Nations forces superior in limited combat but lacking the numbers necessary to engage the main Chinese army. At the same time the North Koreans proved utterly unwilling to conclude peace on any terms other than full conquest of the South, a condition totally unacceptable to the Americans and their United Nations allies.

Meanwhile the American people, who had supported the war at the outset, began to weary of a situation in which victory was not possible. Capitalizing on this mood the Republican candidate in the 1952 presidential campaign, General Eisenhower, promised to "go to Korea" if elected. Undoubtedly this implied intention of resolving the deadlock contributed to his electoral triumph, but his new administration could achieve no more than a tense armistice, and wholly failed to open a peace conference. By this time, however, American commitment to the cause of South Korean "democracy" had become considerably eroded by the extreme corruption and abuse of civil rights practiced by the South Korean regime.

The quick response to North Korea's invasion by the United Nations had raised brief hopes that this new world organization, unlike its predecessor, was prepared to take up arms collectively to resist aggression. Unfortunately this action was only the product of an accident. In the spring of 1950 Russia had withdrawn her representatives from those United Nations agencies that refused to recognize the new Chinese regime, including the Security Council; as a consequence that body was freed from the otherwise automatic veto of the Soviet Union that would have prevented its move against North Korea. After this experience the Russians were unlikely to allow such a situation to be repeated. The real lesson therefore seemed to be that the Soviet Union and its communist allies were relatively free to test anti-communist defenses by armed attack. This position was reinforced by Russia's detonation of her first atomic device in the fall of 1949, thus ending America's monopoly of the new super weapon and reestablishing the Soviet army as a major military power – a position she advertised by following an American nuclear test in 1953 with her own version a few months later.

Vietnam

One consequence of their Korean experience was to make Americans much more sympathetic with the French position in Vietnam. In Vietnam, following the Japanese collapse, the nationalist movement was divided between the communists, under Ho Chi Minh, who insisted on full independence from France, and the non-communists, including the former emperor Bao Dai, who were willing to settle for autonomy within the new French Union. In 1945, directly after the Japanese withdrawal, Ho Chi Minh had proclaimed the Republic of Vietnam, which the French then recognized on the mistaken assumption that the new leader would accept their terms for independence. Instead, Ho Chi Minh and his Viet Minh forces fought against the French as they had fought the Japanese. Finally, to meet this revolutionary threat the French set up a new Vietnamese regime (in 1949) with its capital in Saigon and Bao Dai as emperor. Outright war was now joined between the Viet Minh forces and the French-supported regime, with the Viet Minh at first attempting frontal assaults on the French-led troops, then changing to guerrilla tactics. In 1950 the big powers became involved in the conflict: China and the Soviet Union recognized the Viet Minh and Britain and the United States supported France and South Vietnam.

The French forces in Vietnam, made up of French professional officers and Vietnamese troops, proved no match for Ho Chi Minh's guerrillas, who alternated staging ambushes with fading into the jungle. In 1954, hoping to force the Viet Minh to fight on their terms, the French established a heavily fortified camp with an airstrip far in the north at Dienbienphu, in the midst of communist-held territory. The French plan was based on the assumption that Ho Chi Minh could only concentrate small numbers of troops and no heavy weapons against this installation: instead he achieved the incredible feat of bringing in large field artillery, which totally dominated the French airstrip and the ten thousand troops attached to the fortress, reducing the whole operation to a hopeless siege. The American government offered aid, but nothing effective could be organized in time. After 55 days the French surrendered at Dienbienphu, and conceded defeat in their struggle to stay in Vietnam. An international conference in Geneva worked out an armistice that was based on a division of Vietnam at the 17th Parallel, with the northern part going to the Viet Minh and the southern part remaining under the existing Saigon regime until nationwide elections could be held to reunify the entire country. The Geneva Accords also recognized the complete independence of the other two provinces of Indochina: Cambodia under the established nationalist regime of King Sihanouk, and Laos under a neutralist government originally set up in 1947. The United States did not sign the Geneva agreement, fearing that it might be paving the way for eventual reunification of Vietnam under the communists, and when the French finally withdrew from Vietnam in 1956 the United States assumed the role of supporting the non-communist South Vietnamese regime with financial and military aid.

Algeria

After their defeat in Vietnam the French forces returned home just in time to meet a major rebellion that broke out in Algeria in October of 1954. For over a century France had been the principal colonial power in North Africa, first establishing herself in Algeria with a military expedition against local pirates in 1830, and finally subduing that country after forty years of fighting against fierce native resistance. In 1881 the French had assumed a "protectorate" over Tunisia, and in 1912 over Morocco as well. Although the French ruled Morocco only indirectly, they attempted to make Algeria, and to some extent Tunisia, French colonies; that is, they encouraged French settlement in these areas, and pushed a policy of both political and cultural assimilation. In 1848 Algeria was officially made a part of France, and organized as three departments, which like their counterparts in France had representation in the French parliament. Under the Third Republic – and after – full French citizenship was available to Muslim Algerians who were literate or owned land, and who were willing to renounce Islamic law. After the Second World War, the population of Algeria was made up of about a million "French" settlers (most actually descendants of earlier emigrants from France, with some from Spain and Italy) and some eight million "Muslims." Some of the Muslim Algerians were more or less assimilated to the French society that dominated the fertile coastal strip of the country, but the majority existed either as a distinct urban proletariat or within the age-old tribal society of the interior.

The 1920s and 1930s had seen the birth of independence movements in all three French-controlled territories, with significant nationalist uprisings in Morocco in 1937 and Algeria in 1945. Nevertheless the French were surprised when the Algerian National Liberation Front (FLN) launched its campaign in 1954. It was an unequal contest from the start. Although the rebels could not match the French army in open combat, they did operate freely as guerrillas in the countryside, and increasingly in the cities as well. The strategy of the leaders – virtually all of whom were French-educated intellectuals – was to win over all Muslims to their revolution, by whatever means necessary, and thereby establish such a wide-ranging clandestine operation that the French professional army would be altogether too small to deal with it. The rebels were successful in this endeavor, and the French had to resort to conscripts to fight the war, thereby bringing it directly into the center of French politics.

The Suez crisis

Although the Algerian War was generally perceived as a specifically French affair, it can better be understood as part of a widespread upsurge of Arab nationalism, which was producing political turbulence in the eastern Mediterranean as well. In this area nationalist energies increasingly found a focus in opposition to the new state of Israel, but they were also exercised in efforts to remove the last remaining vestiges of French and British rule, of which the most important was Britain's treaty right to garrison the Suez Canal. In

1952 an army junta overthrew the decadent monarchy in Egypt, establishing a one-party republic that soon came under the domination of its leader, the charismatic Gamal Abdel Nasser. One of Nasser's first acts was to negotiate an agreement with the British calling for their eventual withdrawal from the Canal zone, with the right to return if the Canal was threatened by an outside power. A year later Nasser announced that he had made a deal with the communist bloc countries to exchange cotton and rice for arms. This came as a shock to the British and even more to the Americans, who had been offering the Egyptians aid on the assumption that as Muslims they would necessarily be hostile to atheistic communism. In response, the British and Americans withdrew their offers of aid to build the high dam on the Nile at Aswan, on which Nasser was counting to modernize Egypt's subsistence economy. Nasser reacted by nationalizing the Suez Canal in July of 1956, saying that he would use its revenues to build the dam. This was an act of direct defiance of the western powers, whose efforts to reestablish some international control of the canal were frustrated by Egyptian resistance, and by Soviet opposition in the United Nations Security Council.

As a result, the British prime minister, Anthony Eden, saw Nasser as threatening international law and order. The French took much the same view, their hostility being considerably reinforced by Egypt's open and substantial aid to the rebels in Algeria. Finally the Israelis were seriously threatened by the prospect of such a declared and dedicated enemy of their state as Nasser assuming control of the Suez Canal. Without informing the Americans, these three concerned parties proceeded to plan a joint military attack to seize the canal. In October 1956 the Israelis began the action with a tank invasion of Egypt's Sinai peninsula that bordered the canal; two days later Britain and France vetoed a peace resolution in the Security Council, and opened an air and sea attack on Cairo and the canal zone. Almost immediately, this action was halted by international condemnation, and by a Soviet threat to come to Egypt's aid with missiles against French and British cities. In response, America's President Eisenhower ordered a world-wide alert of American strategic (air) forces, but at the same time, he made it clear that he was not prepared to support his friends in this adventure, and the United States joined with the

Soviet Union in a United Nations vote to demand a ceasefire and evacuation of all conquered territory.

The aggressors now withdrew in confusion, leaving the United Nations to enforce the ceasefire and evacuation. The canal remained securely in Egyptian hands and the whole operation went down in history as a humiliating blunder on the part of Britain and France, as well as an important victory for Arab nationalism in general and Nasser in particular. The Israelis, in contrast to the British and French, had achieved a stunning military success, but to no avail, since they were forced to give up the territory they had occupied, with no effective guarantee of their right of passage through the canal.

Peace with Japan

During this second postwar phase (roughly 1950–6), when the European world was being challenged on its perimeter, the diplomatic and military rehabilitation of the principal enemy states was being arranged. Stimulated by the Korean war, the United States drafted a formal peace treaty with Japan, which was submitted to and accepted by an international conference; the communist bloc countries boycotted these proceedings, in a symbolic demonstration of the new postwar realignment of nations that put Japan squarely in the American camp. This new relationship was reinforced by a mutual security pact between Japan and the United States, and an agreement allowing Japan to increase its "self-defense forces."

Germany and Europe

In 1950 the western powers gave West Germany a military guarantee and began planning a reduction of occupation controls and her eventual restoration to the European community as a full member. This process culminated in Germany's admission to NATO in 1954 – an action which provoked the Communist nations to form their own joint military command, the Warsaw Pact, in response. The intervening time had been marked by a series of proposals for integrating the new Federal Republic into the defense and economic community of Western Europe. Most significant was the Schuman Plan – named after its French sponsor – for the merging of the French and German coal and iron industries as the basic unit of an eventual "common market" of European states. The Schuman Plan was put in operation in 1952, and the Treaty of Rome, which established the European Economic Community (including Belgium, Holland, Luxemburg, France, Germany and Italy), was signed in early 1957. Together these central organizations created the machinery necessary to lift Europe's national economies out of their postwar doldrums. The principal support for this process still came from American aid, however, which in turn was largely spent for American equipment to rebuild Europe's damaged cities and retool her aging factories; the result was the vigorous stimulation of business on both sides of the Atlantic.

Russia after Stalin

In Russia the most important event at the beginning of the 1950s was the death of Stalin in early 1953. The postwar years of his rule had provided no respite from his habitual brutality, although slave labor camps had replaced purges, mass starvation and indiscriminate slaughter as his preferred method of dealing with his real or imagined enemies. What his passing would mean either to the Russian people or to the rest of the world was impossible to predict, but the transfer of power, for which there was no established procedure, went surprisingly smoothly, with a party leader named Nikita Khrushchev gradually emerging as his principal successor. The only showdown was with Stalin's chief of the secret police, Lavrenty Beria, who was overpowered and executed by his Kremlin rivals. This action seemed to promise a move away from Stalin's policy of maintaining control through terror, as did the subsequent release of huge numbers of political prisoners. Then in early 1956, at the Twentieth Communist Party Congress, Khrushchev delivered an astonishing denunciation of Stalin's regime. While this was not a public performance, its tone and content were gradually leaked to an incredulous world. Within the party high command this led to one last attempt to challenge Khrushchev, who turned the threat into victory and finally consolidated his own power.

Widely hailed as a "thaw," this relaxation of Stalin's rule which followed Khrushchev's accession to power extended to foreign as well as domestic policies. Soviet control was eased in East Germany, leading to the outbreak of large and violent workers' protests in 1953 which although suppressed with tanks were also countered by substantial concessions. Then in 1955 Khrushchev visited Yugoslavia, where he made a public apology for Russia's break with that country in 1948. While this overture was accepted by Tito it did not move him to abandon his relations with the West, particularly the United States. During the same year the Soviet government suddenly proposed a full and liberal peace treaty for Austria, thus finally ending her four-power occupation. While these various developments hardly constituted a reversal of the Soviets' hard-line position, they did suggest an amelioration of the general political and diplomatic climate, which provoked an enthusiastic popular response in Western Europe and an upsurge of hopes for independence in Eastern Europe as well.

Unrest in Poland

It was in Poland and Hungary that Khrushchev's "thaw" had its most important effect. In early 1956 the Soviets released Wladyslaw Gomulka, a popular Polish leader who had been imprisoned for deviation from the party orthodoxy. Soon afterwards serious rioting broke out in Poznań over workers' conditions, and the rebellion spread quickly through the rest of the country. The ensuing state trials of the rebels were broken off as tension mounted and Gomulka was brought back into the Central Committee of Poland's Communist party as a concession, while Khrushchev himself went to Warsaw to urge the Poles to maintain the Soviet line. The former Russian officer General Rokossovsky, Poland's defense minister, then ordered Polish troops to take up positions near Warsaw, a move which was seen as threatening Soviet military intervention, and Polish border units responded by opening fire on their Russian counterparts. To avoid a major catastrophe Gomulka was made head of the Polish Communist party, Rokossovsky was relieved of his command, the Russian troops in Poland were ordered to their quarters and the Polish militia was deployed to protect the Russian units from violent demonstrations. This confrontation coincided exactly with the aborted British–French attack on Suez, as well as with the far more serious anti-communist revolt that had just erupted in Hungary.

The Hungarian rising

Although the Hungarians were hardly less nationalistic than the Poles, their postwar history as a Soviet satellite had been less tumultuous, and most of their rebellious energies had been taken up in party infighting. This had produced a deviant communist leader, Imre Nagy, who, like Gomulka in Poland, had a national following. Although Nagy had become premier in 1953, he was forced from office for "reactionary deviationism" in 1955, then hastily readmitted to the Communist party in the early fall of 1956 and reinstated as premier in October, when student riots demanding national independence and democratic government began getting out of hand. Thus whereas the Polish crisis had developed out of a long-standing struggle against Russian communist domination, the Hungarian outburst appears to have been much more a response to the strange and contradictory messages about party discipline being disseminated by Khrushchev.

In the last week of October 1956, anti-Soviet riots spread from Budapest throughout most of Hungary. Russian forces withdrew from the capital, and Nagy promised free elections and the end of one-party rule; but when he denounced the Warsaw Pact and called on the United Nations to take up Hungary's situation, the Soviet forces reversed their direction and moved back into Budapest, completely smashing all resistance. Nagy was taken into custody (he was executed in 1958), and Russian authority was reestablished. In the course of the upheaval, over 150,000 refugees succeeded in crossing the Austrian border to find asylum in the West, many in the United States. The whole tragic affair had a profoundly sobering effect on the west European political and intellectual leaders who had been celebrating the virtues of coexistence with the Soviet Union, and at the same time served to harden the already pronounced anti-communist orientation of the United States. Although the General Assembly of the United Nations voted to condemn the Soviet intervention, the Western powers never contemplated challenging the Soviets militarily on behalf of Hungary, which they had long since conceded to Russian control.

McCarthyism

In the United States, postwar domestic politics took a sordid turn as the Cold War led to exaggerated fears of communist subversion at home. This paranoid response to the communist challenge abroad stemmed from the shock felt by many Americans when their efforts in winning the Second World War did not lead to the expected reward of safety and freedom from all further threats. With its belligerent rhetoric and military actions, Soviet Russia looked frighteningly like another Germany or Japan, intent on conquest if Americans relaxed their vigilance or failed to keep one step ahead of it in military might; and when the Russians exploded their first atomic bomb, in August of 1949, American alarm turned into panic. It was widely feared that an atomic war with Russia was imminent, and many Americans took the challenge by North Korea as Russia's opening gambit in this dreaded war – something she would never have dared risk if she had not possessed the bomb. Further, and despite the testimony of scientists that there was no "secret" to the atomic bomb, there was a widespread belief in the United States that the Russians must have "stolen" it, through the treachery of Ameicans who had access to it. Suspicion came to focus on anyone who had ever belonged to the Communist party, or had even evinced sympathy for communist ideals.

There had been waves of anti-communist hysteria in the United States between the wars, but these suspicions had been put aside when Russia became America's ally against the Nazis – only to reemerge as soon as the Cold War began. In 1949 the Communist party was banned, in effect, by the trial and conviction of eleven of its leaders for "conspiracy to advocate the overthrow of the United States government by force." There followed a series of trials of people who were accused of committing – or "conspiring to commit" – espionage for the Russians, usually on nebulous or suspect evidence. In 1950, however, a German physicist named Klaus Fuchs was arrested in Britain and confessed to passing atomic information to the Soviets. Fuchs, who had worked on the bomb at Los Alamos, had been in a position to give genuine help to the Russians, and because of it they may have gained as much as two years in their race to build the bomb.

Fuchs was tried in Britain and served a moderate prison term. Instead of resting content with his exposure, however, American authorities were all the more convinced by it that there must have been a larger conspiracy to pass information to the Soviets from Los Alamos, and the FBI redoubled its efforts to uncover this postulated spy ring. Four months after Fuchs's arrest the agency fulfilled this mission with the arrest of a man who had been a machinist at Los Alamos during the war and accused his sister and brother-in-law, Ethel and Julius Rosenberg, of having recruited him to provide sketches of the bomb which they passed on to the Russians. Although the case against the Rosenbergs was far shakier than that against Fuchs, the judge and jury at their trial agreed with the prosecution that they were the traitors who were ultimately responsible for the disaster that had befallen the nation, and they were sentenced to death. Insisting on their innocence the Rosenbergs appealed their case all the way to the Supreme Court without success, and President Eisenhower declined to pardon them, with the explanation that "by immeasurably increasing the chances of atomic war the Rosenbergs may have condemned to death tens of millions of innocent people all over the world."

The climate of opinion which led to the execution of the Rosenbergs provided an opportunity for a demagogic politician, Senator Joseph McCarthy, to wield great power in the first half of the fifties as chairman of the Senate Internal Security Committee. Although he was a thoroughly cynical opportunist, McCarthy probably also half-believed his wild charges that the troubles of the United States must be due to the "traitorous actions" of those in high places. With no lack of political support in the nation as a whole, McCarthy faced little opposition in his self-appointed task of uncovering the vast communist conspiracy that he claimed to have uncovered. He began his campaign in 1950 with the charge that many State Department officers were communists; using the device of the Congressional investigation he could interrogate his victims, and if they denied any communist connections, prosecute them for perjury. McCarthy never succeeded in proving any of his allegations but the investigations themselves were often sufficient to lead to the dismissal or electoral defeat of those he accused, with severe damage to many careers and lives as a result.

McCarthy's rampage came to an end in 1954 when the Senate voted (67 to 22) to censure him for abuse of his powers, and the election of a Democratic majority to the Congress resulted in his removal from the committee chairmanship that had served as his platform; this coincided with a subsiding of the national hysteria that had led to the anti-communist investigations and prosecutions. But the long-term effects of the "red scare" were by no means over. In particular it left a legacy of fear among liberals of becoming vulnerable to the kind of charge McCarthy had leveled – with the full weight of voter opinion behind him – of being disloyal to America if they were "soft on communism." Anti-communism thus became the bipartisan orthodoxy in the United States from which no deviation was tolerated – in the government bureaucracies, the political parties, the media, and even the universities. This adherence to dogma not only stifled thought and expression in the country but also made it difficult for Americans to assess their international situation with adequate objectivity.

14

The Emergence of the Modern World

In the spring of 1956, Nikita Khrushchev, on a visit to Britain, announced that the Soviet Union would produce a guided missile capable of carrying a nuclear warhead; later that year, during the double crisis of the Russian invasion of Hungary and the Franco-British attack on the Suez Canal, he issued threats of a rocket strike against western European cities. While these pronouncements provoked less reaction in the west than might have been expected, the Russian launching a year later of a small satellite – or "Sputnik," which circled the globe repeatedly in clear view of those under its path, produced something akin to panic in the United States. Although perfectly harmless in itself, it not only demonstrated Russia's obvious capacity to deploy long-range missiles but also dramatized the Americans' failure to maintain the technical superiority over their adversary which they had come to take for granted.

There could be no further doubt that the Soviet Union was capable of attacking the United States with nuclear weapons, and that the military strength of the two superpowers was therefore essentially equal, despite the continuing efforts of the Americans to maintain a margin of superiority in the arms race. A balance of terror was now established which became the basis of relations between the United States and the Soviet Union, preventing either power from contemplating any direct challenge to the other, as became obvious in their only confrontation since that time, when Russia attempted to put missiles in Cuba in 1962: on that occasion the Soviets rapidly backed away from a military threat that President Kennedy announced he would not tolerate.

Although this nuclear stalemate completely inhibited the two superpowers in their military relations with each other, it imposed no such restraint on the other armed forces of the world, including the liberation movements in the remaining European colonial possessions, which now began to enjoy an increasing military advantage over their imperial adversaries. This marked shift in the balance of conventional power was due in large part to the new availability of weapons to virtually anyone who wanted them: in addition to the stores of matériel left over from the wide-ranging campaigns of the Second World War, sophisticated modern arms could now be purchased, legally or illegally, from their American and European manufacturers. But the main suppliers of the contending military forces of the world were the Soviet and American governments, which vied with each other for control of territory in what was now being called the "Third World" by supporting client regimes and movements with weapons, money, military advisors, and sometimes troops.

Hardly less important in mobilizing the anticolonial movement was the worldwide dissemination of the revolutionary doctrines of Marx and Lenin, adapted to wars of national liberation by Mao Tse-Tung, Ho Chi Minh and others. These theories appealed to the nationalist pride of the peasant masses, who turned guerrilla tactics into a powerful threat to any conventionally armed adversaries. Eventually the contest became so unequal that the European powers were all forced to withdraw from their colonial possessions, in many cases without a struggle.

Only in the economic sphere did the United States and its European allies far outdistance their Soviet rivals. The spectacular economic growth enjoyed by the west during this period was due in part to the organization of the European Economic Community (Common Market) and other measures to facilitate international trade in the west, but most of all to an enormous and rapid expansion in the use of very cheap and apparently inexhaustible petroleum as the basic source of energy in all western economies. The result was an altogether undreamed-of prosperity, which contrasted dramatically with the low productivity of the socialist realm, and reinforced in Americans the unbounded self-confidence that they had gained from their success in the war. Despite any setbacks they might suffer in the international arena, Americans tended to take their country's booming economy as reassuring evidence that they remained superior to the Russians, and even as grounds for believing that they possessed the sheer material wealth to solve all the remaining problems of the world just as they had solved the problem of winning the Second World War. This heady optimism was dramatically symbolized by President John Kennedy's project to help the people in Third World countries by sending American "Peace Corps" volunteers, mostly young college graduates, to live with them and teach them American techniques. Similar in spirit was the president's ambition to land a man on the moon and bring him safely back to earth by the end of the decade. This magnificent if useless feat was America's belated answer to Russia's Sputnik, and in fact it would be achieved on schedule, unlike the plan of abolishing world poverty through sheer good will. It would also clearly demonstrate the great material and technical progress the United States had been able to make without solving any of its own enduring social problems, much less those of the world at large.

FRANCE AND ALGERIA

With the beginning of the second postwar decade, after 1955, life in the European world had pretty well returned to what was thought of as normal. The rubble was finally cleared away, public services were functioning, there was little unemployment, and new or restored regimes were carrying on the affairs of state with assurance and greater or less efficiency. Russia's brutal suppression of the Hungarian revolt in 1956 had dispelled western hopes for a singificant thaw in the Cold War, but Western Europe was confidently engaged in developing its economy and pursuing numerous and promising initiatives toward economic and political unification. In Europe's relations with its former colonies, however, the decade had an inauspicious beginning in the ill-fated Franco-British Suez venture of 1956. For France the defeat of Suez was a double disaster, because it left her in what would prove to be an untenable position in Algeria, where a revolutionary movement had been struggling to overthrow French rule since 1954.

The Algerian revolt presented the French government with an

agonizing problem. In 1956 the French withdrew from both Morocco and Tunisia in response to the nationalist revolts in these countries, and there was growing sentiment in Paris for getting out of Algeria as well. But the French position in Algeria was considerably more complicated by the existence of the long-established and deeply rooted community of approximately one million French settlers who lived in the cities and along the coastal plain, as well as by the anti-independence feeling among the French military establishment, for which Algeria had long served as the major base and training ground. Eager to minimize the conflict, Paris offered sweeping concessions to the Algerian rebels, which they refused to consider.

Finally, confronted by a real threat to the existence of its citizens in Algeria, the French government mobilized half a million men to put down the rebellion, but without success. The leaders of the rebellion were young intellectuals, several of whom had been at the University of Paris, who seemed to be familiar with the guerrilla tactics of Mao Tse-Tung and Ho Chi Minh. Their operations were entirely clandestine, giving the French the least possible target against which to strike. Acting by ambush, assassination, torture and terror, the rebels intimidated the Muslim population into subservience at the same time that they sought to drive out the French, and the French army was helpless to protect either civilians or its own draftees from becoming targets of such tactics. The independence of Tunisia and Morocco, moreover, had the effect of providing the rebels with a safe haven from which to attack the French without risk of pursuit, while the failure of the Suez strike meant continued Egyptian support for the rebels as well.

The French veterans from Vietnam, recognizing this revolutionary pattern and frustrated by the memory of their previous defeat, now made a desperate attempt to counter the rebellion by using its own tactics against it – particularly torture. It was probably only the information they extracted by this means which allowed the French even to hold their own against their elusive enemies, but when word of this practice reached Paris, it caused a public outcry that brought a government order against its continuation. While this order was not always scrupulously obeyed, it served to restrict the French army sufficiently to put it at a growing disadvantage against its uninhibited enemy. As French casualties mounted, the desire to end the war on any terms swept France, leaving the army feeling betrayed and Algeria's French settlers threatened with extinction. Clearly it was only a matter of time before the French would abandon Algeria as they had Vietnam.

By the spring of 1958 the implications of the situation had become clear enough to the settlers so that a group of their leaders, together with some army officers, constituted themselves a "Committee of Public Safety" and seized power in Algeria. This development produced near-chaos in Paris, and no one seemed willing or able to form a government. Charles de Gaulle, who had been waiting for an opportunity to return to power for some ten years, now saw his chance and flew to Algeria, promising the Committee a "French Algeria" and continued French military resistance to the independence forces. Then he returned to Paris where he presented himself as the guardian of the "integrity of France," since he appeared to be the only potential leader who was able to command the allegiance of the Algerian French as well as the rest of the nation.

The president of the Republic duly called on de Gaulle to form a government, and granted his conditions that he receive emergency powers, including the right to submit a new constitution to the electorate. De Gaulle's draft constitution, which transformed the government from a parliamentary to a presidential regime, received an overwhelming endorsement from the French voters, who next proceeded to elect a new assembly and a special electoral college that named de Gaulle president of the Republic for a seven-year term. When this new government (the Fifth Republic) began to function in January 1959, de Gaulle was established as the virtual dictator of France.

With his formidable new authority de Gaulle moved to restore order and confidence in both Algeria and France. His first actions were to curb the inflation in France with currency reforms, to issue an enigmatic statement promising "auto-determination" to Algeria, and to offer to France's other African colonies a choice between political integration with France or independence within the "French Community."

It would be some time before the meaning of "auto-determination" would become clear, but eventually the defenders of French Algeria realized that de Gaulle intended to resolve the conflict by gradual but total surrender of Algeria to the national liberation forces (the FLN). The desperation engendered by this realization led in 1961 to an army revolt in Algiers, which seemed for a few days to threaten an attack on Paris, but order was quickly restored as the conscripts refused to follow the generals in this defiance. A year later, in 1962, the French government signed a ceasefire with the FLN; at the same time an airlift was organized to evacuate all remaining French settlers from Algeria, leaving the country to the rebels. In a national referendum, 90 percent of the French electorate approved of de Gaulle's disposition of the matter.

France and the Common Market

The integration of the Algerian French into the society and economy of metropolitan France was delayed for some five years (probably owing primarily to a housing shortage), but then took place quite rapidly in the expanding economy that France enjoyed in the early 1960s. For simultaneously with de Gaulle's assumption of power, in 1959, France had begun to experience her first flush of prosperity in thirty years. Inevitably – and with official encouragement – this coincidence was attributed to de Gaulle's influence, but whatever his share in the improved economic conditions, it was slight compared with that of the much-maligned Fourth Republic.

The great achievement of that regime had been to maneuver the antiquated economy of France into the mid-twentieth century without provoking a major social confrontation, and in the process to plan and initiate the economic unification of Europe. Credit for these accomplishments is largely due to the statesman Robert Schuman, who even before the war's end had the vision to realize that a new healthy Europe could be built only on French and German economic cooperation, and to the administrator Jean Monnet who showed genius in translating this dream into reality. Schuman's original plan was to merge the German and French coal and steel industries, and by 1951 this plan had been expanded to include the three "Benelux" countries (Belgium, the Netherlands and Luxemburg) and Italy. In 1957 these six cooperating nations signed the Treaty of Rome, creating the Common Market, which eliminated all tariffs between members and provided for the free circulation of labor and capital as well as goods. It was the hope and expectation of the participants that this process of integration would attract new members from among the European states, and that in time it would even develop into a supranational government.

From the beginning the British had remained apart from this European movement, partly from a sense of cultural distance and partly because of a conflict of economic interests. For over a century the British had imported the bulk of their basic foodstuffs, much of it at low prices from Commonwealth countries such as Australia and New Zealand. Agricultural prices in the Common Market were much higher because of the relative inefficiency of Europe's small farms, so that as a full member of the Market Britain would be forced to pay more for food. After long negotiations, however, the British worked out special terms that would ease her transition to membership. This had not been easy, and it was widely assumed that the arrangement was desired by all parties as offering mutual benefit. With Britain's formal application for admission to the Market in 1963, however, President de Gaulle startled the European world with a most undiplomatic veto. He gave no explanation for his sudden move, but it soon became clear that he had nursed a grudge against "les Anglo-Saxons" ever since the English and Americans had excluded him from their military planning in the Second World War – especially for the Normandy landing – and that he did not intend that France should surrender any sovereignty either to the Common Market or to American-dominated NATO. To de Gaulle the Common Market was properly an organization of Continental Europe around French leadership, while NATO imposed unnecessary constraints on a France that he wished to be independent in its strength, strategy, and foreign policy. Accordingly, in 1959 France began a disengagement from NATO that was completed by 1964, and she also proceeded to develop her own atomic and hydrogen weapons, refusing to join with the United States, Britain and Russia in their nuclear test ban treaty of 1963.

De Gaulle's second and last career as leader of France came to an end over an insignificant political issue in 1969, but by that time he had fully demonstrated that neither the wartime nor the postwar military and diplomatic alignments in Europe represented a permanent expression of the French national interest, as he saw it, and that despite all the progress that had been made in the military, political and economic integration of the Western European community, it was still the national self-interest in the narrow, age-old sense that determined policy, at least for one important member of that community.

THE BERLIN WALL

The return of West Germany (the Federal Republic of Germany) to the European community as a free and independent member raised the question of its reunification with East Germany (the German Democratic Republic) in a new form. While virtually no Germans on either side of the boundary were prepared to accept the division as permanent, neither regime was ready to be absorbed by the other, and the problem of political reunification began to recede into the realm of speculation. It was a complete impasse, which citizens of West Germany found themselves more ready to tolerate as they sensed the first stirrings of postwar prosperity, since a merger with the still impoverished Democratic Republic would inevitably dilute their new affluence. But the enclave of West Berlin continued to pose problems that led to increasingly strained relations between the two Germanys and their occupying powers.

Almost from the beginning of the Allied occupation the Soviets had tried to maneuver the British, French and American forces out of the former capital – notably in the blockade of 1948–9 which produced the famous airlift. At no time did the Russians risk a direct military confrontation, however, and the western Allies remained. But when the NATO powers recognized the sovereignty of West Germany, Khrushchev did the same for the East German government (1955), turning over to it control of civilian access to Berlin. This led to a series of diplomatic exchanges and confrontations on the subject of the city's status, which ended in a standoff between Khrushchev and the new American president, John Fitzgerald Kennedy, in July 1961, and the reinforcement of the American garrison in West Berlin with 1,500 troops. On August 15, the

East German government then closed the border between East and West Berlin, and rapidly constructed a wall between the two.

While there were many reasons why the Soviets wanted the western Allies out of Berlin, there is no doubt that the most important factor was the city's double role as a showcase of the differing levels of prosperity in the two parts of Germany and as an escape hatch for dissatisfied and often desperate citizens of the Democratic Republic. Eastern Europe had never enjoyed a standard of living equal to that of the West, except in limited areas for brief periods, and its recovery from the war had been much slower. By 1960 West Germany, along with most of western Europe, was looking affluent: food was abundant, luxuries were becoming commonplace, almost everyone was well dressed, traffic was unmanageable, and streets were full of shoppers. The contrast with the East was painful; there all goods were in short supply, including food, and appearances were drab. For the most part, the two worlds were separated by the "iron curtain" that prevented travel and even the exchange of information between them, but Berlin was the great exception. There the inhabitants of the eastern sector could plainly see the color, lights and crowds of the city on the other side of the barrier, and they could also travel freely to the western side on two subway systems which still circulated throughout the entire city. Sometimes East German police checked the papers of passengers in their sector, but their control was far from complete.

As the prosperity of West Germany increased, and its contrast with the East – vividly advertised in Berlin – became more marked, increasing numbers of East Germans took the opportunity to cross the border in Berlin and claim refuge in the western sector. To meet this challenge, public authorities and private charities in West Berlin collaborated in providing the new arrivals with shelter, air travel to the Federal Republic, and resettlement in jobs, housing, and all other necessities. Since those who fled had to abandon all their belongings, reestablishing them in the West was a considerable undertaking; but in the late 1950s what had been a trickle of refugees became a torrent, and finally a flood that actually threatened to depopulate the East, particularly of the young and well-educated. For the Democratic Republic it threatened economic disaster as well as general demoralization; clearly the East German government and its Soviet sponsors had to staunch the flow or see the whole Soviet satellite system crumble. The wall was their solution. Crude as it was, it stopped the migration, but it also stood as a shameful admission that the citizens of East Germany were being held there against their will.

THE NEW PROSPERITY

The economic progress which made West Germany such a glittering contrast with East Germany and the rest of the Soviet sphere was hailed in the West as the "German miracle." It was variously attributed to Germany's commitment to private enterprise in comparison with the nationalizing tendency of France and Britain, to her freedom from colonial obligations and entanglements, and to the relatively small appropriations she had been called on to make for her own defense. But in fact there was a larger and more general cause behind this new prosperity, which became apparent when the phenomenon began to spread throughout the North Atlantic community and into the Pacific as well: ultimately the unprecedented economic growth of the entire western world in this period derived from a vast expansion in the use of petroleum as the prime source of energy. This time the origin and generating center of the new phase of industrial growth was the United States, which, like England in the previous century, now provided the capital and tools required to make use of the new energy source, while also furnishing the first model of a petroleum-based economy, which would be imitated throughout the western world.

This increase in petroleum consumption came about first because of the wartime development of the automotive industry. America's war production had been concentrated on land vehicles, aircraft, and ships, for transport and combat, all of which depended on petroleum derivatives – mostly gasoline – for fuel. With the end of the war this huge manufacturing capacity was reoriented toward civilian ends, particularly the production of cars, trucks, and planes; the result was a continued postwar expansion of the use of gasoline and oil for automotive transport and travel. And the same sort of transition and development, on a smaller scale, was taking place in Europe. But automotive use was only a part of this expansion; now that the machinery was in place to extract and exploit petroleum, this fuel rapidly began to replace coal in producing heat, generating electricity, and powering ships and trains, while in a related development a new petrochemical industry began producing an amazing array of materials derived from petroleum that would increasingly take the place of the more expensive traditionally used plant, animal, and mineral products.

One reason for the shift from coal to petroleum for fuel was that some of Europe's coal mines were near depletion; but the fundamental cause of the worldwide transformation to a petroleum-based economy was that oil was now very much cheaper, in terms of the amount of energy required to bring it to market, than any other energy source. In other words, the industrial revival that produced one economic "miracle" after another, in Germany, France, Italy, and Japan — not to mention the far greater transformation of the American economy — was fed by what was simply the cheapest and most abundant source of energy on record.

While this fact was generally recognized, its full implications were rarely grasped at this time. The large profits, or margin of surplus energy, that were generated by use of the cheap petroleum were usually reinvested in new enterprises which consumed still more energy, thus producing an apparently endless spiral of accelerating economic growth. But there were fundamental problems inherent in this process, beginning simply with the rapidly growing dependence of the industrial countries on this source of energy. To take an example, in the United States the proliferation of cars, trucks, and highways led not only to an ever-increasing consumption of oil but also to the near-demise of the more fuel-efficient railroad system, and to the growth of suburbs that virtually required their residents to do a great deal of daily driving. Thus by the end of the second postwar decade any interruption of the flow of oil to American vehicles would have seriously disrupted the country's transportation system and hence its entire economy. Although less tied to the automobile, the European economies became almost equally dependent on oil during this period; for example, France doubled both its total consumption of energy and the percent of energy it derived from oil during the decade (1955–65), with almost no public recognition of this development, let alone its political implications.

Oil had been an important factor in international trade since the beginning of the twentieth century, and as a principal producer of oil the Persian Gulf had become the object of imperialist investment and the source of huge profits since before the First World War. It was not until the Second World War, however, that oil became a military necessity, transforming the Persian Gulf into a key strategic area. Unquestionably Germany's failure to reach a major oil field in the Caucasus contributed to her defeat in 1945; and the American wartime Secretary of the Navy, James Forrestal, came to the conclusion – based on his knowledge of the enormous consumption of petroleum by the carrier fleets and their planes in the Pacific – that only the Persian Gulf oil reserves (the largest known) would be adequate to fuel the even larger ships and fleets that he saw as the dominant forces of the future. As a result, Forrestal was convinced that effective control of the Gulf would amount to world power. Clearly he underestimated the military potential of missiles and of nuclear weapons; but in another sense he was right, for the economic survival of the industrial world did increasingly come to depend on access to the Middle Eastern oil reserves. By 1965 Europe's dependence on oil from this region was already critical and growing at an exponential rate, while America's consumption was increasing at the same breakneck pace and by this time had also begun to run ahead of her domestic production.

As long as there was a swelling tide of oil at two dollars a barrel, few of those benefiting from this bounty worried that eventually this resource must run out, or that it would become vastly more expensive as soon as the oil-producing states of the Gulf realized their power to profit from controlling its flow. Even less pressing at this time were any concerns about the waste products of all this booming economic activity. Whatever the drawbacks and dangers of the new oil-based economy, the generations that had survived the Depression and Second World War were inclined to see only its promise to eliminate poverty and hardship, not only in the west but eventually also in the rest of the world.

Epilogue

Narrative histories that approach the present tend to lose their focus in a welter of detail, from which they draw dubious conclusions about prospects for the future. In an attempt to avoid such pitfalls this account will conclude at the end of the second postwar decade, and close with a brief review of some of the chief factors that shaped the modern world, from its emergence on the western edge of Europe in the seventeenth century through its development into the global system of production and power in which we live today.

In the sense that the ancient world was Mediterranean, the modern world was Atlantic in its focus and organization, based on the ocean-going trade that was made possible by advances in ship design and navigation in the sixteenth and seventeenth centuries. London was the natural geographic capital of this growing Atlantic commerce: an excellent ocean port, it also drew on the fertile Thames valley for grain, and had an all-water route to Newcastle to supply its enormous need for coal. The injection of coal into this economic system, and the British development of new ways of using this abundant source of energy, would produce by the middle of the nineteenth century the most powerful economic machine the world had seen.

Throughout the Continental hinterland, meanwhile, the Bourbons and other monarchs were consolidating their hold over the rich farmland that blanketed the European interior, erecting centralized military monarchies based on peasant agriculture that reached relatively stable form by the seventeenth century. In this system, land farmed by peasants was the chief source of wealth and power, and the ruler consequently strove to increase the extent of the territory he could command. Thus at the same time that the oceanic society was developing over the seas, the land-based states were becoming more fixed and focused on their territorial boundaries, and on the military-administrative establishments needed to hold them together. When railroads finally came to the Continent they were built and usually operated by the states, which possessed the only sufficient concentration of wealth to pay for them, with the result that the lines were laid primarily to mechanize administrative and military functions rather than to open the interior to trade.

The ideas and institutions that took shape within the Atlantic commercial society reflected its economic structure and experience. The difficulty of maintaining governmental control across a major body of water was demonstrated by the successful resistance of the American colonies in the War of Independence, and in recent times by the failure of the European imperial powers to maintain their hold on the overseas territories they had seized in the late nineteenth century. With this intrinsic limitation, the oceanic community tended to order its affairs by negotiation rather than military force, and to favor a parliamentary form of government rather than a centralized administration.

The two different kinds of society were drawn into conflict when the territorial ambitions of a land-based ruler threatened the independence of a neighboring commercial society. Both the English Civil War and the American Revolution can be seen in part as the successful struggle of commercial interests to avoid being taxed by a king to pay for the standing army that would enforce his rule over them. And all three of the major European wars since the French Revolution began as attempts by territorial rulers to expand their holdings, and ended when the Atlantic powers mobilized in their own defense. The dual paroxysm of the two World Wars was essentially the result of Germany's attempt to establish military hegemony over the rest of Europe, but this classic land war turned into a struggle for control of the Atlantic in both cases: all the combatants depended on oceanic transportation for supplies and reinforcements, and it was the entry of the United States, with its huge industrial output and the ships to carry it, that twice proved decisive in the outcome.

On the Continent the Second World War split Europe along much the same lines between oceanic and land powers, with Hitler attempting to consolidate everything up to the coast, only to be driven back by the Allied invasion to meet the Russians at the Elbe. This then became the line of demarcation in the new alignment of land and sea powers that emerged after the war, centering around the United States and the Soviet Union. The territorial orientation of the Soviet Union was demonstrated by its administrative government and heavily fortified boundaries, backed by its massive army, and an economy that was tightly controlled in both production and distribution. This kind of organization would be difficult to impose overseas, while over land it was readily installed in each of the Warsaw Pact nations and reinforced as necessary by military intervention. By contrast, the postwar orientation of the United States was oceanic. With peace, the American productivity that had won the war was redirected to restore western Europe and Japan, and in the process created a new level of prosperity in a newly global oceanic economy. Both West Germany and Japan, having failed to realize their territorial ambitions, prospered beyond measure from their forced conversion to commercial ways, providing a striking demonstration of the productivity of the commercial economy in contrast to the economic stagnation that prevailed on the other side of the iron curtain.

For nearly half a century after the war this dual pattern of organization persisted with remarkable stability, while a similar pattern emerged in the contrasting paths taken by China, the second great territorial power of the modern world, and the commercial enclaves around her perimeter that followed the example of Japan. Both communist superpowers were vast inland empires held together by centralized authoritarian governments; both were isolated from the oceanic economy and remained economically underdeveloped despite massive attempts by the state to bring about industrialization; and finally in both states a large proportion of the national wealth was devoted to maintaining large military establishments and modern arsenals that eventually included nuclear weapons.

The existence of nuclear weapons, together with the independent development of missiles, represented the major impact of the Second World War on the postwar period, providing the nuclear

powers with the capacity to wreak unlimited destruction anywhere
on the globe. Thus far this doomsday potential has had an inhibit-
ing effect on the superpowers, compelling them to avoid direct
military conflict. At the same time, however, the confrontation
between the two systems has led to a number of conventionally-
armed wars in the Third World, as the rival powers have sought
to extend their influence and control overseas, through direct
and indirect participation in local political struggles. Moreover in
order to maintain deterrence, the United States and the Soviet
Union have engaged in a long and expensive nuclear arms race,
which paradoxically appears to have brought about the sudden
end of their confrontation, by bankrupting the backward Soviet
economy. In this sense the recent western victory in the Cold War
has followed the familiar pattern once again, having been achieved
primarily through the superior ability of the American economy to
withstand the costs of military production, even if no weapons
were actually loosed between the main combatants.

The fact that no expert predicted the Soviet collapse, or the
reversal of course that would be undertaken by President Mikhail
Gorbachev to deal with it, should serve as a stern reminder of the
limits of all attempts to peer into the future. Still it is probably safe
to say that both the Soviets and their former satellites face a
difficult road ahead in seeking a conversion to democratic government and a market economy, if only because the United States is
no longer in an economic position to provide massive aid to its
defeated enemies, or to the many other nations that are struggling
to follow the western path of development. But a more fundamental difficulty may arise simply from the attempt to follow that
path far from the water's edge, for the geographic conditions that
shaped modern development still continue to exert their influence,
despite all advances in transportation and communication, and the
basic differences and conflicts between oceanic and territorial
societies will therefore probably persist into the foreseeable future.

Chronology

This chronology is intended to help readers date some of the most important political events surveyed in *The Emergence of the Modern European World*.

Additional chronological information is available in several easily found sources. Among the best are William L. Langer, *An Encyclopedia of World History, Ancient, Medieval, and Modern Chronologically Arranged*, 5th edn revised and enlarged (Boston, Houghton Mifflin, 1982); Neville Williams, *Chronology of the Expanding World 1492 to 1762* (London, Barrie and Rockliff, 1969); Neville Williams, *Chronology of the Modern World 1763–1965*, revised edn (Harmondsworth, Penguin, 1975). Bertold Spuler, ed., *Rulers and Governments of the World*, vol. 2, *1492 to 1929* and vol. 3, *1930 to 1975* (London, Bowder, 1977) lists monarchs, presidents, prime ministers, premiers and cabinets, recording internal changes during the life of a ministry. Bruce Wetterau has produced a superb chronological guide to technology, science, the arts, religion, philosophy, education, exploration, architecture, sports and entertainment in *The New York Public Library Book of Chronologies* (New York, Prentice Hall, 1990).

Rulers of Europe

BRITISH MONARCHS
House of Stuart (Stewart)
James I, 1603–25
Charles I, 1625–49

Commonwealth (powers exercised by Parliament), 1649–53
The Protectorate (Oliver Cromwell, 1653–8; Richard Cromwell, 1658–9)
Commonwealth, 1659–60
Charles II, 1660–85
James II, 1685–8.
William III and Mary II, 1689–1702 (Mary died, 1694)
Anne, 1702–14 (England and Scotland joined to form Great Britain, May 1, 1707)

House of Hanover

George I, 1714–27
George II, 1727–60
George III, 1760–1820 (Ireland joined Great Britain to form the United Kingdom, January 1, 1801)
George IV, 1820–30
William IV, 1830–7

House of Saxe-Coburg-Gotha (called House of Windsor from July 17, 1917)

Victoria, 1837–1901
Edward VII, 1901–10
George V, 1910–36
Edward VIII, 1936
George VI, 1936–52
Elizabeth II, 1952–

PRIME MINISTERS OF ENGLAND, GREAT BRITAIN
AND THE UNITED KINGDOM

Date indicates the date the cabinet was formed. For changes in the personnel of each cabinet during its life, consult the list of cabinets in the appropriate volume of the *Oxford History of England* (see Suggestions for Further Reading for a list of these).

Robert Walpole, April, 1721
Earl of Wilmington, February, 1742

Henry Pelham, July, 1743
Duke of Newcastle, March, 1754
William Pitt (Earl of Chatham), November, 1756
Duke of Newcastle, June, 1757
Earl of Bute, 1762
George Grenville, 1763
Marquis of Rockingham, 1765
Earl of Chatham, 1766
Lord North, 1770
Marquis of Rockingham, March, 1782
Earl of Shelburne, July, 1782
Duke of Portland, April, 1783 (Fox–North Coalition)
William Pitt, December, 1783
Henry Addington, February, 1801
William Pitt, 1804
Lord Grenville, 1806
Duke of Portland, 1807
Spencer Perceval, 1809
Earl of Liverpool, June, 1812
George Canning, April, 1827
Viscount Goderich, August, 1827
Duke of Wellington, January, 1828
Earl Grey, November, 1830
Viscount Melbourne, July, 1834
Sir Robert Peel, December, 1834
Viscount Melbourne, April, 1835
Sir Robert Peel, September, 1841
Lord John Russell, July, 1846
Earl of Derby, February, 1852
Earl of Aberdeen, December, 1852
Viscount Palmerston, February, 1855
Earl of Derby, February, 1858
Viscount Palmerston, June, 1859
Earl (previously Lord John) Russell, October, 1865
Lord Derby, 1866
Benjamin Disraeli, February, 1868
W. E. Gladstone, December, 1868
Benjamin Disraeli, February, 1874
W. E. Gladstone, April, 1880

Marquess of Salisbury, June, 1885
W. E. Gladstone, February, 1886
Marquess of Salisbury, August, 1886
W. E. Gladstone, August, 1892
Earl of Rosebery, March, 1894
Marquess of Salisbury, June, 1895
A. J. Balfour, July, 1902
Sir Henry Campbell-Bannerman, December, 1905
H. H. Asquith, April, 1908
H. H. Asquith, May, 1915
David Lloyd George, December 1916
David Lloyd George, November, 1919
Andrew Bonar Law, October, 1922
Stanley Baldwin, May, 1923
J. Ramsay MacDonald, January, 1924
Stanley Baldwin, November, 1924
J. Ramsay MacDonald, June, 1929
J. Ramsay MacDonald, August, 1931
J. Ramsay MacDonald, November, 1931
Stanley Baldwin, June, 1935
Neville Chamberlain, May, 1937
Neville Chamberlain, September, 1939
Winston S. Churchill, May, 1940
Winston S. Churchill, May, 1945
Clement Attlee, July, 1945

TSARS OF RUSSIA, 1613–1917 (HOUSE OF ROMANOV)

Michael III, 1613–45
Alexis, 1645–76
Fyodor III, 1676–82
Peter I ("the Great"), 1682–1725 (Ivan V was nominally co-
    ruler 1682–96)
Catherine I, 1725–7
Peter II, 1727–30
Anna, 1730–40
Ivan VI, 1740–1
Elizabeth, 1741–62
Peter III, 1762 (acceded to the throne January 5, deposed July
    10, died July 17, 1762)

Catherine II, 1762–96
Paul, 1796–1801
Alexander I, 1801–25
Nicholas I, 1825–55
Alexander II, 1855–81
Alexander III, 1881–94
Nicholas II, 1894–1917

AUSTRIA, 1612–1918 (HOUSE OF HABSBURG)

Matthias, 1612–19
Ferdinand II, 1619–37
Ferdinand III, 1637–57
Leopold I, 1658–1705
Joseph I, 1705–11
Charles III, 1711–40
Maria Theresa, 1740–80
Joseph II, 1780–90
Leopold II, 1790–2
Francis II, 1792–1835
Ferdinand I, 1835–48
Franz-Joseph, 1848–1916
Charles, 1916–18

BRANDENBURG-PRUSSIA AND GERMANY

The Electors of Brandenburg were also Dukes of Prussia, August 18, 1618 until January 18, 1701.

Kings of Prussia (House of Hohenzollern)

Frederick I, 1701–13 (Elector of Brandenburg since 1688)
Frederick William I, 1713–40
Frederick II ("the Great"), 1740–86
Frederick William II, 1786–97
Frederick William III, 1797–1840
Frederick William IV, 1840–61
William I, 1861–88 (Kaiser of a united Germany from January 18, 1871)
Frederick III, 1888

William II, 1888–1918 (died June 4, 1941)
(Germany became a republic on November 9, 1918)

Chancellors of the German Empire, 1871–1945

Otto von Bismarck, 1871–90
Count Caprivi, 1890–4
Prince Hohenlohe-Schillingsfürst, 1894–1900
Prince Bulow, 1900–9
Theobald von Bethmann-Hollweg, 1909–17
Georg Michaelis, 1917
Count Hertling, 1917–18
Prince Max of Baden, 1918

Chancellors of the Weimar Republic

(People's Representatives, 1918–19)
Philipp Scheidemann (prime minister), 1919
Gustav Bauer (prime minister), 1919–20
Hermann Müller, 1920
Konstantin Fehrenbach, 1920–1
Josef Wirth, 1921–2
Wilhelm Cuno, 1922–3
Gustav Stresemann, 1923
Wilhelm Marx, 1923–4
Hans Luther, 1925–6
Wilhelm Marx, 1926–8
Hermann Müller, 1928–30
Heinrich Brüning, 1930–2
Franz von Papen, 1932
Kurt von Schleicher, 1932–3

The Nazi Regime

Adolf Hitler, 1933–45
Caretaker government, 1945

Postwar Rule

Occupation government, 1945–9
Konrad Adenauer (German Federal Republic), 1949–63

SPAIN, 1556—1868

House of Habsburg

Philip II, 1556–98
Philip III, 1598–1621
Philip IV, 1621–65
Charles II, 1665–1700

House of Bourbon

Philip V, 1700–24 (grandson of Louis XIV of France)
Louis, 1724
Philip V, 1724–46 (second time)
Ferdinand VI, 1746–59
Charles III, 1759–88
Charles IV, 1788–1808
Ferdinand VII, 1808–33
(Joseph Bonaparte, brother of Emperor Napoleon, 1808–13)
Isabella II, 1833–68
(Spain became a republic on September 30, 1868)
Alfonso XII, 1875–85
Maria de las Mercedes, 1885–6
Alfonso XIII, 1886–1931
(Spain was a republic, 1931–75)
Juan Carlos 1975–

FRANCE, 1589—1792

House of Bourbon

Henri IV, 1589–1610
Louis XIII, 1610–43
Louis XIV, 1643–1715
Louis XV, 1715–74
Louis XVI, 1774–92 (deposed, August 10, 1792; executed, January 21, 1793)

Government during the French Revolution and under Napoleon

Convention, September 21, 1792
Directorate, October 26, 1795

Consulate, November 9, 1799
Empire: Napoleon I (previously First Consul), May 18, 1804–
April 11, 1814 and March 1, 1815–June 22, 1815

House of Bourbon

Louis XVIII, April 11, 1814–24 (reign interrupted by return of
Napoleon, March–July, 1815)
Charles X, 1824–30 (abdicated August 2, 1830)

House of Orléans

Louis–Philippe, August 8, 1830–February 24, 1848 (abdicated)

The Second Republic, 1848–52

Heads of State: Between March and December, 1848, France
was headed by Philippe J. B. Buchez, and after a five-day
military dictatorship in June, by Eugène Cavaignac
President and Emperor: Louis Napoleon Bonaparte, December
10, 1848–December 2, 1852, when he became Emperor
Napoleon III
The Second Empire, 1852–70: Napoleon III (until September 4,
1870, when a republic was declared)

The Dawn of the Modern World

THE THIRTY YEARS WAR

The Bohemian Period, 1618–25

Defenestration of Prague, May 23, 1618
Battle of the White Mountain, November 8, 1620

Danish Period, 1625–9

Edict of Restitution, March 29, 1629
Treaty of Lübeck, May 22, 1629

Swedish Period, 1630–5

Battle of Lützen, November 16, 1632
Treaty of Prague, May 30, 1635

The Swedish–French Period, 1635–48

Treaties of Westphalia, October 24, 1648

BOURBON FRANCE THROUGH THE REIGN OF
LOUIS XIV

Henry IV

Edict of Nantes, April 13, 1598

Louis XIII

Administration of Richelieu, 1624–42
France participated in the Thirty Years War, 1631–48

Louis XIV

The Fronde, 1648–53
Treaty of the Pyrenees, 1659
Death of Mazarin, 1661
Jean Colbert was controller general of finances, 1663–83; the
  Marquis de Louvois was minister of war, 1666–91
War of Devolution, 1667–8
War with Holland, 1672–8
Treaties of Nijmegen, 1678–9
Revocation of the Edict of Nantes, October 18, 1685
War of the League of Augsburg, 1688–97 (Treaty of Ryswick,
  September 30, 1697)
War of the Spanish Succession, 1701–14
  Battle of Blenheim, August 13, 1704
  Battle at Ramillies, May 23, 1706
  Battle of Malplaquet, September 11, 1709
  Treaty of Utrecht, April 11, 1713

ENGLAND 1603–1714

Charles I

Five Knights' Case, November, 1627
Petition of Right, 1628
First Ship Money writs issued, October, 1634
Scottish National Covenant, February 27, 1638
Short Parliament, April 13–May 5, 1640

The English Civil War to the Revolution of 1689

Long Parliament met November 3, 1640
Root and Branch Petition, December 11, 1640

Parliament issued a Grand Remonstrance, December, 1641

Parliament issued Nineteen Propositions, June 2, 1642

Battle of Edgehill, October 23, 1642

Battle of Newbury, September 20, 1643

After Parliament agreed to the Solemn League and Covenant, Scots allied with Parliament, September 25, 1643

Battle of Marston Moor, July 2, 1644

Charles I rejected the Uxbridge Propositions, 1645

Independent faction gained control in the House of Commons; Parliament's army is remodeled as the New Model Army, 1645

Battle of Naseby, June 14, 1645

General Leslie defeated royalist partisans in Scotland, September 13, 1645

Battle of Stow-in-the-Wold ended the first phase of the war, March 26, 1646

Charles I fled to Scotland (May 5, 1646), but the Scots turned the king over to Parliament, January 30, 1647

Charles consented to the Newcastle Proposition, May 31, 1647

New Model Army seized Charles, June 4, 1647

Agreement of the People issued, 1647

Charles escaped (November, 1647) and allied with the Scots, December 26, 1647

Battle of Preston, August 17–19, 1648

Pride's Purge, December 6–7, 1648

Charles I executed, January 30, 1649; England declared a Commonwealth, May 19, 1649

Cromwell suppressed Irish revolt; sacked Drogheda (September 11) and Wexford, October 11, 1649

Cromwell defeated Charles II at Worcester, September 3, 1651

Instrument of Government created a Protectorate, December 16, 1653

Oliver Cromwell died, September 3, 1658

Richard Cromwell resigned; Commonwealth reestablished, May 25, 1659

Coronation of Charles II, April 23, 1660

Cavalier Parliament met, May 8, 1661 (dissolved January 24, 1679)

Clarendon Code passed

    Corporation Act, November, 1661

Act of Uniformity, August, 1662
Conventicle Act, May, 1664
Five Mile Act, October, 1665
Second Dutch War, 1665–7 (concluded by the Treaties of Breda, July 21, 1667)
Treaty of Dover, May, 1670
The Popish Plot, September 1678
Exclusion Crisis, 1679–81
Accession of James II, February 6, 1685
Birth of a son to James, June 10, 1688
William of Orange landed at Torbay, November 5, 1688
James II escaped to France, December 22, 1688
Convention Parliament, January 22, 1689–January 27, 1690
Declaration of Rights, February 13, 1689
Mutiny Act passed, March, 1689
Toleration Act, May 24, 1689

Reign of William III and Mary II

War against France began May 7, 1689 (concluded by the Treaty of Ryswick, September 20, 1697)
Bank of England established, July 27, 1694
Queen Mary died, December 28, 1694
Act of Settlement, June 12, 1701
William died (March 8, 1702), succeeded by the last of the Stuarts, Anne (died August 1, 1714)

The Eighteenth Century

THE NEW MONARCHIES

Russia under Peter I

Wars against the Turks (1695–6), resulting in the capture of Azov, July 28, 1696 (peace concluded, July 4, 1700)
Peter traveled to western Europe, March 21, 1697–September, 1698
Great Northern War, May, 1700–21
  Battle of Poltava, July 8, 1709
  Treaty of Nystadt, August 30, 1721
Foundations of St Petersburg laid, June, 1703

First budget in Russia, January 27, 1710
War with Turkey, November 30, 1710–August 1, 1711
Council of Boyars replaced by a Senate, 1711
Government bureaux, called Colleges, created, 1718

Prussia

Frederick III elector recognized as King Frederick I, January 18, 1701
Frederick William I
   War of the Polish Succession, 1733–5
Frederick II
   War of Austrian Succession, 1740–8
   Seven Years War, 1756–63 (Battle of Rossbach, November 5, 1757)
   War of the Bavarian Succession, 1778–9

THE AMERICAN REVOLUTION

British Parliament declared Massachusetts to be in revolt against the Crown, February 9, 1775
First skirmishes at Lexington and Concord, April 19, 1775
Battle of Bunker Hill, June 17, 1775
British evacuated Boston, March 17, 1776
Congress proclaimed the Declaration of Independence, July 4, 1776
British occupied New York City, September 15, 1776
British campaign in New England began with attack at Fort Ticonderoga (July, 1777) but failed with General Burgoyne's surrender, October 17, 1777
France entered the war (treaty signed February 6, 1778)
British surrendered at Yorktown, October 19, 1781
Treaty of Paris signed, September 3, 1783

The French Revolution

THE IMPASSE

Assembly of nobles convened in Versailles, February 22, 1787
Louis agreed to call the Estates General, November 20, 1787

Estates General met May 5, 1789

Third Estate demanded that the Estates meet as a single body; debate about voting in the Estates General

Third Estate voted to constitute itself as a National Assembly, June 17, 1789; the king closed the meeting hall for repairs; Tennis Court Oath, June 20, 1789

The first two estates joined the new National Assembly, June 27, 1789

THE CONSTITUTIONAL MONARCHY

Attack on the Bastille, July 14, 1789

The Great Fear, summer, 1789

Abolition of the vestiges of feudalism, August 4, 1789

Declaration of the Rights of Man, August 27, 1789

March on Versailles, October 5, 1789; Louis accompanied the marchers back to Paris; the National Assembly followed Louis to Paris

Emigration of nobles increased during October, 1789

Nationalization of Church property, November 2, 1789

Administrative reform abolished the old provinces, replacing them with 83 smaller departments, November 12, 1789

Reform of finances: paper currency (assignats) issued, December 21, 1789

Civil Constitution of the Clergy, July 12, 1790

Louis attempted to flee the country, June 20, 1791

Elections (September) and a new Legislative Assembly met on October 1, 1791

THE REVOLUTIONARY REPUBLIC

France declared war on Austria (April 20), and Prussia, July 8, 1792

Duke of Brunswick's Manifesto, July 25, 1792

Louis stripped of all authority and imprisoned August 10–13, 1792

The September Massacres in Paris, September 2–7, 1792

Victory at Valmy stopped the advance of foreign armies, September 20, 1792

French National Convention met September 21, 1792

Monarchy abolished by the new Convention, September 21; French Republic proclaimed, September 22, 1792

Louis executed, January 21, 1793

War declared against Great Britain and Holland, February 1, 1793; against Spain, March 7, 1793

Committee of Public Safety established, April 6, 1793

Reign of Terror, 1793–4

Final overthrow of the Girondins, June 2, 1793

Levée en masse, August 23, 1793

Law of Suspects, September 17, 1793

Law of the Maximum, September 28, 1793

Law of June 10, 1794 permitted mass executions

Fall of Robespierre, July 27 (9 Thermidor); executed July 28, 28, 1794

French military victories, spring, 1795: Flanders ceded to France; the Batavian Republic, a French puppet regime, installed in Holland

The White Terror, May 20–June, 1795

THE DIRECTORY

The constitution of 1795 (August 22) created a government known as the Directory (1795–9)

General Napoleon Bonaparte stopped a threatening popular demonstration with a "whiff of grapeshot," October 5, 1795

Revolts in the Vendée and Brittany finally put down, March, 1796

Two French armies invaded Germany, 1796

General Bonaparte's Italian campaign, 1796–7 (Preliminary Peace of Leoben, April 18, 1797; Treaty of Campo Formio, October 17, 1797)

Napoleon's Egyptian expedition 1798–9

Alliance between Great Britain and Russia (December 24, 1798) leads to the War of the Second Coalition against France

French military reverses during 1799 set the stage for Napoleon's *coup d'état* of Brumaire, November 9, 1799

THE CONSULATE

A new government formed as the Consulate, 1799–1804

New constitution, December 24, 1799

A new campaign against Austria began in spring, 1800; French victories produced the Treaty of Lunéville, February 9, 1801

Administrative reform: Act of February 17, 1800 created new departments

Concordat between French and the Papacy, July 15, 1801–April 8, 1802

Treaty of Amiens (March 27, 1802) brought a temporary peace in the war between France and Britain (war renewed, May 16, 1803)

Napoleon was recognized as Consul for life, August 2, 1802

Napoleon assembled troops in Boulogne, possibly to invade England, 1803

Napoleon raised tariffs, 1803

THE EMPIRE

Napoleon proclaimed Emperor on May 18, 1804; consecrated as Emperor Napoleon I by Pope Pius VII on December 2, 1804

Napoleon's codification of French law
    Civil Code, 1804
    Code of Civil Procedure, 1806
    Commercial Code, 1807
    Criminal Code, 1808
    Penal Code, 1810

The Third Coalition formed against France (1805), consisting of Britain, Austria, Russia and Sweden (Spain allied with France)

Napoleon defeated the Austrians at the Battle of Ulm, October 17, 1805

Battle of Trafalgar: the British admiral, Nelson, destroyed the combined French and Spanish fleets, October 21, 1805

Battle of Austerlitz (also called the Battle of the Three Emperors), December 2, 1805: Napoleon defeated the combined Austrian and Russian armies, forcing the Austrians to accept a truce and the Russians to retreat; Austrian capitulation was formally recognized at the Treaty of Pressburg, December 26, 1805

The Confederation of the Rhine (July 12, 1805) made most of Germany, except Prussia, Austria and Brunswick, a French protectorate. The death blow to the Holy Roman Empire was delivered when Francis II formally relinquished its crown to become Austrian Emperor

Prussia went to war with France but was defeated decisively in the Battles of Jena and Auerstädt, October 14, 1806

Napoleon proclaimed the Berlin Decree (November 21, 1806), which declared Continental ports closed to British trade, (the Continental System, reiterated in the Milan Decree, December 17, 1807)

After being defeated by the French at the Battle of Friedland (June 14, 1807), the Russians signed the Treaty of Tilsit, July 7–9, 1807. Prussia and France also joined this effort to settle differences and further agreed to the Treaty of Königsberg, July 12, 1807

Napoleon invaded Spain (March, 1808), substituting his brother, Joseph, for the previous ruler, but this occasioned a rebellion by the Spaniards. Britain sent an army, commanded by Sir Arthur Wellesley (later titled as the Duke of Wellington) to fight the French in Portugal and Spain, 1808

Austria renewed the war with Napoleon in April, 1809, but was defeated at the Battle of Wagram (July 5–6, 1809), and agreed to the Treaty of Schönbrunn on October 14, 1809

The marriage of Archduchess Marie Louise, daughter of the Austrian Emperor, and Napoleon (April, 1810) was supposed to seal the reconciliation of the two powers

War between France and Russia, 1812

  Battle of Borodino, September 7, 1812

  Moscow was burned, September 15–19, 1812

  Retreat from Moscow, October 19, 1812

The Wars of Liberation

  Treaty of Toeplitz pledged joint Russian, Prussian and Austrian action to defeat France, September 9, 1813

  Battle of Leipzig, October 16–19, 1813: Napoleon's army

was defeated and French influence in Germany was dealt a mortal blow

French forces suffered a series of defeats in Spain (June–October, 1813) and were driven back to their side of the Pyrenees

The Allies entered Paris, March 31, 1814

Napoleon abdicated unconditionally (April 11, 1814) and went to live on the island of Elba, May, 1814

Napoleon left Elba and landed in France, March 1, 1815

French troops rallied to their former leader, and Napoleon entered Paris on March 20, 1815

The Hundred Days' rule was brought to an end by Napoleon's defeat at the Battle of Waterloo (June 18) and his second abdication, June 22, 1815

Napoleon was exiled to the island of St Helena, where he remained until he died on May 5, 1821

The Concert of Europe

After the Allies took Paris (March 31, 1814), they invited Louis XVIII (the oldest surviving brother of Louis XVI) to return to rule France

The First Treaty of Paris, May 30, 1814

The Congress of Vienna, September, 1814 to June, 1815 (Act of the Congress of Vienna, June 8, 1815)

Return of Louis XVIII to Paris, July 7, 1815

The Holy Alliance, September 26, 1815

The Second Peace of Paris (November 20, 1815) reallocated territory; at the same time the Allies renewed the Quadruple Alliance to meet in the future to settle differences and to supply soldiers for an army to enforce the Paris Peace Treaty

Congress of Aix-la-Chapelle (September, 1818) was the first of the post-Vienna Congresses

Revolutionary uprisings in Naples (July 2, 1820), Portugal (August 24, 1820) and Piedmont (March 10, 1821)

Congress of Troppau, October 23, 1820

Congress of Laibach, January 12–May 12, 1821

Greek War of Independence to overthrow Turkish rule began

1821 and lasted until Greece was granted full independence (Treaty of Adrianople, 1829)

Congress of Verona, October, 1822

Rebellion in Spain provided an opportunity for Spain's colonies in the Western Hemisphere to rebel and establish national independence

Decembrist Revolt in Russia, 1825

The Revolutions of 1830–1

  France, July 27–9, 1830

  Belgium, August 25, 1830

  Revolts in Saxony, Hesse and Brunswick, September, 1830

  Poland, October 29, 1830

  Revolutionary outbreaks in Modena, Parma and the Papal States, February, 1831

Postwar England

  Corn Laws, 1815

  Spa Fields Riot, December 2, 1816

  Coercion Acts, March, 1817

  Peterloo Massacre, August 16, 1819

  Six Acts, December, 1819

  Cato Street Conspiracy, February 23, 1820

  Repeal of the Combination Acts, June 21, 1824

  Trade Union Law, July 6, 1825

  Test Act repealed, May 9, 1828

  New Corn Law, July 15, 1828

  First Reform Bill fails in the committee stage, March 22, 1831

  Second Reform Bill passes the House of Commons, but does not pass the House of Lords, September 21, 1831

  Third Reform Bill passed to become the First Reform Act, March 23, 1832

  Abolition of slavery in the colonies, August 23, 1833

  Factory Act, August 19, 1833

  Grand National Consolidated Trades Union, January, 1834

  The New Poor Law passed, August 14, 1834

  The Municipal Corporations Act, September 9, 1835

  Workingmen's Association formed, 1836

  Anti-Corn Law League, 1839

  Chartist riots in Birmingham, Newport and elsewhere, July–

November, 1839; second National Convention of Char-
tists, April 12–May 12, 1842
Anti-Corn Law agitation, 1845–6
Repeal of the Corn Laws, June 6, 1846
Crimean War (1854–6), concluded at the Congress of Paris,
February 25–March 30, 1856
The American Civil War
South Carolina seceded from the Union, December 20, 1860
Conferederates fired on Fort Sumter and the war began, April
2, 1861
Emancipation Proclamation issued, January 1, 1863
Battle of Gettysburg, July 1–3, 1863
Surrender of Vicksburg, July 4, 1863
General Lee surrendered to General Grant, April 9, 1865
President Lincoln assassinated, April 14, 1865

The Demographic Revolution

THE REVOLUTIONS OF 1848

France

Revolt in Paris, February 22–4, 1848
Louis-Philippe abdicated; a republican provisional government
was proclaimed under Alphonse de Lamartine, February 24,
1848
National Workshops based on Louis Blanc's proposals were
established, February 26, 1848
Elections to the National Assembly, April 23, 1848
Insurrection of June 23–6, 1848
New constitution, November 4, 1848
Presidential elections, December 10, 1848
Louis Napoleon Bonaparte sworn in as President of the French
Republic, December 20, 1848

The Habsburg Dominions

Louis Kossuth denounced Hungary's place in the current governmental arrangement, March 3, 1848

Hungarian Table of Deputies adopted the March Laws, which were, in effect, a constitution, March 15, 1848

The Emperor accepted the March Laws and made further concessions during April, which gave Hungary much autonomy

Demonstrations in Vienna, March 12–13, 1848

Prince Metternich resigned, March 13, 1848

Demonstrations in Milan (18–23, 1848) March started a revolution in Lombardy

Piedmont responded to Milanese request for aid by declaring war on Austria, March 22, 1848

Austrian control over Lombardy confirmed by the Battle of Custozza, July 24, 1848

Venetians proclaimed a Republic (March 22). After a siege and bombardment (July 20–April 28, 1848), the Austrians retook the city

Czechs obtained a concession for a constituent assembly for Bohemia, April 25, 1848

The first Pan-Slav Congress met in Prague, June, 1848

Prague bombarded, June 17, 1848

Hungary was invaded (September 17) but the Hungarians repulsed the attack and in response invaded Austria, approaching Vienna, October 3, 1848

Rebellion in Vienna (October 6) was suppressed by bombarding the city into submission, October 31, 1848

Emperor Ferdinand abdicated (December 2, 1848) in favor of Franz Joseph I (1848–1916)

Joined by Russian forces, the Austrians defeated the Hungarians, August, 1849

The Revolution in Germany

The Berlin "March Days" began March 15, 1848

The Frankfurt National Assembly met, May 18, 1848

New constitution in Prussia, December, 1848

A federal state created by the Frankfurt Constitution, March 27, 1849

The old Germanic Confederation restored at the Dresden Conference, December, 1850–March, 1851

Mazzini and the Republic of Rome

Insurrection in Rome began November 16, 1848; Pope Pius fled the city, November 25, 1848

Republic of Rome proclaimed, February 9, 1849

French troops took Rome after a lengthy siege, July 2, 1849

THE UNIFICATION OF ITALY

Count Camillio Benso di Cavour became Premier of Piedmont, November 4, 1852

Piedmont entered the Crimean War on the side of England and France, January 26, 1855

Cavour and Napoleon III met secretly at Plombières (July 20, 1858) and signed the Treaty of Plombières on December 10, 1858

Austrians invaded Piedmont (April 29, 1859) and were defeated at the Battles of Magenta and Solferino

Preliminary peace between France and Austria concluded at Villafranca on July 11 and confirmed on November 10, 1859 by the Treaty of Zurich

Plebiscites in Parma, Modena, Tuscany, Emilia and Romagna in favor of union with Piedmont, March 11–15, 1860

Giuseppe Garibaldi and the Redshirts sailed from Genoa (May 5), landed on Sicily (May 11) and took Palermo, May 27, 1860; Garibaldi took Naples September 7, 1860; Naples and Sicily voted to join northern Italy, October 21–2, 1860

Piedmontese soldiers entered the Papal States, September 10, 1860

An Italian Parliament proclaimed the Kingdom of Italy, March 17, 1861

Venice conceded to Italy, July 3, 1866

Rome annexed to Italy after a plebiscite, October 2, 1870

THE UNIFICATION OF GERMANY

Otto von Bismarck appointed Prussian Premier, September 22, 1862

King Frederick VII of Denmark issued a proclamation annexing Schleswig to Denmark, March 30, 1863

Following the vote of the Germanic Confederation (October 1, 1863) to take federal action against Denmark, Austria joined Prussia in an alliance, and both sent an ultimatum to Denmark, January 16, 1864; Austrian and Prussian troops entered Schleswig, February 1, 1864

The London Conference (April 25–June, 1864) failed, and war resumed, June 26; in the Peace of Vienna (October 30), Denmark gave Schleswig, Holstein and Lauenburg to Austria and Prussia

The Seven Weeks War (June–August, 1866) was concluded by the Treaty of Prague, August 23, 1866

North German Confederation created with Prussian leadership, April 16, 1867

The Franco-Prussian War began, July 19, 1870

William I proclaimed Emperor of Germany, January 18, 1871

FRANCE

Louis Napoleon Bonaparte made Emperor (Napoleon III), December 2, 1852; his powers were extended December 25, 1852, but modified in favor of the legislature, November 24, 1860, and November 4, 1861

Napoleon III capitulated at Sedan, September 2, 1870; Prussian armies besieged Paris, September 19, 1870; Paris capitulated, January 28, 1871; the Franco-Prussian War was ended by the Peace of Frankfurt, May 10, 1871

National Assembly met at Bordeaux, February 13, 1871

The Paris Commune (March–May, 1871), fell in the Bloody Week, May 21–8

L. A. Thiers elected President, August 31, 1871

Marshal MacMahon elected President, May 24, 1873

The Constitution of 1875 created the Third French Republic, January 30, February 24, and July 16, 1875

Jules Grévy elected President, January 30, 1879

Primary education law, March 19, 1882

Divorce legally re-established, July 27, 1884

Trade Union Act, July 27, 1884

Since 1886, General Georges Boulanger led political attacks on the government, but his movement failed when he refused to seize power on January 27, 1889

The trial of corrupt practices during the construction of the Panama Canal, which began on March 8, was concluded on March 21, but the sentences were set aside on June 15, 1893

The Dreyfus Affair, 1894–1906

Church and state legally separated, December 9, 1905

BISMARCKIAN GERMANY

The Kulturkampf, 1871–83

Anti-socialist Law, October 19, 1878

Sickness Insurance Law, May, 1883

Accident Insurance Law, June, 1884

Old Age and Invalid Insurance Law, May, 1889

Bismarckian Foreign Policy

    Three Emperors' League, June, 1873

    Alliance between Germany and Austria, October 7, 1879

    The Three Emperors' Alliance, June 18, 1881

    The Triple Alliance, May 20, 1882 (renewed February 20, 1887)

    Secret Russian–German Treaty, June 18, 1887

Bismarck dismissed, March 18, 1890

INTERNATIONAL RELATIONS BEFORE THE FIRST WORLD WAR 1890–1914

Germany decided not to renew the Reinsurance Treaty with Russia, March, 1890

France and Russia became allies by the August Convention, 1891

First Hague Peace Conference, May 18–July 29, 1899 (Second Hague Peace Conference, June 15–October 18, 1906)

Anglo-Japanese alliance, January 30, 1902

The Russo-Japanese War (February 4, 1904), concluded by the Treaty of Portsmouth, September 5, 1905

Anglo-French Entente, April 8, 1904

First Moroccan crisis (March 31, 1905) settled by the Algeciras
Conference, January 16–April 7, 1906

HMS *Dreadnought* launched, February 10, 1906; Germany revised its naval construction policy, May, 1906

Triple Entente, August 31, 1907

Austria annexed Bosnia and Herzegovina, October 6, 1908

Second Moroccan crisis, June–November, 1911

The First Balkan War (October 18, 1912) concluded by the
Treaty of London, May 30, 1913

The Second Balkan War (June 29–July 30, 1913), concluded by
the Treaty of Bucharest, August 10, 1914

The First World War

Assassination of Archduke Franz Ferdinand at Sarajevo, June
28, 1914

Austrian ultimatum given to Serbia, July 23, 1914

Austria declared war on Serbia, July 28, 1914

Germany declared war on Russia, August 1, 1914

Germany declared war on France, August 3, 1914

Britain declared war on Germany, August 4, 1914

Austria declared war on Russia, August 6, 1914

Japan declared war on Germany, August 23, 1914

Germany invaded Belgium, August 4, 1914

Germans occupied Brussels, August 20, 1914

Russian invasion of East Prussia was turned back by the Battle
of Tannenberg, August 26–30, 1914

Battle of the Marne, September 5–12, 1914

After a German thrust to the English Channel, their attempt to
break the Allied line at the first battle of Ypres (October
30–November 24, 1914) failed

German submarine warfare resulted in the sinking of the *Lusitania* (May 7, 1915)

Allied autumn offensive (September 22–November 6, 1915)
yielded little change on the Western Front

Battle of Verdun began, February 21, 1916

Battle of Jutland, May 31–June 1, 1916

General Brusilov opened Russian offensive, June 4, 1916

Battle of the Somme began, July, 1916

Italy declared war on Germany, August 28, 1916

United States of America declared war on Germany, April 6, 1917

British and Canadian forces attacked at the Battle of Arras, April 9–May 4, 1917

French army attacked the Hindenburg Line, April 16–May, 1917

The Third Battle of Ypres, July 31–November 10, 1917

Woodrow Wilson stated his Fourteen Points, January 8, 1918

Treaty of Brest-Litovsk, March 3, 1918

A German offensive in the West (begun March 21) was stopped at the Second Battle of the Marne, July 15–August 7, 1918

Allied counteroffensive against Germany, September 26–October 15, 1918

General Ludendorff demanded that his government ask for an armistice, September 29, 1918; German and Austrian governments appealed to President Wilson for an armistice based on his Fourteen Points, October 4, 1918

Mutiny in the Germany navy began in Kiel (November 3, 1918) and spread to other ports in northwestern Germany

Revolution in Munich, November 7–8, 1918

Kaiser William II abdicated, November 9, 1918

An armistice stopping the war on the Western Front took effect at 11 a.m. on November 11, 1918

THE PEACE

Paris Peace Conference opened, January 18, 1919

Versailles Treaty signed, June 28, 1919

Treaty of St Germain, September 10, 1919

Treaty of Trianon, June 4, 1920

Treaty of Sèvres, August 20, 1920

The Russian Revolution and the Soviet Union

Rasputin assassinated, December 30, 1916

Demonstration in St Petersburg (March 8, 1917) led to strikes and riots

Troops mutinied in St Petersburg, March 10, 1917

A provisional government was created, March 12, 1917

Tsar Nicholas II abdicated in favor of his brother, Michael, who declined in favor of the provisional government, March 15, 1917

Lenin arrived in St Petersburg (April 16, 1917), and issued his April theses

Bolsheviks attempted a *coup d'etat* in St Petersburg, (July 16–18), but it failed

Alexander Kerensky succeeded Prince Lvov as head of the government, July 22, 1917

General Lavr Kornilov attempted to overthrow the government, September 9–14, 1917

Kerensky proclaimed a Russian Republic, September 15, 1917

Successful Bolshevik revolution in St Petersburg, November 6, 1917

Lenin became chairman of the Council of People's Commissars, November 8, 1917

Control of some factories given to workmen, November 28, 1917

Delegates from Russia and Germany signed an armistice at Brest-Litvosk, December 5, 1917

Church property was confiscated by the government, December 17, 1917

Civil War, 1918–20

The Tsar's debt was repudiated, January 28, 1918

Treaty of Brest-Litovsk signed, March 3, 1918

Law of June 28, 1918 nationalized larger factories

Soviet constitution promulgated, July 19, 1918

Tsar Nicholas II, his wife and their children were executed, July 16, 1918

War with Poland (April 25–October 12, 1920), was concluded by the Treaty of Riga, March 18, 1921

Mutiny of the Kronstadt sailors, February 23–March 17, 1921

Lenin's New Economic Policy, March 17, 1921

Treaty of Rapallo between the USSR and Germany, April 16, 1922

Lenin died, January 21, 1924

Joseph Stalin launched a campaign to defeat Leon Trotsky (July–October, 1926), which culminated in the expulsion of

Trotsky and Grigori Zinoviev from the Politbureau, October 15, 1926. Stalin consolidated his victory at the meeting of the Communist party on December 27, 1927, when Trotsky was expelled from the party. Trotsky was expelled from the USSR., January 21, 1929. Bukharin and other opponents of Stalin were expelled from the Politbureau, November 17, 1929

Introduction of a Five-Year Plan for economic development (effective October, 1, 1928)

Second Five-Year Plan began, January 22, 1932

Stalin's purge of the Communist Party

    Assassination of Serge Kirov, December 1, 1934

    Zinoviev, Kamenev and others tried for treason, January 15–17, 1935

    Zinoviev, Kamenev and others were tried again, convicted and executed, August 19–23, 1935

    Georgei Piatakov, Karl Radek and others tried and convicted, January 23–30, 1937

    Seven generals and Marshal Tukhachevski executed, June 12, 1937

    Bukharin, Rykov, Yagoda, and others tried and executed, March 2–15, 1938

    New constitution adopted, December 5, 1936

The Aftermath of the First World War

Little Entente created by treaty between Czechoslovakia and Yugoslavia, August 14, 1920. Romania joined Czechoslovakia in the Little Entente (April 23, 1921) and completed the alliance by a treaty with Yugoslavia on June 7, 1921.

Treaty of Rapallo between Italy and Yugoslavia, November 12, 1920

Paris conference discussed reparations, January 24–30, 1921. This was followed by a London conference, February 21–March 14, 1921. Germany was declared in default, March 24, 1921. The amount of the reparations was announced on April 27, and another conference was held in London (April 29–May 5, 1921) to demand German payment.

Washington Conference, November 12, 1921–February 6, 1922

France and Belgium sent troops into the Ruhr district, January 11, 1923; passive resistance lasted until September 26, 1923

Dawes Plan, April 9, 1924

Locarno Conference, October 5–16, 1925; treaties signed December 1, 1925

Germany joined the League of Nations, March 17, 1926

Kellogg–Briand Pact signed August 27, 1926

Young Plan, June 7, 1926

London Naval Conference, January 21–April 22, 1930

Post-First World War Germany and the Rise of Hitler

Spartacist revolt in Berlin, January 5–15, 1919

A National Assembly elected, January 19, 1919

Weimar Constitution adopted, July 31, 1919

Kapp Putsch, March 13–17, 1920

Munich ("Beer Hall") Putsch, November 8–11, 1923

Hitler's National Socialists became a major party in the Reichstag elections September 14, 1930

Hindenburg defeated Hitler in the presidential election March 13, 1932

Hitler appointed Chancellor, January 30, 1933

Reichstag fire, February 27, 1933

Reichstag elections, March 5, 1933

Enabling Act passed, March 23, 1933

Civil Service Law, April 7, 1933

Strikes and lockouts forbidden, May 17, 1933

National Socialist party declared the only political party, July 14, 1933

Germany withdrew from the League of Nations, October 14, 1933

People's Court established, May 3, 1934

Great Blood Purge, June 30, 1934

Universal military service made compulsory, March 16, 1935

Nuremberg Laws, September 15, 1935

Germany denounced the Locarno Pacts and reoccupied the Rhineland, March 7, 1936

Berlin–Rome axis formalized, October 25, 1936
Pact between Germany and Japan concluded, November 25, 1936
Germany invaded and annexed Austria, March 12–13, 1938
Crisis created by German claims to part of Czechoslovakia (September 12–29, 1938) led to conference at Munich
German annexation of Bohemia and Moravia, March 15, 1939
Non-aggression Pact signed with USSR, August 23, 1939
Germany invaded Poland, September 1, 1939

Spain and the Spanish Civil War

Military coup established General Primo de Rivera as dictator under King Alphonso XIII, September 13, 1923
General Rivera resigned, January 28, 1930
Municipal elections gave the Republicans a victory, April 12, 1931
King Alphonso left Spain without abdicating, April 14, 1931
New constitution adopted, December 9, 1931
Elections of April 23, 1933 gave a victory to the Right
Elections of February 16, 1936 gave victory to the Popular Front
Spanish Civil War began, July 18, 1936 (until the surrender of Madrid and Valencia, March 28, 1939)

Japan

Shōwa Hirohito became Emperor, December 25, 1926
Revival of China's boycott of Japanese goods, July, 1931
Japan landed troops at Shanghai, January 28, 1932
League of Nations report disparaged Japanese action in Manchuria, October 2, 1932; on May 27, 1933, Japan announced its intention to withdraw from the League of Nations two years hence
Incident at Lukouchiao during the night of July 7, 1937 caused Japanese troops to begin hostilities in China (1937–45): Nanking fell to the Japanese, December 13, 1937; Canton, October 21, 1938; Hankow, October 25, 1938

The Second World War

EUROPE 1939—40

Germany invaded Poland, September 1, 1939

Great Britain and France declared war on Germany, September 3, 1939

USSR invaded Poland from the East, September 17, 1939

Germans reached Warsaw, September 28, 1939

USSR concluded pacts with Estonia (September 29), Latvia (October 5) and Lithuania (October 10) allowing the Soviet Union to occupy military bases in those countries

USSR invaded Finland (November 30, 1939) starting the Russo-Finnish War (until March 12, 1940); the Soviet Union was expelled from the League of Nations, December 14, 1939

Germany invaded Norway and Denmark, April 9, 1940; British naval forces landed in Norway, April 14, 1940

Winston Churchill became British Prime Minister, May 10, 1940

Germany invaded Holland, Belgium, and Luxemburg, May 10, 1940; Dutch army surrendered, May 14; Belgium capitulated, May 28

British forces evacuated Dunkirk, May 29–June 3, 1940

Italy declared war against Great Britain and France, June 10, 1940

Germans took Paris, June 13, 1940

Marshal Pétain made head of French state (June 16), and agreed an armistice with Germany, June 22; armistice signed with Italy, June 24, 1940

USSR invaded Romania, June 27, 1940

The Battle of Britain (1940–41), entailed heavy German air bombardment of Britain and British counterattacks on the Continent

Lend-Lease approved in the USA, March 11, 1941

German–Italian–Japanese Pact concluded, September 27, 1940; endorsed by Hungary (November 20) and Romania (November 23, 1940), and by Yugoslavia, March 25, 1941

German troops entered Romania to occupy the oil fields, October 8, 1940

THE MEDITERRANEAN AREA 1940—1

Italian army invaded British Somaliland, August 6, 1940

Italian army invaded Egypt, September 13–15, 1940

Italy invaded Greece, October 28, 1940

British victory over the Italian fleet at the Battle of Taranto, November 13, 1940

British attacked the Italians in North Africa by launching a counterattack, December 8, 1940

Germany invaded Yugoslavia and Greece, April 6, 1941

German and Italian forces under General Erwin Rommel counterattacked the British in Libya (April 3, 1941), driving them back to Egypt

Germans parachuted troops into Crete, May 20; British forces in Crete evacuated to Cyprus and Egypt, May 31, 1941

RUSSIA

Germany invaded Russia, June 22, 1941

Germans reached the outskirts of Leningrad, September 3, 1941

First Soviet Protocol promised that Britain and the USA would supply material help for the next nine months, October 1, 1941; this was supplemented by a lend-lease agreement between the USA and Russia on June 11, 1942

Germans advanced from Smolensk toward Moscow, October 1, 1941; by October 16, a German army was only sixty miles from Moscow

German army took Kharkov, October 24, 1941; the siege of Sebastopol began on November 15, 1941; Sebastopol captured by the Germans, July 2, 1942

The first German offensive against Moscow failed, October 25, 1941

Russian counteroffensive launched in two sectors, October 27 and 29, 1941

German offensive against Stalingrad began, August 22, 1942; Soviet forces counterattacked, September 21, 1942; Germans surrendered January 31, 1943

Soviet army began new offensive (November 25 and December 16, 1942) that inflicted a series of defeats on the Germans, January 1–18, 1943

German drive was opened on March 15, 1943, that temporarily stabilized the German lines

Soviet summer campaign (begun July, 1943) forced Germans to retreat; by February, 1944, a USSR army reached the Polish border

Russia began an offensive in the Ukraine, March 4, 1944

Sebastopol liberated, May 9, 1944

The Romanian government surrendered to Russia, August 24, 1944

NORTH AFRICA AND EUROPE, 1942–5

Germany and Italy declared war on the United States, December 11, 1941

Battle of El Alamein began, October 23, 1942

Allies, commanded by Dwight D. Eisenhower, landed in French North Africa, November 8, 1942

US Eighth Army repulsed German counter-attacks in Tunisia, March 7–11, 1943

Allies took Tunis and Bizerta, May 7, 1943; Axis resistance in North Africa ended

Allies landed in Sicily, July 10, 1943

Benito Mussolini forced to resign, July 25, 1943

Allies landed near Salerno, September 8, 1943;

Italy's unconditional surrender announced, September 8, 1943. Allies landed at Anzio, January 22, 1944

US Fifth Army entered Rome, June 4, 1944

Invasion of Normandy, June 6, 1944 ("D-Day")

First V-1 flying-bomb fell on London, June 13, 1944

German army plot to kill Hitler failed, July 20, 1944

Charles de Gaulle and French army entered Paris, August 25, 1944

Brussels was liberated, September 5, 1944

First V-2 rocket landed in Britain, September 8, 1944

Battle of the Bulge, December 16–25, 1944; American counter-attack, January 3, 1945

Soviet army began an offensive in Silesia, January 13, 1945

Russians took Warsaw, January 17, and reached the Oder River, January 23, 1945

Yalta Conference, February 4–11, 1945

Franklin Roosevelt died, April 12, 1945
Russians reached Berlin, April 20, 1945
Allies crossed Elbe River, April 28, 1945
Benito Mussolini killed, April 28, 1945
Adolf Hitler committed suicide, April 30, 1945
"VE Day," May 8, 1945

THE PACIFIC

Japan attacked Pearl Harbor, the Philippines, Hong Kong and
    Malaya, December 7, 1941; the United States declared war on
    Japan, December 8, 1941
Japan attacked Guam and Wake Island, December 8, 1941
Japan attacked the Dutch East Indies, January 2, 1942
Japan victorious in the Battle of the Java Sea, February 27–
    March 1, 1942
Battle of the Coral Sea disrupted a possible Japanese invasion of
    Australia or New Zealand, May 7, 1942
Heavy losses inflicted on the Japanese when they attacked Mid-
    way Island, June 4–7, 1942
Chinese defeated Japanese army in Kiangsi Province, July 9,
    1942
US marines landed on Guadalcanal, August 7, 1942
Naval Battle in the Solomon Islands, November 13, 1942
Allied forces began an offensive in the South Pacific, July 1,
    1943
US landed troops in the Philippines, October 19, 1944; Second
    Battle of the Philippine Sea, October 21–2, 1944
US invaded Iwo Jima, February 19, 1945
Atomic bomb dropped on Hiroshima, August 6, 1945; a second
    atomic bomb was dropped on Nagasaki, August 9, 1945
Japan surrendered, August 10, 1945

The World after the Second World War

RECONSTRUCTION OF EUROPE

Potsdam Conference, July 17–August 2, 1945
Churchill's "Iron Curtain" speech, March 5, 1946

Elections in Greece, March 31, 1946; guerrilla attack on the Greek government, May, 1946; civil war in Greece, May, 1946–October, 1949

Elections made Italy a republic, June 2, 1946

French ratified the constitution of the Fourth Republic, October 13, 1946

Truman Doctrine, March 12, 1947; George Marshall called for a European Recovery Program, June 5, 1947 (Congress passed the legislation, March 31, 1948)

Cominform, October 5, 1947

Coup d'état in Czechoslovakia, February 25, 1948

Organization of European Economic Cooperation drafted a European Recovery Program, April 16, 1948

Stalin stopped road traffic between Berlin and West Germany, June 24, 1948; Berlin airlift until May 12, 1949

NATO Treaty signed, April 4, 1949

EUROPEAN ECONOMIC INTEGRATION

Benelux created, March 13, 1949; France and Italy joined, March 26, 1949

Schuman Plan, May 9, 1950

Treaty of Rome, March 25, 1957

British application to join EEC rejected by France, January 29, 1963

THE SOVIET UNION AFTER STALIN

Stalin died, March 5, 1953

Warsaw Pact signed, May 14, 1955

Soviets accepted peace treaty with Austria, May 15, 1955

Khrushchev denounced Stalin, February 14, 1956

Hungarian uprising crushed, November 14, 1956

Sputnik, October 5, 1957

Construction begun on Berlin Wall, August 15, 1961

Cuban missile crisis, October 22, 1962

ISRAEL

Britain withdrew and referred the Palestinian problem to the UN, April 2, 1947

UN proposed a partition into two separate states, November 29, 1947; Arabs refused this plan, December 17, 1947

David Ben-Gurion proclaimed a State of Israel, May 14, 1948

Arab League invaded Palestine, May 14, 1948 UN ordered a truce in Palestine, July 15, 1948

Israel was admitted to the UN, May 11, 1949

EGYPT

King Farouk overthrown, July 23, 1952

Agreement for British withdrawal from Canal zone, October 19, 1954

Nasser concluded deal with Communist bloc countries, September 27, 1955

US and Britain withdrew their Aswan dam aid, July 19–20, 1956

Suez Canal nationalized, July 26, 1956

Israel, joined by France and Britain, attacked Egypt, October 29, 1956;

Evacuation of British and French forces completed, December 22, 1956

CHINA

Communist troops clashed with Nationalists, who took Nanking and Shanghai, August, 1945

General George Marshall sent to mediate nationalist–communist conflict, December 14, 1945

Truce between Nationalists and Communists was signed, January 10, 1946

Nationalists ignored Communists' demand for joint control in Manchuria, February 17, 1946

Communist troop attacked Peking–Mukden railroad, April, 1946

Second truce, May 12–June 30, 1946

Communist offensive in Yangtze region, July, 1946; Mao ordered a total offensive, August, 1946

Kuomintang reelected Chiang Kai-shek president, October 10, 1946

Nationalists began offensive in Shantung region, February, 1947

Communists completed their conquest of Manchuria, October, 1947

Communists formed North China People's Government, September 1, 1948

After a month-long siege, communists took Peking, January, 1949

Negotiations between communists and nationalists broke down, April, 1949

People's Republic of China proclaimed, October 1, 1949

KOREA

North Korea invaded South Korea (June 25) and captured Seoul, June 28, 1950

UN voted to send assistance, June 27, 1950

MacArthur appointed leader of UN force, July 8, 1950

Inchon landing, September 13, 1950

China entered the war, November 26, 1950

Armistice signed, July 26, 1953

Suggestions for Further Reading
by Glenn O. Nichols

There are so many books written about various aspects of modern European history that perhaps readers will find the following suggestions helpful. To begin, it is often possible to satisfy one's immediate desire to know more about a person, country or historical period by consulting the solid, readable essays in volumes of the *New Cambridge Modern History* (all published by the Cambridge University Press). The volumes appropriate for the centuries since 1600 are: J. P. Cooper, ed., *The Decline of Spain and the Thirty Years War, 1609–48/59* (1971); F. L. Carsten, ed., *The Ascendancy of France, 1648–88* (1961); J. S. Bromley, *The Rise of Great Britain and Russia, 1688–1715/25* (1970); J. O. Lindsay, ed., *The Old Regime, 1713–63* (1957); A. Goodwin, *The American and French Revolutions, 1763–93* (1968); C. W. Crawley, ed., *War and Peace in an Age of Upheaval, 1793–1830* (1969); J. P. T. Bury, ed., *The Zenith of European Power, 1830–70* (1964); F. H. Hinsley, ed., *Material Progress and World-Wide Problems, 1870–1898* (1967); David Thomson, ed., *The Era of Violence, 1898–1945* (1960).

Unfortunately the *New Cambridge Modern History* does not include bibliographies, but that deficiency can be remedied somewhat by consulting the books in *The Rise of Modern Europe* series edited by William L. Langer & Row. Unlike the *New Cambridge Modern History*, which employs different authors to write each chapter, each book in Langer's series is written by a single author. Some of these volumes now show their age, but they were initially written with such good sense and pleasing style that they can still be recommended to new readers. Volumes considering the last four centuries are: Carl J. Friedrich, *The Age of the Baroque, 1610–1660* (1952); Frederick L. Nussbaum, *The Triumph of Science and Reason, 1660–1685* (1953); John B. Wolf, *The Emergence of the Great Powers, 1685–1715* (1951); Penfield Roberts, *The Quest for Security, 1715–1740* (1947); Walter L. Dorn, *Competition for*

Empire, 1740–1763 (1940); Leo Gershoy, *From Despotism to Revolution, 1763–1789* (1944); Crane Brinton, *A Decade of Revolution, 1789–1799* (1934); Geoffrey Bruun, *Europe and the French Imperium, 1799–1814* (1938); Frederick B. Artz, *Reaction and Revolution, 1814–1832* (1934); William L. Langer, *Political and Social Upheaval, 1832–1852* (1969); Robert C. Binkley, *Realism and Nationalism, 1852–1871* (1935); Carlton J. H. Hayes, *A Generation of Materialism, 1871–1900* (1941); Oron J. Hale, *The Great Illusion, 1900–1914* (1971); Raymond Sontag, *A Broken World, 1919–1939* (1972); Gordon Wright, *The Ordeal of Total War, 1939–1945* (1968).

Oxford University Press has published a multi-volume series describing the history of England in its *Oxford History of England*. Authors of the individual volumes are Godfrey Davies, George N. Clark, Basil Williams, J. Steven Watson, Llewellyn Woodward, Robert Ensor, and A. J. P. Taylor. Each volume also contains a bibliographic essay. A *New Oxford History of England* has been commissioned, and the first volume, Paul Langford, *A Polite and Commercial People: England 1727–1783* (1989), raises great expectations for the new series.

After finding the importance of the physical environment so persuasively stated in the present volume, readers will want to know more about European geography. The following atlases and accounts of historical geography are useful: Edward Whiting Fox, *Atlas of European History* (New York, Oxford University Press, 1957); *The Times Atlas of World History*, ed. Geoffrey Barraclough, rev. edn (Maplewood, Hammond, 1985); vol. 14 of the *New Cambridge Modern History*, which is H. C. Darby and Harold Fullard, eds, *Atlas* (Cambridge, Cambridge University Press, 1970).

Comparative studies, by their very nature, often encompass several nations, cultures, or periods of time, and lend themselves to the application of the ideas and methods of other social sciences. At its worst, this type of analysis risks distorting history to fit ahistorical categories or "prove" universal laws; when done skillfully, however, comparisons assist in sorting out the unique from the typical, and can often suggest explanations for those elements of history that are common enough to be considered typical. Some of the more evocative examples of the application of comparison to history can be found in the following books. Theda Skocpol, *States and Social Revolutions: A Comparative Analysis of France, Russia, and China* (Cambridge, Mass., Harvard University Press, 1979) identifies common attributes of the revolutions in these three nations in spite of a considerable passage of time, and an even larger difference between European and Asian cultures. Michael Mann, *The Sources of Social Power*, vol. 1: *A History of Power from the Beginning to A.D. 1760* (Cambridge, Cambridge University Press, 1986) presents a superb general discussion of power networks, and is worth examining even though only the final chapters of this volume are germane to the early modern period. Reinhard Bendix, *Kings or People: Power and the Mandate to Rule* (Berkeley, University of California Press, 1978) examines how popular sovereignty succeeded in replacing hereditary monarchy as the preferred form of government in western Europe after 1500; to do this, Bendix deftly compares European beliefs and practices to those of non-Western cultures. Many of the attempts to explain economic development over a long time, or for a geographic area comprising several countries, also make extensive use of comparisons. Immanuel Wallerstein, *The Modern World System*, 3 vols (New York, Academic Press, 1974–89) offers a bold explanation of the expansion of capitalism. Political development is acutely assessed in the essays published in Charles Tilly, ed., *The Formation of National States in Western Europe* (Princeton, Princeton University Press, 1975). E. L. Jones, *The European Miracle: Environments, Economies, and Geopolitics in the History of Europe and Asia*, 2nd edn (New York, Cambridge University Press, 1987) is a brilliant ecologically oriented examination of the development of the modern capitalist economy. Finally J. H. Shennan, *Liberty and Order in Early Modern Europe: The Subject and the State, 1650–1800* (London, Longman, 1986) explains the emergence of an impersonal centralizing state in a brief essay.

Examples of interesting military history abound. Geoffrey Parker, *The Military Revolution: Military Innovation and the Rise of the West, 1500–1800* (Cambridge, Cambridge University Press, 1988) looks at the nature of Western military supremacy in an enjoyable essay accompanied by informative illustrations. Paul M. Kennedy, *The Rise and Fall of the Great Powers: Economic Change and Military Conflict from 1500–2000* (New York, Random House, 1987) examines the relationship of economic and military power, and speculates about the reasons for the rise and fall of empires. Michael E. Howard, *War in European History* (New York, Oxford, 1976) is a brief inquiry written by one of the masters of this field. Geoffrey Best, *War and Society in Revolutionary Europe, 1770–1870* (New York, St Martin's Press, 1982) discusses the consequences of the introduction of popular participation in warfare, in revealing explanation of the economic and sociological aspects of armed forces. Gordon Craig, *The Politics of the Prussian Army, 1640–1945* (New York, Oxford University Press, 1964) considers the role of the army in shaping Prussian policy. Brian Bond, *British Military Policy between the Two World Wars* (Oxford, Clarendon Press, 1980) relates the formulation of British military strategy to the nation's foreign policy.

Economic history has not lacked historians who proposed large schemes or grand explanations. Fernand Braudel, *The Mediterranean and the Mediterranean World in the Age of Philip II*, trans. Siân Reynolds, 2 vols (New York, Harper & Row, 1972) and *Civilization and Capitalism 15th–18th Century*, trans. and revised by Siân Reynolds, 3 vols (New York, Harper & Row, 1981–4) characterize the combination of detailed investigation and sweeping analysis for which this historian is known. The latter work examines the European economy from the fifteenth to the eighteenth century, from the fascinating detail of everyday life and local self-sufficiency to impersonal market mechanisms at the national and international level. Douglass C. North, *Structure and Change in Economic History* (New York, Norton, 1981) applies the assumptions of neoclassical economics to the problem of economic change in a sweeping survey of this vital topic from the Greeks to modern times. A very different explanation of European economic development is found in Peter Kriedte, *Peasants, Landlords and Merchant Capitalists: Europe and the World Economy, 1500–1800* (Cambridge, Cambridge University Press, 1983), where class conflict is seen as shaping European economic growth. Markets, the self-regulating "invisible hand" traditionally depicted in the accounts of historians who base their work on neoclassical economics, are not a generally beneficent mechanism of development as portrayed in Kriedte's short controversial survey. Taxes and government spending are indeed prosaic topics, but Carolyn Webber and Aaron Wildavsky show the influence of these institutions on political and economic development in a most readable form in *A History of Taxation and Expenditure in the Western World* (New York, Simon and Schuster, 1986).

Social history has received extensive attention from historians during the last twenty-five years. Peter Laslett, in *The World We Have Lost – Further Explained* (London, Methuen, 1983), extends his pioneering demographic study of England before the industrial revolution. Edward Shorter, in *The Making of the Modern Family* (New York, Basic Books, 1975), has written an entertaining, sometimes extravagant, history of the family, which is the starting point for much that has been written about this growth area of social history during the last decade and a half. Other explorations of family life are Lawrence Stone, *The Family, Sex and Marriage in England, 1500–1800 (New York, Harper & Row, 1977)* and P. Ariès, *Centuries of Childhood: A Social History of Family Life* (Harmondsworth, Penguin Books, 1979). Interest in the history of women has produced many superb social histories. Good places to start are Marilyn Boxer and Jean Quataert, eds, *Connecting Spheres: Women in the Western World, 1500 to Present* (New York, Oxford University

Press, 1987), Antonia Fraser, *The Weaker Vessel* (New York, Knopf, 1984), and L. Tilly and Joan Scott, *Women, Work and Family* (New York, Holt, Rinehart and Winston, 1978). Michel Foucault, *The History of Sexuality*, trans. Robert Hurley, 3 vols (New York, Pantheon, 1978–86) deconstructs sex and culture. Urban life has been successfully surveyed in Paul M. Hohenberg and Lynn Hollen Lees, *The Making of Urban Europe, 1000–1950* (Cambridge, Mass., Harvard University Press, 1985), which covers a millennium of urban history in a readable account that utilizes relevant theoretical constructs of geographers. Jan de Vries, *European Urbanization 1500–1800* (Cambridge, Mass., Harvard University Press, 1984) argues that cities changed from medieval administrative and marketing centers to communities based on expansion of government and overseas trade; the modern industrial city is then superimposed on the latter without really changing them.

There are several outstanding works that tackle large subjects that should be mentioned before examining books of a more specialized orientation. Keith Thomas, *Religion and the Decline of Magic: Studies In Popular Beliefs in Sixteenth and Seventeenth Century England* (New York, Scribner, 1971) is a groundbreaking study of religious beliefs in the sixteenth and seventeenth centuries. James H. Billington, in *The Icon and the Ax: An Interpretative History of Russian Culture* (New York, Knopf, 1966), has written a masterful synthesis of modern Russian history and culture in engaging prose. Frank E. Manuel and Fritzie P. Manuel, in *Utopian Thought in the Western World* (Cambridge, Mass., Belknap Press, 1979), explore the myriad efforts to transform society in a book that requires a sense of irony to be fully appreciated. Charles Tilly, *The Contentious French: Four Centuries of Popular Struggle* (Cambridge, Mass., Belknap Press, 1986) focuses on the efforts of the French people to make their claims against both the intrusions of the centralizing state and the changes accompanying the growth of capitalism during the last four centuries. Tilly's sympathies are clearly with the losers in this struggle, and his vigorous prose makes it unlikely that readers will not be touched by those sympathies. Finally, curiosity about history often leads to curiosity about the people who write it. *The Blackwell Dictionary of Historians*, ed. John Cannon et al. (Oxford and Cambridge, Mass., Blackwell, 1988) makes this information available conveniently.

CHAPTER 1   *The Dawn of the Modern World*

Geoffrey Treasure, *The Making of Modern Europe, 1648–1780* (New York, Methuen, 1985) is a large book that can be recommended both as the source of detailed explanation of the events of the period, and as a convenient summary of the conclusions of many other early modern historians. R. J. W. Evans, *The Making of the Habsburg Monarchy 1550–1700* (Oxford, Clarendon Press, 1979) is a well-written, lengthy contribution to the political and cultural history of central Europe. The question of political crisis is explored in three suggestive books: Trevor Aston, ed., *Crisis in Europe, 1560–1660* (Garden City, Anchor Books, 1967); Theodore K. Rabb, *The Struggle for Stability in Early Modern Europe* (New York, Oxford University Press, 1975); and P. Anderson, *Lineages of the Absolutist State* (London, NLB, 1974).

The study of early modern France should begin with Edward Whiting Fox, *History in Geographic Perspective: The Other France* (New York, Norton, 1971), which shows the influence of geography on French political development. Any student of absolutism will ultimately have to consult Roland E. Mousnier, *The Institutions of France under the Absolute Monarchy 1598–1789*, trans. Brian Pearce, 2 vols (Chicago, University of Chicago Press, 1979–84). William Beik, *Absolutism and Society in Seventeenth-Century France: State Power and Provincial Aristocracy in Languedoc* (Cambridge, Cambridge University Press, 1985) demonstrates that absolutism worked because the profits arising from administering the taxes were shared by the Crown and provincial elites. The notion that support for the central government is bought by privileges, subsidies, and the like has been used by some historians to explain change in French history, at least until the "modernization" of the peasants in the late nineteenth century. Julian Dent, *Crisis in Finance: Crown, Financiers and Society in Seventeenth Century France* (Newton Abbot, David & Charles, 1973) and Richard Bonney, *The King's Debts: Finance and Politics in France, 1589–1661* (Oxford, Clarendon, 1981) elucidate the important connection between finance and politics. Two highly readable studies of early modern France by Pierre Goubert are *Louis XIV and Twenty Million Frenchmen*, trans. Anne Carter (New York, Pantheon Books, 1970) and *The Ancient Régime: French Society, 1600–1750*, trans. Steve Cox (New York, Harper & Row, 1973). The essays in Natalie Z. Davis, *Society and Culture in Early Modern France: Eight Essays* (Stanford, Stanford University Press, 1975) include elucidations of important subjects such as the history of women, violence, printing, and poor relief.

Lawrence Stone, *The Causes of the English Revolution 1529–1642* (New York, Harper, 1972) sorts out earlier interpretations of the English Civil War and approaches it with exemplary historical analysis. G. E. Aylmer, *Rebellion or Revolution? England, 1640–1660* (Oxford, Oxford University Press, 1986) also surveys competing methodologies and ideologies skillfully in a vigorously written introduction to the English Civil War. David Underdown, *Revel, Riot and Rebellion: Popular Politics and Culture in England, 1603–1660* (Oxford, Oxford University Press, 1987) is a fascinating and important book about the development of political culture in England. William A. Speck, *Reluctant Revolutionaries: Englishmen and the Revolution of 1688* (New York, Oxford University Press, 1989) is an excellent summary of the events before and during the revolution. The crucial place of finance in the development of the English state in the eighteenth century is demonstrated in two important studies: P. G. M. Dickson, *The Financial Revolution in England: A Study in the Development of Public Credit, 1688–1756* (New York, St Martin's Press, 1967); and John Brewer, *The Sinews of Power: War, Money and the English State, 1688–1783* (New York, Knopf, 1989). J. C. D. Clark, *English Society, 1688–1832: Ideology, Social Structure, and Political Practice during the Ancien Régime* (Cambridge, Cambridge University Press, 1985) places far less emphasis on the transformations resulting from the financial revolution, concluding that traditional society, as represented by Church and king, continued to prevail during the eighteenth century.

Intriguing attempts to explain the origins of assumptions common in modern culture are found in Albert O. Hirschman, *The Passions and the Interests: Political Arguments for Capitalism before Its Triumph* (Princeton, Princeton University Press, 1977) and Joyce Appleby, *Economic Thought and Ideology in Seventeenth-Century England* (Princeton, Princeton University Press, 1978). Richard Ashcraft, *Revolutionary Politics and John Locke's Two Treatises of Government* (Princeton, Princeton University Press, 1986) recreates the intellectual and political context of Locke's political thought. Thomas Kuhn, *The Structure of Scientific Revolutions*, 2nd edn enlarged (Chicago, University of Chicago Press, 1970) examines the manner of creating and changing scientific thought. Herbert Butterfield, *The Origins of Modern Science, 1300–1800*, revised edn (New York, Free Press, 1957) is a survey with a more conventional explanation of change in scientific thought. Michael Hunter, *Science and Society in Restoration England* (New York, Cambridge University Press, 1981) considers Robert K. Merton's thesis that Puritanism and the rise of modern science were connected. Paul Hazard, *The European Mind, 1680–1715*, trans. J. Lewis May (Cleveland, World, 1963) and *European Thought in the Eighteenth Century: From Montesquieu to Lessing*, trans. J. Lewis May (Cleveland, Meridian Books, 1963) successfully convey the excitement of the intellectual history of this period. The Enlightenment is conveniently anthologized in Peter Gay, ed., *The Enlightenment: A Comprehensive Anthology* (New York, Simon and

Schuster, 1973). Professor Gay's understanding of the Enlightenment is published in *The Enlightenment: An Interpretation*, 2 vols (New York, Knopf, 1966–9).

CHAPTER 2   *The Eighteenth Century*

C. B. A. Behrens, *Society, Government, and the Enlightenment: The Experiences of Eighteenth-Century France and Prussia* (New York, Harper & Row, 1985) compares the weaknesses of French government with the strengths that enabled the Prussian monarchs to avoid revolution. Other surveys of Prussia are Hans Rosenberg, *Bureaucracy, Aristocracy, and Autocracy: The Prussian Experience, 1660–1815* (Cambridge, Mass., Harvard University Press, 1958) and F. L. Carsten, *The Origins of Prussia* (Oxford, Clarendon Press, 1954). Isabel de Madariaga, *Russia in the Age of Catherine the Great* (New Haven, Yale University Press, 1981) is a brilliant biography of Catherine that also provides a superb assessment of her reign. Its careful placement of Catherine and Russia in a wider context makes this an important book for all students of the second half of eighteenth-century Europe.

The emergence of a single community on different sides of the Atlantic is the subject of Ian K. Steele, *The English Atlantic, 1675–1740: An Exploration of Communication and Community* (New York, Oxford University Press, 1986). Bernard Bailyn, *The Ideological Origins of the American Revolution* (Cambridge, Mass., Belknap Press, 1967) examines the intellectual background of the revolution. Robert R. Palmer, *The Age of Democratic Revolution. A Political History of Europe and America, 1760–1800*, 2 vols (Princeton, Princeton University Press, 1959–64) puts the American Revolution in the context of revolutions in other countries. Lawrence H. Gipson, *The Coming of the Revolution, 1763–1775* (New York, Harper, 1954) summarizes the conflicts leading up to the revolution in the context of the old British Empire. Three good accounts of the revolution are Robert Middlekauff, *The Glorious Cause: The American Revolution, 1763–89* (New York, Oxford University Press, 1982), Charles Royster, *A Revolutionary People at War: The Continental Army and American Character, 1775–1783* (Chapel Hill, University of North Carolina Press, 1979), and Gordon Wood, *The Creation of the American Republic, 1776–1787* (Chapel Hill, University of North Carolina Press, 1969).

CHAPTER 3   *The French Revolution*

Historians of the French Revolution have given us imaginative and insightful accounts of the these events. William Doyle, *Origins of the*

French Revolution (Oxford, Oxford University Press, 1980) is a work of thoughtful synthesis of almost a half-century's publications, presented in an eminently accessible style. The following general works analyze the background and early years of the revolution distinctively: James C. Riley, *The Seven Years War and the Old Regime in France: The Economic and Financial Toll* (Princeton, Princeton University Press, 1986); Alexis de Tocqueville, *The Old Regime and the French Revolution*, trans. Stuart Gilbert (Garden City, Doubleday, 1955); Alfred Cobban, *The Social Interpretation of the French Revolution* (Cambridge, Cambridge University Press, 1964); Norman Hampson, *A Social History of the French Revolution* (Toronto, University of Toronto Press, 1963); François Furet, *Interpreting the French Revolution* (Cambridge, Cambridge University Press, 1981); Simon Schama, *Citizens: A Chronicle of the French Revolution* (New York, Knopf, 1989); and David P. Jordan, *The King's Trial: The French Revolution vs. Louis XVI* (Berkeley, University of California Press, 1979). The revolutionary republic is analyzed in Robert R. Palmer, *Twelve Who Ruled: The Year of the Terror in the French Revolution* (Princeton, Princeton University Press, 1970; reissued Princeton and Oxford, Blackwell, 1989) and David P. Jordan, *The Revolutionary Career of Maximilien Robespierre* (New York, Free Press, 1985). Lynn Hunt, *Politics, Culture, and Class in the French Revolution* (Berkeley, University of California Press, 1984) shows the extent to which democracy and egalitarianism were permanently injected into French political culture.

CHAPTER 4   *The Industrial Revolution*

It is unlikely that the debate on the question of whether the industrial revolution was "a good thing" or "a bad thing" will ever be settled to everyone's satisfaction. For those interested in the classic indictment of the industrial revolution, Friederich Engels, *The Condition of the Working Class in England*, trans. and ed. W. O. Henderson and W. H. Chaloner (Oxford, Blackwell, 1958) is the place to start. A far more sanguine conclusion is reached by the authors of the essays in Friedrich A. von Hayek, ed., *Capitalism and the Historians* (Chicago, University of Chicago Press, 1954). W. O. Henderson, *The Industrial Revolution in Europe, 1815–1914* (Chicago, Quadrangle Books, 1961) is a general study without the usual heavy dose of ideology or revisionism. The significance of the development of transportation on the continent is explored in Rondo Cameron, *France and the Economic Development of Europe, 1800–1914: Conquests of Peace and Seeds of War* (Princeton, Princeton University Press, 1961). Two useful surveys by Alan S. Milward and S. B. Saul are *The Economic Development of Continental*

Europe, 1780–1870, 2nd edn (London, Allen & Unwin, 1979) and *The Development of the Economies of Continental Europe, 1850–1914* (Cambridge, Mass., Harvard University Press, 1977).

The seemingly elementary questions of what the industrial revolution was, and when it occurred, have not been answered to the satisfaction of many historians. N. F. R. Crafts, *British Economic Growth During the Industrial Revolution* (New York, Oxford University Press, 1985) denies that there was an industrial "take-off" in Britain before 1830. Indeed, "revolution" is appropriate only as a description of a very limited part of British economic history from 1750 to 1850. The traditional interpretation of the process of British industrialization, including David Landes's magisterial explanation of the technology of industrialization in *The Unbound Prometheus* (cited below), is questioned in Maxine Berg, *The Age of Manufactures: Industry, Innovation and Work in Britain, 1700–1820* (Towanda, Barnes and Noble, 1985); her laudable attempt to show how social life helped structure the industrial revolution has been criticized as being better at stating the questions than at answering them. One survey of the industrial revolution stands out from the others: Peter Mathias, *The First Industrial Nation: An Economic History of Britain, 1700–1914*, 2nd edn (London, Methuen, 1983). E. L. Jones, *Agriculture and Economic Growth in England, 1650–1815* (London, Methuen, 1967) provocatively examines the agricultural foundation of the industrial revolution. David Landes, *The Unbound Prometheus: Technological Change and Industrial Development in Western Europe from 1750 to the Present* (Cambridge, Cambridge University Press, 1969) is a *tour de force* of economic history. The same author's *Revolution in Time: Clocks and the Making of the Modern World* (Cambridge, Mass., Harvard University Press, 1983) helps us appreciate the role of culture in creating a concept of time, but he has really written a brilliant synthesis of economic and technological history from early times to the quartz watch.

CHAPTER 5   *The Napoleonic Empire*

A stimulating sample of the variety of historical interpretation surrounding Napoleon is found in Pieter Geyl, *Napoleon, For and Against* (New Haven, Yale University Press, 1949). G. Lefebvre, *Napoléon*, 6th edn (Paris, Presses Universitaires de France, 1969) may be considered somewhat dated, and its size may be daunting, but there is a grandeur to its scope that is entirely appropriate to its subject. It has been translated into English and published in two volumes by Columbia University Press. Louis Bergeron, *France Under Napoleon*, trans. R. R. Palmer (Princeton,

Princeton University Press, 1981) is a concise survey, with a brilliant portrait of Napoleon. Like Lefebvre, Bergeron considers Napoleon to have been challenged by industrialism and capitalism; the question of "turning-points" in French history therefore arises again, but Bergeron carefully emphasizes those elements of continuity between the eighteenth and nineteenth centuries. Additional perspectives are offered in Felix Markham, *Napoleon* (New York, New American Library, 1963), J. M. Thompson, *Napoleon Bonaparte: His Rise and Fall* (Oxford and Cambridge, Mass., Blackwell, 1952; reissued in paperback, 1990), and Owen Connelly, *Napoleon's Satellite Kingdoms* (New York, Free Press, 1965). Irene Collins, *Napoleon and his Parliaments, 1800–1815* (New York, St Martin's Press, 1979) examines the legislative process under Napoleon, finding a surprising amount of opposition to the emperor. Richard K. Riehn, *1812: Napoleon's Russian Campaign* (New York, McGraw-Hill, 1990) puts his well-written account of the military campaign in the context of spreading nationalism and the contemporary diplomatic situation. A survey of Napoleon's campaigns is to be found in Owen Connelly, *Blundering to Glory: Napoleon's Military Campaigns* (Wilmington, Scholarly Resources, 1987).

General Studies for the Period 1815–1945

Eric Hobsbawm has completed his three-volume survey of the years from the French Revolution to the First World War: it begins with *The Age of Revolution: Europe, 1789–1848* (New York, Praeger, 1969), continues in *The Age of Capital, 1848–1875* (New York, Charles Scribner's Sons, 1975), and concludes with *The Age of Empire, 1875–1914* (New York, Vintage, 1989). Hobsbawm's interpretation is informed by his understanding of Marxism, but these eminently readable treatments are not doctrinaire. A. J. P. Taylor, *The Struggle for Mastery in Europe, 1848–1918* (Oxford, Clarendon Press, 1969) makes relations between the great powers exciting reading.

Peter N. Stearns, *European Society in Upheaval: Social History since 1750*, 2nd edn (New York, Macmillan, 1975) is an accessible survey of social history. Arno Mayer, *Persistence of the Old Regime: Europe to the Great War* (New York, Pantheon, 1981) is more specifically a history of the durability of the aristocracy, who continued to possess great wealth and political influence until 1914. In Mayer's book monarchy remains the main form of government, with representative institutions restricted in the authority allowed to them. The countryside and agriculture, not towns and industry, were the focus of life for most Europeans.

Books investigating the history of women during the last two centuries are numerous. Some good examples of recent work are Patricia Branca, *Women in Europe Since 1750* (New York, St Martin's Press, 1978), Martha Vicinus, *Suffer and Be Still: Women in the Victorian Age* (Bloomington, Indiana University Press, 1972), Renate Bridenthal and Claudia Koonz, eds, *Becoming Visible: Women in European History* (Boston, Houghton Mifflin, 1977), and Francine du Plessix Gray, *Soviet Women: Walking the Tightrope* (New York, Doubleday, 1990). Peter Gay examines sexuality in the nineteenth century in *The Bourgeois Experience: Victoria to Freud*, vol. 1: *The Education of the Senses* and vol. 2: *The Tender Passion* (Oxford, Oxford University Press, 1984, 1986). Early twentieth-century society is depicted with great panache in Barbara Tuchman, *The Proud Tower: A Portrait of the World before the War, 1890–1914* (New York, Macmillan, 1966). See also E. R. Tannenbaum, *1900: The Generation Before the Great War* (Garden City, Anchor, 1976) for a special treatment of the social history of pre-World War I years.

The powerful political currents of liberalism and conservatism are gauged in Guido de Ruggiero, *The History of European Liberalism*, trans. R. G. Collingswood (Boston, Beacon Press, 1959), Peter Viereck, Conservatism Revisited: The Revolt Against Revolt, 1815–1949 (New York, C. Scribner's Sons, 1949), and John Weiss, *Conservatism in Europe 1770–1945: Tradition, Reaction and Counter-Revolution* (New York, Harcourt Brace Jovanovich, 1977). Many courageous attempts have been made to explain nineteenth-century nationalism, but at the present the subject seems to have escaped capture. E. Kedourie, *Nationalism*, rev. edn (New York, Praeger, 1961) is a brief but distinguished account. Students of socialism are fortunate to have a Albert S. Lindemann, *A History of European Socialism* (New Haven, Yale University Press, 1983) to guide them. Written primarily as an introduction for general readers, each chapter also includes an annotated bibliography.

Histories of individual countries or regions offer readers a different focus. E. H. Kossmann, *The Low Countries, 1780–1940* (Oxford, Clarendon Press, 1978) deserves the gratitude of readers interested in the modern history of Belgium and the United Provinces by conveniently surveying the history of those countries. Gordon Wright, *France in Modern Times: From the Enlightenment to the Present*, 4th edn (New York, Norton, 1987) has long been a favorite of students. Theodore Zeldin, *France, 1848–1945*, 2 vols (Oxford, Clarendon Press, 1973, 1977) is a provocative attempt to synthesize French social history, defined to include politics and culture as well as society. It is also published in five paperbound volumes with the subtitles *Politics and Anger, Ambition and Love, Intellect and Pride, Taste and Corruption*, and *Anxiety and*

Hypocrisy (Oxford, 1979–80). As these titles indicate, Zeldin does not adopt a strict chronological approach in his attempt to explain the central themes of French national identity. *The Cambridge History of Modern France* (all published at Cambridge by Cambridge University Press) includes the following volumes: André Jardin and André-Jean Tudesq, *Restoration and Reaction, 1815–1848* (1984); Alain Plessis, *The Rise and Fall of the Second Empire, 1852–1871* (1985); Jean-Marie Mayeur and Madeleine Rebérioux, *The Third Republic from its Origins to the Great War, 1871–1914* (1984); Philippe Bernard and Henri Dubief, *The Decline of the Third Republic, 1914–1938* (1985); and Jean-Pierre Rioux, *The Fourth Republic, 1944–1958* trans. Godfrey Rogers (1989). An authoritative survey of modern Spain is Raymond Carr, *Spain 1808–1975*, 2nd edn (Oxford, Clarendon Press, 1982).

The Woodward and Ensor volumes in the *Oxford History of England* occupy the middle ground of surveys of nineteenth-century England. Elie Halévy, *A History of the English People in the Nineteenth Century*, trans. E. I. Watkin and D. A. Barker, 2nd edn, 6 vols (1949–52) is a survey that requires commitment, but Halévy's engaging prose and a felicitous translation make this work far less formidable than the number of volumes suggests. Norman Gash, *Aristocracy and People: Britain, 1815–1865* (Cambridge, Mass., Harvard University Press, and London, Arnold, 1979) is a laudable survey of the major areas of British life, outstanding in its elucidation of political culture. While Robert K. Webb's, *Modern England from the Eighteenth Century to the Present*, 2nd edn (New York, Harper & Row, 1980) was written to be a text-book, its beautiful prose and masterful analysis put it in a class by itself among one-volume surveys of the last two centuries. Trevor Lloyd, *Empire to Welfare State: English History, 1906–1985*, 3rd edn (Oxford, Oxford University Press, 1986) is an engaging account of modern British political history. Cecil Woodham Smith, *The Great Hunger: Ireland 1845–1849* (New York, Harper & Row, 1962) gives a poignant account of the famine in Ireland. The title of Sean Cronin, *Irish Nationalism: A History of Its Roots and Ideology* (New York, Continuum, 1981) accurately describes the book's contents.

Two volumes of Hajo Holborn's history of Germany touch this period: *A History of Modern Germany, 1648–1840* (New York, Knopf, 1964) and *A History of Modern Germany, 1840–1945* (New York, Knopf, 1969). Theodore Hamerow, *Restoration, Revolution, Reaction: Economics and Politics in Germany, 1815–1871* (Princeton, Princeton University Press, 1966) examines the period from the Congress of Vienna to the end of the Franco-Prussian War. Gordon Craig, *Germany, 1866–1945* (New York, Oxford University Press, 1978) surveys the history of united Germany until the hiatus at the end of World War II and conveys an enormous amount of information in less than 800 pages. Three surveys of Austria and its empire can be recommended: Barbara Jelavich, *Modern Austria: Empire and Republic, 1815–1986* (Cambridge, Cambridge University Press, 1987); A. J. P. Taylor, *The Hapsburg Monarchy, 1809–1918: A History of the Austrian Empire and Austria-Hungary* (New York, Harper, 1965); and Robert A. Kann, *The Multinational Empire: Nationalism and National Reform in the Habsburg Monarchy, 1848–1918*, 2 vols (New York, Octagon Books, 1964). Leften S. Stavrianos, *The Balkans, 1815–1914* (New York, Holt, Rinehart and Winston, 1963) splices the seperate strands of Balkan history into a coherent history of this frequently unsettled region. Robert Lee Wolff, *The Balkans in Our Time*, rev. edn (Cambridge, Mass., Harvard University Press, 1974) concentrates on the period since the late nineteenth century.

Donald Westwood, *Endurance and Endeavour: Russian History 1812–1986* 3rd edn (Oxford, Oxford University Press, 1987) is beautifully written (except for occasional awful puns), and his thorough bibliography is very helpful. Franklin D. Scott's survey of *Sweden: The Nation's History* (Minneapolis, University of Minnesota Press, 1977) is wonderful history from first to last page, with the nineteenth and twentieth centuries receiving special emphasis. Denis Mack Smith, *Italy: A Modern History*, rev. edn (Ann Arbor, University of Michigan Press, 1969) will be found useful by students of the Mediterranean. Some recommended general surveys of extended periods of the present century are Elizabeth Wiskemann, *Europe of the Dictators, 1919–1945* (New York, Harper & Row, 1966), Robert Paxton, *Europe in the Twentieth Century* (New York, Harcourt, Brace, 1975), and Paul Johnson, *Modern Times: The World from the Twenties to the Eighties* (New York, Harper & Row, 1983).

Carlo. M. Cipolla, *The Fontana Economic History of Europe: The Twentieth Century* (Glasgow, William Collins Sons, 1976) provides essays by specialists on the component parts of the twentieth-century European economy. Karl Hardach, *The Political Economy of Germany in the Twentieth Century* (Berkeley, University of California Press, 1980) is economic history for readers who are not specialists; like most books that survey history into contemporary times, it concludes before today's most pressing questions are answered (or raised, for that matter), continuing only through the "postindustrial" economy of the 1960s. Keith Middlemas, *Politics in Industrial Society: The Experience of the British System since 1911* (London, André Deutsch, 1979) views the decade between 1916 and 1926 as critical in forming the relationship between government, trade unions, and big business that is the key to modern

British politics. Michael Biddiss, *Age of the Masses: Ideas and Society since 1870* is a lively survey of twentieth-century culture.

CHAPTER 6 *The Concert of Europe*

Harold Nicolson, *The Congress of Vienna: A Study in Allied Unity, 1812–1822* (New York, Harcourt, Brace, 1946) is stylishly written, but represents the interpretation of a now distant age. The same comment can be made of Henry Kissinger, *A World Restored: Metternich, Castlereagh and the Problems of Peace, 1812–22* (Boston, Houghton Mifflin, 1957). French social and intellectual history is discussed in F. B. Artz, *France Under the Bourbon Regime, 1814–1830* (New York, Russell & Russell, 1963). David H. Pinkney, *The French Revolution of 1830* (Princeton, Princeton University Press, 1972) describes the overthrow of the Bourbon dynasty. The same author's *Decisive Years in France, 1840–1847* (Princeton, Princeton University Press, 1986) states his argument in the title of his book: the sudden expansion of industrialization and road and railroad construction altered France decisively. This is indeed a valuable correction to early interpretations of the July Monarchy, but it also employs the "take-off" concept that is now discredited among economists. C. Morazé, *The Triumph of the Middle Classes: A Study of European Values in the Nineteenth Century* (Cleveland, World Publishing Company, 1966) offers a generally sympathetic account of the bourgeoisie and capitalism.

Romanticism is most enjoyably explored by sampling the contents of Howard E. Hugo, ed., *The Portable Romantic Reader* (New York, Viking Press, 1960). Jacques Barzun's affection for his subject is evident in his study of the life and music of Hector Berlioz in *Berlioz and the Romantic Century*, 3rd edn, 2 vols (New York, Columbia University Press, 1969); some readers may prefer reading David Cairns, ed., *Memoirs of Hector Berlioz* (New York, Knopf, 1969). Aspects of German romanticism are explored in the essays in Siegbert Prawer, *The Romantic Period in Germany* (New York, Schocken Books, 1970).

CHAPTER 7 *Pax Britannica*

Vol. 5 of *The Cambridge History of India* is a convenient compendium of information; see Henry H. Dodwell, ed., *British India, 1497–1858* (Cambridge, Cambridge University Press, 1929). François Crouzet, *The Victorian Economy*, trans. Anthony Forster (New York, Columbia University Press, 1982) was originally intended to be a textbook explaining research on the British economy to advanced French undergraduates and makes few demands of its readers. Edward P. Thompson, *The Making of the English Working Class* (New York, Vintage, 1966) describes some of the social consequences of industrial growth.

Eugene Genovese, *Roll, Jordan, Roll; The World the Slaves Made* (New York, Pantheon Books, 1974) examines the institution that was a major cause of the American Civil War. Studies of various other aspects of the war are James McPherson, *Battle Cry of Freedom: The Civil War Era* (New York, Oxford University Press, 1988) and Henry Hattaway and Archer Jones, *How the North Won: A Military History of the Civil War* (Urbana, University of Illinois Press, 1983).

Asa Briggs, *Victorian Cities* (New York, Harper & Row, 1965) and Richard Dennis, *English Industrial Cities of the Nineteenth Century* (Cambridge, Cambridge University Press, 1984) are good general introductions to this important segment of Victorian society. Readers interested in following the history of one of these cities may do so in the exemplary urban history by P. J. Waller, whose *Democracy and Sectarianism: A Political and Social History of Liverpool 1868–1939* (Liverpool, Liverpool University Press, 1981) captures the extraordinary heterogeneity of this city. Harold Perkin, *The Origins of Modern English Society, 1780–1860* (London, Routledge & Kegal Paul, 1969) is a classic study of English social history.

CHAPTER 8   *The Demographic Revolution*

Theodore Hamerow, *The Birth of a New Europe: State and Society in the Nineteenth Century* (Chapel Hill, University of North Carolina Press, 1983) examines the social consequences of changes in the methods of producing goods, which he considers to be the principal transformational force during the nineteenth century. Sidney Pollard, *Peaceful Conquest: The Industrialization of Europe, 1760–1970* (Oxford, Oxford University Press, 1981) offers a readable description of industrial changes.

Early socialist thought can be examined in F. E. Manuel, *The New World of Henri Saint-Simon* (Cambridge, Mass., Harvard University Press, 1956); E. Durkheim, *Socialism and Saint-Simon*, ed. Alvin W. Gouldner (Yellow Springs, Antioch Press, 1958); J. F. C. Harrison, *The Quest for the New Moral World: Robert Owen and the Owenites in Britain and America* (New York, Scribner, 1969); *The Utopian Vision of Charles Fourier: Selected Texts on Work, Love, and Passionate Attraction*, trans. and introduced by J. Beecher and R. Bienvenu (Boston,

Beacon Press, 1972); and George Lichtheim, *The Origins of Socialism* (New York, Praeger, 1969).

The most comprehensive view of the events of 1848 is to be found in Priscilla Robertson, *Revolutions of 1848: A Social History* (New York, Harper, 1960), which surveys the revolutions in several countries. L. B. Namier, *1848: The Revolution of the Intellectuals* (London, Oxford University Press, 1962) is critical of his topic. The years of consolidation immediately following the revolution in France are described in Maurice Agulhon, *The Republican Experiment, 1848–1852*, trans. Janet Lloyd (New York, Cambridge University Press, 1983).

Edward Crankshaw, *Bismarck* (New York, Viking Press, 1981) is a popular biography of the principal architect of German unification. Otto Pflanze, *Bismarck and the Development of Germany: The Period of Unification, 1815–1871* (Princeton, Princeton University Press, 1973) is a balanced and thorough appraisal of this controversial subject. Michael Howard, *The Franco-Prussian War: The German Invasion of France, 1870–1871* (New York, Macmillan, 1961) is an enjoyable examination of the Prussian triumph.

CHAPTER 9   *The Consolidation and Expansion of Europe*

Eugen Weber, *Peasants into Frenchmen: The Modernization of Rural France, 1870–1914* (Stanford, Stanford University Press, 1976) emphasizes education and modern communications in his description of social change in France after 1870. P. M. Jones, *Politics and Rural Society: The Southern Massif Central, c. 1750–1880* (Cambridge, Cambridge University Press, 1985) rejects much of this; the peasantry in his region were brought into the political mainstream by republican politicians' success in winning them away from traditional local loyalties with government subsidies and jobs. Maurice Agulhon, *The Republic in the Village: The People of the Var from the French Revolution to the Second Republic*, trans. Janet Lloyd (New York, Cambridge University Press, 1982) looks at the social roots of politics and concludes that the interplay of the forms of sociability, peasant and bourgeois alike, was essential to political modernization. Students interested in examining the application of some of the methodologies of anthropologists to a large historical problem would be well-advised to read Agulhon's book.

Roger Price, *The Modernization of Rural France: Communications Networks and Agricultural Market Structures in Nineteenth Century France* (New York, St Martin's Press, 1983) illustrates the effect of the introduction of railroads on peasants and their agriculture, and provides extensive information about the construction of French railways as well.

There are many treatments of the Dreyfus affair, ranging from fictional renditions to historical accounts. There is no single volume that stands above the others, but readers interested in this case may want to start their reading with D. Johnson, *France and the Dreyfus Affair* (New York, Walker, 1967) or Robert L. Hoffman, *More than a Trial. The Struggle over Captain Dreyfus* (New York, Free Press, 1980).

Carl E. Schorske, *Fin-de-Siècle Vienna: Politics and Culture* (New York, Knopf, 1980) is a spirited assessment of Austrian politics and culture. The vast and sometimes unfamiliar terrain of eastern Europe can be viewed in Arthur E. Adams, Ian M. Matley, and William O. McCagy, *An Atlas of Russian and East European History* (New York, Praeger, 1967). Nineteenth-century Russia is put into perspective by Marc Raeff, *Understanding Imperial Russia: State and Society in the Old Regime*, trans. Arthur Goldhammer (New York, Columbia University Press, 1984), H. Seton-Watson, *The Russian Empire, 1801–1917* (Oxford, Clarendon Press, 1967), and Richard Pipes, *Russia under the Old Regime* (New York, Scribner, 1974). More concise descriptions of individuals, events, and places are found in Archie Brown et al., eds, *A Cambridge Encyclopedia of Russia and the Soviet Union* (New York, Cambridge University Press, 1982). The importance of peasants and agrarian reform is confirmed in several important studies. There is much to be learned about the daily life of the peasantry in Wayne S. Vucinich, ed., *The Peasant in Nineteenth Century Russia* (Stanford, Stanford University Press, 1968). George Yaney traces agrarian reform between 1860 and the first years of Stalin's first Five-Year Plan in *The Urge to Mobilize: Agrarian Reform in Russia, 1861–1930* (Urbana, University of Illinois Press, 1982). The critical importance of Russian railways is well demonstrated in J. N. Westwood, *A History of Russian Railways* (London, Allen & Unwin, 1964), while R. M. Haywood considers the influence of pre-rail transport on later policy in *The Beginning of Railway Development in Russia in the Reign of Nicholas I, 1835–1842* (Durham, N.C., Duke University Press, 1969).

Policy toward the non-Russian nationalities comprehended in the Russian Empire is described in the essays in W. Gurian, ed., *Soviet Imperialism: Its Origins and Tactics: A Symposium* (Notre Dame, University of Notre Dame Press, 1953). Most studies of this as yet unsettled problem focus on specific groups or regions. Examples that may be of special interest currently are Edward C. Thaden, ed., *Russification in the Baltic Provinces and Finland, 1855–1914* (Princeton, Princeton University Press, 1981), Serge A. Zenkovsky, *Pan-Turkism and Islam in Russia* (Cambridge, Mass., Harvard University Press, 1960), and Edward C.

Thaden, *Russia's Western Borderlands, 1710–1870* (Princeton, Princeton University Press, 1984).

D. K. Fieldhouse approaches imperialism from two perspectives: his survey of the earlier period is *Economics and Empire, 1830–1914* (Ithaca, Cornell University Press, 1973), followed by *Colonialism, 1870–1945: An Introduction* (New York, St Martin's Press, 1981). Among the better attempts to assess national motives for late nineteenth-century imperialism are Bernard Semmel, *The Rise of Free Trade Imperialism: Classical Political Economy, the Empire of Free Trade and Imperialism, 1750–1850* (Cambridge, Cambridge University Press, 1970), J. Gallagher and Ronald Robinson, *Africa and the Victorians: The Climax of Imperialism in the Dark Continent* (New York, St Martin's Press, 1961), and Winfried Baumgart, *Imperialism: The Idea and Reality of British and French Colonial Expansion* (New York, Oxford University Press, 1982). Motives of the Continental powers are examined in W. Mommsen and J. Osterhammel, eds, *Imperialism and After: Continuities and Discontinuities* (London, Allen & Unwin, 1986). William Woodruff, *Impact of Western Man: A Study of Europe's Role in the World Economy, 1750–1960* (New York, St Martin's Press, 1967) has a large, if now somewhat dated, bibliography, while Daniel Headrick assesses the impact of western technology on imperialism in *Tools of Empire: Technology and European Imperialism in the Nineteenth Century* (New York, Oxford University Press, 1981). Headrick's *The Tentacles of Progress: Technology Transfer in the Age of Imperialism, 1850–1940* (New York, Oxford University Press, 1988) builds on his earlier work; he argues that importation of western technology into African and Asian colonies led to underdevelopment, not industrialization.

The context of Japanese history can be obtained from Edwin O. Reischauer's well-known *Japan: The Story of a Nation*, 3rd edn (New York, Knopf, 1981). W. G. Beasley, *The Meiji Restoration* (Stanford, Stanford University Press, 1972) examines this decisive event of nineteenth-century Japanese history.

Three important intellectual developments are considered in Michael Ruse, *The Darwinian Revolution: Science Red in Tooth and Claw* (Chicago, University of Chicago Press, 1979), Philip Rieff, *Freud, the Mind of the Moralist*, 3rd edn (Chicago, University of Chicago Press, 1979), and Lincoln Barnett, *The Universe and Dr. Einstein*, 2nd edn (New York, W. Sloane Associates, 1957).

CHAPTER 10   *Peace or War*

L. L. Farrar, Jr., *Arrogance and Anxiety: The Ambivalence of German Power, 1848–1914* (Iowa City, University of Iowa Press, 1981) examines state interests in the half-century before the First World War and maintains that war was essential to the great-power system of the nineteenth century, even though it was incompatible with it. In Paul Kennedy's *The Rise of Anglo-German Antagonism, 1860–1914* (London, Allen & Unwin, 1980) special emphasis is placed upon economic competition as the most profound cause of estrangement between these two great powers. Fritz Fischer, *War of Illusions: German Policies from 1911 to 1914*, trans. Marian Jackson (New York, Norton, 1975) views German foreign policy as being consistently conservative and expansionist from 1897 until 1914.

Laurence Lafore, *The Long Fuse: An Interpretation of the Origins of World War I*, 2nd edn (New York, Lippincott, 1971) is a beautifully written, balanced consideration of the causes of the First World War. A more recent evaluation of the same subject is James Joll, *The Origins of the First World War* (London, Longman, 1984). Luigi Albertini, *The Origins of the War of 1914*, trans. and ed. I. M. Massey, 3 vols (New York, Oxford University Press, 1952–7) sets a more leisurely pace in his investigation of the war's origins.

Barbara Tuchman, *The Guns of August* (New York, Macmillan, 1962) describes the beginning of the war. B. H. Liddell Hart, *History of the First World War, 1914–1918* (London, Faber & Faber, 1938) is a masterful military history. German ambition is discussed in Fritz Fischer, *Germany's Aims in the First World War* (New York, Norton, 1967), and this began a controversy that is summarized in John A. Moses, *The Politics of Illusion: The Fischer Controversy in German Historiography* (New York, Barnes & Noble, 1975). Norman Stone, *The Eastern Front, 1914–1917* (New York, Scribner, 1975) explains Russia's participation in the war. Richard Wall and Jay Winter, eds, *The Upheaval of War: Family, Work and Welfare in Europe, 1914–18* (Cambridge, Cambridge University Press, 1989) examine the destabilizing consequences of the war.

Harold Nicolson, *Peacemaking 1919* (London, Constable, 1933) is an account of the Paris Conference by a historian who was a member of the British delegation. Variant interpretations of the Versailles Treaty, including a telling excerpt from John Maynard Keynes, *The Economic Consequences of the Peace*, are set forth in Ivo J. Lederer, *The Versailles Settlement: Was it Foredoomed to Failure?* (Boston, Heath, 1960).

Marc Ferro, *October 1917: A Social History of the Russian Revolution*, trans. Norman Stone (London, Routledge & Kegan Paul, 1980) views the Bolshevik revolution in terms of a framework of historical interpretation that comprehends a broad range of causes, as opposed to the customary close focus on Lenin, Trotsky, and St Petersburg. When Ferro attempts to apply his valuable analytical framework to Stalinist

Russia, the results are more questionable. Alexander Rabinowitch, *The Bolsheviks Come to Power. The Revolution of 1917 in Petrograd* (New York, Norton, 1976) examines the revolution in the most important city. Edward Hallett Carr, *The Bolshevik Revolution, 1917–1923*, 3 vols (London, Macmillan, 1950–3), is an important survey of the field. Studies of individuals are L. Fischer, *The Life of Lenin* (New York, Harper & Row, 1964), Isaac Deutscher, *The Prophet Armed: Trotsky, 1879–1921* (New York, Viking, 1965), and B. D. Wolfe, *Three Who Made a Revolution: A Biographical History*, rev. edn (New York, Dial Press, 1964).

CHAPTER 11 *A World Safe for Democracy*

H. Seton-Watson, *Eastern Europe Between the Wars, 1918–1941*, 3rd edn, rev. (New York, Harper & Row, 1967) depicts the nearly universal collapse of democracy in eastern Europe. Erich Eyck, *A History of the Weimar Republic*, trans. H. P. Hanson and R. G. L. Waite, 2 vols (Cambridge, Mass., Harvard University Press, 1962–3) is a standard account of the political history of Germany from the fall of the empire to 1933; Peter Gay, *Weimar Culture: The Outsider as Insider* (New York, Harper & Row, 1968) is a satisfying account of the intellectual life of that period. An older, briefer political history of the Weimar Republic is S. W. Halperin, *Germany Tried Democracy: A Political History of the Reich from 1918 to 1933* (New York, Norton, 1965).

C. P. Kindleberger, *The World in Depression, 1929–1939*, rev. edn (Berkeley, University of California Press, 1986) is an excellent book; examination of one aspect of the Great Depression is found in John Garrity, *Unemployment in History: Economic Thought and Public Policy* (New York, Harper & Row, 1978).

Three studies of fascism are F. L. Carsten, *Rise of Fascism*, 2nd edn (Berkeley, University of California Press, 1980), Hanna Arendt, *The Origins of Totalitarianism*, 2nd edn (Cleveland, World Publishing, 1958), and Walter Laqueur, ed., *Fascism: A Readers's Guide: Analyses, Interpretations, Bibliography* (Berkeley, University of California Press, 1976).

Studies of Italian fascism naturally focus on Mussolini. Denis Mack Smith, *Mussolini* (New York, Knopf, 1982) is a solid biography. A. James Gregor has published two enlightening complementary studies: *Italian Fascism and Developmental Dictatorship* (Princeton, Princeton University Press, 1979) and *Young Mussolini and the Intellectual Origins of Fascism* (Berkeley, University of California Press, 1979). Mussolini was no shallow intellectual adventurer, according to Gregor, and fascism was more than just political opportunism; it was a scheme of national development. Stanley G. Payne, in *Fascism: Comparison and Definition* (Madison, University of Wisconsin Press, 1980), does not try to write descriptive accounts of fascism, but ponders the general characteristics of this twentieth-century ideology.

W. Shirer, *The Rise and Fall of the Third Reich: A History of Nazi Germany* (New York, Simon and Schuster, 1960) is a fascinating survey of Hitler's Germany. There are ample alternatives for readers seeking a biography of Adolf Hitler: Alan Bullock, *Hitler: A Study in Tyranny*, rev. edn (New York, Harper & Row, 1964); John Toland, *Adolf Hitler* (Garden City, Doubleday, 1976); and Joachim C. Fest, *Hitler*, trans. Richard and Clara Winston (New York, Harcourt Brace Jovanovich, 1974). Gerhard Weinberg surveys German foreign policy in *The Foreign Policy of Hitler's Germany*, vol. 1; *Diplomatic Revolution in Europe, 1933–1936*; vol. 2; *Starting World War II, 1937–1939* (Chicago, University of Chicago Press, 1970, 1980).

Isaac Deutscher describes the struggle for power between Trotsky and Stalin in *The Prophet Unarmed: Trotsky, 1921–1929* (New York, Oxford University Press, 1959). Given Deutscher's preference for Trotsky, his biography of Stalin, *Stalin: A Political Biography* 2nd edn (New York, Oxford University Press, 1967) is surprisingly balanced, but readers might prefer the alternative view offered by Adam Ulam, *Stalin: The Man and His Era* (New York, Viking, 1973). Robert C. Tucker, ed., *Stalinism: Essays in Historical Interpretation* (New York, Norton, 1977) is an examination of the components of Stalin's regime. Robert Conquest, *The Great Terror: Stalin's Purge of the Thirties*, rev. edn (Harmondsworth, Penguin, 1971) is a chilling account of his purges. Soviet foreign policy is explained in George F. Kennan, *Russia and the West under Lenin and Stalin* (Boston, Little, Brown, 1961).

Hugh Thomas, *The Spanish Civil War*, rev. edn (New York, Harper & Row, 1977) and Raymond Carr, *The Spanish Tragedy: The Civil War in Perspective* (London, Weidenfeld & Nicolson, 1977) represent good surveys of greatly different length.

A. J. P. Taylor, *The Origins of the Second World War* (New York, Atheneum, 1961) stressed the element of continuity in German policy during the 1930s and ignited a heated debate. G. Martel, ed., *The Origins of the Second World War Reconsidered: The A. J. P. Taylor Debate After Twenty-Five Years* (Boston, Allen & Unwin, 1986) instructively sifts through the ashes. P. M. H. Bell, *The Origins of the Second World War in Europe* (London, Longman, 1986) is admirably balanced and well written; it is an introductory survey to the subject that is highly recommended.

CHAPTER 12   *The Second World War*

In addition to Gordon Wright's superior general survey in the Langer series (mentioned previously), B. H. Liddell Hart, *History of the Second World War* (New York, Putnam, 1971) and Chester Wilmot, *The Struggle for Europe* (New York, Harper, 1952) explain the course of the war. Alan S. Milward, *War, Economy, and Society, 1939–1945* (Berkeley, University of California Press, 1977) is a thorough and accessible account of the economic side of the war. Literature on the Holocaust is extensive: Vera Laska, *Nazism, Resistance, and Holocaust in World War II: A Bibliography* (Metuchen, Scarecrow Press, 1985) is a good place to start. The memoirs of the chief participants in the war offer the insiders' point of view at the risk of distortion by special pleading. Those by Winston Churchill, *The Second World War* (Boston, Houghton Mifflin, 1948–53), Charles de Gaulle, *The Complete War Memoirs of Charles de Gaulle*, trans. J. Griffen and R. Howard, 3 vols in one (New York, Simon and Schuster, 1964), and Albert Speer, *Inside the Third Reich: Memoirs*, trans. Richard and Clara Winston (New York, Macmillan, 1970) are examples of this sort of history. Correlli Barnett, *The Desert Generals* (New York, Viking Press, 1961) gives the British view of this campaign. John Toland examines the end of the war in *The Last 100 Days* (New York, Random House, 1966).

CHAPTER 13   *The Postwar Decade*

Students of the reconstruction of postwar Europe have several excellent choices among historical surveys. Maurice Crouzet, *The European Renaissance since 1945*, trans. Stanley Baron (New York, Harcourt Brace Jovanovich, 1970) is concise, but ambitious in its scope. Alan S. Milward, *The Reconstruction of Western Europe, 1945–51* (Berkeley, University of California Press, 1984), Walter Laqeur, *Europe Since Hitler*, rev. edn (London, Weidenfeld & Nicolson, 1982), and J. Robert Wegs, *Europe Since 1945: A Concise History*, 2nd edn (New York, St Martin's, 1984) survey the postwar years. The Marshall Plan is sympathetically portrayed in Imanuel Wexler, *The Marshall Plan Revisited: The European Recovery Program in Economic Perspective* (Westport, Conn., Greenwood Press, 1983). Relations between two of the great powers of western Europe are examined in F. Roy Willis, *France, Germany, and the New Europe, 1945–1967*, rev. edn (Stanford, Stanford University Press, 1968), which is continued by Haig Simonian, *The Privileged Partnership: Franco-German Relations in the European Community, 1969–1984* (Oxford, Clarendon Press, 1985). Walter LaFeber, *America, Russia, and the Cold War, 1945–1984,* 5th edn (New York, Knopf, 1985) is a balanced assessment.

Richard Whelan, *Drawing the Line: The Korean War, 1950–1953* (Boston, Little, Brown, 1990), Max Hastings, *The Korean War* (New York, Simon and Schuster, 1987), and Jon Halliday and Bruce Cummings, *Korea: The Unknown War* (New York, Pantheon, 1988) examine and analyze the history of this "police action." W. G. Beasley, *The Rise of Modern Japan* (New York, St Martin's, 1990) is a solid and enjoyable survey of Japan from the Tokugawa period to the death of Hirohito.

Jonathan Spence, *The Gate of Heavenly Peace: The Chinese and their Revolution, 1895–1980* (New York, Viking Press, 1981) interprets modern Chinese politics. Spence's textbook, *The Search for Modern China* (New York, Norton, 1990), covers some of the same ground, and supplies a good bibliography as well. Immanuel C. Y. Hsu, *China Without Mao: The Search for a New Order,* 2nd ed. (New York, Oxford University Press, 1990) is a revised explanation of recent Chinese history.

CHAPTER 14   *The Emergence of the Modern Word*

William B. Quandt, *Revolution and Political Leadership: Algeria, 1954–1968* (Cambridge, MIT Press, 1969) contemplates this segment of the dissolution of France's empire. Jack Schick, *The Berlin Crises, 1958–62* (Philadelphia, University of Pennsylvania Press, 1974) probes the Cold War confrontation that produced the Berlin Wall.

Edward Crankshaw, *Khrushchev* (New York, Viking Press, 1966) is an eminently readable biography of the Soviet leader. Richard J. Walton, *Cold War and Counterrevolution: The Foreign Policy of John F. Kennedy* (New York, Viking Press, 1972) considers the actions of the United States.

W. Polk, *The Elusive Peace: The Middle East in the Twentieth Century* (New York, St Martin's, 1979) puts contemporary Middle Eastern history into perspective.

Karen Dawisha, *Eastern Europe, Gorbachev and Reform: The Great Challenge* (Cambridge, Cambridge University Press, 1988) has attempted an especially difficult task: bringing us up to date on Eastern Europe. Dusko Doder and Louise Branson, *Gorbachev: The Last Tsar* (New York, Viking, 1990) dispassionately analyzes the efforts of Gorbachev to hold the Soviet Union together while reforming the state.

Daniel Yergin, *The Prize* (New York, Simon & Schuster, 1991) analyzes the role of oil in the history of the last two centuries.

Index